THE FIRST WORLD WAR

The Outbreak of the
First World War

THE OUTBREAK
OF THE FIRST
WORLD WAR

HEW STRACHAN

OXFORD
UNIVERSITY PRESS

OXFORD

UNIVERSITY PRESS

Great Clarendon Street, Oxford OX2 6DP

Oxford University Press is a department of the University of Oxford.
It furthers the University's objective of excellence in research, scholarship,
and education by publishing worldwide in

Oxford New York

Auckland Bangkok Buenos Aires Cape Town Chennai
Dar es Salaam Delhi Hong Kong Istanbul Karachi Kolkata
Kuala Lumpur Madrid Melbourne Mexico City Mumbai Nariobi
São Paulo Shanghai Taipei Tokyo Toronto

Oxford is a registered trade mark of Oxford University Press
in the UK and in certain other countries

Published in the United States
by Oxford University Press Inc., New York

© Hew Strachan 2004

British Library Cataloguing in Publication Data

Data available

Library of Congress Cataloging in Publication Data

Data available

ISBN 0-19-925726-4

1 3 5 7 9 10 8 6 4 2

Typeset by Kolam Information Services Pvt. Ltd, Pondicherry, India
Printed in Great Britain on acid-free paper by
Biddles Ltd., King's Lynn, Norfolk

PREFACE

It is now over forty years since the Hamburg historian, Fritz Fischer, published his first book on the First World War, and thirty-five since his major book on the war's origins, *Krieg der Illusionen*. In his hands the First World War became the 'prequel' (to use a horrible neologism for which we presumably have Hollywood to thank) to the Second. Germany was guilty of causing both, and therefore Hitler was less *sui generis* than apologists for Germany liked to pretend. Fischer's books divided not just the German academic community but also the German nation, as it struggled with its post-war identity and the incorporation of its recent past. Outside Germany, historians swallowed the argument. Beginning in the late 1960s and carrying on through the 1970s research on the origins of the war and on the aims developed during it proliferated. I was in Cambridge at the time, and a roll call of those then working on the lead-up to the First World War—Christopher Andrew, Sir Harry Hinsley, Richard Langhorne, Jonathan Steinberg, Norman Stone, Zara Steiner, Clive Trebilcock—is testimony to the intellectual vitality of the subject. Their students included John Keiger, John Leslie, Dominic Lieven, and David Stevenson. A cursory glance at the bibliography to this book will show how much it stands on their shoulders.

What remains curious is how little the debates about why the war was fought were linked to those concerned with how it was conducted. By the 1930s, a consensus had been established that Germany was probably not guilty of causing the war, for all that the treaty of Versailles had said it was. The conclusion was that the war had broken out through a combination of misunderstanding and miscalculation. The corollary of that conclusion was deeply disturbing for those widows and mothers who sought meaning for their own bereavement. Their loved ones' deaths had been in vain. From here it was but a brief step to characterise the trenches of the western front as the embodiment of waste and futility. Fischer should have given those who mourned fresh hope. If he was right, then the purpose and necessity of the First World War were reaffirmed. It could not have been avoided because Germany was bent on fighting it, in order to re-create the European and even world order according to its own lights. In Britain, at about the same time, John Terraine set about rescuing the reputation of the British Expeditionary Force and its commander-in-chief: his most important book, *Douglas Haig: The Educated Soldier*, was published in 1963. Terraine endured almost as much criticism in Britain as Fischer did in Germany. Like Fischer, he overstated his case, However, as with Fischer, it is almost impossible now to imagine the topic without his contribution. And yet no major work put together Fischer's basic point, that Germany was a danger to the world in 1914, alongside Terraine's, that the war was bloody and horrible but was a job that had to be done. In part that lack of convergence said something about the intellectual divisions between diplomatic historians and military historians, but it also revealed the gap between academic historians and those like Terraine, who wrote for a more popular market.

Those fissures are now less deeply etched. Academic historians have moved into the territory which Terraine once inhabited, and the pace of publication on the war's origins—although far from halted—has slowed. Those who worked on war aims found that other belligerents as well as Germany developed schemes for annexation during the war, even if in most cases they did not get fully into their stride until 1916. But that last point tells its own story. The fact that neither Britain nor France had well-developed war aims packages in the autumn of 1914 suggested that it would be hard to blame them for deliberately provoking the war. To that extent Fischer's legacy is still with us. The issue of German war guilt remains central to the discussion as to how the war began.

Nonetheless, the dust has settled. Historians may be no nearer a consensus on the war's causes, but in embracing explanations that are multi-factorial they have moved away from the crude generalisation that it was all Germany's fault. Much of the evidence used to beef up Fischer's case, both by Fischer himself and by his followers, rested on inference and hindsight. The testimony of German leaders during the war was used to explain what was intended or planned before the war. This is an approach to evidence that is not applied to any other belligerent. If it were, the state of the debate would be much more volatile, and also much less securely grounded.

If this book has a simple message (and I rather think it has not), it is that war changed everything. Its first half is an account of what historians used to call high politics. In some ways it is very traditional history, following the behaviour of diplomats and foreign ministers in much the same way as did those who wrote about the outbreak of the war in the 1920s and 1930s. Readers may be struck by how similar are its major points. The crisis of July 1914 did have a dynamic of its own, but any analysis of the behaviour of its principal players has to take into account their experiences over the previous decade. Where it departs most profoundly from Fischer, however, is in its conviction that much of the blame for causing the war lies in Vienna, rather than Berlin. Here I have been influenced in particular by the work of Sam Williamson, who was also in Cambridge in the late 1970s, as a visiting fellow at Churchill College. Austria-Hungary certainly did not intend to cause a European war, let alone a world war, but it did want a Balkan war—the third in as many years.

If the first half of the book comes close to resurrecting the inter-war consensus, that is not intended to suggest that the war could have been avoided. That seems to me as unhelpful as the idea that it was 'inevitable'. In July 1914 the statesmen of the great powers in Europe were confronting issues that they saw as deeply serious. They were aware that they were courting war, and that the war would be of a horror and intensity unequalled in the history of mankind. Many of them—Theodor von Bethmann Hollweg of Germany, Tsar Nicholas II of Russia, and Sir Edward Grey of Britain among them—recognised that it could be a revolutionary moment. They went ahead nonetheless.

They were right, and the second half of the book describes the beginning of that process. Popular enthusiasm and intellectual conviction did not cause the war. They were important to the statesmen guiding policy in July 1914: all of them belonged to states (even Russia) where public opinion had to be taken into account in reaching a decision as fundamental as that for war or peace. The fact that most of their peoples saw this as a war of national self-defence is crucial in recognising the legitimacy of the demand which their statesmen imposed upon them. Without that the war could not have been sustained over four and more years.

In the process beliefs crystallised and differences hardened. European societies before the war were more internally diverse than characterisations written after 1918 or 1945 allowed for. Germany could be seen either as a conservative, reactionary, militarised state run by an autocracy, or as the home of academic excellence, of innovation in science and technology, a state on the brink of liberalisation and possessed of the largest socialist party in the world. Britain characterised itself as the home of constitutional government, the guardian of liberalism, and the defender of morality and international law. But in 1914 it had the most restrictive male franchise of any European country outside Hungary, and it was home to jingoism, navalism, and imperialism. Evidence not dissimilar to that used by Fischer to castigate the Germans could also be deployed to mount an attack on Britain. Similar observations could be made about France, Austria-Hungary, and Russia.

What part II of the book reveals is how quickly and irrevocably these internal subtleties and variations disappeared. Immediately the war broke out, previously polymorphous societies were overtaken by uniformity in thought and deed. Ideas which the other side had also entertained before the war became the monopoly of one. Germany could now see no good in capitalism or liberalism, Britain none in collectivism or militarism. Thus the war became the stuff of 'low' politics as well as 'high'. A war that began through calculations about great power status and strategic advantage became a battle for big and irreconcilable concepts for the ordering of society. A war entered into for reasons of national self-interest was defined in terms of universal values. This paradox is central to understanding the First World War. Ultimately it was why its outcome continued to matter even when the cost-benefit calculus had outstripped the issues which had been stake in July 1914. It says something about war as an existential act. The policy which determines why nations go to war in the first place may not determine why they carry on with that war. We must be wary of too simplistic a rendering of Clausewitz. Precisely because war stands on the extremes of human experience—and that can be said more truthfully of the First World War than most—it transforms how people see themselves and see each other. That of course is also why the First World War shaped the twentieth century.

The text is unaltered since its first publication in 2001. However, the opportunity has been taken to correct a number of misprints, and I owe a particular debt to Knut Bücker-Flürenbock, Richard J. Collins jr, Jürgen Förster, John Hussey, Sir John Keegan, J. G. Lucas, P. G. Urben, and, above all, N. C. Palmer for bothering to write to me with corrections. I have added a guide to further reading and taken the opportunity to update the bibliography.

CONTENTS

LIST OF MAPS

PART I

THE ORIGINS OF
THE WAR

1

GERMANY AS
A WORLD POWER

To begin at the end.[1] At Versailles, on 28 June 1919, the Germans, albeit reluctantly, acceded to the peace terms imposed upon them by the victorious powers. Although Britain, France, and the United States had made most of the running, twenty-five other states were signatory to the treaty. By it, in article 231, they asserted not only the responsibility of the defeated for the loss and damage incurred as a result of the war, but also that the war had been 'imposed upon them by the aggression of Germany and her allies'.

The Germans had already made clear their rejection of the charge. On 27 May, in a fruitless endeavour to overcome the intransigence of the victors, four distinguished professors—two of them of seminal importance in the world of scholarship: Hans Delbrück, the effective founder of academic military history, and Max Weber, the political theorist—signed a memorandum claiming that Germany had fought a defensive war against Russian tsarism. Although beaten in the short-term debate, the German government fought back. A long-term project, examining not merely the immediate causes of the war but the entire range of

---

[1] In addition to books specified in subsequent footnotes, the following works have been of general assistance throughout this chapter: Albertini, *Origins of the war*; Berghahn, *Germany and the approach of war*; Bridge and Bullen, *Great powers and the European states system*; Droz, *Les causes*; Fischer, *War of illusions*; Jarausch, *Enigmatic chancellor*; Joll, *Origins*; Kaiser, *Journal of modern history*, LV (1983), 442–74; Keiger, *France and the origins*; Kennedy, *Rise*; Koch (ed.), *Origins*; Krumeich, *Armaments*; Steiner, *Britain and the origins*; Williamson, *Politics of grand strategy*.

international relations since 1871, was put in train. The Foreign Office assumed responsibility for the volumes, and ensured that the activities which it sponsored and the publications which it produced became the basis for all serious research working on the war's causes. Access to the documents once they had been published was denied to subsequent and possibly more independent scholars; a separate Reichstag inquiry—designed originally by the left to put the blame on the right, and then by the right to blame the left—dragged on and was overtaken; and the tactic of placing the events of July 1914 in the context of the previous decades successfully muddied the precise issue of war guilt.[2] Gradually the Germans' rejection of article 231 gained ground, although more conspicuously in Britain and America than in France. The Versailles Treaty itself was not ratified by the United States Senate and it became abundantly clear that the peace settlement had not resolved the frontier problems of eastern and central Europe in a convincing manner. In particular, the injustices done to Germans residing in the successor states of the Austro-Hungarian empire came to be widely recognized.

In Britain in 1933 Lloyd George, who in July 1911—three years before the outbreak of the war—had as chancellor of the exchequer delivered a clear warning to Germany, and who in December 1918 had been returned to power as prime minister on a wave of anti-German sentiment, began his war memoirs by stating that nobody in July 1914 had wanted European war, that nobody had expected it, and that 'the nations slithered over the brink'.[3] In the United States Sidney B. Fay, professor of history at Harvard, wrote in *The origins of the world war*, first published in 1928, that 'all the powers were more or less responsible', and that 'the War was caused by the system of international anarchy involved in alliances, armaments and secret diplomacy'.[4] By shifting the blame to '-isms' rather than individuals, to militarism, nationalism, and economic imperialism, Fay exculpated Germany. Only by re-emphasizing the immediate causes of the war, by stating that it was the resolve of Germany and Austria-Hungary during the crisis of July 1914 that enabled the war to occur, could the doyen of France's war historians, Pierre Renouvin, put

---

[2] Langdon, *July 1914*, 20–65; Herwig, *International Security*, XII (1972), 5–44; Droz, *Les causes*, 12–19.
[3] Lloyd George, *War memoirs*, i. 32.
[4] Fay, *Origins of the world war*, i. 2.

across a Germanophobe perspective.[5] In the 1930s, for most of the English-speaking world, as indeed for Germany, the arguments of Fay and Lloyd George were the current orthodoxy.

The Second World War changed this perspective, albeit gradually rather than immediately. From the vantage-point of the second half of the century the two world wars could be seen as part of a whole, the years 1918 to 1939 representing a truce rather than a definitive break. Furthermore, given the relative lack of controversy about the origins of the second war, that it was caused by German aggression, and that Hitler—whether as leader of an enraptured German people or as embodiment of a deeply-rooted national will—was the prime culprit, it became possible to project back onto Germany before 1933 the insights and continuities derived from a study of Nazi Germany.

In particular, the causes of the First World War could be re-examined in the light of those of the Second. The debate was also set in a general context, that of the peculiarities of Germany history, of Germany's *Sonderweg* (special path). Simply put, Germany was portrayed as a state where militarism and authoritarianism—partly owing to its Prussian origins, partly to its strategically vulnerable position—had been more easily exploited by leaders of a conservative and expansionist bent. The political thought of the Enlightenment and the bourgeois legacy of industrialization, which in west European states left a grounding of constitutionalism, in Germany was suborned by nationalism. The right used nationalism for its own conservative ends, and liberalism—in 1813, 1848, and 1919—did not take strong root. Hitler was presented as the climax of what went before.

It was against this background that the more specific controversy over the origins of the First World War was renewed. The key works, *Griff nach der Weltmacht* (*Germany's aims in the First World War*) and *Krieg der Illusionen* (*The war of illusions*), both by Fritz Fischer and published in 1961 and 1969 respectively, placed the burden of war guilt once again at the feet of Germany. Much of the detail of Fischer's case will be considered later in this book. Despite their opaque and dense presentation and despite the lack of a succinct argument, Fischer's books rent German historians into deeply entrenched camps. For them, more than for

---

[5] Renouvin, *La Crise européenne*, 1939 edn., 183.

historians of other nationalities, the issue was fraught, since the overall thesis—the arguments about *Sonderweg* and the ongoing preoccupation with the effect of Hitler—concerned continuity in German history, and therefore was as much about Germany's current identity as about its past. The subtleties and differences of the interpretations put forward within the two camps were subsumed by the fundamental divide. Fischer's opponents, who constituted the majority, had to accept combat on Fischer's terms: in other words, they had to address the question of German expansionism before 1914, to ask whether Germany was prepared to go to war in fulfilment of its aims, to decide whether all the dominant groups in pre-war German society could be found culpable, and to consider whether their motivation was to use foreign policy to avert an internal social and political crisis. Fischer himself, in the foreword to *Krieg der Illusionen*, spelled out the primacy of domestic policy:

the aim was to consolidate the position of the ruling classes with a successful imperialist foreign policy, indeed it was hoped a war would resolve the growing social tensions . . . By 1912 at any rate the domestic crisis was apparent. The decision to go to war in 1914 was, in addition to the domestic considerations, based above all on military reflections which in turn depended on economic and political objectives. All these factors—and as regards both the masses and the Emperor there were also the psychological elements—the Government was forced to consider. If one looks at all these forces it is possible to see a clear continuity of aim before and during the war.[6]

In 1967 Immanuel Geiss, a pupil of Fischer, put it more pithily:

The determination of the German Empire—the most powerful conservative force in the world after Tsarist Russia—to uphold the conservative and monarchic principles by any means against the rising flood of democracy, plus its *Weltpolitik*, made war inevitable.[7]

In practice, this sort of argument is very hard to substantiate in precise terms from the evidence now available. But the challenge that Fischer, Geiss, and others issued compels historians—in addition to undertaking a fundamental reconsideration of the role of Germany—to make two connections not so readily made in the 1930s. Both are connections which

---

[6] Fischer, *War of illusions*, pp. viii–ix; on Fischer's reaction to the debate, see Fisher *World power or decline*; Droz, *Les causes*, provides an excellent historiographical survey.

[7] I. Geiss, 'Origins of the first world war', in Koch (ed.), *Origins*, 46.

come more easily to a generation to whom nuclear weapons—by finding their role as deterrents rather than as weapons of war—link more closely the issues of war and peace, and at the same time obscure the divisions between purely military functions and those of civilian society. First, the Fischer controversy forces historians to dispense with their traditional division between the causes of a war, a long-standing interest of academics and exhaustively worked over in undergraduate essays, and its course, the task of military historians and all too often neglected by those same undergraduates. Fischer's revisionism began with the development of German war aims during the war itself, and worked backwards to the war's origins, finding continuity between the two and using one to illuminate the other. In 1934, by contrast, C. R. M. F. Cruttwell's history of the war, reprinted as recently as 1991, felt it unnecessary to discuss the war's origins. Secondly, Fischer restated the interconnection between domestic policy and foreign policy. The point was well taken: recent studies of other nations and the origins of the war, and of their subsequent aims, have not been able to treat foreign policy as a discrete entity. Even more must this apply to the conduct of the war itself, frequently described as the first total war and entailing the mobilization of all the belligerents' industrial and economic resources.

Therefore, the initial task must be—as it was for the peacemakers of 1919—to consider Germany and its role in the origins of the war.

On 18 January 1871, at Versailles, in the same hall where, almost five decades later, the leaders of the new republic would have to accept defeat and humiliation, the king of Prussia was declared emperor of a united Germany. Technically the new nation was a federation: the independent German states retained their own monarchs, assemblies, taxation, and—in the cases of Saxony, Württemberg, and Bavaria (as well as Prussia)—their own armed forces. To balance the national parliament, the Reichstag, which was elected by universal manhood suffrage and by a secret ballot, there was an upper chamber, the Bundesrat, made up of representatives of the individual federal states. But in practice the achievement of unification, although long sought by liberal nationalists, was not a triumph for constitutionalism but for the monarchical-aristocratic principle on the one hand and for Prussia on the other. In ousting Austria from Germany, and in effecting unification, Bismarck and Prussian junkerdom had made fellow-travellers of the national liberals, had usurped nationalism for conservative ends, and had thus split liberal loyalties. Furthermore, universal suffrage, by linking the lower classes more closely as allies of the monarchy, was designed to isolate the liberals yet further. The Reichstag was therefore weak because its political parties were weak; furthermore, even should they manage to co-operate effectively, the constitution was so designed that Prussia would act as a counterweight. Prussia held seventeen out of fifty-eight votes in the Bundesrat: it was therefore in a position to block legislation. And the Prussian Chamber of Deputies was elected not by universal suffrage, but by a complicated three-class franchise weighted according to the amount of tax paid. The majority of federal ministers either held office by virtue of their Prussian appointment (the Prussian minister of war was de facto minister for all Germany) or were themselves Prussian: including the chancellor, they were accountable not to the Reichstag but to the Kaiser. The Kaiser himself, in addition to being the king of Prussia, had direct control of those areas of government where Germany most manifested itself as a nation, in foreign policy and in control of the army.

Implicit, therefore, within the new Germany was a host of interlocking structural tensions that required the mollifications of national success and victory on the battlefield. Fundamental was Germany's status as an industrializing power: Germany industrialized late but very rapidly, the value of her output increasing well over six times between 1855 and 1913. In 1870 agriculture still contributed 40 per cent of the total national product and employed 45 per cent of the total active population, but by 1910 it constituted 25 per cent of the total national product and as early as 1895 employed only 36 per cent of the workforce.[8] A political structure designed to meet the needs of an agricultural aristocracy abetted by a compliant peasantry increasingly did not reflect the true range of German society. Economic power shifted from Westphalia to the Ruhr, from East Prussia to Silesia; the contrast between Germany's ill-adapted constitution on the one hand and the envy of western liberals for the quality and rigour of its secondary and higher education on the other became more pronounced. With the growth of the urban working class, the device of universal suffrage posed a new threat to the Bismarckian settlement, that of socialism. A united and effective majority in the

---

[8] Tables in Trebilcock, *Industrialisation*, 433–5.

Reichstag could upset the checks and balances so carefully built into the constitution. If this were to happen, the highly personalized nature of Germany's government and the latent differences between the states could be exposed. Germany in 1871 was sufficiently centralized to upset the feelings of individual states, particularly those of Bavaria but also of Prussia, and yet insufficiently united to get the true benefits of central government. Given the divisions within the Reichstag, the chancellor's role was to manage the parties, to play one off against another; and yet he himself remained without a true party base. His authority rested on the support of the Kaiser and on the personal relationship between the two of them. This combination of socio-economic trends at one extreme and of individual primacy at the other highlighted the central ambiguity with regard to the constitution itself: because it was given from above, it could as easily be taken away. Political rights were not axiomatic.

In 1888 Wilhelm II ascended the throne, his father's reign cut short by cancer of the throat. The new Kaiser was young, energetic, and for many the representative of the waxing vigour of Germany itself. But the immaturity concomitant with these qualities was never outgrown, never supplemented with the wisdom of experience. 'Not quite sane' was a description that readily occurred to observers. His withered arm had prompted the withdrawal of his mother's love, leaving him deeply insecure, with a strong animosity towards her and towards her native land of Britain. He constantly asserted his personality and prejudices, but proved himself unable to sustain the hard work or the serious thought required to endow them with consistency. Anxious to be the shining leader, he succeeded only in endowing his decisions with theatricality rather than substance. The aged Bismarck concluded that, 'The Kaiser is like a balloon. If you do not hold fast to the string, you never know where he will be off to.'[9]

The Kaiser was the public image of Germany: both before and during the war his upturned moustache and spiked helmet shaped foreigners' perceptions. Nor was the image without reality. The Kaiser exercised personal rule, in which he devoutly believed, and which was allowed him by the ambiguities of the constitution, in two key ways. First, he had the

[9] Quoted by Paul Kennedy, in Röhl and Sombart (eds.), *Kaiser Wilhelm II*, 155. Much of what follows rests on the essays in this book, particularly those of Röhl and Deist, and on Isabel V. Hull, *The entourage of Kaiser Wilhelm II*.

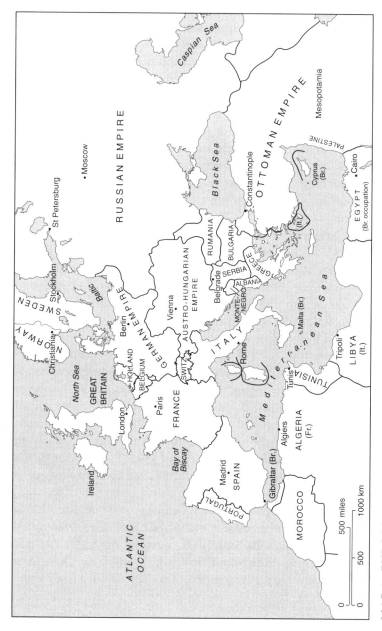

MAP 1. EUROPE IN 1914

right of appointment to all major governmental and service posts; and secondly, once appointed, a large number of those officials had the privilege of direct audience with the monarch. The army was the main buttress to Wilhelm's idea of monarchical authority, and by 1914 over forty officers—including all those commanding the military districts of Germany—had access to him. In addition, his personal entourage at court was increasingly dominated by military influences. Wilhelm himself said that it was in regimental life that he found the security, the family and friends that he had hitherto lacked. But the officers with whom he surrounded himself were even more conservative and traditional than the officer corps as a whole. Nine out of ten came from noble families, and nineteen out of twenty from landowning or military backgrounds; the cavalry dominated over the technical arms, and the guards over other types of infantry. Furthermore, once attached to the court an officer might stay a very long time: 108 served continuously throughout the reign. The entourage constituted a cocoon into which the influences of industry and commerce, western and southern Germany could only rarely penetrate. The dominance of these military and traditional influences was never complete, but gradually—and especially after 1906–8—it grew. And as it grew the contrast between it and the rest of the army increased also. A major plank of the Kaiser's personal rule was his supreme command of the armed forces, but his grasp of the complexities of exercising that command remained rudimentary.

Moreover, it was in foreign policy that the Kaiser's personal rule remained most clearly untrammelled by constitutional considerations, and it was through imperialism that the Kaiser sought to legitimize the authority which he craved.

Germany's position in Europe after 1871 was at once threatening and vulnerable—threatening because central Europe was now dominated by a major power, casting shadows over Russia to the east and France to the west, and vulnerable because the new state had long, exposed land frontiers in the same directions. For Germany the danger of a revivified France, anxious to revenge the defeat of 1870–1 and to regain the provinces of Alsace-Lorraine, was real enough: the memory of Napoleon's victories and the subsequent French occupation of Germany coloured Bismarck's determination that France should be weak and isolated as long as possible. But simultaneously Bismarck sought to reassure the states of Europe, to accustom them to the presence of a united and powerful Germany. The alliance with Austria-Hungary of 1879, guaranteeing mutual support in the event of an attack by Russia, therefore had stability as its primary objective. Bismarck hoped to restrain Austria in its dealings with Russia, and to persuade Russia that, rather than war with Germany, it should seek better relations. In 1882 Italy joined Germany and Austria-Hungary, and thus the Triple Alliance came into being.

In 1890 Wilhelm dismissed Bismarck—with good reason, as the chancellor was increasingly dominated by his own vanities and decreasingly able to manage the Reichstag. The situation which Bismarck left was in large measure the legacy of the settlement which he had achieved in 1871. Agricultural depression and economic recession had highlighted the differences between East Elbian grain producers anxious to protect their frontier with high tariffs against imported food (particularly from Russia) on the one hand, and the representatives of new industry keen to free trade so as to secure markets for their manufactured goods on the other. The mutually reinforcing weaknesses of the Reichstag and of its parties encouraged these economic interest groups to form extra-parliamentary pressure groups, which themselves confirmed the weakness of the political structures. Within the Reichstag the effects of universal suffrage began to be felt as the social democrat vote almost trebled between 1877 and 1890, and reached over 2 million—or 27 per cent of the whole—in 1898. The split in the liberal vote, already exploited by Bismarck, was deepened as the national liberals supported the interests of industry, while the left-wing liberals, the Progressives, lacked organization and were unclear in their response to social democracy. The independent peasant farmer, the small shopkeeper, the white-collar worker—the so-called *Mittelstand* of Germany—alienated by big business and hence by national liberalism, turned to conservatism, or—if Catholic—to the Catholic Centre party. To combat these fissiparous tendencies and, above all, to rally industry and agriculture to a common cause and to oppose socialism, Germany needed—it was argued increasingly from 1895—a policy that would unite and reconcile rather than divide, a *Sammlungspolitik*.

The instrument chosen to effect the rallying of Germany was one that lay specifically within the Kaiser's competence, a more nationalist and imperialist foreign policy. It was Wilhelm who appointed the main architect of *Weltpolitik*, Bernhard von Bülow, first as foreign minister in 1897 and then in 1900 as chancellor, and in 1897 Bülow himself stated that he would be a 'tool' of the Kaiser's personal rule.[10] Bülow subscribed to the feeling of inevitability associated with German overseas expansion, the product of Germany's status as a major power and of the need for markets to satisfy its burgeoning manufacturing industry. In the late nineteenth century interstate relations frequently employed the vocabulary of social Darwinism. The belief that man's environment, rather than his individuality, determined his behaviour challenged liberal views of the relationship between the individual and the state. Rather than a minimalist role for the latter to allow the fruition of the former, social Darwinism suggested the subordination of the first to the second, and went on to clothe the nation with an identity and vitality of its own. States were dynamic entities, rising or declining according to fitness. Max Weber, in his inaugural lecture as professor of political economy at the University of Freiburg in 1895, reminded his countrymen:

We must understand that the unification of Germany was a youthful prank performed by the nation in its old age and that, because of its expensiveness, it would have been better left undone if it was meant to be the end and not the beginning of a German policy of world power.[11]

But the connection between *Weltpolitik* and the war's outbreak is not a direct one. What *Weltpolitik* certainly did not imply was territorial expansion within Europe: the incorporation of subordinate non-national groupings into a greater *Reich* could only promote the fissiparous tendencies *Weltpolitik* was designed to dampen. Rather, the first focus of *Weltpolitik* could not have been geographically more distant—its hub was China and its apogee the acquisition of Kiaochow in 1897.[12] That Germany should wish to obtain colonies did not in itself surprise or alarm to an excessive degree the power most likely to be affected by that decision, Great Britain. In 1890 the two countries collaborated to the extent of exchanging Heligoland and Zanzibar. But as the disparate threads of domestic, colonial, and naval policy were woven together, so

[10] Hull, *The entourage of Kaiser Wilhelm II*, 97; see also Craig, *Modern Germany*, 273.

[11] Quoted by Craig, in *New York Review of Books*, 18 Feb. 1988 (referring to Mommsen, *Weber*).

[12] Peter Winzen, 'Zur Genesis von Weltmacht—Konzept und Weltpolitik', in Röhl (ed.), *Der Ort Kaiser Wilhelms II*.

the whole acquired a vocabulary that was much more threatening to the status quo. The notion of pax Germanica replacing the pax Britannica, however irenic in theory, promised radical revisionism in practice. By 1914 the reality had not come close to matching the rhetoric. The empire which Germany had acquired barely deserved the title: it covered a million square miles, attracted one in a thousand of Germany's emigrants, absorbed a paltry 3.8 per cent of Germany's overseas investment, and accounted for 0.5 per cent of its overseas trade.[13] It was the manner of German foreign policy more than its objects, let alone its achievements, which was to provoke the other powers before 1914.

Nor was the conclusion that German objectives remained consonant with peace a misplaced one. For all the provocative phrases of Weber or his publicist, Friedrich Naumann, Bülow's objectives remained domestic. The purpose of *Weltpolitik* was to achieve integration within Germany, to reconcile agriculture and industry, to woo social democracy. By pointing liberalism overseas, in the pursuit of markets, Bülow hoped to minimize the friction with conservatism, and to produce the economic benefits which might still the political demands of the workers. Politically, *Weltpolitik* manifested itself in a series of bargains between interest groups; externally, it aimed at a sequence of minor successes. It spoke the language of a grand design but practised short-term expediency. However, the longer it survived the more its rhetoric created exaggerated popular expectations. And, given that *Sammlungspolitik* rested on ad hoc compromise, it had constantly to present itself with new targets.[14] Furthermore, the principal method used to implement *Weltpolitik*, the creation of a sizeable German navy, carried with it all the elements that would generate fresh problems—the challenge to Britain as a seapower, the need for hyperbolic and expansionist propaganda to get financial support for ship construction, and the potential subordination of diplomacy to arms policy. Much of Bülow's effort in foreign policy was to be directed to providing the cover for the fleet's creation.

As with *Weltpolitik* and Bülow, so with the navy and its architect, Alfred von Tirpitz, the Kaiser's role was direct and vital. Wilhelm's personal passion for his fleet was the customary blend of absurdity and

---

[13] Steiner, *Britain and the origins*, 68–71; Herwig, *Luxury fleet*, ch. 6, esp. pp. 106–7.
[14] Amidst the vast literature on this subject, Kaiser, *Journal of Modern History*, LV (1983), 442–74, speaks much sense.

energetic enthusiasm. He felt it appropriate to wear his admiral's uniform to performances of Wagner's *Der fliegende Holländer,* and yet was fired by technical interests in the ships of the British navy and in 1894 read Alfred Thayer Mahan's influential book *The influence of seapower upon history.* Seeing Germany as a potential colonial power, Wilhelm at first advocated the construction of cruisers, but in 1895 the naval high command recommended the creation of a battle fleet able to meet the French or the Russians in a major action in home waters. It argued that Germany's ability to flex its oceanic muscles was entirely dependent on its capacity to break out of the North Sea, and thus cruisers could not be effective in isolation but only as adjuncts to battleships. The Kaiser was convinced and ordered the planning of a fleet of twenty-five battleships. The Reichstag was less easily persuaded, and so in 1896–7 the need for a press campaign to popularize the navy and thus win over the Reichstag had become clear. In June 1897 the Kaiser appointed Tirpitz, still a relatively junior admiral, to head the Imperial Naval Office; his was the responsibility of guiding the naval programme through the Reichstag.[15]

The domestic functions of the navy laws were conciliatory. The navy was above all a creature of the new Germany, not of the old Prussia: unlike the army, it was a product of unification, an armed service that belonged to all the nation, and particularly to the industrialized middle class. Its officer corps was more bourgeois than that of the army (although its members were socially divided from within, and its middle-class origins did not prevent it from aping the mannerisms of the Prussian aristocracy). The creation of a regular building pattern was designed to please heavy industry, to provide a buffer against cyclical depression, and to take the sting out of socialism by ensuring full employment. These were the strengths on which Tirpitz could base his propaganda effort: he established an information service in the naval office to liaise with the press, and by 1914 the Navy League—which was founded in 1898—could boast a membership of over a million. Tirpitz proved a consummate manager of the Reichstag, of its parties and its parliamentary committees, persuading its deputies that the fleet was a vital auxiliary to the expansion of German overseas trade, that its size

---

[15] The main works in English on the naval programme are Herwig, *Luxury fleet,* and Steinberg, *Yesterday's deterrent.*

would be modest and its purpose defensive, and that a fixed programme which would tie the Reichstag was not a programme without controls. When opposition within parliament became too strong, when liberal imperialism began to smell a rat, Tirpitz cowed it with the popular support of the pressure groups—the Colonial Society and the Pan-German League, and in due course the Navy League. The broad lines of his policy—the emphasis on battleships rather than cruisers, and the calculation of the fleet's overall size on the basis of arithmetic rather than combat efficiency—had already been established before he took up office. In 1898 the Reichstag approved a target of nineteen battleships, eight armoured cruisers, and twelve large and thirty light cruisers, to be completed by April 1904; it also agreed that battleships should be replaced every twenty-five years. In 1900 a new law aimed for thirty-eight battleships, twenty armoured cruisers, and thirty-eight light cruisers. Tirpitz planned that Germany should possess sixty capital ships by 1920, and hoped to have the cycle of their replacement so fixed that the Reichstag's approval would be redundant and the Kaiser's whims irrelevant.

Tirpitz had hoodwinked the Reichstag, both as to his domestic object-ives and as to his international aims. The naval staff continued to plan for war with France or Russia, and viewed the possibility of hostilities against Britain with horror. But from the outset Tirpitz's putative enemy was the Royal Navy. He shared the Anglophobia of his royal master, and he linked commercial rivalry with Britain to the navalist propaganda emanating from the Imperial Naval Office. Tirpitz hoped to create a sufficiently large fleet to ensure that the Royal Navy would not risk a naval battle with the Germans for fear that—even if it won the engagement—it would then be too weak to face a third naval power. He recognized the possibility of a pre-emptive strike by the British before the German fleet was complete, a rerun of Nelson's sinking of the Danish fleet in harbour at Copenhagen, and so required Bülow's foreign policy to create the right conditions to cover the period of vulnerability by mollifying the British and even seeking agreement with them. On almost every count, Tirpitz's calcula-tions with regard to likely British responses proved to be wrong.

Britain put its foreign policy through a rapid and dramatic reorien-tation after 1900. However, this was less the product of the new circum-stances in Europe, and more a response to an accumulation of older and more global pressures. Until the middle years of the nineteenth century

Britain led the world in industrial production; free trade guaranteed access to world markets because no other country could manufacture so much so cheaply. But from then on other countries—particularly the United States and Germany—began to catch up: in 1870 Britain commanded 32 per cent of the world's manufacturing capacity, but by 1910 it had only 14.7 percent, behind both Germany (15.9 per cent) and the United States (35.3 per cent).[16] London remained the hub of the world's banking, insurance, and shipping markets until 1914, and Britain's invisible exports therefore helped mask its relative industrial decline. Nonetheless, it followed that for some the doctrinaire commitment to free trade—appropriate to the days of easy industrial supremacy—became an increasing, if self-imposed, burden. Given British opposition to protection, formal empire, the direct control of territory, with its guaranteed markets made more economic sense in 1900 than it had in 1850. However, the empire itself was enormously expensive, particularly in relation to the costs of its defence. The colonial ambitions of the other, now industrialized, European powers meant that the yardsticks by which the forces had to be judged were not simply—if they ever had been—the technological and military margin sufficient to defeat Zulus or Pathans. Seapower was the primary means by which free trade had been sustained, and by which both the home country and the colonies guarded against external attack. But what had been a source of stability before the industrialization of the continental powers became a well-spring for insecurity thereafter. Other nations transformed their financial administration and their banking systems, and proved willing to contract debts to fund naval programmes. The introduction of the iron-clad, steam-powered battleship in 1860, and the decision in 1889 that the Royal Navy should be maintained at sufficient strength to be at least equal to the next two ranking naval powers assumed that Britain's maritime rivals would restrain themselves. They did not, and Britain's defence spending soared. In 1884 British naval expenditure was £10.7 million; by 1899—in a period of relatively constant prices—it was £24.1 million (and it was to double again by 1914). Britain's total expenditure on the navy in the seven-year period 1897 to 1904 was 78 per cent higher than in the previous septennium.[17] Britain had

---

[16] Kennedy, *Anglo-German antagonism*, 291.
[17] Offer, *First World War*, 6; Sumida, *In defence of naval supremacy*, 7, 13–23.

perforce to adopt policies which eased the fiscal burdens of naval and imperial responsibility. The Boer War, which had cost £200 million and in which not far short of half a million men had served, vividly highlighted in double fashion the precarious nature of Britain's position. The war had been marked by early defeats and had been protracted; the commitment to it had left Britain's other possessions vulnerable and exposed. In 1901 Britain eased its problems in the western hemisphere with an agreement with the United States. In January 1902 it followed this up with a treaty with Japan, like America a rising naval power: the purpose of the treaty was limited and local, to help Britain balance Russia in the Far East and to ease the Royal Navy of its burdens in Chinese waters.

The German naval laws and the tub-thumping Teutonic exploitation of British embarrassment in South Africa did not at this stage produce a Eurocentric reconstruction of British strategy and diplomacy. German behaviour between 1898 and 1901 did mean that whatever attractions an Anglo-German alliance might have had for Britain were dissipated. But the end of British isolation in relation to Europe was determined by the relative position of the European powers in Africa and Asia, not within Europe itself. Improved relations with France and Russia, the former aspiring to control North Africa and the Mediterranean, and thus challenging British control of Egypt and the Suez route to India, and the latter expanding south and east, also towards India, were the keys of future imperial policy.

Russia, spurned by a Germany focusing its foreign policy on the simplicities of the Triple Alliance after Bismarck's fall in 1890, and anxious for French loans to finance its industrialization, had come to terms with France between 1891 and 1894. The two powers ratified a military convention by which each agreed to defend the other in the event of a German attack, or of a German-supported attack by Austria-Hungary on Russia or by Italy on France: French and Russian mobilization was to follow immediately on the mobilization of any member of the Triple Alliance. Thus, in 1904 the Russo-Japanese War in Manchuria found France allied to the former and Britain to the latter; one pressure for an Anglo-French rapprochement was that both were wedded to a policy of mutual restraint in relation to Manchuria. However, the key motivation for France behind the affirmation of the *entente cordiale*, effected on 8 April of that year, was—as for Britain—imperial. After the drubbing of 1870, French ambitions—or those in France possessed of ambition—had looked away from the metropolis to North Africa. Delcassé, foreign minister from 1898, was anxious to expand France's influence from its colony, Algeria, into Morocco, to the exclusion of Germany. Britain, by agreement with France on the Moroccan question, in return secured its own controls over the gates of the Mediterranean, Gibraltar and Egypt, and hence over the route to India, the focus of the empire. The Entente was intended to affect the naval balance here and not in the North Sea.[18]

By 1904, therefore, the context in which Bülow's *Weltpolitik* was set seemed very different from that of 1897. The composing of French and British differences, the existence of secret clauses in this agreement (which actually concerned the division of Morocco), and the more formal Franco-Russian alliance, conjoined to play on German insecurities. Convinced that France wanted revenge for the loss of Alsace-Lorraine, determined that Britain would be challenged by the naval programme, and terrified by the strategic dilemma of a war on both its western and eastern fronts simultaneously, Germany projected its fears onto its putative opponents and in due course gave its imaginings a reality which in origin they need not have had.

German policy therefore aimed to woo Russia from France or to split France from Britain. Given Russia's weakness in 1904–5, its defeat at the hands of the Japanese and its subsequent revolution, the opportunities for the former seemed somewhat greater. In the event Russia saw any treaty with Germany as incompatible with its commitments to France, resisting the German offer of a defensive alliance in October 1904 and refusing to ratify the agreement reached between the Kaiser and the Tsar at Björkö in July 1905. The opportunity to divide Britain and France was presented by French policy in Morocco. Moroccan independence was guaranteed by the 1880 Madrid Convention. Delcassé's advancement of French interests was hardly compatible with Moroccan integrity, and on 31 March 1905 the Kaiser landed at Tangiers and declared his support for the Sultan's bid to maintain his independence.

On the face of it, despite its provocative nature, the Kaiser's action was fully justified and deserving of success. Both the French prime minister and French public opinion seemed to think so, and Delcassé—the author

---

[18] Williamson, *Politics of Grand Strategy*, chs. 1 and 2.

of France's Moroccan policy—was ousted by June. But divided counsels within Germany, themselves a reflection of the lack of centralized control, and the absence of diplomatic sensitivity turned success into humiliation.

What it seems fairly clear that Germany did *not* want was war. Many of those who argue that Germany did not plan for war in 1914 point to the 1905 crisis and show how much more favourable to Germany the international position was at that juncture. The French army was still reeling from the Dreyfus affair and from the Third Republic's continuing uncertainty as to its political loyalties. The British army was both small and focused on India. Above all, Russia's preoccupation with Japan removed the threat of a war on two fronts. The chief of the German general staff, Alfred von Schlieffen, recognized the opportunity for a preventive war. But the focus of the general staff's planning was German security in Europe; whatever German objectives in Morocco, they were not in the first instance concerned with that. Furthermore, Schlieffen's was not necessarily the dominant voice in German military counsels, let alone in Germany more generally. Of late the navy had enjoyed the higher profile, and yet Tirpitz did not regard the German fleet as ready to take on the Royal Navy. Indeed, the German navy in 1905 had no operational plan for war with Britain or with Britain and France.[19] Schlieffen recognized that the army did not have the means to attack Britain should Britain support France. Moreover, both Germany's allies, Italy and Austria-Hungary, looked as militarily weak as did Germany's putative opponents. In these circumstances, the caution uttered by the Prussian minister of war, von Einem, was compelling—and gained force when Schlieffen fell sick in the summer. Von Einem was particularly concerned by the fact that France had completed the re-equipment of its army with quick-firing field artillery but Germany had not.[20]

Weltpolitik, in other words a diplomatic success, not war, was Germany's purpose in 1905. But, behind the overall aim of disrupting the Entente, middle-distance German objectives diverged. Wilhelm stood for little more than he had publicly declared: an open door to Morocco was necessary given the volume of German trade. But others saw the

---

[19] On German naval plans, see Lambi, *Navy and German power politics*, esp. 242–4, 257–60.
[20] Bucholz, *Moltke, Schlieffen, and Prussian war planning*, 207–8; Herrmann, *Arming of Europe*, 30–5, 37–41, 52–5; Stevenson, *Armaments and the coming of war*, 68–75.

opportunity to exchange concessions to the French for German gains elsewhere, and Friedrich von Holstein of the Foreign Ministry—to whom Bülow gave a free hand—wanted to emphasize to France the dangers of disregarding Germany.[21] The foreign office realized that militarizing the crisis, threatening war, albeit with no intention of going to war, could help it achieve these wider objectives. Delcassé regarded this posturing as bluff, but others in France, all too conscious of their military weakness, were less sure. Germany insisted on the summoning of a conference at Algeçiras in January 1906 to discuss the Moroccan question. But at the same time the Kaiser made it clear that Germany would not fight. Thus, in the subsequent deliberations Germany harvested all the disadvantages and none of the benefits that its earlier high-handedness had promised. Britain was provoked into hardening its support of France; furthermore, the Triple Alliance showed its weakness, Italy backing the Entente (and thus reflecting its own awareness of the relative naval balance in the Mediterranean) and Austria-Hungary urging Germany to be more conciliatory. The conference left France in a dominant position in Morocco.

The consequence of this, the first Moroccan crisis, was thus the reverse of that intended by Germany. The Entente gained a dynamism which it had hitherto lacked. Germany was plainly using colonial questions as an instrument in European and great power politics. Such an approach found a ready response within France. French colonial activity had been in part a substitute for the loss of status in Europe, the acquisition of empire a compensation for forfeiting Alsace-Lorraine. Popular enthusiasm for colonialism was therefore yoked to continental rivalries. Delcassé had, after all, sought out an alliance with Britain precisely to enable France the better to counter Germany. Many of the permanent civil servants within the Foreign Ministry, particularly those of the younger generation, were characterized by a blend of nationalism, colonialism, and anti-Germanism: with Delcassé's fall, French foreign policy lacked a guiding ministerial hand, and the civil servants became correspondingly more powerful.[22]

But it was the change in British attitudes that was really decisive in confirming the shift, and in directing colonial rivalries back into a

---

[21] Balfour, *Kaiser*, 252–4.
[22] Keiger, *France and the origins*, ch. 2; Hayne, *French foreign office*, 139–40.

European context. Late-nineteenth-century colonial rivalry has often been portrayed as an extra-European safety valve for the tensions of the great powers. In 1898 the French Colonel Marchand and Britain's General Kitchener had glared at each other at Fashoda, but both countries had treated their competition for the Upper Nile as a purely African problem. In 1902 and 1904 Britain had settled with Japan and France at least in order to remain isolated from Europe. But during the course of 1905 German behaviour caused the British to see the Moroccan crisis less as a colonial issue and increasingly as a European one. The Anglo-German rivalry, whose roots extended back over the previous three decades, and which had been nurtured by economic competition, now found clear political expression.

Germany's naval challenge was only a part, although the most concrete manifestation, of the two powers' mutual antagonism. The build-up of the Royal Navy pre-dated the 1898 German naval law: it was a product of the introduction of the iron-clad battleship, the two-power standard, and the need to sustain a consistent pattern of orders in order to use shipyard and industrial capacity effectively. But by 1901 the Admiralty was seriously worried by Germany's plans, and thereafter Germany provided the thrust to British naval policy. On the day before Trafalgar Day 1904 'Jackie' Fisher was appointed First Sea Lord. His brief was to cut naval spending, an objective which he believed he could achieve while simultaneously delivering gains in efficiency. By December the main outlines of his reforming programme were already clear. The combination of a steam-powered fleet with the Japanese and French agreements allowed Britain's battleships to concentrate on the North Sea without sacrificing their global mission. The redistribution scheme, which used the Atlantic Fleet at Gibraltar as a potential support for the Channel Fleet, meant that three-quarters of Britain's battleships were available to face the Germans.[23] Secondly, Fisher decided to begin work on a new and revolutionary class of battleship, the Dreadnought. In so doing he rendered obsolete Britain's existing naval superiority, but in practice he had little choice since other powers were on the brink of taking comparable decisions. Fisher's early thinking on warships was conditioned by rivalry with France and Russia, and put speed ahead of armour.

[23] Marder, *From the Dreadnought*, i. 40–2.

Envisaging war in the Atlantic or the Pacific, he wanted a vessel whose speed would enable the Royal Navy to keep its opponents at a distance and so defeat them through long-range gunnery: he dubbed this the 'battle cruiser'. But by 1905, when the first Dreadnought was laid down, the likely enemy was Germany and the probable theatre of operations the more confined spaces of the North Sea. The ship that therefore resulted was a battleship, and her most striking feature was not her speed of 22 knots but her armament.[24] Her size enabled her to mount five twin-turrets with 12-inch guns: her broadside and her effective range were double those of a pre-Dreadnought. The battleship had secured a fresh lease of life by being able to operate outside torpedo range. Fisher's anti-Germanism was as pronounced as Tirpitz's Anglophobia, and his hopes for a preventive war with Germany in 1905 were quite sufficient to justify German fears of another Copenhagen. But in his calmer moments Fisher, like Tirpitz, rationalized his fleet as a deterrent.[25]

Simultaneous with the anti-German shift in British naval thought was a comparable and similar growth within the British Foreign Office. Some members of the diplomatic service, like Eyre Crowe, were not immune to the navalism which accompanied Fisher's reforms. But most important was a belief in the balance of power in Europe, and the conviction after 1905 that Germany represented a threat to it. In the British case, ministerial direction from December 1905 was firm and continuous. Henry Campbell-Bannerman, who became prime minister when the Liberals were returned to power that month, appointed Sir Edward Grey as his foreign secretary. Grey, a liberal imperialist, used a cross-party appeal to win Conservative support for his policies, and to remove foreign policy from party-political debate and endow it with consistency and direction. Indeed, he managed to remain remarkably independent of his own cabinet, and thus minimize any challenge from the government's own left wing. The Liberals' programme of social reform, and after 1910 the preoccupations of domestic problems, meant that both parliament and cabinet were happy to collude in the separation of Britain's foreign policy from the mainstream. Thus Grey was left free to pursue a design that aimed at maintaining peace in Europe by preparing for war, and that saw

---

[24] Sumida, *In defence of naval supremacy*, 37–61.
[25] Marder (ed.), *Fear God and dread nought*, ii. 51, 55.

Britain's role as the arbitrator in balancing power in Europe. Grey's stance
was moral and high-minded, but it was also shrewdly realistic: a dominant power in Europe would threaten Britain's command of the sea at its
most vulnerable point—the Channel—and so the European balance was
an integral component in imperial security.[26]

The immediate threat to European stability, it was clear by 1906, came
from Germany. Thus British policy leaned towards France and towards
giving the Entente firmer shape and direction, albeit without a formal
commitment. Paul Cambon, France's ambassador in London, picked up
the mood in 1905, and worried that the Liberals might back-pedal
encouraged the French to seek ways of making the Entente a defensive
alliance. In December 1905 and January 1906 the two powers arranged
and conducted military staff talks which continued until May 1906. Grey
was a driving force in these conversations, but he insisted to the French
that they did not compromise British neutrality, and to begin with set
them directly in the context of the Moroccan crisis. Even when he later
acknowledged that the maintenance of the Entente would itself be a cause
for war, he omitted to inform the cabinet of the talks.[27]

Therefore, when in 1907 Britain settled its differences with Russia, the
treaty could not, like the earlier agreements with Japan and France,
remain set solely in a local and colonial context. The arena for British
and Russian rivalry was Asia, and for Britain the worry of Russian
penetration through Persia and Afghanistan to the frontiers of India
itself. In November 1904 fears of Russians at the Khyber led the viceroy
in India to demand a potential reinforcement of 143,686 men in addition
to the army already in India.[28] Therefore, Britain's rapprochement with
Russia was not a revolution in British foreign policy: it was a diplomatic
conclusion determined by strategic and financial common sense, and one
which Grey himself had espoused ever since he had been parliamentary
under-secretary at the Foreign Office in the early 1890s. The main domestic obstacle had been Liberal sentiment, averse to any agreement with
a reactionary autocracy. Such sensibilities were eased by the constitutional reforms introduced in Russia after the 1905 revolution, and were

---

[26] Howard, *Continental commitment*, 51–2; on the British position in general, see Steiner,
Britain and the origins.
[27] Williamson, *Politics of grand strategy*, ch. 3, esp. 72–4, 81–3.
[28] Gooch, *Plans of war*, 217.

further consoled by the treaty's Asiatic context, which rendered it the solution to a long-standing imperial rivalry. But the implications were much greater than the fact that not so many troops would have to go to India. The Anglo-Russian convention was the coping-stone of the Anglo-French Entente. The Triple Entente had become simultaneously the means by which Britain could contain Germany in Europe, and also a contrivance for moderating relations with France and Russia. If Britain wanted to support France, it had also to accommodate Russia. French capital was increasingly—by 1914 it would be a quarter of all French investments—committed to Russia; the falling French birth rate—the lowest of the major powers in Europe—rendered France reliant on Russia's military manpower. Thus, for Conservatives the settlement was the first stage in facing a fresh threat, that of Germany.

What made the Anglo-Russian convention possible was less change in Britain than change in Russia. The twin blows of defeat in Manchuria and revolution at home convinced the Tsar's advisers that war prompted domestic upheaval. The principal objective of P. A. Stolypin, the chairman of the Council of Ministers from 1906 to 1911, was the corollary of this point: peace was necessary to enable domestic consolidation. Thus, both Stolypin and Russia's foreign minister, A. P. Izvolsky, were anxious not merely to end Russia's forward policy in the Far East but also to secure its frontiers elsewhere. Settlement with Britain in Central Asia was one element in a package that might also embrace Germany in the Baltic and Austria-Hungary in the Balkans. But Russia lacked the strength to shape its own policy. Although in certain senses both Britain and France needed Russia more than Russia needed them, the latter was handicapped by its inability to set and follow its own agenda. As the first Moroccan crisis had shown, it had to choose between the emerging blocs. Although Russia would persist in seeking understandings with Germany and Austria-Hungary, in the last resort it remained wedded to France and Britain, finding on each occasion that it did so that the Entente tightened.[29]

In Germany, therefore, the overriding consequence of the 1905 Moroccan crisis was an unravelling of *Weltpolitik*. There can be no greater indictment of German diplomacy than the fact that the deep-seated

[29] McDonald, *United government and foreign policy in Russia*, 4, 97–110; Neilson, *Britain and the last Tsar*, pp. xiv, 11–12, 267–9; D. W. Spring, *Slavonic and East European Review*, LXVI (1988), 583–91.

hostilities of Britain, France, and Russia had been resolved so rapidly. The constellation which faced it in 1907 had seemed unimaginable: before 1904 a Franco-British Entente was improbable, then in 1904–5 it had been hoped that the *entente cordiale* would weaken the Franco-Russian convention, and throughout there had remained the assumption that Britain and Russia were irreconcilable. More specifically, the false assumptions which Tirpitz's naval policy had made of Britain were now writ large. The calculations of German naval deficiency had not reckoned on Fisher's redistribution of the British fleet; the gradualism of the naval build-up was no longer tenable with the commissioning of the first Dreadnought; and Britain—despite a hiccough in 1907—declared its determination to continue building to the two-power standard, which meant that Germany could never reach a sufficient level for effective deterrence. To use epithets like 'paranoid' and 'fatalistic' of Germany after 1905—adjectives more appropriate to individuals than nations—does not seem so misplaced. German expansion, conceived in limited terms and apparently no more ambitious than that allowed to other powers, had triggered the creation of a power bloc which not only seemed to prevent the flexing of Germany's own industrial and commercial muscle but also to encircle Germany by land to the east and west and by sea to the north.

The vocabulary of personal emotion is of course rendered more appropriate in the context of personal rule. Bülow and *Weltpolitik*, Tirpitz and the navy—these were the creatures by which the Kaiser had attempted to legitimize his own position; Wilhelm himself had been Germany's emissary in Tangiers. His principal adviser, and indeed the architect of the means by which the Kaiser's personal rule might be effected, was Philipp von Eulenburg. In 1908 Eulenburg was arraigned on a charge of homosexuality. The implications for the imperial court as a whole went beyond scandal and loss of prestige; Eulenburg's departure left the Kaiser's entourage dominated by the military. Furthermore, in November of the same year Wilhelm gave a typically vainglorious interview to the London *Daily Telegraph*, which aroused the fury of all parties in the Reichstag and opened a split between the monarch and his foreign office. The accumulation of these blows marks the point at which personal rule can be accounted to have failed. Given the fact that Germany's constitution was designed to rest on the Kaiser's command—above all in the areas of war and diplomacy—Wilhelm's subsequent loss of confidence left a vacuum which was probably even more dangerous to Germany than his earlier assertions of authority.

No comparable self-doubts seem to have assailed Tirpitz. In 1906 he used the mood generated by the Moroccan crisis to pass a supplementary naval bill, increasing the annual spending on the fleet by 35 per cent. However, it was the 1908 bill that accepted the acceleration of the German programme in the light of the Dreadnought, and which institutionalized a naval arms race between the two powers. The life of a capital ship was reduced from twenty-five years to twenty, so that Germany would build not three but four ships a year between 1908 and 1911, and would therefore have a total of fifty-eight capital ships by 1920. Privately, Tirpitz was aiming at a rate of three—not the agreed two—ships a year in the period 1912–17.

The cost of such a programme revealed the fragility of any compromise on which *Sammlungspolitik* might rest. In the 1907 elections Bülow fought a successful campaign on an appeal to *Weltpolitik*, convincing the left-liberals, the Progressives, that they should join his bloc so as to balance reactionary influences within it and avoid the threat of a Centre party–socialist coalition; the socialists actually lost thirty-six seats. But Bülow had little with which he could hold the Progressives over the long term. Even more importantly, the financing of the navy would split conservatives and national liberals. The additional cost per ship when built to Dreadnought standards was 7 million marks, and a further 60 million marks were required for improved port facilities.[30] The deficit anticipated by the 1908 naval programme was 500 million gold marks. The national debt was almost double that of 1900. To put federal finances on a sound footing Bülow had to diminish the powers of the individual states, which were still largely responsible for their own taxation: he would therefore expose a sore which *Weltpolitik* had been designed to heal. To meet part of the deficit he planned to increase inheritance tax; thus the navy came home to roost, directly challenging the interests of conservative landowners. The Centre party joined with the Conservatives in calling for a tax on mobile capital: together they crushed the inheritance tax proposal, and passed the burden of taxation on to business and urban interests. The economic consequences of *Weltpolitik* had divided,

---

[30] Epkenhans, *Wilhelminische Flottenrüstung*, 26.

not united, the different forms of property-ownership. In June 1909 Bülow, no longer able to manage the Reichstag and held responsible by the Kaiser for the *Daily Telegraph* affair, resigned the chancellorship.

Bülow had the satisfaction of nominating his successor, Theodor von Bethmann Hollweg, a Prussian bureaucrat and former secretary of state for the interior. Bethmann Hollweg was a cabinet politician, not a popular national leader. Reserved, conscientious, and honest, he never mastered the office of which he was to be the incumbent until 1917. Fritz Fischer has bracketed Bethmann with the military and Prussian influences that were to dominate Germany during the war; by contrast, Sir Edward Grey and other contemporary observers imagined that in him rested Germany's hopes for liberalism and true parliamentary government. Neither view is wholly correct. Bethmann Hollweg was a conservative and saw the position of government as above—not dependent on—the political parties. But he was also pragmatic enough to recognize that reform, albeit limited, of the Prussian suffrage was required: typically, the measure he proposed in 1910 was sufficient to alienate the right and insufficient to please the left. Thus, even more than was the case with Bülow, his management of the Reichstag constituted a succession of short-lived compromises. Not even the conservatives, who now acted as an agrarian interest group rather than as the supporters of the political status quo, were reliable. In any case, in the 1912 elections all the parties of the right and centre lost ground to the socialists, who won sixty-seven seats to become the largest party in the Reichstag. Bethmann Hollweg's power, therefore, rested to an increasing degree on external pressure groups and on his relationship—always lukewarm—with the Kaiser himself.[31]

Bülow had managed the Reichstag by use of *Weltpolitik.* But when Bethmann Hollweg became chancellor the financial implications of the navy's expansion ensured that *Weltpolitik* was deeply divisive in its effects. Bethmann therefore forswore *Weltpolitik,* at least in its more aggressive forms, for a policy of détente. He did so for reasons not of foreign policy, a field in which he had no previous experience, but of domestic political necessity. Indeed, even had he tried to manipulate the parties by the use of nationalist appeals, he might well not have succeeded. The 1909 budget had still not resolved Germany's economic problems. Nor was it only

[31] Jarausch, *Enigmatic chancellor,* 71–91.

among conservatives—with their fears of increased inheritance taxes—
that opposition to naval spending was now to be found. Industry itself
was divided: between 1904 and 1914 Britain was Germany's best overseas
customer, and Germany was Britain's second best; twenty-two out of
forty international producer cartels were Anglo-German organizations.[32]
Thus, while some German concerns welcomed the steady orders which
the naval arms race generated, others—including not only bankers but
also iron and steel exporters—stood to lose by any further deterioration
in Germany's relations with Britain.

An Anglo-German naval agreement was therefore the main means by
which Bethmann sought to extricate himself from his problems. By 1908
Bülow had already been thinking along similar lines, but Tirpitz had
proved strongly opposed and he had been abetted by the Kaiser. The
argument that naval construction might browbeat the British into a
German agreement was no longer deemed relevant. This is not to say
that Tirpitz now wanted war with Britain. He recognized full well that
such a conflict would be futile. The opportunity to exploit the *tabula rasa*
which the Dreadnought revolution had, at least in theory, created had
not been seized; Germany's implementation of it lagged three years
behind Britain's, and its building targets still did not aspire to equiva-
lence. However, Tirpitz did aim to break Britain's commitment to the
two-power standard. He proposed a formula under which ostensibly
Germany would build two ships a year for every three built by Britain,
but whose effects in practice would produce three and four. Germany
would not reduce its programme, and Britain would have to increase its
own if it wished to maintain its lead. Furthermore, because Britain had a
larger fleet in the first place, more of its new construction would be
replacing obsolete ships rather than adding to the total size of the fleet.
Thus the gap in the effective size of the two forces would be narrowed.
Tirpitz derived some comfort from the fact that radical pressures on
Britain's Liberal government produced a rationale for the fleet that
eschewed reference to the two-power standard, but in reality the talks
held out little prospect of a successful outcome. Bethmann Hollweg
wished to use the specific issue of a naval agreement to secure a much
wider objective, that of British neutrality. In April 1910 the Germans

---

[32] Steiner, *Britain and the origins*, 60–4.

actually proposed that Britain commit itself to neutrality before a naval agreement was concluded: to the Foreign Office in London it seemed that Germany was using a naval lever to secure British isolation and German domination of the continent.[33]

Bethmann Hollweg's efforts at détente were not limited to Britain. Germany's rivalry with France and Russia found its focus in Europe and not further afield; the roots of the Triple Entente were to be traced to colonial questions, and thus the chances that long-term imperial tensions between the Entente partners might reappear seemed good. Bilateral arrangements with France and Russia on extra-European questions promised some loosening of the Entente. Furthermore, they accorded well with Bethmann's increasing personal sense that Germany needed colonies of its own. The détente which France and Germany achieved between 1909 and 1910 was limited, and primarily motivated by economic links (German exports to France increased 38 per cent in 1905–9), which the governments—and particularly Jules Cambon, France's ambassador in Berlin—endeavoured to clothe with political formulae. In February 1909 the Germans recognized French political interests in Morocco, and France recognized Germany's economic interests; discussions took place about possible co-operation in the Congo and the Cameroons, and French short-term capital was loaned to Germany for the construction of the Baghdad railway.[34] The latter also provided the basis, in November 1910, of an agreement between Germany and Russia: Russia approved of the extension of the Baghdad railway, while Germany undertook to help in the opening of railways in Russia's sphere of interest in Persia.

By early 1911 France was worried by the implications of Bethmann's policy for Entente unity, although it does not seem to have conceived of its next step in that light. Indubitably, however, one of the repercussions of the 1911 Moroccan crisis was a reinvigoration of Anglo-French links. The resumption of a forward French policy in Morocco was largely the responsibility of the younger generation of French Foreign Ministry bureaucrats, who dominated a weak and inexperienced foreign minister.[35] Their target was as much Germany and an end to the détente

[33] Ibid. 54–6; Epkenhans, *Wilhelminische Flottenrüstung*, 32–91.
[34] Duroselle, *La France*, 12–19; Keiger, *France and the origins*, 37–40; Kaiser, *Politics and war*, 321–2.
[35] Keiger, *France and the origins*, 34; Hayne, *French foreign office*, 199–214.

which Jules Cambon had fostered as it was an expansion of French influence in North Africa. 'The solution of the Moroccan crisis', Charles Maurras wrote in *Action française*, 'is not to be found in Fez but among the pines of the Vosges. What is afoot in Morocco makes sense only if we are prepared to fight in the Vosges.'[36] The second Moroccan crisis made explicit what had been implicit in the first: colonial questions were not to be dealt with simply on their own terms but were projected back into European rivalries. Indeed, the geographical position of Morocco— affecting as it did the balance of power in the Mediterranean—was bound to make the isolation of problems here from problems in Europe that much more difficult than it was for any disputes over spheres of responsibility in Central Asia or Equatorial Africa.

Using the excuse of riots against the Sultan in Fez, the French ordered troops into Morocco on 17 April 1911. Once in, the soldiers were slow to depart. The French were clearly in contravention of the Algeçiras act. Neither the Spanish nor the British were very pleased, and the Germans gave the French a specific warning. However, the French having reopened the Moroccan question, the Germans, and specifically Kiderlen-Wächter, the foreign minister, saw the opportunity for a diplomatic success in true *Weltpolitik* style. Joseph Caillaux, France's prime minister from June, was conscious of the weakness of the French position, and was more conciliatory than his Foreign Office. Through secret negotiations—which bypassed the Foreign Office—he encouraged Kiderlen in the pursuit of German objectives. Kiderlen wished to trade German recognition of the French position in Morocco for concessions in the Congo. On 1 July, on the pretext of protecting German commercial interests, the German warship, *Panther*, appeared at Agadir.

Such sabre-rattling—although the Germans had no intention of going to war, and indeed were still without a naval plan for operations against Britain—could only provoke. Germany had seen the issue as one between France and Germany only. The employment of sea-power, however limited, immediately raised the hackles of Britain. Paramount was the fear of Germany acquiring an Atlantic port. The inadequacy of British naval and military intelligence only served to reinforce Germanophobe prejudice: the whereabouts of the German fleet was

uncertain in July, and in September false indications of German preparations on the Belgian frontier suggested imminent invasion.[37] During
July Grey's attitude hardened: the crisis was no longer concerned with
the irresponsibility of French imperial policy but with the survival of the
Entente. On this occasion the cabinet was involved: evidence of the degree
of Britain's commitment would be calculated to infuriate the radicals and
pacifists within the Liberal party, and increase the reliance of a government that lacked an overall parliamentary majority on Conservative
support. On 21 July Lloyd George, as chancellor of the exchequer, spoke
in the Mansion House: without naming Germany, he clearly stated that
Britain would fight rather than let its status as a great power go un-
acknowledged. The Mansion House speech was designed above all for
domestic purposes: by supporting Grey's foreign policy, Lloyd George—
the hero of the left and the author of the Liberals' package of social
reforms—split the radicals and assured the Liberal imperialists of support in the cabinet and in the party. But it also had an international effect.
It faced Germany with the threat of war, however veiled, and Kiderlen-
Wächter could not command the support either of Germany's ally,
Austria-Hungary, or of the Kaiser to play for such stakes. In the event
Kiderlen got what he had asked for; Caillaux continued to bypass his
foreign ministry and on 4 November Germany—in exchange for recognizing a French protectorate over Morocco—was guaranteed respect for
its economic interests and received a slice of the French Congo. But
popular feeling in Germany was characterized by a sense of humiliation.
The iron and steel industries had hoped for concessions to mine the ores
of southern Morocco itself. Expectations had been roused and then
disappointed. Both the Kaiser and Bethmann Hollweg lost credit. The
frustration at diplomacy's failure to gain for Germany the status its power
warranted grew apace.

Much of this feeling was directed against Britain, and in Britain too the
crisis had the effect of hardening popular sentiment. Britain was the
power that had taken the initiative in elevating a colonial dispute into a
European crisis: henceforth it was not to be deflected from having
Europe, rather than the empire, as the focus of its foreign policy. At the
Committee of Imperial Defence on 23 August 1911 strategy followed suit.

---

[37] Hiley, *Historical Journal*, XXVI (1983), 881–4.

It is tempting to argue that British military thought had already anticipated diplomacy in assuming a continental thrust. In 1903 and 1908 the Committee of Imperial Defence had concluded that British naval supremacy ensured that there was little prospect of a successful hostile invasion of Britain. Furthermore, the succession of alliances, ending with the 1907 Anglo-Russian convention, lessened the number of strategic options which the newly created general staff had to consider. The possibility of operations against Germany in Europe, first adumbrated in 1902 and the object of a war game in 1905, gradually grew in importance. But until 1907 any major continental operations which the army envisaged were centred on India, not—despite the 1906 Anglo-French staff talks—on Europe. The purpose of the latter was diplomatic, not strategic. They were fostered by the politicians, Grey and the secretary of war, Haldane, rather than by the soldiers, who had formed a low estimate of the French army.[38] The British Expeditionary Force of six divisions, ready to be dispatched to any quarter of the globe, and fashioned by Haldane, was the fruit of cash constraints, not strategic reappraisal. The burgeoning costs of the navy, plus the Liberals' domestic reforms, necessitated savings: between 1905/6 and 1909/10 Haldane had lopped £2.5 million from the army estimates. Haldane's army was still the projectile of the navy, relying on sea-power for ubiquity and concentration, and so gaining in effectiveness and in flexibility while remaining small.[39]

Two factors contributed to the emerging dominance of continentalism in British military thought. First, the navy itself showed little interest in amphibious operations: the fleet wanted a big sea battle in the event of European war not the more mundane tasks of transporting and supplying limited land warfare on the European periphery. The one plan it did develop, that for a landing on the Baltic coast, was dismissed as unworkable by the army as early as the winter of 1908–9.[40] Secondly, Henry Wilson, a noted Francophile, convinced that war in Europe was inevitable and possessed of political instincts few British soldiers could match,

[38] Herrmann, *Arming of Europe*, 55–6, 84.

[39] Gooch, *Plans of war*, 165–73; Gooch, *Prospect of war*, pp. vii–viii, 93–112; Spiers, *Haldane*, 3–4, 9, 38–44, 64–5, 71–3, 77–81, 193–5.

[40] Paul Hayes, 'Britain, Germany and the Admiralty's plans for attacking German territory 1906–1915', in Freedman *et al.* (eds.), *War, strategy and international politics*.

became director of military operations in August 1910. Wilson promptly began to give substance to the 1906 staff talks; he conveniently calculated that the British contribution of six divisions was sufficient to swing the balance in a Franco-German conflict, and set about planning the transport of those divisions to France. Thus, when in the wake of the Agadir crisis the Committee of Imperial Defence met on 23 August 1911 to review British strategy in the event of a European war, the army's case was well developed and specific. By contrast, the presentation of Sir A. K. Wilson, Fisher's successor as First Sea Lord, was shambling and ill-thought-out. The navy's potential supporters were not present at the meeting; instead, Lloyd George and Winston Churchill—representatives of the radicals in the government—were convinced by the arguments for rapid continental intervention in the event of a Franco-German war. In the wake of that meeting Churchill was appointed First Lord of the Admiralty. The effect was to divide Churchill from Lloyd George, so weakening the radicals' voice in the cabinet. The significance of this move became increasingly evident in late 1913 and early 1914, by which stage the chancellor of the exchequer regarded the European scene as increasingly peaceful and the case for a reduction in naval spending in 1915 as correspondingly stronger.[41] Ostensibly Churchill's task was to create a naval staff, so that the senior service could prepare itself as well as the army had done for strategic discussions, but it was also to bring the navy into line with continental thought. The French navy in 1906 had already decided to concentrate its strength in the Mediterranean, and Fisher's redistribution had weighted the British navy towards the Atlantic and the Channel; these independent decisions were made complementary by the institution of Anglo-French naval talks in 1912. The Royal Navy was prepared to accept operational plans that confirmed its existing deployment, and consigned what was seen as a subsidiary theatre to the secondary naval power.

Although the consequence of the second Moroccan crisis was a closer identification between British strategy and French, no formal alliance resulted. The cabinet was informed in November 1911 of the Anglo-French staff talks, and a year later agreed, as the culmination of the naval discussions, that the two powers would consult each other in the event of an attack by a third party. In German eyes British diplomacy was

[41] Grigg, *Lloyd George*, 133; Gilbert, *Lloyd George*, 76.

now focused on the Entente, not on the concert of Europe, with the Foreign Office too ready to interpret every crisis, however fomented, as the consequence of a Berlin-driven conspiracy.[42] Nonetheless, Grey warded off French pressure for an even tighter commitment, citing his fear of radical opposition in parliament and the accompanying danger that even these limited agreements could thus be undermined. The concert of Europe remained his ideal means of managing the continent; the Entente was a device by which Britain could maintain its free hand, while simultaneously cautioning the Germans and moderating French and German behaviour.[43] Britain's refusal to align itself unequivocally created an ambiguity in great power relations between 1911 and 1914, for Grey's faith in the concert system was not reciprocated elsewhere. Conferences had, after all, not proved to be to Germany's advantage.

French foreign policy, while not pursuing an entirely straight course after 1911, gained considerably in coherence and direction. Caillaux's secret communications with Germany were intercepted and deciphered by the intelligence service of the very Foreign Ministry he was trying to bypass. In January 1912 the Germanophobe and radical, Georges Clemenceau, used this information to engineer the fall of Caillaux's government. Raymond Poincaré, who formed the new ministry, had been rapporteur of the Senate commission to examine the Franco-German treaty of 4 November 1911, and assumed the foreign office portfolio himself. In January 1913 Poincaré became president, an office that he was to hold until 1920. He was thus able to provide the continuity which proved so elusive, given the endemic ministerial instability of the Third Republic. Partly by sheer hard work, partly by creating his own administrative structure, and partly by his direct access to intercepted diplomatic messages, he contrived to be independent of the machinations of the bureaux of the foreign ministry, and to a considerable degree to insulate foreign policy from the seven changes of government experienced by France between 1912 and 1914.

Poincaré himself was a Lorrainer; he was a patriot and he distrusted Germany. But it would be mistaken to conclude that France either sought

---

[42] Gregor Schöllgen, 'Germany's foreign policy in the age of imperialism: a vicious circle?', 129–30, and Gustav Schmidt, 'Contradictory postures and conflicting objectives: the July crisis', 138, in Schöllgen (ed.), *Escape into war?*.

[43] Steiner, *Britain and the origins*, 244–5; also 113, 117.

war or did so to recover Alsace-Lorraine. If Germany and France found themselves at war for other reasons, the lost provinces would, quite clearly, become a war aim for France. *Révanche* figured large in German projections of French ambitions, but in practice mattered little to most Frenchmen. The provinces increasingly identified themselves with Germany, and not even the Zabern incident of 1913, which made abundantly clear the high-handedness of the German military presence, evoked an official French response.

Poincaré's foreign policy had two main aims. Domestically, he hoped to establish a political consensus, drawing support from the left and right of the centre, and weakening *Action française* on the extreme right and socialism on the left. His chances of success were boosted by the fact that radicalism, like liberalism in Germany, was being split between left and right: at the beginning of the century anticlericalism had sponsored a fusion of the radicals and socialists, but after 1906 the socialists had been pulled away from the bourgeois radicals by the need to respond to the trades-union movement. Externally, Poincaré saw the Triple Alliance and the Triple Entente as creating a European balance of power and fostering continental security through mutual rivalry. To that end, the coalition of the opposing alliance was as important as that of his own. The activities of Jules Cambon in Berlin, fostering Franco-German détente, were rebuffed as a threat to Entente solidarity; but so too were the efforts of Barrère, France's ambassador in Rome, to draw Italy out of the Triple Alliance by exploiting Italian hostility for Austria-Hungary. One of the paradoxes of European security before 1914 was that each of the major players—Grey, Bethmann Hollweg, and Poincaré himself—sought to create stability, but each used different means as appropriate to its achievement.

It followed from Poincaré's commitment to the Entente that Franco-Russian relations, as well as Anglo-French, should be strengthened in 1912. From the German perspective such moves were far from reassuring: they cut across Bethmann Hollweg's policy of détente and they confirmed fears of a two-front war. Poincaré's policy did nothing to lessen the tensions in European relations, and to that extent he promoted war rather than averted it.[44] Moreover, his policy in relation to Russia in 1912 was open to more than one interpretation. Poincaré's defenders argue that his

---

[44] Hayne, *French foreign policy*, 242–3.

object was to manage Russia, not egg her on: the lack of Russian support for France during the 1911 crisis and German efforts to woo Russia combined with a desire to restrain Russia in her policies towards the Ottoman empire and the Balkans. But to the Russians themselves, and even to Henry Wilson, Poincaré could seem an adventurist.[45] In July 1912 the French and Russian general staffs met, as they had been doing since 1892 under the terms of the military convention. The following month Poincaré visited Russia in order to learn more of Russian involvement in the Balkans. He assured the Russians that should Russia and Austria-Hungary come to blows over the Balkans, and should the Germans then support the Austrians, they could rely on French support. Poincaré gave this undertaking knowing that in all probability the Germans would strike against France first, in order to secure their rear before turning east. The commitment did not, therefore, represent a major shift in the French position; rather, it was vital to the plans of the French general staff who hoped thus to secure Russian support against any German attack on France. On 17 November 1912 Poincaré reiterated his undertaking to Russia: France's concern for its own defence therefore allowed Russia to be more adventurous—not less so—in the Balkans. Poincaré reaffirmed his Russian policy by appointing Delcassé as France's ambassador in St Petersburg in February 1913.[46] In the summer, the French government intervened in Russian negotiations on the French stock market for a loan to finance railway construction. The French objective was to bring pressure to bear on the speed of Russian mobilization, so as to co-ordinate mutually supporting attacks on Germany from east and west: the French said they would concentrate 200,000 more troops than they had undertaken to do in 1892.[47]

All the threads of Poincaré's foreign policy were brought together during the course of 1913 by the debate on the extension of the period of military service to three years. At one level this was a purely technical question. In 1905 the term of service was set at two years: loud and long were the complaints of regular soldiers, who felt that all their time was

[45] Stevenson, *Armaments and the coming of war*, 239–41.

[46] On Poincaré's policy in general, see Keiger, *France and the origins*; on the importance of the 1912 guarantees, L. C. F. Turner, 'Russian mobilisation in 1914' in Kennedy (ed.), *War plans*, 252–6.

[47] Krumeich, *Armaments*, ch. 6.

taken up with basic training and that the level of training then acquired was inadequate. Force was given to their arguments by the relative decline in the French population (France in 1910 had to take 83 per cent of her available manpower to produce the same size army as Germany did with 57.3 per cent),[48] and by the need to match the increases authorized for the Germany army in 1912–13. Professional military wisdom therefore calculated that a longer period of service would produce an army that was both larger and more competent. The domestic arguments of the French army were of course at one with the strategy which the alliance with Russia now demanded: both Poincaré and the French general staff had committed France to taking the offensive against Germany if need be. The alliance and the three-year law therefore interlocked.[49] So powerful were these arguments that the radicals could not unite on the issue, but split, some acknowledging the threat posed by the level of German military preparedness and others accepting the socialists' preference for a short-term citizen army. The debate showed how relatively little French politics were polarized when foreign policy was employed in a domestic context: the radicals and socialists did form a fresh bloc in October 1913, but the issue that united them was less opposition to three-year service and more the advocacy of income tax as a means to finance it. Finally, although set in the context of popular nationalism, the three-year service law was presented by the government as a means of reassurance and of deterrence in Franco-German relations. The minister of war, addressing the army committee of the Chamber of Deputies on 11 March 1913, accepted that defensive requirements necessitated German manpower increases, given the threats to east and west: 'Quite frankly, and I mean this most sincerely,' he declared, 'I do not think that at this moment, as I utter these words, or even yesterday, Germany has or had the intention to pounce upon France.'[50]

While the Moroccan crisis hardened the Entente, and in particular France's advocacy of robustness as a means to deterrence, it alarmed Bethmann Hollweg. He did not abandon *Weltpolitik*, but he did soften it, recognizing that its pursuit should be harmonized at least with Britain. Furthermore, the chances of domestic support for a renewed attempt at

[48] Ritter, *Sword and the sceptre*, ii. 223.   [49] Krumeich, *Armaments*, esp. 17–18, 125.
[50] Quoted in ibid. 74.

an Anglo-German naval agreement seemed, on the face of it, reasonable. The naval budget had grown 134 per cent between 1904 and 1912, against an army increase of 47 per cent; naval spending now exceeded half the total military expenditure.[51] By espousing the army's case for attention Bethmann could deflect the navy's, and so play off one against the other. Furthermore, the navy itself was divided by Tirpitz's building programme: Henning von Holtzendorff, the commander of the High Seas Fleet, wanted to improve training and efficiency rather than to have more ships. On the political front, the composition of the Reichstag did not augur well for the navy's chances of further funds: the January 1912 elections had been a triumph for the left and, in March 1912, introduction of a new inheritance tax undermined any residual support from the right. The Treasury and the Bundesrat—for similar financial reasons— backed Bethmann against Tirpitz. Finally, German hopes that the British Liberal government would be more amenable than it had been in 1909 and 1910 were buoyed by the anxiety of its more radical members at the heightened Anglo-German tension; Herbert Asquith's cabinet (Asquith succeeded Campbell-Bannerman as prime minister in 1908) had to show its supporters that it had at least tried to reach an understanding with Germany.

In practice, the prospects of success were remote. Tirpitz was now openly set on a rate of construction that would proceed independently of Britain, and would give Germany a ratio of 2:3 in capital ships. He proposed a supplementary naval law, that would prevent a return to a building rate of two vessels per year as planned, and would instead commit Germany to three ships in each of 1912, 1914, and 1916. Domestic-ally his cards were stronger than first appearances suggested. To those supportive of détente he could argue that Britain would never negotiate if Germany embarked on reductions unilaterally. The case for firmness was of course equally attractive to those who identified Britain as the primary author of Germany's humiliation at Agadir. And for Tirpitz himself, conscious of the domestic political pressures now mounting against the naval programme, an international agreement fixing rates of shipbuilding would at least secure the programme's independence of the Reichstag. The Kaiser, listening to the naval attaché in London rather than to

[51] Herwig, *Luxury fleet*, 75.

the German ambassador, backed Tirpitz and not Bethmann Hollweg. Bethmann's domestic position was further weakened on 9 February 1912 when Churchill sarcastically and provocatively characterized the German navy as a 'luxury fleet'.

Therefore, when the British emissary Haldane, the secretary of state for war and a student of German philosophy, arrived in Berlin, his expectations were not great. The Kaiser, it is true, was as usual using bluster and declamation as a substitute for diplomacy, and at bottom hoped and even believed that a strong line would bring Britain to terms more readily than overt conciliation. But Bethmann Hollweg still wished for a general undertaking of neutrality on Britain's part, and his hopes were raised by Haldane's apparent inclination to discuss political issues rather than naval matters. Even more encouraging was Churchill's suggestion on 18 March of a 'naval holiday'. For most Germans this suggested that their strong line had triumphed; however, Tirpitz was momentarily nonplussed, since Churchill's suggested ratio of sixteen British Dreadnoughts for ten German implied a break in the building tempo. Four days later the 1912 German supplementary naval law was published. Churchill calculated that it would compel Britain to build five ships in one year and then four the next year over a six-year period, at a cost of an extra 3 million pounds a year.[52] Whatever the financial burden, Britain was not prepared to be neutralized, to leave France to German domination, and so undermine its own strategic position. The talks reached an impasse. The Anglo-French naval agreement of 1912 was therefore in part a gesture of solidarity towards France after the flirtation with Germany. It was also profoundly pragmatic: to control naval building Britain had—given the 1912 German law—to ask France to take on responsibility for the Mediterranean in the name of the Entente.

The naval balance in the Mediterranean highlighted the fact that by the summer of 1912 both sides, and particularly Britain, were pursuing policies that were increasingly driven by factors in addition to those that determined their relationship with each other. Britain maintained a one-power standard in the Mediterranean, so that it would be equivalent to the next largest local navy after that of France. Thus the decision

---

[52] Marder, *From the Dreadnought*, i. 275–6; Epkenhans, *Wilhelminische Flottenrüstung*, 114–42.

by Austria-Hungary to lay down two Dreadnoughts in 1910 and a further two in 1912 (so matching Italy's programme) was both a driving force in the Anglo-French naval agreement and a factor in the abandonment of the idea of a 'naval holiday'.[53] Similarly Australia, New Zealand, and to a lesser extent Canada showed an interest in contributing to the Dreadnought programme, not so much because of the German threat in the North Sea as because of their worries about Japan in the Pacific. The equivalent German pressure was the Russian decision to replace the Baltic fleet lost at Tsushima. The effect of these secondary naval arms races was to compound the principal one, each side aggregating the forces of its opponent, although elements of its own building were a response to other pressures. In May 1912 Churchill declared that Britain would build two new ships for every additional German ship; the implication of his programme was that by 1917 Britain would have fifty-one Dreadnoughts to Germany's twenty-eight.

Nonetheless, by late 1912 the heat had gone out of the Anglo-German naval arms race. This was due primarily neither to Churchill's determined response nor to Bethmann Hollweg's pursuit of détente. The core explanation was the implosion of *Sammlungspolitik* itself. By 1912 the latter had become more of a vehicle by which to drive Germany's armaments policies than an end in itself.[54] Arms spending in 1913 accounted for only 4.7 per cent of Germany's net social product, and it was therefore too small to have any stabilizing effect in the economy as a whole; much of it was spent on personnel rather than plant, and its consequences were to reduce the capital available for further investment while driving up interest rates. Bethmann Hollweg's response was contradictory. On the one hand he publicly rejected international competition over arms, while on the other he espoused the army's case against that of the navy.[55] The latter was the ultimate loser. Crucially, the Kaiser withdrew his support for Tirpitz, and at the same time elements within the navy itself demanded that manning and training should take priority over matériel. On 6 February 1913 Tirpitz announced to the Reichstag's budget committee that he now found Churchill's proposed 16:10

[53] Stevenson, *Armaments and the coming of war*, 174–5, 215.
[54] Geyer, *Deutsche Rüstungspolitik*, 89.
[55] Kroboth, *Finanzpolitik des Deutschen Reiches*, 306, 312.

Dreadnought ratio acceptable. Germany's renunciation of the Anglo-German naval arms race was effectively unilateral.[56]

The other bridge to détente open to Bethmann Hollweg was through colonial policy. Here Bethmann enjoyed greater success. Neither France nor Britain was opposed to German colonialism per se, provided it did not clash with their own interests. In the Moroccan agreement France accepted German ambitions in Central Africa; so did Britain in its negotiations with Germany over the Portuguese colonies, and specifically Angola. Between 1912 and 1914 Britain and Germany found that their interests in the Baghdad railway could, by dividing the line at Basra, be rendered complementary rather than contradictory: simultaneously Germany—short of capital because of the demands of its own rapid industrialization—welcomed French finance and involvement in the project. Within France the formation of the radical–socialist bloc in October 1913 forced Poincaré to appoint a radical, Doumergue, as prime minister, and Doumergue brought back Caillaux as his finance minister. By late 1913 both Poincaré's orientation of French foreign policy and even his status as president looked less secure, and when in January 1914 Germany and Russia argued over their respective interests in Turkey, French support for Russia was more cautious than Russia might have expected. Furthermore, the question of the three-year law was reopened for debate. Bethmann's hope, that extra-European interests carefully played would show more points of contact between France and Germany and would reveal the underlying tensions between the imperial ambitions of the Entente powers, seemed to be well founded. Certainly it provided the basis for much of the optimism with which many Europeans greeted 1914. But Bethmann's policy worked because it was limited. It was effective in certain geographical areas where tensions were already low; it did not push any of the Entente powers into breaking with its allies. And it came too late. Colonial antagonisms had already shaped European alliances; it would take a long time and considerable patience before colonial agreements could loosen those alliances.

Bethmann Hollweg had come to share Bülow's position, to recognize that Germany's economic strength and great-power status made expansionist pretensions legitimate. To that extent détente was his version of

---

[56] Epkenhans, *Wilhelminische Flottenrüstungspolitik*, 312–24, 343, 396.

Weltpolitik. Furthermore, it was clear that in Bethmann's hands, even more than in Bülow's, *Weltpolitik* could be accommodated in international politics. The events of 1905–14 showed that Franco-German and Anglo-German disputes could be settled without war. Even the naval rivalry had become institutionalized to the point where Churchill could claim, admittedly after the event, that it was increasingly irrelevant to Anglo-German controversies.[57] Bethmann's confidant the youthful Kurt Riezler, in his pseudonymous work of 1913, *Grundzüge der Weltpolitik* (the fundamentals of world policy), concluded that the dangers of defeat were such that war had lost its utility and that, although it might occur through irrationality or dire necessity, it would not occur through calculation. In particular, he saw the alliance system as a restraint, since in no one crisis would all allies simultaneously view their interests as so threatened that they would support each other to the point of war.[58]

Riezler's analysis, however, also revealed exactly how destructive *Weltpolitik* had been to the tenor of west European relations. All nations, he thought, conceived of coexistence 'as a preparation for hostility, as a postponement of hostility'; armaments were therefore a form of that postponement and were an essential component of the bluff necessary in diplomacy. *Weltpolitik* had militarized international relations. The naval arms race had assumed a momentum of its own, with ship construction planned up to a decade ahead, and with national budgets and patterns of employment shaped round it. The alliances had been given substance and direction by staff talks and war plans. Despite the very great level of economic interdependence between France, Britain, and Germany in 1914, and the genuine need of most businessmen and industrialists for peace, economic rivalry was increasingly expressed in national terms. Most important of all, the effect of the two Moroccan crises was to subordinate colonial questions to European. They had shown that, geographically, the division between Europe and the rest of the world was not as neat as the populations of north-west Europe sometimes seemed to imagine. The problems of the North African coastline, the balance of power in the Mediterranean, could not but affect the other powers on the Mediterranean littoral—Turkey, which was simultaneously of Europe and Asia, and Italy and Austria-Hungary. Nor had

[57] Churchill, *Unknown war*, 49.   [58] Thompson, *In the eye of the storm*, 60–5.

Weltpolitik succeeded in resolving Germany's domestic tensions: at best it had postponed them. Germany did not in the end go to war in pursuit of its *Weltpolitik*. But the conduct of *Weltpolitik*, and the setbacks which it entailed, contributed to its sense of humiliation, beleaguerment, and fatalism in 1914. And, once war was declared, the continuity of *Weltpolitik*—both in terms of Germany's war aims and in terms of Germany's domestic political and social pressures—was to become all too evident.

2

AUSTRIA-HUNGARY
AND THE BALKANS

In both the major crises triggered by Germany in the pursuit of *Weltpolitik*, the two Moroccan confrontations of 1905 and 1911, Germany enjoyed less than fulsome support from its major ally, Austria-Hungary.[1] During the war German generals were apt to cite Nibelung loyalty when referring to the Austro-German alliance, but they did so between clenched teeth. The shared Germanic traditions to which such comparisons appealed suggested a common identity that was in practice largely superficial—or, if real, was subscribed to only by a minority (since in 1910 Germans constituted a quarter of the total) of the Austro-Hungarian population. The more recent history of the two countries suggested division rather than fusion. In 1866 Prussia had summarily ended Austria's leadership of the Germanic states on the battlefield, and although the memory of that war seems to have rankled remarkably little, the subsequent thrust of Germany's development highlighted differences

---

[1] In addition to the works cited in n. 1 above, the following books and articles have been of general assistance in the writing of this section: Beztuzhev, *Journal of Contemporary History*, I (1966), 93–112; Bridge, *From Sadowa to Sarajevo*; Dedijer, *Road to Sarajevo*; Lieven, *Russia and the origins*; Leslie, *Wiener Beiträge*, XX (1993), 307–94; Linke, *Miltärgeschichtliche Mitteilungen*, 32 (1982), 9–34; May, *Passing of the Hapsburg monarchy*; Mommsen, *Central European History*, VI (1973), 3–43; Mommsen, 'Topos of inevitable war in Germany in the decade before 1914', in Berghahn and Kitchen (eds.), *Germany in the age of total war*; Pares, *Fall of the Russian monarchy*; Renouvin, *Crise Européenne*; Röhl, *Historical Journal*, XII (1969), 651–73; C. J. Smith, *Russia's struggle for power*; Stone, *Past and Present*, 33 (1966), 95–111; Turner, *Origins*; Valiani, *End of Austria-Hungary*; Williamson, *Austria-Hungary*; Zeman, *Break-up of the Habsburg Empire*.

as much as points of contact. German unification elevated the idea of nationalism, but Austria-Hungary—as a multinational empire—had perforce relied for its continued integrity throughout the nineteenth century on supra-nationalism. In order to consolidate its legitimacy as a government, Austria-Hungary had used the networks of international relations, the authority of treaties, to buttress the domestic status quo; the creation of Germany, the cuckoo in the European nest, had upset the Concert system and the balance of power. Most important of all, economic development had transformed these otherwise implicit distinctions into direct and overt competition. Although the growth rate in industry in Austria-Hungary was impressive between 1890 and 1914, it started from a low point and its effect was patchy. Over that period railway construction in the empire all but matched that of Germany, but by 1913 the density of track per square kilometre of territory was only a third that of its ally. In Hungary the number of industrial workers rose by 76 per cent between 1898 and 1913, but industrial workers only constituted 17 per cent of the working population. In Austria industrial productivity increased 50 per cent between 1900 and 1910, but in that latter year 56.5 per cent of the workforce of Austria-Hungary were still in agriculture. Agricultural productivity had risen, but remained low relative to other states and, even in those years when yields were sufficient, protectionism acted as a block to food exports.[2] The dual monarchy was therefore in no position to compete with Germany, which used its productive capacity as an arm of its foreign policy. Throughout the decade before the First World War Austria-Hungary saw its Balkan markets fall to its ally. In 1901–5 Romania drew 28.5 per cent of its imports from Austria-Hungary and 27.1 per cent from Germany; by 1913 these figures were 23.4 and 40.3 per cent.[3] Most galling of all was the outcome of Austria-Hungary's decision to impose economic sanctions on Serbia in 1906. In retaliation for Serbia's decision not to order arms from the Skoda works in Bohemia but from the French, Austria-Hungary refused to import Serbian livestock, in particular pigs. Serbia's response was to find alternative markets, including Germany: by 1910, when Austro-Serb

[2] Macartney, *Habsburg Empire*, 755–6; Trebilcock, *Industrialization*, 443–4; Valiani, *End of Austria-Hungary*, 4.

[3] Fischer, 'World policy, world power and German war aims', in Koch (ed.), *Origins*, 150–1.

commercial relations were resumed, Germany had replaced Austria-Hungary as one of Serbia's principal trading partners.[4]

It was therefore necessity rather than affection which fuelled the Nibelung compact. For Germany, Austria-Hungary was better than no ally at all. The dual monarchy broke the ring of encircling and seemingly hostile powers; more positively, and increasingly more importantly, Austria-Hungary was the land bridge not merely to the Balkans but to Asia Minor. For the Habsburg monarchy the Austro-German alliance replaced the Concert of Europe as the bulwark behind its fragile identity. For Germans within Austria the alliance removed any possible conflict of loyalty: 1866 had seemingly sundered them from Germany proper, but the alliance and its potentialities had reunited them. Moreover, Germany's support also extended to the Magyars, whose landowning aristocracy dominated Hungary in power if not in numbers, and whom the Kaiser portrayed as honorary Teutons in their battle against the Slav. The alliance therefore provided the *Ausgleich* of 1867 with an external validation which its parlous domestic condition made indispensable.[5]

Although in 1815 and again in 1848 the Habsburgs had evaded the threat of nationalism, in 1867 they had struck a compromise with Hungary. Franz Joseph became simultaneously emperor of Austria and king of Hungary. Each state had its own assembly, the Austrian Reichsrat and the Hungarian Diet. Delegations of the two convened once a year, albeit in separate buildings, to approve common expenditure. Ministers for the two nations were answerable to the emperor. The two national ministers president, plus the three joint ministers—the foreign minister, the minister of war, and the common minister of finance—together constituted the common ministerial council. The foreign minister set the agenda for the common council and thus became the de facto chancellor of the dual monarchy. The army itself was also common to both parts of the empire, and in many ways the most effective embodiment of its supra-national and multinational status, although in addition Austria and Hungary each had a separate territorial army. The *Ausgleich* was a pragmatic and sensible response which lasted until 1918. Its strength rested on its application of internal imperialism: the Germans, albeit in a

---

[4] Bridge, *From Sadowa*, 277–80; see also 268–9; Dedijer, *Road to Sarajevo*, 368–9.
[5] Shanafelt, *The secret enemy*, 4–6.

somewhat more liberal and enlightened clothing, were left free to dominate Austria, while Hungary was consigned—by virtue of a very restrictive franchise—to the Magyars. Its weaknesses were twofold. First, the
Ausgleich was renewable every ten years: Austria-Hungary was therefore
on perpetual notice as to its future. Secondly, it was a compromise that
commended itself to only one group, the Magyars. For everybody else it
was a halfway house. A few wanted a return to centralism. More saw the
relative independence achieved by the Magyars as an indication that
comparable devolution might be possible for the other ethnic groups.
Of the 20 million inhabitants of Hungary, less than half were Magyars
and the remainder included Romanians (nearly 3 million), Slovaks and
Croats (nearly 2 million of each), and Serbs (less than a million). Austria
was even more variegated: 10 million Germans formed the largest group
in the total population of 28 million, but 4.9 million Poles and 3.2 million
Ruthenes lived in Galicia, 6.5 million Czechs in Bohemia, and there
were smaller groupings of Slovenes, Italians, Serbs, and Croats. For
many of these the *Ausgleich* became not a stopping point, but an inter-
mediate stage to trialism (a third, Slav, component in the empire) or even
federalism.[6]

The major block to change, and indeed the key element in domestic
politics in the decade before the First World War, was the intransigence of
the Magyars. Either trialism or federalism would diminish Hungary; the
Magyar solution was one of repression and of Magyarization, particularly
in relation to the use of the Hungarian language. In 1903 the Hungarian
Diet declined to increase the recruit contingent for the army in line with
the growth in population without the effective formation of a separate
Hungarian army. Franz Joseph refused, a challenge to the unity of the
army being a challenge to Habsburg authority itself. The Diet was twice
dissolved in an effort to form a fresh government, and even the possibility
of a military occupation mooted. However, the solution to the impasse
most attractive to the monarchy was to widen the Hungarian franchise:
the power of the Magyar aristocracy would be broken and at the same
time sufficient national divisions created to allow the possibility of
enhanced Habsburg influence. By the same token the major Magyar

  [6] Williamson, *Austria-Hungary*, 14–30; Renouvin, *Crise européene*, 94; Leslie, *Wiener Beiträge*, XX (1993), 367–8.

parties, and in particular Count Istvan Tisza, Hungary's minister president in 1903–5 and again from 1913, were determined to block suffrage reform. Magyar compliance with Franz Joseph's instructions was so minimal that in 1914 only 6 per cent of Hungary's population enjoyed the vote and only fifty of the 453 deputies in the Diet were not Magyars.[7] On the other hand, the threat of universal suffrage contributed to the renewal of the *Ausgleich* (albeit on terms which left the Austrians paying 63.6 per cent of the common expenses). Furthermore, Tisza forced through the army bill in 1912 and reformed the Diet so as to make its proceedings more workable. He also moderated policy towards the Croats, second only to the Romanians as the largest and most independent of the non-Magyar groupings in Hungary. Tisza was shrewd enough to realize that Magyar bloody-mindedness must not go so far as to make the *Ausgleich* unworkable: that would only hasten its demise. Hungary would maximize its power, he calculated, if it established itself as the key element in a continuing empire, and indeed if that empire remained a member of a major international alliance. The by-products of such policies—effective government and the enhancement of the army— pleased Franz Joseph, and were sufficient to persuade him to abandon the pursuit of real political reform.

But the Magyars knew that the confrontation was only deferred. Franz Joseph had come to the throne in 1848, and his succession could not be long postponed. His heir, Franz Ferdinand, was notorious for his anti-Magyar views. Both trialism and federalism had been canvassed within Franz Ferdinand's circle, although the heir apparent ultimately embraced centralism through the idea of a greater German Austria.[8] Whatever the means, the Magyars could expect a renewed challenge to their position in the not too distant future and this alone was sufficient to confirm the precarious state of the *Ausgleich*.

Franz Joseph's espousal of a moderate liberalism did not proceed from any love of liberalism per se but from its attraction as a device to soften national opposition and thus indirectly to buttress Habsburg power. Within Austria liberalism of this sort was progressively applied, but without achieving the expected effects. South Slav and Czech culture and education received a considerable boost from ordinances in 1880 and

---

[7] May, *Hapsburg monarchy*, 394.   [8] Dedijer, *Road to Sarajevo*, ch. 7.

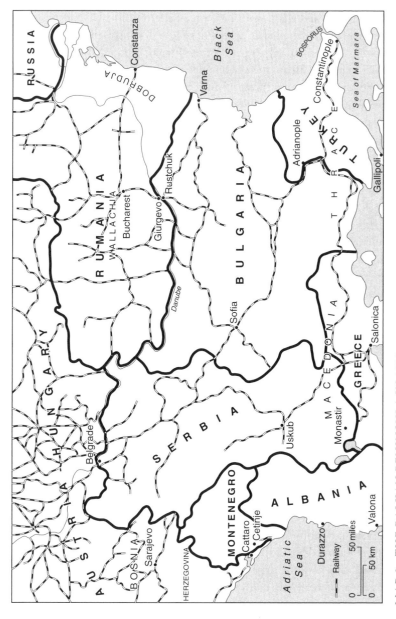

MAP 2. THE BALKAN PENINSULA IN 1914

1881 which allowed official languages other than German. The suffrage of 1882 progressively enfranchised the lower middle class, the shopkeeper and the artisan. The Poles in Galicia became effectively self-governing. The final step, that of universal suffrage introduced in 1907, was in part the corollary of Franz Joseph's attempt to carry through the same reform in Hungary. It was also prompted by an exaggerated fear of socialism, the 1905 Russian revolution having stimulated disturbances in Vienna and Prague. Socialism, if brought within the Reichsrat, might be channelled towards reformism, not revolution; it might—as a supra-national movement, committed to the benefits of large economic units—buttress the larger forum of the empire as a whole; and it was hoped that the clerical parties would react and organize a more conservatively inclined lower-class vote. In the 1907 elections the socialists duly increased their representation sixfold, to eighty-six seats out of 516. But socialism in Austria was not the threat or the force it was in western Europe: nationalism splintered it too, and the Czechs broke away from the Austrian socialists to form their own party. The 1907 franchise had been calculated on the basis of national groupings, and indeed had had to rest on the existence of the divisions which nationalism would create in order to prevent a Slav coalition outnumbering the German representation within the Reichsrat. Therefore, although party loyalties reflecting class and occupational factors were formed, ethnic division was pre-eminent. Czech obstruction was particularly vociferous. Only the Poles, driven into loyalty by their fear of the Russians and of the latter's support for the Ruthenes in Galicia, could be counted on. Parliamentary government, even parliamentary debate, was rendered impossible, and in March 1914 Count Karl Sturgkh, Austria's minister president since 1910, adjourned the Reichstag altogether. It was not to reconvene until 1917. The trappings of constitutionalism thus proved more resilient and more continuous in Hungary, where they were buttressed by a form of domestic colonialism, than they did in the more liberal conditions of Austria.

Because one of the most important political changes to emerge from the First World War was the fragmentation of the Austro-Hungarian empire into a number of new nation states, it is tempting to conclude that the disintegration was well in train before the war broke out. It is true that major change, presumably on Franz Joseph's death, was generally expected, and that the vulnerabilities of the *Ausgleich* and hence of

Austria-Hungary as a whole were acknowledged. But most national groups derived benefits as well as disadvantages from membership of the empire, and therefore the majority before 1914 looked to federalism, not independence.

The cultural diversity of Vienna, home before 1914 to Freud and the philosopher Wittgenstein, the writers Rilke and Karl Kraus, the painter Gustav Klimt, and the composers Mahler, Richard Strauss, and Schoenberg, and the relative liberalism of the Habsburg empire compared with the autocracy of its Slav neighbour, Russia—all these were plus points for the inhabitants of Austria-Hungary. The strength and size of the bureaucracy, consciously expanded to embrace the nationalities of the empire, meant that effective administration continued regardless of parliamentary paralysis. Ministers were drawn from the civil service and were enabled to govern by virtue of paragraph 14 of the Austrian constitution, which conferred emergency powers when the Reichsrat was not in session.

What was, however, true was that if any state manifested a close connection between domestic policy and foreign policy, if in any country the former directed the latter, it was not so much Germany as Austria-Hungary. Generally speaking, and with notable exceptions, Austria-Hungary was neither a bellicose nor expansionist actor in international relations after 1866. The defence budget declined from the 1890s until 1912, and the war of 1866 ought to have been sufficient reminder that fighting did not necessarily resolve problems in a satisfactory manner. But in the debate on the *Ausgleich* and its future the funding and the recruitment of the army were pivotal; for some, its employment in war would be the best way to cut through the debate and the procrastination. Furthermore, the dual monarchy's ethnic groups prevented the empire from lapsing into any form of isolation. With the exception of the Magyars, each of them could look to a national homeland that lay outside the frontiers of the empire—to Serbia, to Romania, to Italy, to Russia, and even to Germany. Domestic and foreign policy were therefore inextricably linked. In 1815 Metternich had used the Concert of Europe to give this racial pot-pourri external validation and support; by 1914 the relative decline of the Concert system could only enhance Austria-Hungary's dependence on the Austro-German alliance as a substitute.

However unstable the dual monarchy might appear, however much it might seem a relic of the eighteenth century, its survival was much less remarkable than that of its immediate eastern neighbour, the Ottoman empire. The origins of the tensions in the Balkans which became the immediate cause of the First World War lie not so much in Austrian aggression (although in time this came to play its part) as in Ottoman senescence. In July 1908 the Young Turks, a group of Turkish patriots, backed by the III army corps at Salonika (the army being an agent of modernization), staged a revolution against the oriental despotism of Sultan Abdul Hamid II. Abdul Hamid granted the constitution which the Young Turks demanded, but then in April 1909 staged a counter-revolution. The Young Turks rallied, ousted Abdul Hamid, and installed his brother, Mohammed V, as the new Sultan.

The Young Turks' revolution threatened to transform the situation in European Turkey. Over the last half of the nineteenth century the great powers of Europe had endeavoured to manage Turkey's decline, and in particular its withdrawal from the Balkans, in as gradual a manner as possible. In 1878 they had stepped in after the Russian defeat of Turkey, and at the Congress of Berlin had acknowledged the independence of Serbia, Romania, Montenegro, and Bulgaria, the latter albeit under Ottoman suzerainty, and had entrusted to Austria-Hungary the administration of Bosnia-Herzogovina while leaving it technically in Turkish possession. Turkey's lingering status as a European power was confirmed by its continued direct rule over Rumelia and Macedonia. Russia, although understandably peeved at not reaping any return from its success on the battlefield, had come to accept that it must collaborate with Austria-Hungary in the management of Ottoman decline. Neither power, least of all Russia after the Manchurian defeat and the subsequent revolution, could afford disturbance on its frontiers. By July 1908, however, both had acknowledged an interest in revising the Congress of Berlin—Russia, thwarted in its Far Eastern ambitions, had turned south-west and wanted the use of the Black Sea straits for its warships, and Austria-Hungary was anxious to regularize its position in Bosnia-Herzogovina.

Austrian urgency derived from its relationship with Serbia: the latter, rather than be content with its position as a client of the dual monarchy, was touting itself as the 'Piedmont' of the South Slavs—the nation that would lead the way to the formation of a large independent South Slav state. A greater Serbia would not only draw in Bosnia-Herzogovina but also the Serbs and possibly Croats resident within the empire proper: external problems would be projected back into the domestic arrangements of the dual monarchy. In 1907 Austria-Hungary had planned a railway line to link the Austrian and Turkish networks south of Serbia, so as to consolidate the empire's stabilizing influence in the Balkans and at the same time outflank Serbia. Britain (which wrongly saw the proposal as an extension of German ambitions, and part of a Berlin-to-Baghdad railway) and Russia opposed, and by 1908 Austria-Hungary was confronted with a loss of prestige in the Balkans. Then in July the Young Turks' revolution put all the assumptions underpinning Austrian and even Russian policy into reverse. The Young Turks might apply the principles of democracy and nationalism to the Balkans, in which case Austro-Russian abilities to manage the situation would be considerably dented. Similar effects would follow on any precipitate completion of Turkish withdrawal from Europe. Alternatively, a reinvigorated Ottoman empire might try to reassert its crumbling position in the Balkans. However, that was likely only to provoke the insurrectionary talents of Turkey's Slav subjects.

On 16 and 17 September 1908 the foreign ministers of Austria-Hungary and Russia, Aehrenthal and Izvolsky, met at Buchlau to discuss the position.[9] Both were acting independently of their alliance partners. Aehrenthal brought to the meeting a self-confidence unwarranted by the overall situation in the Balkans but no doubt buttressed by his awareness of Russia's relative weakness. In this he was right: when confrontation loomed in March 1909 the Russian minister of war said that the Russian army was not fit even for defensive operations. But Aehrenthal's aim was not aggression. Like Izvolsky, he intended to improve, not worsen, Austro-Russian relations, albeit at Serbia's expense. More specifically, he wanted a clear demarcation between Austrian interests in the Balkans and Turkey. He therefore proposed the annexation of Bosnia-Herzogovina. What he had in mind was a foreign policy success sufficient to rally the Habsburg loyalties of the national groupings and

---

[9] Bridge, *From Sadowa*, 297–324, provides much detail on the Bosnian crisis; for the Russian perspective, see Lieven, *Russia and the origins*, 33–7; McDonald, *Union government and foreign policy*, 102, 130–51.

especially of the Magyars. In this he picked up the schemes of Stephan Count Burian, who felt that the incorporation of Bosnia within the empire would divide South Slav nationalism between Zagreb and Belgrade, and so weaken its impact that the threat of trialism would be removed. Moreover, if Bosnia-Herzogovina were attached to Hungary rather than to Austria, the expansion of the former would enhance the *Ausgleich* by making it more truly a marriage of equals. For Aehrenthal, the domestic benefits of putting the dual monarchy's Balkan policy back on track went further: by focusing the army's attention elsewhere, it would still the efforts of the general staff to resolve the military budget by demands for preventive war against the empire's ostensible ally, Italy.[10]

The lure for Izvolsky was the prospect of getting something for nothing. By his reckoning Austria-Hungary already exercised control over Bosnia-Herzogovina: formalizing the arrangement would leave Russia no worse off and would further Russia's wider foreign policy objectives after the defeat by Japan. The Balkan settlement imposed by the powers in the Treaty of Berlin, which still rankled in St Petersburg, would have been reopened, but through unilateral action by Austria, not Russia. Izvolsky would then be able to call for an international conference to review the treaty, and could appear as the protector of the Balkan Slavs. Most important, he could use the opportunity to ask that the straits be opened to Russian warships. Aehrenthal had indicated that he would support such a request, and Izvolsky reasoned that Russia's new-found ally, Britain, might also be expected to back the proposal.

Izvolsky's strategy began to unravel almost immediately. In Sofia Bulgaria declared its independence from Turkey without waiting for Russia's support. In Vienna, on 6 October, Aehrenthal announced the Austrian annexation of Bosnia-Herzegovina earlier than anticipated, and presented Russian acceptance of it as unconditional. And in St Petersburg Stolypin was outraged to discover that the foreign minister had been developing a policy which had not been concerted in the Council of Ministers and was more ambitious than Russia's weakened state would allow. Technically, Stolypin had no cause for complaint: neither the

---

[10] Leslie, *Wiener Beiträge*, XX (1993), 314, 326–8; Stevenson, *Armaments and the coming of war*, 85, 114, 141–2; Hermann, *Arming of Europe*, 108–10.

Council of Minsters nor the Duma had responsibility for foreign affairs, which remained a fiefdom of the Tsar, and in this case the Tsar was both informed about and supportive of his foreign minister's policy.[11] But Stolypin and, ironically, Izvolsky himself had promoted the idea that Russia's domestic strength and international status were linked, and that foreign affairs should be subject to wider accountability. This line had been easier to advance after the Tsar's humiliation in the Far East and the rejection of the Björkö agreement. The publication of the details of the Buchlau agreement produced widespread outrage in Russia. Izvolsky received no credit for ingenuity in relation to the straits or the Treaty of Berlin, and earned equal opprobrium for having handled the interests of the Balkan Slavs with so much cynicism. His only hope of salvaging either his domestic position or Russia's external authority resided in his plan that the whole question should go to a European congress.

In this too he was disappointed. Germany had no intention of promoting another conference, with its attendant danger of diplomatic defeat. This is not to say it was particularly pleased by Austria-Hungary's independent line, since it endangered Germany's wooing of Turkey, but by December it had come round to the idea of backing its ally. Bülow recognized that, if Austria-Hungary was to be an effective support in the event of a war in Europe, it must relieve Germany of some of the burden on its eastern front. At the time Austria-Hungary seemed more likely—if it were to make war at all—to do so on Italy rather than Russia, and antagonism towards Italy weakened the Triple Alliance. On 14 December Bülow gave Austria-Hungary Germany's support.[12] In January 1909 Conrad von Hötzendorff, the Austrian chief of the general staff, made contact with Helmuth von Moltke the younger, his German counterpart and Schlieffen's successor, in an effort to establish German operational plans in the event of war with Russia. Moltke warned that Germany's initial concentration would be against France, but assured Conrad of German support against Russia if Russia acted with Serbia. Neither Bülow nor Moltke expected the Bosnian crisis to result in war, but their attitudes were decisive in stiffening Austrian resolve. They had

---

[11] Fuller, *Strategy and power in Russia*, 419–20; Neilson, *Britain and the last Tsar*, 289, 296–302.

[12] Lambi, *Navy and German power politics*, 304.

simultaneously strengthened the Triple Alliance, relieved Germany's own sense of encirclement, and exposed the weaknesses of the Triple Entente. Russia, by contrast, was not able to elicit similar backing from its allies. France made it clear that no support against Austria-Hungary would be forthcoming. Britain reverted to a more traditional policy than the 1907 Anglo-Russian Entente had suggested likely. Long-established concerns about Russian naval penetration into the Mediterranean, and the defence of the route to India, manifested themselves in a reluctance to underwrite Russia's claim to use of the Black Sea straits. What 1908 offered Britain was a renewed opportunity for a role in Turkey: anxiety not to affront the Young Turks overrode any obligations to Izvolsky.

Thus, the most important consequence of the Bosnian crisis was Russian humiliation. The withdrawal of Turkey from Europe removed any buffer between the Habsburg and Romanov empires. The Russians could only interpret the annexation of Bosnia-Herzogovina as evidence of Austrian expansionism in the Balkans, an expansionism which might eventually take the dual monarchy to the gates of Constantinople and to a landward domination of the straits. Arguably Russo-Austrian collaboration in the Balkans could not have been long sustained independently of the Bosnian crisis. But now latent hostility was unavoidable if Russia was not to forfeit its great power status in the west as well as in the east. The Duma happily approved arms appropriations. Henceforth Russia's policy was to revolve around the creation of an anti-Austrian bloc in south-east Europe.

Nor was Austria-Hungary's own position much improved, despite the apparent gains. Russian involvement in the Balkans, particularly in Bulgaria and Serbia, was not consonant with Austrian objectives in the region. Aehrenthal had hoped to compensate Serbia for Austria's annexation of Bosnia by economic concessions sufficient to draw Serbia back into Austria-Hungary's orbit. Serbia rejected Austria-Hungary's proposals. Aehrenthal's response was to invoke the threat of military action. On 29 March 1909 the mobilization of the Austro-Hungarian army was approved. Two days later Serbia climbed down, promising to be a good neighbour. Aehrenthal had not entered the crisis with any intention of applying coercion, and not until December had he been willing to countenance the Conrad–Moltke exchange of views. But now he was convinced of the value of military pressure in Balkan diplomacy. At one

level this change of heart reflected the views of Conrad, who had transferred his advocacy of preventive war from Italy to Serbia, arguing that
Russia's weakness gave the dual monarchy a unique opportunity to settle
with Serbia. But Conrad wanted war, not the threat of war. He was
furious that the opportunity for the former had been forfeited in favour
of the latter. Next time, he warned, Russia would not be so compliant.[13]

Nor did long-term relations with Serbia look much more auspicious.
Serb sentiment, both in the population as a whole and in the army
specifically, was not in sympathy with its government's actions. When
Narodna Odbrana (National Defence), a Serb society committed to
revolutionary activity in Bosnia, was forced by the government in the
light of its undertaking to Austria to modify its position and concentrate
on cultural activities, its place was promptly taken by a secret organization, *Ujedinjenje ili Smrt* ('Unification or Death' but known to its enemies
as 'Black Hand'), committed to Serbia's fulfilment of its self-appointed
role as the Piedmont of the South Slavs, and to fighting beyond Serbia's
frontiers for the achievement of that goal.[14]

Therefore Austria's relations with Serbia showed little hope of
improvement. Furthermore, at home the acquisition of Bosnia-
Herzogovina failed to resolve the conflicts generated by the *Ausgleich*.
The new province was not incorporated into either Austria or Hungary,
but administered jointly. The difficulties of concerting a wider Balkan
policy were compounded: the case for a South Slav component within
the empire, for trialism, was strengthened by the annexation, and thus
Hungary's fears that it would lose its control over Croatia heightened.
And finally, the crisis which Austria-Hungary had initiated independently of Germany had had the effect of confirming Austrian subordination to its northern partner. Although Austria-Hungary would try to
pursue an independent policy on other occasions before 1914, in the eyes
of the Triple Entente—and especially of Britain—Austria was now no
more than Germany's stalking-horse in south-eastern Europe.

This analysis was right in so far as the Bosnian crisis did mark the
beginnings of a reorientation in German foreign policy. By 1909 the
domestic repercussions of *Weltpolitik*—the budgetary consequences of

---

[13] Tunstall, *Planning for war*, 60–8; Hermann, *Arming of Europe*, 128–30; Stevenson, *Armaments and the coming of war*, 114–22.

[14] Dedijer, *Road to Sarajevo*, 371–8.

Tirpitz's fleet and the associated problems of managing the Reichstag—had begun to make that particular form of imperialism unsustainable, at least at such a high tempo. The process of disillusionment was completed with what was perceived as humiliation over Morocco in 1911: not only were ships expensive but they did not even guarantee diplomatic success. In place of *Weltpolitik*, the idea of Germany as the dominant continental power gained strength. Blocked by Britain at its western maritime exits, Germany should instead turn east, to central Europe and even, via Austria-Hungary, to south-east Europe and to Turkey. In 1912 Walther Rathenau of the *Allgemeine Elektrizitatsgesellschaft* sketched out to the Kaiser and Bethmann Hollweg a plan for a central European customs union. Germany's volume of trade was the highest in the world, but it was unbalanced: between 1887 and 1912 imports rose 243.8 per cent but exports increased by only 185.4 per cent. Each of its major economic rivals, the United States and Britain, had carved out an area of effective domination, in the Americas and in the British empire respectively; Russia had the potential to do the same in Asia. Germany, not least in order to balance its trade, should become the pivot of a European economic bloc, an enclosed free-trade area, a *Mitteleuropa*.[15]

It is too simplistic to see a direct switch from *Weltpolitik* to *Mitteleuropa* occurring between 1909 and 1912. The German fleet and the now-flourishing expectation of 'a place in the sun' could not simply be put to one side. *Weltpolitik* would continue as a theme of German policy. Nor had *Mitteleuropa* arisen *de novo*. German economic penetration into south-east Europe was, as we have seen, already generating friction with Austria-Hungary. Rathenau's idea was to reinvigorate and give direction to an existing element in Germany's activities. Furthermore, *Weltpolitik* and *Mitteleuropa* were not mutually exclusive. 'Germany', Bethmann Hollweg told the Reichstag in 1911, 'can conduct a strong policy in the sense of *Weltpolitik* only if she maintains her power on the Continent.'[16] Part of *Mitteleuropa*'s attraction was that it provided a land route into Turkey and Asia: it showed once again how European and colonial concerns could no longer be neatly compartmentalized. The nature of Germany's imperialism had received a new emphasis, economic

---

[15] Fritz Fischer's writings are the main source for these points; see *Germany's aims*, 9–11, 28–9; *War of Illusions*, 6–11, 139–40; Fischer, in Koch (ed.), *Origins*.

[16] Herwig, 'Imperial Germany', in E. May (ed.), *Knowing one's enemies*, 82.

and diplomatic rather than naval and maritime, but in the long run and in its furthest reach it was just as likely to upset the interests of the existing imperial powers, particularly Britain and France, but also Russia.

Mitteleuropa in its proper sense, relating to central Europe, had a strategic justification as well as an economic one. *Weltpolitik* was a German policy; it did not in any way accord with the interests of the Triple Alliance as a whole. Italy as a Mediterranean power was dependent on Anglo-French good will for commercial freedom, and in particular derived almost all its coal (which met 87.6 per cent of its energy needs) from Britain.[17] Nor did Austria-Hungary, as it showed through its lack of support in 1905 and 1911, identify with Germany's Moroccan ventures. By pursuing *Mitteleuropa*, Germany might bring its alliance commitments and its economic imperialism into line, thus integrating its strategy. To give expression to this, the army—which had seen the navy's budget grow to 55 per cent of its own between 1897 and 1911—now began to make up for lost time, and to have increases of 29,000 men in 1912 and 136,000 in 1913. By switching the spotlight back to their land forces many Germans felt—with good reason—that they were affirming their natural strengths rather than—as they had been doing with the navy—trying to build from weakness.

If all this had amounted to a consistent policy the events of 1912 to 1914 in the Balkans might not have been as confused as they became, or at least might not have had such wide repercussions. To Austria-Hungary in particular Germany seemed unable to follow a steady course. Partly this was because Germany continued both to affirm the alliance and yet at the same time to undercut Austria-Hungary's economic position in the Balkans. Furthermore, Germany's efforts could as often reflect dynastic sympathies (there were Hohenzollerns on the thrones of Greece and Romania) as Austrian interests. Not least because of its doubts about Romania's loyalty, Austria-Hungary saw Bulgaria, a power without ethnic interests in the population of the empire, as its natural ally in the Balkans: Germany did not. Ironically, too, the very pace of German industrialization confused and weakened Germany's policies in south-east Europe. By 1913 over half Germany's foreign investment in Europe and almost 40 per cent in the world was concentrated in the area between

---

[17] Bosworth, *Italy and the approach*, 17.

Vienna and Baghdad.[18] But, despite such figures, Germany was disconsolate. German capital was so absorbed by domestic production that the aggregate left over for foreign investment was small; France—as a power that was industrializing more slowly and where capital therefore remained uncommitted—proved a much more attractive money market for the emergent Balkan states. In Serbia, Greece, and Bulgaria French capital won out over German, and even in Romania—where Germany made special efforts—Germany's share of state loans and in the oil market fell after 1911. But this was a competition from which Austria-Hungary itself could not derive benefit. Twenty-five per cent of all German foreign loans went to the dual monarchy; the latter imported more from the former than it exported; and yet Austria-Hungary could not diminish its dependence by raising loans on the French Bourse, as the French (with Russian support) would not allow them to do so. Thus Austria-Hungary's dependence on Germany increased, but its ability to influence German policy declined.[19]

Austria-Hungary's loss of control in the Balkans was not simply the result of German activities. The substitution in the region of Austro-Russian antagonism for their erstwhile détente created opportunities for the newly emergent Balkan states. The latter could exploit great-power rivalry for their own ends in a way that great-power collaborative action had in the past made impossible. Thus, while superficially the Balkans appeared to be the focus of Austro-Russian hostility, the inner dynamism of the situation was provided by the opposition of the Balkan states to Turkey. This put Austria-Hungary at a yet greater disadvantage, for the dual monarchy had strapped itself to a losing policy, the maintenance of a Turkish presence in Europe. It hoped thereby to keep the Slav states on its frontiers, and particularly Serbia, in a state of dependence.

The next stage in Ottoman decline was not, however, initiated by the Balkan states themselves, but by the third member of the Triple Alliance, Italy. Despite its humiliation at Abyssinian hands at Adowa in 1896, Italy had not abandoned its colonial aspirations. Growing French strength in the Mediterranean and in Morocco fuelled Italian jealousy, born of the conviction that Italy too was a Mediterranean power. Floated by the

[18] Herwig, in May (ed.), *Knowing one's enemies*, 86.
[19] Fischer, *War of Illusions*, 291–8; Fischer, in Koch (ed.), *Origins*, 141–8.

patriotic rhetoric celebrating the fiftieth anniversary of the Risorgimento, and anxious to exploit a favourable constellation on the international scene, Italy declared war on Turkey on 29 September 1911 and launched an expedition to seize Libya. Proof was once again to be provided that colonial interests could not be pursued without European consequences.

The threat to Turkey increased Russian sensitivities over the future of the Black Sea straits. Between 1903 and 1912 37 per cent of Russian exports and three-quarters of Russia's grain shipments passed through the straits.[20] Russia's anxiety that no other state should control such a vital waterway was second only to its desire to control the straits itself. The presence of the Italian navy in the Dodecanese and its bombardment of the Dardanelles in April 1912 gave as concrete expressions to Russian fears as had Austria-Hungary's behaviour in the Bosnian crisis. Good relations with Bulgaria seemed to be the first step in neutralizing the landward approaches to the straits. Russia's task was made more easy by Austria-Hungary's support of Turkey, a policy with little appeal in Sofia. But, alongside this defensive motivation on Russia's part, there flourished in some quarters a more virulently pan-Slav and anti-Austrian sentiment. N. V. Hartwig, the Romanovs' representative in Belgrade, was fired by such considerations and played a key role in effecting, on 13 March 1912, a most unlikely rapprochement, an alliance between Serbia and Bulgaria.

Hartwig's policy was not necessarily the same as that of Sazonov, Izvolsky's successor as foreign minister. In 1910 and 1911 Russo-German relations improved. The Kaiser and the Tsar met; Sazonov's visit to Berlin produced an agreement over the Baghdad railway in exchange for German willingness to restrain Austria-Hungary in the Balkans; and the following year Russia—in revenge for its allies' failure to support it in 1909—stood aloof over Morocco. Even a thawing in Austro-Russian relations was not beyond the bounds of possibility: Franz Ferdinand, somewhat far-fetchedly, found his enthusiasm for the monarchical principle favouring a resuscitation of Bismarck's *Dreikaiserbund*, an alliance of Germany, Russia, and Austria-Hungary. In 1910 Russia began a redeployment of its forces to the east, so threatening a weakening of its commitment to France and a reawakening of its antagonism for Japan.[21]

[20] Lieven, *Russia and the origins*, 45–6.
[21] Fuller, *Strategy and power in Russia*, 396, 427–30, 433.

Therefore Poincaré's visit to Russia in August 1912 had a dual aim: he wished to restrain Russia in the Balkans, but he also had to reaffirm the Triple Entente.[22] However, Poincaré's efforts to achieve the latter could only undermine the former: France's repeated affirmation of the Entente in 1912 encouraged Russia to feel confident that, if its Balkan manoeuvres led to a clash with Austria-Hungary and then Germany, France would back it up. Such expectations, once formed, were not undermined by other signals from Paris. In a memorandum prepared for Poincaré on 2 September 1912 the French general staff welcomed war in the Balkans as likely to weaken Austria-Hungary, so freeing Russia to take on Germany: 'Under these conditions, the Triple Entente . . . could achieve a victory permitting it to remake the map of Europe.'[23] Delcassé, appointed as France's ambassador to St Petersburg in 1913, affirmed France's support of Russia's grievances against the Austrians. With France standing by Russia just as surely as Germany stood by Austria-Hungary, the alliance blocs of the great powers were ranged against each other in the Balkans. Their problem was that none of them was a prime mover in Balkan politics.

Russia's policy, whether embodied by Sazonov or Hartwig, was not at bottom that of Serbia and Bulgaria. The aim of the Serb–Bulgar treaty was to complete the Ottoman ejection from Europe by the conquest and partition of the one surviving piece of Balkan Turkey, Macedonia; the terms contained a secret clause concerning possible attack against Austria-Hungary only if the dual monarchy itself intervened. The policy of Turkey in Macedonia was zealously repressive. In the course of 1912 Greece and Montenegro fell in behind Serbia and Bulgaria. While Germany, Russia, and Austria-Hungary spoke piously of restraint, the Balkan League—conscious of the opportunity created by the Italian attack on Libya—prepared for hostilities. On 8 October Montenegro declared war on Turkey. On 15 October Turkey came to terms with Italy, forfeiting Libya in its bid to concentrate on the danger closer to home. On 17 October Serbia, Bulgaria, and Greece joined Montenegro. The rapidity and scale of the Balkan League's success took the great powers by surprise. A high growth rate in the population, without any accompanying industrialization to soak up the available labour, had

[22] See p. 29.   [23] Hermann, *Arming of Europe*, 178.

permitted the Balkan states to form huge peasant armies.[24] The Turks, outnumbered by almost two to one, spurned the counsel of their German military advisers and opted for encounter battles rather than defensive ones. By mid-November the Turks had been driven out of Thrace and Macedonia, and stood with their backs to Constantinople.

Turkey's defeat was a major setback for Germany and for Austria-Hungary. A strong Turkey, putting pressure on Russia in the Black Sea and the Caucasus, and on Britain in Egypt and Persia, relieved the burden on Germany.[25] For Austria-Hungary such stunning Slav triumphs could only foster irridentism within the empire. In the immediate term, Serbia's expansion—and claim to head a South Slav state outside Austria-Hungary—continued. To baulk Serbia, to continue its dependence on other powers, Berchtold, Aehrenthal's successor as Austria's foreign minister, insisted on the creation of Albania. His purpose was to prevent Serbia acquiring a Mediterranean port, but on 15 November the Serbs reached the Adriatic. The Austrian army, which had increased its annual intake of conscripts by 42,000 men in October, called up 200,000 reservists in Bosnia-Herzogovina. In Russia the Council of Ministers was divided. Both its chairman, Kokovtsov, and Sazonov feared another humiliation to put alongside the Bosnian crisis, and privately urged Serbia to compromise. Publicly Russia sprang to Serbia's support. The victories of the Balkan states boosted pan-Slav sentiment, and this found expression in a more bellicose grouping headed by the minister of agriculture, Krivoshein. Russia conducted a trial mobilization in Poland during October and November, and on 22 November (although the order was cancelled the following day) the Tsar succumbed to the war party's advocacy of a partial mobilization in response to Austrian concentrations in Galicia.[26] On 12 December Conrad von Hötzendorff, the advocate of a preventive war against Serbia in 1909, who had been dismissed for his continued espousal of a similar line against Italy, was recalled as chief of the general staff. As in 1909 Austria was using military signals to beef up its diplomacy. Germany had so far seen its task as restraining its ally:

[24] Zeman, 'The Balkans and the coming of war', in Evans and Pogge von Strandmann (eds.), *The coming*, 31.

[25] Schulte, *Europäische Krise*, 295–6; also *Vor dem Kriegsausbruch*, 14–15, 39–46.

[26] Bridge, *From Sadowa*, 348; Williamson, *Journal of Interdisciplinary History*, XVIII (1988), 800; L. C. F. Turner, 'The Russian mobilisation in 1914', in Kennedy (ed.), *War plans*, 252–6; McDonald, *United government*, 180–6.

neither Wilhelm nor Moltke felt war with Russia could be justified by a dispute over Albania. But alliance obligations could not be totally denied. On 2 December 1912 Bethmann Hollweg declared in the Reichstag that, if Austria-Hungary was attacked by a third party while pursuing its interests, Germany would support Austria-Hungary and would fight to maintain its own position in Europe.[27] On 5 December the Triple Alliance was renewed: the danger of Serbia, a possible proxy for a great power, having possession of an Adriatic port alarmed Italy as much as Austria-Hungary. Meanwhile, on 3 December Britain threatened to abandon its erstwhile policy of restraining Russia and France. Haldane warned the German ambassador in London that Britain would not accept a French defeat if a Russo-Austrian war led to a German attack on France. For both powers alliance loyalties outweighed the Concert of Europe.

Wilhelm was outraged by Haldane's statement. He had been persuaded that the First Balkan War was a war that Russia had fought by proxy, and that presented real dangers for the dual monarchy. Austria-Hungary was therefore in the right and the British reaction revealed the futility of Bethmann Hollweg's efforts to neutralize them. On 8 December he summoned a meeting at his palace. In attendance were Moltke, Tirpitz, August von Heeringen (the chief of the naval staff), and Georg Alexander von Müller (chief of the Kaiser's naval cabinet). Austria-Hungary, the Kaiser said, should be encouraged to persist in a strong line with the Serbs. If Russia came to Serbia's aid, Germany would fight. Wilhelm assumed that, in such a war, Bulgaria, Romania, Albania, and Turkey would stand with the Triple Alliance. Therefore Austria-Hungary would be freed from its Balkan commitments to concentrate against Russia, and Germany in turn could face west, with its full strength against France. Moltke greeted this scenario by saying that war was inevitable, and that the sooner it came the better for Germany. Tirpitz, on the other hand, reported that the fleet could not be ready for another twelve to eighteen months, by which time the Heligoland fortifications and the widening of the Kaiser Wilhelm canal to allow the passage of Dreadnoughts between the Baltic and the North Sea would be completed. Moltke remarked, not without justice, that the navy would never be ready.

---

[27] Jarausch, *Enigmatic chancellor*, 133–4.

Fritz Fischer has dubbed the meeting of 8 December 1912 a war council, and has seen a direct link between it and the outbreak of war in 1914.[28] The meeting ended with only one resolution, that a press campaign should prepare the German public for war with Russia. There is no evidence that the press chief of the Foreign Ministry attempted to orchestrate such a campaign, or that the newspapers could have been so manipulated if he had.[29] Fischer reckons two further conclusions were implied—that the army should be increased and that food stocks should be amassed. The 1913 law did give the army an increase of 136,000 men. In itself, however, the law does not prove Fischer's point. The navy was over-represented at the meeting, naturally enough as its immediate cause was the attitude of Britain. The minister for war, the man charged with implementing any increase to the army, was not present. In reality the new army law was already in preparation before the meeting of 8 December and its target was an additional three corps, to enter the order of battle in 1916 (and not 1914). Moreover, the bill was less a bid for strategic supremacy than a reflection of military weakness. Turkey's defeat cast doubts on the wisdom of German tactical doctrine and simultaneously removed an Asiatic counterweight to the Russian army. Both the latter and the French army, by the virtue of the three-year service law, were being increased.

What is more supportive of Fischer's position is the change in the law's priorities and the tempo of its implementation. The general staff's worries about manpower in relation to Germany's external threats had had to compete with the Ministry of War's concerns for the army's internal order. At one level these were a demand for quality rather than quantity: ideally, growth should have been gradual, to allow first for the expansion of the army's training cadres, its officers and NCOs, and secondly to provide for the army's infrastructure, its equipment and accommodation. In the event, however, the measured growth towards 1916 was discarded in favour of an immediate increase in numbers. The army's field training, already compromised in part by its role as an agent of domestic order, was put second to its size. Heinz Pothoff, writing in the *Berliner Tageblatt* on 3 April 1913, thought such measures could only be

---

[28] Fischer, *War of illusions*, 160–203; Röhl, *Historical Journal*, XII (1969), 651–73; Röhl, *Kaiser and his court*, 162–89. A constructive critique is Lambi, *Navy and German power politics*, 382–4.
[29] Rosenberger, *Zeitungen als Kriegstreiber?*, 213.

justified if war occurred within a year: it 'is no longer a peacetime measure, but simply a mobilization'.[30]

On the second point, that of food stocks, nothing was done in relation to the population as a whole—although preparations were put in hand for feeding the army. Germany's high tariffs limited its ability to stockpile grain. This omission did not indicate that Germany was not planning a war from December 1912 if it assumed that such a war would be short: but it did not follow that it definitely was preparing for war (albeit a short one), and such discussion as did occur on the food question suggests a distinct lack of urgency.

In addition to countering Fischer's claims for the so-called 'war council', two further points need to be made. First, the meeting's most logical consequence would have been a large navy bill. The Kaiser's ire was directed at Britain, and it was the navy that said it was not ready for war. But, although the Kaiser endorsed the three–ships-a-year tempo which Tirpitz had been advocating, Bethmann Hollweg was able to head off a new naval law. An increase in the navy would have cut across the needs of the army, and it was to those that the enthusiasms of the Reichstag could now be directed. The High Seas Fleet continued to plan for war against France and Russia, despite Wilhelm's injunction that it concentrate on Britain. Moltke's expectation was proved right: the navy was not ready in July 1914 and probably would not have been in 1920. Tirpitz's fleet was a weapon forged for cold war only. Secondly, Bethmann Hollweg was not present at the meeting and did not endorse its conclusions. The close relationship between the Kaiser and his service chiefs would probably permit a gathering that excluded the political leadership nonetheless being called a 'war council'. But Bethmann Hollweg, not the service chiefs, took centre stage in the crisis that did lead to war. The policy which he—and Germany—followed between December 1912 and July 1914 is not marked by the consistency which would endorse Fischer's argument. It is even hard to sustain the case for an increase in anti-Russian propaganda in 1913.

What remains striking about the meeting on 8 December is that the decision for peace or war was made conditional not on the objectives of

---

[30] Quoted in Hecker, *Rathenau*, 148. The fullest discussion of the needs of training and civil order is in the writings of Schulte, *Die Deutsche Armee*; *Vor dem Kriegsausbruch*; *Europäische Krise*. See also Stevenson, *Armaments and the coming of war*, 295–6.

policy but on the state of military readiness.[31] The shift in attitudes to
which this points was not confined to Germany, although it is probably
true to say that the land arms race which it reflects was primarily a
consequence of the 1912 German army law. Until 1910 the high-profile
arms races had been between navies; in armies the modernization of
equipment, and in particular the acquisition of quick-firing artillery, had
acted as a brake on expansion. But after the second Moroccan crisis
quantity not quality stoked the competition in land armaments. Very
often the targets which the general staffs set were long term: in 1914 none
of the current programmes of Germany, France, or Russia had been fully
implemented. But the arguments which ministers of war used in order to
secure the necessary appropriations revolved around present crises. Thus
the Balkan wars sustained the momentum which Agadir had initiated.
The trial mobilizations which became a feature of the diplomacy of those
wars confirmed the emphasis on immediate readiness. Two independent
but convergent consequences followed. First, external threats played key
roles in parliamentary debates on finance, and the linking of public
rhetoric to diplomacy narrowed the options open to foreign ministries.
Secondly, foreign policy itself became militarized. This in turn gave
general staffs greater political leverage in the formation of state strategy.
As windows of opportunity seemed to close, so the idea of preventive war
gained a hold.

This, then, is the real significance of the 'war council' meeting—the
fact that Moltke advocated a preventive war. Nor was this the first time:
he had done so in his exchanges with Conrad during the 1909 Bosnian
crisis. For Moltke and the German general staff, war was endemic in
international relations. Such a view was not the personal property of the
Prussian soldiery: social Darwinism, the belief that states were rising and
declining and would fight for position, was a prevailing orthodoxy that
was just as capable of being embraced by liberal circles in more democratic states. The soldier's duty was to prepare for that war, and so fight
it on the best possible terms. Preventive war was therefore the acceptance
of an inevitable war at the right time. Moltke's predecessors in office
had canvassed the idea—Alfred Graf von Waldersee against Russia in

---

[31] Geyer, *Deutsche Rüstungspolitik*, 88; the discussion which follows rests on Hermann,
Arming of Europe, and Stevenson, *Armaments and the coming of war.*

the 1880s,[32] and on some interpretations Schlieffen in 1905[33]—and it is to be found incorporated in the popular military literature of the day, most notoriously in Friedrich von Bernhardi's *Deutschland und der nächste Krieg* (*Germany and the next war*) (1912). But none of these advocates of preventive war saw it as Fritz Fischer sees it, as a deliberate step to resolve an impending domestic crisis. Nor did Moltke approach the subject with the same calculation that previous chiefs of the general staff had brought to its consideration. Moltke talked in general terms of a coming struggle between Slav and Teuton: he was both pessimistic and fatalistic. He did not then combine these world views with the more specific military picture. As chief of the general staff he concentrated on operational plans for war against France, but did little to co-ordinate those plans with those of Conrad, and he did not attempt to formulate what we would now call a grand strategy, integrating operations with the overall picture in a specific way. Moltke's attitude accustomed both Bethmann Hollweg and the Kaiser to the possibility of war, but it did not affect policy in any immediate sense.[34]

At its most negative, the December 1912 meeting made clear what Germany did not want—a European war at that juncture. Thus Germany resumed its original policy, that of an alliance leader co-operating with the British in managing the situation. Superficially at any rate, the Concert of Europe was resuscitated. A conference of ambassadors in London rapidly agreed that an independent Albania stretching from Montenegro to Greece should be created. However, it then proceeded to emasculate the new state by allocating large chunks of its interior to Serbia and Montenegro, so depriving it of its original *raison d'être*, to be an effective barrier against the Serbs. Berchtold, caught between Conrad advocating war with Serbia and a finance minister predicting that war would entail economic collapse, gave in to his German ally and accepted the enlargement of Serbia. In February 1913 Turkey renewed hostilities against the Balkan states, and Conrad again pressed the opportunity for pre-emptive action. But Bulgaria's rapid success against the Turks, bringing it to Adrianople, led Russia to fear that Bulgaria would control the Black Sea

---

[32] Kitchen, *German officer corps*, 65–6, 72.

[33] Ritter, *Sword and the sceptre*, ii. 106–7, 194, denies this; but see Lambi, *Navy and German power politics*, 242–4, 259–60.

[34] Hull, *Wilhelm II*, 239–42, 255–9, 262–5; see also Groener, *Lebenserinnerungen*, 136.

straits: for the moment Russia tried to restrain the bellicosity of the Balkan states. Thus, when Montenegro seized Scutari, the port which the powers had allocated to Albania, Austria-Hungary's renewed threat of military action was backed up by an international naval demonstration, and Montenegro withdrew.

By May 1913 Conrad's demands for preventive war seemed to have been as ineffectual as those of Moltke. In reality the civilian front against military action was cracking. Aehrenthal's death removed its cement. Although expansionist in his policies, the former foreign minister rejected war as an option and curbed Conrad. His successors were less resolute in their brinkmanship. Repeated mobilization was expensive: the December 1912 crisis had cost almost 200 million crowns. The common finance minister, Bilinski, argued that war might be cheaper than recurrent mobilizations. Bilinski was a Pole, and for him the fact that the case for war, which had hitherto assumed Russian neutrality, might now embrace Russia enhanced its attractions.[35] The competition between the two states for influence in Galicia made Poland and the Ukraine almost as inflammatory elements in their relationship as Serbia. At the same time those civilians who favoured rapprochement with Russia— Magyars, like Tisza and Burian—did not therefore oppose a forward policy. They argued that two large, dynastic, multinational states should not allow themselves to be the puppets of the Balkan powers. For them the corollary of détente in the north was assertiveness in the south-east, building on Bulgaria and forcing Romania to declare its hand.[36]

For the time being the new foreign minister, Berchtold, who favoured better relations with Russia, held the line against war, but he was as aware as anyone of the dividends that Austria had reaped by its threat. Furthermore he headed a ministry that drew three further major and interrelated lessons from the events of the preceding six months. First, the Concert system was no longer the external buttress to Austro-Hungarian integrity that it had been in the past. Secondly, unilateral action, not conferences, had achieved Austrian objectives. Thirdly, the Austro-German alliance,

[35] März, *Austrian banking*, 103.
[36] Leslie, *Wiener Beiträge*, XX (1993), 315–17, 333–40, 360–9, 377–9; Leslie, 'Österreich-Ungarn vor dem Kriegsausbruch', 667–70; Stevenson, *Armaments and the coming of war*, 253–5, 267–75; Rauchensteiner, *Tod des Doppeladlers*, 20–1.

although vital to both parties, was nonetheless not supported with consistency by Germany: it paid Austria-Hungary to lead the way.

Austrian distrust of its northern partner was only confirmed by the events of the summer of 1913. In May the Serbs and Bulgars fell out over the division of Macedonia. On 1 June the Serbs and Greeks formed a defensive alliance, partitioning Macedonia and limiting Bulgaria to the line of the River Vardar. The Bulgarians, seething with indignation since they claimed that they had borne the burden of the fighting, declared war on the Serbs. The Russians were unable to check the Bulgarians, and saw their Balkan policy—and the Balkan League—disintegrate as the Second Balkan War took hold. The Greeks came to Serbia's support, and the Romanians—fearful of Bulgarian preponderance in the region and covetous of Silistria (which the Bulgarians were willing to let them have) and the southern Dobrudja (which they were not)—entered the war on 10 July. The Turks seized the moment to retake Adrianople. Further Serb victories were unacceptable to Austria-Hungary, and once again the dual monarchy prepared for war in the Balkans, this time to support Bulgaria. But Germany aligned itself with the opposition. Wilhelm backed Romania and Greece, and hence also Serbia. Italy pointed out to the Austrians that any action they might take in the Balkans would be offensive, not defensive, and consequently the Triple Alliance could not be invoked. Therefore Bulgaria stood alone, and on 10 August 1913 signed the Treaty of Bucharest. Greece got southern Macedonia, Serbia northern Macedonia, and Romania southern Dobrudja. Bulgaria and Austria-Hungary had hoped that the great powers would subsequently revise these concessions. But Germany, anxious to curry favour with the victorious Balkan states, blocked any such proposal. Therefore Austria-Hungary's conclusions from May were reinforced in August—any passivity on its part was exploited; German support was capricious and therefore to be utilized when it was available; and the Concert system had irretrievably broken down. Four minor Balkan nations had flagrantly breached the Treaty of London and had not been called to order. As a result, Serbia had virtually doubled its territory and increased its population from 2.9 million to 4.4 million, to the point where its claim to head a South Slav state outside the empire had gained validity as well as shrillness. Romania, fired by its easy success in the Dobrudja, now fostered irridentism among its fellow-nationals in Hungarian

Transylvania. And, even more significantly, Russia had learned that restraint in the Balkans simply resulted in the loss of influence. With Bulgaria a broken reed, Russia transferred its attentions to the waxing power of Serbia.

Those, like Fischer, who seek to trace a straight line from the December 1912 meeting to the events of July 1914 argue that Germany's support for Austria-Hungary never wavered in 1913.[37] Furthermore, its desire to restrain the dual monarchy in the Balkans derived not from any rejection of war per se, but from the fear that it might break out prematurely. Part of the problem with the pursuit of such consistency is that its fountain-head must be the Kaiser. In that case the consistency lies in the respect for dynastic loyalties, whether in his support for the Hohenzollerns of Romania and Greece in the summer of 1913, or his affirmation of the Habsburgs that same autumn.

Both Germany and Austria-Hungary were sufficiently aware of the fractured state of their relations to make efforts to mend the bridges in October 1913. Serbia, continuing its forward policy, and justifying its actions by the revolts against Serb rule, occupied towns in northern Albania, thus clearly contravening the peace settlement. Austria-Hungary, anxious to use any opportunity to reverse the Treaty of Bucharest and even more anxious to curb Serbia, determined on a hard line. This time Germany stood by its ally: there was little risk in doing so since neither Russia nor France was prepared to condone Serb behaviour. Berchtold dispatched an ultimatum to Serbia, and Serbia gave way. In late October Wilhelm followed up Germany's affirmation of the alliance by a visit to Franz Ferdinand. The Kaiser charmed the archduke by his courteous treatment of the latter's wife Sophie, who as a Czech countess was treated as a commoner at the Austrian court. Most importantly, Wilhelm insisted that Serbia should be a client of Austria-Hungary; if Austria-Hungary had to fight to achieve this, then Germany would back the empire.[38] The centenary of the battle of Leipzig, when Habsburg and Hohenzollern had combined to overthrow Napoleon, helped bathe the Austro-German alliance—at least for the moment—in a warm light.

[37] Fischer, 'Kaiser Wilhelm II und der deutschen Politik vor 1914', in Röhl (ed.), *Der Ort Kaiser Wilhelms II*, 264–8.
[38] Dedijer, *Road to Sarajevo*, 155–8; Fischer, *War of Illusions*, 221–3.

Neither power saw fit to remember that a third dynasty, that of the Romanovs, had also participated in the victory of 1813. In practice the Romanovs' attention was focused on another anniversary that fell in the same year. The tercentenary of Romanov rule persuaded Tsar Nicholas II that a revival of his autocracy could be rooted in popular sentiment. In due course a stronger foreign policy would emerge as a means for the achievement of that end.[39] What marked the winter of 1913–14 and the following spring was an end to the ambivalence which had characterized Russo-German relations for so long (despite their membership of opposing alliances) and its replacement with categorical hostility.

Antagonistic commercial relations between the two countries meant that the Russian right, many of whom were naturally inclined to favour an alliance with autocratic, monarchical Germany rather than liberal, republican France, found its position increasingly hard to sustain. East Elbian landowners, as a reward for their agreement to Tirpitz's naval appropriations, had secured a tariff that effectively excluded the import of Russian grain into Germany. The effect was not reciprocal: by 1914 German rye had found its way into Finland and Russian agriculture was threatened with the loss of Scandinavian markets. Russia responded in the summer of 1914 by imposing a heavy tariff on imported grains, and the prospects for the renewal of the Russo-German commercial agreements of 1904—due in 1917—did not look good. Thus, Russian farmers found their views on foreign policy coinciding—albeit for different reasons—with those of industry. For German commercial policy cut two ways. German heavy industry wanted the reverse of German agriculture: it was anxious to lower tariff barriers between the two countries, thus opening the Russian market to German goods. Russian industry for its part needed—in its fledgling, if burgeoning state—the protection of high tariffs. Both agriculture and industry were therefore united in identifying national interests with economic policy, and both sectors saw themselves as exploited by Germany. In 1910–11 sections of the Russian press were advocating rapid industrialization as a foundation for waging war.[40]

[39] McDonald, *United government*, 187.
[40] Siegelbaum, *Politics of industrial mobilization*, 13–14; also Linke, *Militärgeschichtliche Mitteilungen*, 32 (1982), 11; D. Geyer, *Russian imperialism*, 307–9.

In these circumstances foreign policy could become the unifying and soothing balm which the fractured state of Russian society so urgently needed. In the wake of the 1905 revolution the Tsar had accepted the establishment of a legislative assembly, the Duma, based on a wide, if indirect, franchise. But Nicholas was unhappy with the concession which he had made. The army, the navy, and the raising of foreign loans were all excluded from the Duma's competence. Under article 87 of the constitution the government was free to legislate while the Duma was not sitting provided the law was confirmed by the Duma within two months of its next sitting. Thus the Tsar had available the means to re-establish his authority, to assert that Russia's ministers were his servants and were not answerable to the Duma. In 1906 he dissolved the first Duma, an assembly that contained the flower of the Russian intelligentsia. The leaders of the Kadets—a liberal party representing the professional middle classes—decamped to Viborg in Finland, where they issued a manifesto rejecting the dissolution and called for civil disobedience until the Duma was restored. The Viborg manifesto produced little response: its effect was to divide and weaken the Kadets, since those who signed the appeal were disqualified from re-election to the Duma. The Tsar's efforts to limit the Duma were carried forward a stage further with the appointment of Stolypin as prime minister. He got the weakened second Duma to accept a revised electoral law, which favoured the countryside in preference to the towns and boosted Russian representation at the expense of the other nationalities. After 1907 the cycle of revolution and terrorism abated. Good harvests aided Stolypin's efforts to re-establish domestic order. However, the Duma—although more compliant than in 1905—was still a legislative forum where open and uncensored debate was permitted. Nationalism expressed within Russia was potentially almost as domestically divisive as it was within Austria-Hungary. But used externally, cloaked in pan-Slavism and embracing state support for the Orthodox church, it became a means to rally and manage the Duma. Liberal imperialism found powerful advocates among some of the Kadets: P. B. Struve argued that such a policy could reconcile the people and the state, and V. A. Maklakov supported Serb unification at Austria-Hungary's expense. Within the administration this sort of thinking found expression with the appointment in 1912 of the Slavophil liberal, Prince G. N. Trubetskoy, as head of the foreign ministry department concerned with the Balkans and Turkey. For Trubetskoy, and for many Russians before 1914, Austro-Hungarian policy in the Balkans was only rendered effective by virtue of German support. Furthermore, Trubetskoy—like other liberals—derived strength and encouragement from the alliance with France and Britain.[41]

Thus anti-Germanism had, by the end of 1913, come to characterize the views of Russian farmers and industrialists, had the support of many of the intelligentsia, and had become a means by which domestic politics seemed capable of regulation and management. The penetration of German influence through the Balkans and into Turkey, the presence of German commercial interests in the Ottoman empire, symbolized most clearly by the Baghdad railway, triggered Russian anxiety with regard to the future control of the Black Sea straits. In 1912 the Turks had briefly to close the straits during the Italian war, and the Russian grain trade had lost 30 million roubles a month, with the adverse effects on the Russian balance of trade causing the state bank to raise its discount rate half a per cent in 1913.[42]

In October 1913 all these currents found their focus with the appointment of a German general, Liman von Sanders, to command I Corps of the Ottoman army at Constantinople. A German military mission, designed to train and upgrade the Turkish army, was not in itself a legitimate cause for objection. Liman was not the first German officer to undertake such a task in Turkey, and the British were performing a similar function in relation to the Turkish navy. But the Turks appointed Liman to a command, not to an advisory post. Furthermore, Wilhelm—in his usual bombastic way, and far exceeding the brief favoured by the German foreign ministry—had instructed Liman to Germanize the Turkish army and to make Turkey an instrument of German foreign policy and a counterweight to Russia.[43] Given the strength of Russia's reaction, the diplomats' more cautious approach prevailed over Wilhelm's instructions, military objectives were subordinated to political, and Liman von Sanders became inspector-general of the Turkish army instead. But the consequences of the affair stretched beyond its

[41] Lieven, *Russia and the origins*, 90–100, 126–32; on Russia generally in this period, see Pares, *Fall of the Russian monarchy*.

[42] C. Jay Smith, *Russian struggle for power*, 63–5.

[43] Fischer, *War of illusions*, 330–54.

apparent solution. It consolidated Sazonov's desire that Russia control the straits, and by February 1914 he was clear that this would be a Russian war aim if war came. Even more importantly, it confirmed his fears of German ambitions, and revealed his preference for war rather than to have the Triple Alliance regard Russian interests as of no consequence. A conference convened by Sazonov in the middle of the crisis, and attended by the ministers for the services as well as by the chief of the general staff, revoked the renunciation of war that had guided Russian policy since 1905. Instead, war was deemed to be 'fully permissible', and the conference set out a series of escalatory steps designed to get Germany to comply with Russia's wishes. Sazonov was not so foolhardy as to imagine that Russia was suddenly able to take on Germany and Austria-Hungary unaided. Thus, a necessary corollary of this shift was a much firmer allegiance to the Entente, and a determination to convert it into a fully-fledged alliance. Indeed, Sazonov had overreacted to Liman's appointment not least to test the Entente.[44]

France, through Poincaré, duly expressed to Izvolsky—now the Russian ambassador in France and working tirelessly for the promotion of the Triple Entente—its support for Russia. Such expressions were seen as inadequate by Sazonov, but they were more than sufficient to reveal the limitations of Bethmann's foreign policy. By emphasizing joint Franco-German interests in the Middle East, Bethmann had in 1913 achieved a measure of détente. Caillaux's return to office as minister of finance, the acrimony generated by the debate on the three-year service law, and the apparent waning of Poincaré's influence had all been good omens for Germany. But the Liman affair showed that, when driven to make a choice, the first priority in French foreign policy remained the Franco-Russian alliance. And, to add insult to injury, in 1914 once again French capital won out over German, with Turkey increasing its borrowings so that the level of French investment was three times greater than that of Germany.

By early 1914, therefore, the sole remaining plank in Bethmann Hollweg's foreign policy was the hope that Britain might yet be neutralized. In playing the Turkish card, Bethmann Hollweg had at least exploited the underlying and traditional weakness in Anglo-Russian relations. If

---

[44] McDonald, *United government*, 190–5.

Russia was unhappy about Germany's involvement with the Turkish army, it could hardly be ecstatic about the Royal Navy's comparable role with the Turkish navy—especially as the imminent arrival of two British-built Dreadnoughts would give the Turks supremacy in the Black Sea. Furthermore, other British Asian interests, particularly in Persia but also in Afghanistan, Tibet, and China, helped foster tension between the two powers. Bethmann Hollweg could console himself with the thought that, given time, the Anglo-Russian alliance showed every likelihood of collapsing from within.

Bethmann Hollweg's hopes were the stuff of Entente nightmares. Although Grey remained determined that Britain should retain a free hand, France could only endorse Sazonov's appeal in February 1914 that the Entente become a formal defensive alliance designed to deter Germany and Austria-Hungary. In April 1914 Grey agreed to the French suggestion that Russo-British naval conversations should take place, a proposal to which the cabinet gave remarkably ready approval. The naval talks were of course secret, but a German agent in the Russian embassy in London passed on their details to Berlin. On 22 May the *Berliner Tage-blatt* published the details, and on 11 June questions were asked in the House of Commons. Grey denied that Britain was under any obligations and denied that any negotiations were in progress—a technical truth in terms of treaty commitments, but a strategic fiction.[45]

Grey had feared that, if known, the naval conversations would confirm German fears of Russia and strengthen the hand of what he saw as the war party in Germany against that of Bethmann Hollweg. His worries were realized. Grey saw the German ambassador on 6 and 9 July, and insisted that, although staff talks had taken place, the governments of the Entente were not politically committed to one another. But such artfulness, 'seeking a compromise between isolationism and a policy of alliance in order to gain the advantage of both at the same time',[46] smacked of deceit. Grey hoped to appeal to liberalism in Germany and yet betrayed his own sense of democratic accountability by misleading parliament—or at least so it seemed to Bethmann Hollweg. For Bethmann the possibility of a German–British rapprochement as a basis for German overseas

---

[45] Williamson, *Politics of grand strategy*, 335–8.
[46] Egmont Zechlin, 'Cabinet versus economic warfare in Germany' in Koch (ed.), *Origins*, 199.

expansion was now gone; threatened too was the idea that each could manage its own alliance in the event of a crisis, as it had in November–December 1912.

Far more important, however, than these diplomatic setbacks was Germany's conviction that its encirclement was now complete. The fear which had accompanied German assertiveness gained the upper hand: the bull in the china-shop of European diplomacy began to see itself as a resigned sacrificial victim. For the Anglo-Russian naval talks gave the cue to the latent but pervasive Russophobia that gripped not only Bethmann Hollweg but also Moltke. The press and popular feeling played on the inevitability of a clash between Teuton and Slav. This emotive vocabulary did not seem inappropriate given the reality of the position. The Russian army's budget—independently of extraordinary capital grants—had grown from 406 million roubles in 1907/8 to 581 million in 1913/14. Spending on the navy nearly tripled over the same period, and in 1914 exceeded that of Germany. In 1913 the Russians introduced the 'grand programme', enacted in 1914, which aimed to increase the annual contingent of recruits for the army from 455,000 to 585,000, and to expand the total number of divisions from 114.5 to 122.5.[47] The Russian war minister accompanied these enlargements with statements calculated to stoke German anxieties. The German and Austro-Hungarian armies were already inferior to those of France and Russia by over a million men in the summer of 1914;[48] by 1917 the Russian army alone would be three times the size of Germany's. The argument that, objectively, there was no chance of a Russian challenge in economic terms did not figure in the calculations on the military balance. By 1914 French loans had enabled the construction of strategic railways so that Russia's mobilization could be accelerated, and the first troops be into battle within fifteen days. German plans drawn up in 1905 rested on the then-valid assumption that Germany would have six weeks in which to deal with France before turning east: the very existence of that planning assumption, which by 1913 was demonstrably wrong, added to Germany's sense of panic. In May 1914, therefore, Moltke's advocacy of preventive war took on greater

---

[47] David Jones, 'Imperial Russia's forces at war', in Millett and Murray, *Military effectiveness*, i. 265–6; Stone, *European society*, 334–5; Knox, *With the Russian army*, vol. i. p. xviii; D. Geyer, *Russian imperialism*, 200–1.

[48] Schmidt-Richberg, *Der Regierungszeit Wilhelms II*, 38.

urgency, if no more precision: 'we must wage a preventive war', he told Gottlieb von Jagow, the foreign minister, 'to conquer our opponents as long as we still have a reasonable chance in this struggle.'[49]

Both Jagow and Bethmann Hollweg resisted Moltke's suggestion.[50] But the case for doing so seemed, in the self-absorbed atmosphere of Wilhelmine politics, to be growing weaker. As early as December 1912 Bethmann—who had visited Russia in that year—confessed: 'One must have a good deal of trust in God and count on the Russian revolution as an ally in order to be able to sleep at all.'[51] The increases in the army necessary to meet the Russian threat exposed the delicacy of his own ability to manage the Reichstag. In 1913 90 per cent of central government spending was devoted to the armed forces, and the national debt had increased 125 per cent in 1898.[52] The conservatives still opposed property taxes, and the introduction of direct Reich taxation threatened the balance between Prussia and Germany as well as increasing Bethmann's reliance on liberal support. In addition, it was not clear that spending at such levels could be maintained. By the end of 1913, the German economy was in recession, 5 per cent of the labour force was out of work, and fears of depression followed.[53] Bethmann's ability to manage the domestic situation seemed as doubtful as his competence to overcome Germany's succession of diplomatic setbacks. Bethmann himself increasingly gave way to fatalism: the death of his wife on 11 May 1914 can only have confirmed his sense of resignation.

Optimists in 1914 took comfort from the fact that the great powers had successfully surmounted a succession of crises since 1905. On the surface, it seemed that the international system could regulate itself. But none of those crises had resolved the underlying problems which had given them birth. Above all, nobody saw the Treaty of Bucharest and the end of the Second Balkan War as more than an armistice. Austro-Serb relations remained locked in rivalry. Germany's own ability to manage another

---

[49] Jarausch, *Central European History*, II (1969), 59.

[50] Mommsen, 'The topos of inevitable war in Germany in the decade before 1914', in Berghahn and Kitchen (eds.), *Germany in the age of total war*, 40; also Jarausch, *Enigmatic chancellor*, 146–7.

[51] Jarausch, *Enigmatic chancellor*, 96.

[52] Herwig, *Luxury fleet*, 78; Kennedy, *Anglo-German antagonism*, 357–8, gives slightly different figures.

[53] Berghahn, *Germany and the approach of war*, 156–60; Fischer, *War of illusions*, 355–68.

confrontation was diminished by its need to support its ally, a dependence made more pressing by Russia's military and economic growth. The fact of direct Russo-German antagonism would change the dimensions of the next Balkan crisis. And the remoteness of Balkan politics, the fratricidal nature of their warfare, did not diminish their importance for Europe as a whole. In the Balkans imperial rivalries intersected and overlapped with the cold war of the alliances. The Balkans were also the point where three empires—the Russian, the Ottoman, and the Austro-Hungarian—came face to face with the imminent prospect of their own decline as great powers.

3

THE JULY CRISIS

In 1914 the annual summer manoeuvres of the Austro-Hungarian army were centred on XV and XVI corps in Bosnia.[1] In March it was announced that the Archduke Franz Ferdinand would attend the manoeuvres and would visit Sarajevo. Franz Ferdinand himself was somewhat apprehensive about the trip. On one level the Austrian occupation of Bosnia-Herzogovina had been enlightened: the road mileage of the province had increased over seven times since 1878, the railways had arrived, and new coal- and iron mines had been opened. But the administration of the crown-lands smacked of colonialism. Divide and rule was the Austrian path, retaining Moslem feudal landlords and so setting them against the Christian population. The army, increasingly frustrated by what it saw as lax government in Austria and Hungary, determined that its administration of Bosnia-Herzogovina should be a model of effectiveness. Franz Ferdinand himself advocated repression and active Germanization. He was also a staunch Catholic: in Bosnia Catholics were the minority (18 per cent) and 42 per cent of the population were Orthodox. Many Bosnians looked wistfully to Serbia. They were impressed not only by Serbia's growth in 1912 and 1913 but also by its schooling: young Bosnians crossed

[1] In addition to the works listed in nn. 1 and 59 above, the following have been of general assistance throughout this section: Evans and Pogge von Strandmann (eds.), *Coming of the first world war*; Geiss, *July 1914*; id., *Journal of Contemporary History*, I (1966), 75–91; Jarausch, *Central European History*, II (1969), 48–76; Kennedy (ed.), *War plans*; Stone, *Journal of Contemporary History*, I (1966), 153–70; Langdon, *July 1914*; Thompson, *In the eye of the storm*; Trumpener, *Central European History*, IX (1976), 58–85; Williamson, 'Vienna and July 1914', in Williamson and Pastor (eds.), *War and Society in East Central Europe*, v. 9–36; K. Wilson, *Policy of the Entente*; id. (ed.), *Decisions for war*.

the border to Belgrade for further education. Franz Ferdinand's appre-
hension had good grounds. Five assassination attempts had been made
against representatives of the Habsburg administration in the previous
four years. In the circumstances, and even without the benefit of hindsight, the early announcement of the visit of the heir-apparent, and the
extraordinarily lax security associated with it, were inexcusable.

On Sunday, 28 June, the archduke and his wife were driven from the
station at Sarajevo to the town hall, along the Appel quay. No soldiers lined
the route. Nedeljko Cabrinovic, a Bosnian youth, threw a bomb, which
bounced off the archduke's car, and then exploded, wounding two officers
in the following car and a number of bystanders. The archduke went on to
the town hall. He then decided to visit the wounded officers. At the junction
of Franzjosefstrasse and the Appel quay confusion arose as to the route to be
followed. The driver began to back the car. An associate of Cabrinovic,
Gavrilo Princip, was at the corner, having failed earlier in the day to take his
opportunity on the Appel quay. He stepped forward and shot both the
archduke and his consort. Franz Ferdinand, whose unattractive character
was at least redeemed by his affection for his family, called on his wife to live
for the sake of their children. But by the time the car had conveyed their
bodies to the governor's residence both husband and consort were dead. It
was their wedding anniversary. It was also the day of the battle of Kosovo: in
1389 a single Serb, after defeat at the hands of the Turks, had penetrated the
Ottoman ranks and killed the Sultan. For the Serbs and the Bosnians
tyrannicide had retained a pedigree which no longer seemed so appropriate
to the revolutionaries of industrialized societies.

The assassination led directly to the outbreak of the First World War.
And yet, for all the subsequent efforts to trace its authorship to one of the
great powers, it remains true that the prime responsibility rested with
none of the major belligerents but with an amateurish student revolutionary body, Young Bosnia, whose success owed far more to luck than to a
sophisticated conspiracy.

Princip—'a character from a Chekhov play except that when he fired he
did not miss'[2]—was born in 1894, the son of a Bosnian Christian peasant
family, had received his early education in Sarajevo but had completed it

[2] Taylor, *Politics in wartime*, 68; for a full account of the circumstances of the assassination,
see Dedijer, *Road to Sarajevo*. Also, on Young Bosnia, see Wayne S. Vucinich, 'Mlada Bosna and
the First World War', in Kann *et al.* (eds.), *The Habsburg empire*.

in Serbia, and had aspirations to being a poet. His brief life therefore embraced not only the Bosnian tradition of resistance to foreign, and specifically Ottoman, rule, which had been so easily transferred into opposition to Austria-Hungary, but also the fusion of romanticism and revolution characteristic of his hero Mazzini. Young Bosnia did not reflect a broad current of opinion but was one of a number of small student groups. The aims of these groups were diverse, but certainly Princip and his colleagues embraced the idea of a Yugoslavia, of a South Slav independent state, and rejected gradualism and reformism as means to achieve that end. Violence, they reckoned, would provoke Austro-Hungarian repression and so increase South Slav hatred of Habsburg government. Terrorism, tyrannicide, direct action, the decisive role of the individual in history—all these themes appealed to the Young Bosnians.

It is therefore hard to see how an assassination attempt would not have taken place even without support from outside. But the assassins did not operate alone. Two members of *Ujedinjenje ili Smrt*, acting under the cover of *Narodna Odbrana* and so eluding the detection of Austrian intelligence, played key roles. Major Vojin Tankosic of the Serb army provided the four revolvers and six bombs with which the conspirators were equipped; Captain Rade Popovic commanded the Serb guards on the Bosnian frontier and had seen Princip and his associates safely into Bosnia from Serbia some four weeks before. The key figure behind both officers, and the driving force in *Ujedinjenje ili Smrt*, was Colonel Dragutin Dimitrijovic, known as Apis. Apis was chief of intelligence in the Serb general staff: he had used his position to help *Ujedinjenje ili Smrt* penetrate the army, and also to create the frontier organization which Popovic represented and which allowed *Ujedinjenje ili Smrt* to carry its activities into Austria-Hungary. His objective, and that of his organization, was not the federal Yugoslavia favoured by the Young Bosnians but a Greater Serbia, with the implication that the Serbs would dominate the Croats and Slovenes in the new state. Apis was in contact with Artamanov, the Russian military attaché in Belgrade, but it does not follow that Russia was privy to the assassination. Apis's stock in trade, regicide, was not congenial to the Romanovs. Apis, for his part, wanted the achievement of a Greater Serbia to be that of Serbia itself, not that of Russia.[3]

---

[3] In addition to the works already cited, see Zeman, *Break-up*, 24–34.

Serb subjects were therefore implicated in Franz Ferdinand's assassination. Austria-Hungary's assumption, and indeed determination, that
this was so was shared by most of the other great powers. But the
involvement of the Serb government specifically remains a moot point.
Although the tariff war of 1906 with Austria-Hungary (the so called 'Pig
War', because the border was closed to Serbian livestock) had given Serbia
a sharp push towards independent industrialization, this was a recent
development and Serbia was predominantly a society of self-sufficient
peasants.[4] In such circumstances the army, with its provision of professional education and its possession of sophisticated equipment and
weaponry, enjoyed considerable political influence. In 1903 a group of
officers, Apis among them, had effected a particularly brutal coup in
which King Alexander and his wife had been murdered and the pro-
Russian, albeit westernizing and liberal, Petar Karageorgevich, installed
in his stead. Petar translated J. S. Mill into Serbo-Croat, and the constitution of 1903 contained all the trappings of democracy, including equality before the law, a free press, and an independent judiciary. But the
cabinets which followed the coup were short-lived, and the conspirators
themselves continued in the army, their authority and influence increased by their king's indebtedness to them. The army was frustrated
by the realistic stand taken by Serbia's ministers during the Bosnian crisis,
but it was the aftermath of that affair which gave status and reality to the
army's pretensions for Serbia as the Piedmont of the South Slavs. The
gains of the Balkan wars hallowed the Serb army with the aura of victory.
Re-equipped with French artillery (the cause and the fruit of the 'Pig
War'), its peacetime strength standing at 200,000 men, it saw Serbia as an
independent political actor.

Pasic, the prime minister, was more cautious, using the backing of
Russia to hold the army in check, and seeking a modus vivendi with
Austria-Hungary. Although he too was supportive of Serbia's expansion
and of its inclusion of Serbs currently within the dual monarchy, he
accepted that the achievement of that aim would be more gradual and
piecemeal than did *Ujedinjenje ili Smrt*. The administration of the newly
acquired areas of Macedonia brought the clash between Pasic and
Apis, between the civilian government and the army, into the open.

---

[4] Petrovich, *Modern Serbia*.

In December 1913 civilians were given priority over soldiers at public functions in Macedonia. Pasic's response to the outrage of Serb officers was to oust the minister of war. Apis and the opposition parties then rallied to oppose Pasic, and through Putnik, the chief of the general staff, put pressure on the king to dismiss Pasic's government. On 2 June 1914 Pasic resigned, and on 24 June elections were announced for 1 August. However, Apis's position was weak. King Petar abdicated, and his son Alexander backed Pasic against Apis. Both Alexander and Pasic looked to Russia for support; Apis turned to the army, but when he ordered a coup on 7 June it would not follow him. It has been suggested that so desperate had Apis's position become within Serbia that his motivation in backing Princip and his accomplices was to try to force a confrontation between Austria-Hungary and Serbia, in which the latter would be humiliated and the overthrow of the government thus become possible.[5]

In the circumstances of June 1914, therefore, Pasic could gain little from the assassination of Franz Ferdinand. But his responses were inevitably dilatory. It seems that he was informed that students armed with bombs and revolvers had crossed into Bosnia: it required little imagination to guess their likely target. Pasic therefore ordered an inquiry into the arrangements at the border, into the illegal traffic of weapons, and into Apis himself. But he did not dispatch a specific warning to the government of Austria-Hungary. An attempt does appear to have been made to halt the conspirators, but its author was probably Apis himself after the central committee of *Ujedinjenje ili Smrt* had belatedly been informed and had opposed his and Tankosic's actions. Although Pasic may not have approved of the assassination, domestically he was not in a sufficiently strong position to check it. He could not overtly antagonize the army any further, and anti-Austrian feeling and Greater Serb sentiment were genuinely popular in Belgrade. When the news of the assassination broke, his policy was to treat the matter as an incident internal to Austria-Hungary: it had occurred within the empire and had been carried out by its own subjects. But neither Serbia's ambassadors nor Serbia's press reacted with the same restraint; the enthusiasm of their responses to Franz Ferdinand's death did much to confirm Vienna's presumption of Serbia's guilt. Whatever Pasic's more sensible reflections suggested, the

---

[5] Geiss, in Koch (ed.), *Origins*, 83.

Serbian government after the assassination was not in a position force-fully to condemn it.

Whether an unequivocal and early response by Serbia to the assassin-ation would have made any difference to Austria-Hungary's behaviour must be doubtful. Franz Ferdinand was not the sort of personality who commanded popularity, and his demise in itself did not cast the empire into deepest mourning: indeed, in Vienna the Prater continued its jollifications without interruption. But as the Serb press crowed, so the Austrian and even Hungarian newspapers retaliated, and indignation that the heir-apparent should have been eliminated—apparently—by a foreign power took on a totally justifiable note of grievance.

Well before this mood was common the minds of all but one of Franz Joseph's ministers were firmly set. In the preceding Balkan crises the strongest voice for restraint had been that of Franz Ferdinand himself. He had appreciated that, for all his advocacy of Germanization, the majority of the empire's population was Slav and that war against the Slavs outside the empire was not a sensible way to cement the loyalty of those within it. Furthermore, he recognized that such a war could not be restricted to Austria-Hungary and Serbia, but would draw in Russia. Not only would Austria-Hungary find a two-front war difficult to sustain, it would also automatically sacrifice his own foreign-policy objective of a renewed *Dreikaiserbund*. By his own death the archduke had made war possible in more ways than one.

The opinion that the archduke's moderation had had most frequently to counter in the previous eight years was that of his own nominee as chief of the general staff, Conrad von Hötzendorff. Conrad was a social Darwinist. He believed that a recognition that the struggle for existence was 'the basic principle behind all the events on this earth' was 'the only real and rational basis for policy making'.[6] Conrad regarded it as self-evident that Austria-Hungary would at some stage have to fight to preserve its status as a great power. For much of the early part of his tenure of office his focus had been on a preventive war against Italy, but from 1909 he came to see Serbia as the more important issue. The irridentism of both powers threatened the southern belt of the empire, and war against one could provoke the other. Two cardinal points

---

[6] Peball (ed.), *Conrad*, 148.

therefore followed. First, Serbia and Italy were both as much domestic as foreign problems, and their resolution was an essential preliminary to greater Austrian strength at home as well as abroad. Secondly, it was important to fight each power separately and independently rather than to face both simultaneously. War should therefore be undertaken logically or preventively: 'politics', he averred, 'consists precisely of applying war as a method.'[7] Conrad first advocated preventive war against Serbia in 1906, and he did so again in 1908–9, in 1912–13, in October 1913, and May 1914: between 1 January 1913 and 1 January 1914 he proposed a Serbian war twenty-five times.[8]

Ironically, by the summer of 1914, although his enthusiasm for war had not diminished, it resided less on the calculation of previous years and more on the resigned fatalism which characterized so much of German thought at the same time. The Hungarian parliament's opposition to the army's reforms had delayed the new service law's introduction until 1912, and the consequent reorganization would not be complete until 1915.[9] In conjunction, the Balkan states (without Russian support) could outnumber the Austro-Hungarian army, and the Serbs alone—Conrad was wont to reckon—could field 500,000 men (although only 200,000 would be available on mobilization, the balance being made up of reserves). Conrad saw the Balkan League as an Entente-sponsored organization which threatened the dual monarchy with encirclement.

Thus he added to his frustration with the Magyars the expectation of a life-and-death struggle between Teuton and Slav. But in so revealing his own Austro-Germanism, he placed himself at odds with the multinationalism of the army's Hapsburg loyalties. During the course of 1913 he had become increasingly distant from Franz Ferdinand, and in September, stung by the latter's acerbic (if warranted) criticisms of the army and its general staff, he had sought permission to retire. Cut off from his royal patron and distant from the key government ministers, he was becoming politically isolated once more.[10] Then the assassination and its consequences put him back at the fulcrum. His pessimism caught the apocalyptic mood prevalent in Vienna, suggesting that Austria-Hungary

[7] Ritter, *Sword and the sceptre*, ii. 229; see also Peball (ed.), *Conrad*, 128, 148, 152.

[8] Dedijer, *Road to Sarajevo*, 145.   [9] Stone, *Past and Present*, 33 (1966), 103–11.

[10] Jerabek, *Potiorek*, 76–9; Leslie, 'Antecedents of Austria-Hungary's war aims', 310–13; Deak, *Beyond nationalism*, 72–4.

was already the victim of Conrad's Darwinian contest. War, he said on 29 June, would be 'a hopeless struggle, but even so, it must be because such an ancient monarchy and such an ancient army cannot perish ingloriously'.[11]

He was determined, too, that this time the outcome would not just be more sabre-rattling: a repetition of the mobilizations used in earlier crises without actual fighting would, he warned, be bad for the army's morale. Nobody in Vienna on 29 and 30 June could misinterpret his resolve, even if its basis was no longer rational calculation but, in his own words, 'va banque'.[12] And the fact that he was listened to was itself in part a result of that previous enthusiasm for preventive war. By that enthusiasm, he had won Moltke's undertaking in 1909 that, if Russia mobilized to support Serbia against Austria, Germany too would mobilize: in other words, he was confident that he could turn against Serbia, with Germany either deterring or fighting Russia. He seems to have been remarkably slow to consider what France would do. That enthusiasm, too, had enabled him to accustom Franz Joseph's ministers to the idea and expectation of war. The domination of the chief of the general staff over the minister of war had been accomplished by 1900. Conrad's efforts to achieve comparable sway over the foreign minister had been thwarted by Aehrenthal, and indeed it was Aehrenthal's pacific line which had headed Conrad off in 1909.[13] But Berchtold was made of weaker stuff.

The foreign minister was not under pressure just from Conrad. His ministry was staffed by a group of younger diplomats, protégés of Aehrenthal, who were committed to the fulfilment of Aehrenthal's pro-gramme for an Austrian domination of the Balkans. Berchtold's conciliar style meant that he listened to their views. Each day during the July crisis he held meetings with his principal subordinates, and mapped his tactics on the basis of their advice. It was these men who shaped Berchtold's Balkan strategy before the assassination, and kept the foreign minister to his resolve as the crisis unfolded.[14]

---

[11] Rothenberg, 'Habsburg army in the first world war', in Kann *et al.* (eds.), *The Habsburg empire*, 75.

[12] Herrmann, *Arming of Europe*, 218.

[13] Rothenberg, *Army of Francis Joseph*, 125; Regele, *Conrad*, 60–4.

[14] Leslie, 'Österreich-Ungarn vor dem Kriegsaubruch', 662–6; id. *Wiener Beiträge*, XX (1993), 378–81; Fritz Fellner, 'Austria-Hungary', in Wilson (ed.), *Decisions for war*, 11–12.

Like Conrad, Berchtold was keen to frustrate an Entente-sponsored Balkan League. Late in June his ministry was considering a diplomatic offensive designed to create an alternative Balkan structure. Ideally its pivot would be Romania. This would please the Germans and it would give Conrad sixteen extra divisions and a secure flank in Hungary. But Austrian negotiations begun in November 1913 had foundered, in part on the Hungarians' refusal to make concessions over Transylvania. Realistically, therefore, Austria's hopes were pinned on Bulgaria, and possibly Turkey. The aim was to isolate Serbia and to block Russia. In a memorandum of 24 June Franz von Matscheko portrayed Belgrade as manipulating Russian aggressiveness in the Balkans for its own ends. Matscheko's tone was deliberately alarmist: he hoped thereby to rally both the Germans and the Magyars in support of Austrian diplomacy.

The Sarajevo assassination presented this long-term policy with an immediate crisis. Matscheko's memorandum became the blueprint, not for forceful negotiation but for the negotiation of force. It seemed that Serb terrorism would lead to a Balkan League sponsored not by the Triple Alliance but by Russia. Swift military action—and it should be emphasized that Berchtold envisaged a war without the issue of an ultimatum and without the mobilization of Austrian resources—should eliminate Serbia's power in the Balkans, and so pre-empt a new league and destroy Russian influence. Potiorek, the governor of Bosnia-Herzogovina, no doubt anxious to cover over his inadequate security arrangements, exaggerated the unrest in Bosnia and pressed on Vienna the need for decisive and early steps against Belgrade. Berchtold and his colleagues were convinced of Serbia's culpability, and that inaction would be tantamount to diplomatic humiliation and would lead to a further decline in Austria-Hungary's status in the Balkans. By 30 June Berchtold was already proposing a 'final and fundamental reckoning' with Serbia. He told the royal household that the Entente heads of state should not be invited to Franz Ferdinand's funeral.[15] Franz Joseph did not demur, and on 2 July he reworked the Matscheko memorandum in a letter to Kaiser Wilhelm seeking his support. Count Alexander Hoyos, Berchtold's *chef de cabinet*, a

---

[15] Herwig, *First World War*, 12; Rauchensteiner, *Tod des Doppeladlers*, 68.

protégé of Aehrenthal and a noted hawk, was chosen to bear the imperial letter to Berlin.[16]

Austria-Hungary had received no formal expression of Germany's views before Hoyos boarded his train. Hoyos had met the German journalist Victor Naumannn on 1 July, and Naumann, an acquaintance of Bethmann Hollweg and of Jagow, had assured him that the Kaiser would support the dual monarchy, even to the point of war.[17] But Germany's ambassador in Vienna, Heinrich von Tschirschky, had kept silent. Austria-Hungary's decision to fight Serbia was its own.

Firmness had worked in 1908 and 1913; on other occasions a willingness to negotiate had led the empire into restraint and loss of face. The interaction between domestic and foreign policy was not simply a contrivance, as has to be argued in the German case, but an iron law. As Conrad had remarked to Franz Ferdinand in December 1912, South Slav unification was inevitable. It could be achieved within Austria-Hungary or at Austria-Hungary's expense. If the former, given the power and strength Serbia had acquired, a showdown with Serbia could not be avoided. It was the Austrian general staff, not the German, for whom war was a strategic necessity.

Franz Joseph's letter to Wilhelm was delivered by Hoyos to Count Szögeny, Austria-Hungary's aged and somewhat ineffectual ambassador in Berlin. The Kaiser had visited Franz Ferdinand and Sophie at their home as recently as 12 June, and his sense of personal loss gave him uncharacteristic decisiveness. He invited Szögeny to Potsdam on Sunday, 5 July, and over lunch—while stressing that he had yet to consult Bethmann Hollweg—expressed his conviction that Austria-Hungary should deal rapidly and firmly with Serbia, and that such action would have Germany's support. This typical display of apparent determination and swift resolve was effectively endorsed by the Kaiser's advisers. That same afternoon Wilhelm held a crown council at which Bethmann Hollweg, Zimmermann (standing in for Jagow, the foreign secretary being away on his honeymoon), Erich von Falkenhayn (the minister of war), Moritz von Lyncker (the chief of the military cabinet), and Hans von Plessen (the

---

[16] Bridge, *From Sadowa*, 368–74, 448–9; Williamson, *Austria-Hungary*, 165–89; id., in Williamson and Pastor (eds.), *War and society*, v. 9–36; id., *Journal of Interdisciplinary History*, XVIII (1988), 806–8; A. J. May, *Hapsburg monarchy*, 22–50, 55–8.

[17] Rauchensteiner, *Tod des Doppeladlers*, 70.

adjutant-general) were present; significantly neither Moltke, who was taking the waters at Karlsbad, nor any naval representative was in attendance. The meeting agreed to support the Austro-Hungarian desire to reconstruct a Bulgaria-centred Balkan League favourable to the Triple Alliance; as for Serbia, the dual monarchy's action was its own affair, but it was assured of German support in the event of Russian intervention. The following morning, 6 July, Bethmann Hollweg conveyed the council's views to Szögeny and Hoyos. Equipped with this 'blank cheque', Hoyos returned to Vienna.

What is striking about the 'blank cheque' is not that it was issued but that it was indeed blank. The council had made little effort to discuss the implications of what it was doing. Its decisions followed from previous events rather than from a projection as to the future. Falkenhayn wrote to Moltke expressing the view that neither he nor Bethmann Hollweg believed that Austria-Hungary would follow through the forceful language which it had so far employed.[18] But Bethmann Hollweg had done little to inform himself on precisely this point. When on 9 July he told the minister of the interior, Clemens von Delbrück, of the impending Austrian ultimatum he confessed that he had no idea of its contents; furthermore, so little was he disturbed by his own ignorance that he used it as a device to still Delbrück's alarm.[19] The fatalism which had increasingly gripped the chancellor had become a device to ease him of responsibility for his actions. Later in the same month he was to express the view that 'a fate greater than human power hangs over the situation in Europe and over the German people'.[20] The Kaiser too felt that the affairs of nations were beyond individual control and were subject to the inscrutable will of God.[21] Thus, nobody in Germany attempted to guide and manage events in July 1914.

Such an extraordinary abdication of responsibility is all the more remarkable in view of the fact that Bethmann Hollweg's calculations did not exclude the possibility of a major European war. The key question was the Russian response to an Austro-Hungarian invasion of Serbia. Assuming that Russia would intervene, Zimmermann told Hoyos that

---

[18] Quoted in Fay, *Origins*, ii. 212–13.
[19] Delbrück, *Der wirtschaftliche Mobilmachung*, 96.
[20] Diary entry for 27 July 1914, Riezler, *Tagebücher*, 192.
[21] Moses, *War & Society*, V (1987), 31.

there was a 90 per cent probability of a European war. But such realism—or pessimism—does not seem to have been widespread. By 11 July Zimmermann—whose reputation rested on his forthright but not necessarily consistent views—was confident that there would not be war because Austria and Serbia would come to terms. More widespread was the expectation that there would be war, but that it would be localized because Russia would stay out. That had been Plessen's view at the meeting of 5 July, and it was the line taken by Zimmermann's superior, Jagow.[22] Germany's ambassador in Russia, Pourtalès, continued to insist that the dangers of domestic revolution in the event of a major war would inhibit Russia. After all, Russia had backed down during the Bosnian crisis, and as recently as 1913 had endeavoured to restrain the Balkan states. Furthermore, its rearmament programme was not completed. If such calculations proved ill-founded, a second line of argument suggested that Britain and France would hold their eastern ally back from precipitate action. The Kaiser took comfort in the notion that his imperial cousin could not afford to condone the assassination of royalty. Outrage at the murders of the archduke and his wife seemed to have created a mood in Europe sympathetic to the Habsburgs. Bethmann Hollweg did not, therefore, embrace the probability of general war, but he was indubitably using its threat as an instrument in foreign policy, to isolate Russia both from its Entente partners and from its Balkan friends. His intentions were to strengthen the Triple Alliance by endorsing the Austro-German pact, and then, assuming the Austrians moved fast enough, to repeat the moderating role of 1912–13. The culmination of this process, according to Kurt Riezler, who was as close to Bethmann Hollweg as anyone in the July crisis, would be both a satisfied Austria and, eventually, a Russo-German agreement.[23] However, alongside the ideas of deterrence Bethmann Hollweg, and also Jagow, placed the calculations of preventive war. Serbia would be a good test as to how justified German Russophobia was: if Bethmann's bluff was called, and Russia did want war, then it was better for the two powers to fight it out in 1914, before

---

[22] Pogge von Strandmann, 'Germany and the coming of the war', in Evans and Pogge von Strandmann (eds.), *The Coming*, 115; Johannes Hürter, 'Die Staatssekretäre des Auswärtigen Amtes im Ersten Weltkrieg', in Michalka (ed.), *Erste Weltkrieg*, 223–4; Epkenhans, *Wilhelminische Flottenrüstung*, 404.

[23] Röhl, *1914*, 22.

Russia completed its rearmament programme in 1917. Furthermore, a war triggered by Serbia would ensure Austro-Hungarian support for Germany, and the fact that imperial Russia would have to initiate hostilities promised that within Germany the socialists would rally to the defence of the Reich. If European war was genuinely inevitable, the circumstances of July 1914 seemed as propitious for Germany as could be reasonably expected.

Bethmann Hollweg was playing fast and loose with the possibility, however remote he thought it, of a European war. He could only do so because his image of such a war—although widely held—was confused. The victories of 1866 and 1870 had achieved in short order and with minimal complications the political objectives for which they had been fought: Bethmann Hollweg's mental image of war in July 1914—at least as it related to an Austrian attack on Serbia—was of Königgrätz and Sedan, not of Verdun and the Somme. But also present in his mind was the idea of a long war with its concomitants, economic strain and social and political disruption. He saw a Russo-German war in such terms, for the possibility of war leading to revolution was a consequence he could envisage for Germany as well as Russia, and such a picture had to be present if he imagined that Russia might be deterred from intervention. Bethmann's policy in July was therefore made even more obscure by its ambivalence as to what war would be like—simultaneously it was a reasonable way to achieve policy objectives and the agent of total upheaval. The former implied that war could be an appropriate means to conduct policy, the latter that only its threat could so operate.

The chancellor himself made no attempt to resolve this dilemma, although his actions suggest that his hopes continued to be shaped by the prospect of a Bismarckian campaign. No preparations for a long war were made in July, and even on the 24th the Treasury rebuffed the general staff's suggestion that Germany build up its food stocks with wheat purchases in Rotterdam. Falkenhayn had assured the crown council on 5 July that the army was ready, but the authority with which he spoke was that of the minister of war, not of the chief of the general staff. He may have been buoyed up by the comparative success with which the 1913 army law had been rushed into effect, especially compared with the disruption which the three-year law was reported as having created in France. But the argument that the army was using this window of opportunity to exploit the idea of preventive war is hard to sustain. Falkenhayn thought that any conflict would remain localized, and promptly went on leave; he did not return until 27 July. Moltke, who was actually responsible for war plans, was not recalled until 25 July. Four days later the chief of the general staff was predicting 'a war which will annihilate the civilisation of almost the whole of Europe for decades to come'.[24] Bethmann had made no attempt to consult the service chiefs earlier in July, in the first half of the month, when Germany might still have been able to fashion the progress of events. Not the least of the ambiguities that such a discussion could have clarified was Germany's support of Austrian operations against Serbia when Germany's war plans required the Austrians to turn against Russia. If, as has been claimed,[25] the 'blank cheque' was designed to get Austria-Hungary to pin down Russia, so leaving Germany free to knock out Belgium and France, then its strategic and operational assumptions were remarkably ill-thought-out.

The focus of much recent historiography with regard to the 'blank cheque' has been on Berlin. But although Berlin issued the cheque, it was Vienna that had requested it and it was Vienna that cashed it. After 6 July, and until 23 July, decisions were taken not by Germany but by Austria-Hungary. The Kaiser departed on a cruise. Jagow returned to the foreign office, but Nicolai, the head of espionage and counter-intelligence on the general staff, only came back to work on the same day as Moltke, 25 July, and Groener, the head of the railway department, not until the following day.[26] On 11 July Berlin informed its ambassadors of the possibility of Austrian action against Serbia, and in Rome the German ambassador inadvisedly told San Giuliano, the Italian foreign minister. Habsburg distrust of Italy, and in particular fears that Italy could exercise its claim to compensation in the Balkans (embodied in article 8 of the Triple Alliance), caused Berchtold to look on his northern ally with almost as much suspicion as a result of this leak as he did on his Mediterranean ally. Communications from Vienna to Berlin were therefore kept to a minimum.[27] The Germans had no direct share in drafting the ultimatum

[24] Quoted in Turner, *Origins*, 105; see also Afflerbach, *Falkenhayn*, 149–53; for an opposing view, see Stevenson, *Armaments and the coming of war*, 298, 303, 407.

[25] Pogge von Strandmann, in Evans and Pogge von Strandmann, *The Coming*, 116.

[26] Trumpener, *Central European History*, IX (1976), 62–6; Groener, *Lebenserinnerungen*, 141.

[27] Williamson, *Journal of Interdisciplinary History*, XVIII (1988), 809.

which Austria-Hungary planned to send to Serbia, although they were aware of its main points and knew that its contents were designed to be unacceptable to the Serbs. Germany's immediate purpose remained relatively consistent: an Austrian coup against Serbia, while Germany worked to localize and limit the repercussions.

On 7 July Hoyos, having returned to Vienna, attended a ministerial council summoned by Berchtold. It was the third time in twenty months that the common council had confronted the issue of war: diplomacy which carried the threat of war came naturally to it. The task which confronted Hoyos was the corollary of that which he had already fulfilled in Potsdam: having displayed Austria's resolve in order to be sure of German backing, he now had to emphasize Geman determination to forestall any backsliding in Vienna. He presented Germany's support in unequivocal terms, and as a result the Austrian prime minister, Sturgkh, shuffled off his customary ineffectiveness with a 'firm intention of concluding the whole affair with war'.[28] Sturgkh knew how fickle Germany's support for Austria-Hungary had been in the last couple of years: it was necessary to seize the moment before Berlin changed direction, rely on Germany to deter Russia, and so shore up the empire by resolving the Balkan question once and for all. Speed was as essential to the calculations of Berchtold as to those of Bethmann Hollweg: any debate should follow a *fait accompli*, not precede it. He used Germany's support to shelve any worries about Russia and to narrow the council's focus on to Serbia alone. Self-deception led to simplification. That same day instructions went out to the Austrian ambassador in Belgrade which were unequivocal: 'However the Serbs react to the ultimatum, you must break off relations and it must come to war.'[29] But from 7 July delay set in, and with delay came loss of control.

Part of the delay was attributable to diplomatic calculation. Poincaré and the French prime minister, Viviani, were due to visit Russia from 20 to 23 July. Given the Austrian desire to limit the crisis, it made sense to postpone delivering the Austrian ultimatum to Serbia until the French leaders had quitted St Petersburg, and so avoid a co-ordinated Franco-Russian response which—on the evidence of 1912—would egg on

[28] Leslie, 'Österreich-Ungarn vor dem Kriegsausbruch', 666; Stone, *Journal of Contemporary History*, I (1966), 164.

[29] Fellner, 'Austria-Hungary', in Wilson (ed.), *Decisions for war*, 15.

the Russians. Much attention has been devoted to the other factors explaining Vienna's slowness in mid-July. But in the event the Austrian ultimatum was delivered as early as this reckoning would allow.

It also made sense to accompany the ultimatum with evidence of Serb complicity in the assassination. Many in Europe saw the Serbs as brigands, and were predisposed, given the 1903 regicides, to accept Austrian accusations on the basis of circumstantial evidence alone. In the event that was as much as they got. The Young Bosnians themselves were at pains to insist that the assassination was all their own work. Furthermore, even if they had Belgrade links, they—like the authors of the earlier assassination attempts—were Habsburg subjects. On 13 July the foreign ministry's investigator reported that he could find no evidence that the Serbian government had played a direct role, and by October, and the trial of Princip and his associates, the Austrian case against Serbia rested on the argument that the Young Bosnians had been the dupes of Serb propaganda. The Austrian investigation was not helped by its continuing ignorance of *Ujedinjenje ili Smrt*, and its consequent determination to pin the blame on the relatively innocent *Narodna Odbrana*.

However, the efforts to establish Serbia's guilt may not have been entirely fruitless, for Tisza, the Hungarian prime minister, maintained that they convinced him of the need to support the Austrian ultimatum. Franz Ferdinand's death had left Tisza as the single most important figure in the politics of the empire. He had been the only minister to oppose the strong line advocated at the ministerial meeting of 7 July. Indeed, his position was clear from 30 June. He saw Russia's entry in the event of an Austrian attack on Serbia as inevitable, and argued that Austria-Hungary should first engage in a diplomatic offensive to restructure a Balkan League embracing Bulgaria, Romania, and Turkey, which would support the Triple Alliance and leave Serbia isolated. Fundamental to Tisza's opposition was the issue of Magyar supremacy in Hungary. If Austria-Hungary successfully overran Serbia and then tried to digest it within the empire, the consequences would be a trialist restructuring of the empire, and a reduction in status and size for Hungary. Far more worrying to Tisza than the threat of Serbia was that of Romania. Romania, in the ascendant after its gains in 1913, was fostering irridentism among its fellow-nationals in Hungarian Transylvania. Magyar satisfaction with the *Ausgleich* as it currently stood combined with awareness of its vulnerability to produce caution. Furthermore, Tisza was well aware of the economic strains which war would impose on the empire, and which the 1912 mobilization had made manifest.

In the event, Tisza's opposition did no more than put down a marker for some of the dual monarchy's future problems. By 14 July he had been convinced by his fellow Magyar, Stephan Burian, who was effectively deputy foreign minister, that he should change his position. He was now prepared to accept an ultimatum designed for Serbia to reject. Politically, his earlier stance had become unsustainable. Popular passions against the Serbs had been roused in Budapest as well as in Vienna. The corollary of not crushing Serbia was a recognition of South Slav demands whose ramifications would impinge on Magyar interests in Croatia and southern Hungary no less than on other interests within the empire. In the shorter term Romania clearly intended to remain neutral, but its loss, Burian contended, could be compensated for by the acquisition of Bulgaria as an ally. In the longer term Romanian aspirations in Transylvania might well be influenced by the success of Serb irridentism if the latter was not crushed.[30] Finally, Tisza was fearful of forfeiting German support, not so much for the empire as a whole but for the *Ausgleich* specifically, and therefore for Magyar predominance. Berchtold was able to use the blank cheque to reinforce that fear. Tisza's earlier objections now found expression, not in opposition to going to war but in the aims of that war: on 19 July, the day on which the empire's ministers finalized the ultimatum to Serbia, they agreed in deference to Magyar concerns that Austria-Hungary would not annex any part of Serbia, but that chunks would be allocated to Bulgaria, Greece, and Albania, and the rump would be treated as a Habsburg client.

Therefore, it was not Hungary that produced the major domestic hiccough in the dual monarchy's timetable for war; surprisingly, that was a role reserved for Conrad von Hötzendorff. On previous occasions Conrad had demanded mobilization with an initial urgency that had then given way to calls for delay. In July 1914 he repeated the pattern. Much of the army was on leave to help bring in the harvest. Conrad argued that to cancel the leave would alert other powers to Austrian intentions. Most soldiers were due to return from leave on 21 and 22 July,

---

[30] Leslie, *Wiener Beiträge*, XX (1993), 341–7, 381.

and therefore 23 July—in addition to being the earliest date compatible with Poincaré's and Viviani's departure from Russia—was also the first that would suit the Austro-Hungarian army. Conrad dragged his feet even beyond 23 July. He reckoned that 12 August was the first day by which he could attack Serbia, and so was opposed to any declaration of war before then. Conrad's fatalism of 1914 was a product not simply of the realities of Austria-Hungary's position, but also of an inner mood. A shrewd observer, Josef Redlich, commented at the end of August: Conrad 'lacks greater inner verve. Inwardly, he does not believe in his historical calling as Austrian commander-in-chief.'[31] Preoccupied with his long-standing love for Gina von Reininghaus, the wife of an industrialist, his thoughts were of a married life with her rather than of Austria-Hungary.

Conrad's fantasies were not very different from the reality for many in Europe in mid-July. Llewellyn Woodward, the British historian, heard the news of the archduke's murder while staying in a hotel in the Black Forest, but considered it 'nothing more than another political assassination in the Balkans'.[32] Some saw its implications, but for the majority in western Europe Bosnia and Serbia were too remote and too primitive to be of direct consequence in their lives. Previous Balkan crises had been surmounted without a general war. It was a hot summer. July was a month of relaxation. The affluent, reflecting the increasingly cosmopolitan atmosphere of the continent's capitals, were taking their holidays abroad. General Brusilov and his wife were among a group of Russians undergoing cures at Kissingen in Germany. The Serb chief of the general staff, Putnik, was in Budapest (where he was interned, but on 28 July released). Wilhelm Groener, head of the railways section of the German general staff, was in Switzerland. Such international contacts made the danger of war seem particularly inappropriate. Commerce, education, and culture were drawing the nations together, not driving them apart. Five of the seven honorary graduands of Oxford University in June 1914 had been German;[33] Tirpitz's daughters had an English governess and were educated at Cheltenham Ladies' College. For those who had stayed

---

[31] Wank, *Austrian History Yearbook*, I (1965), 86; also 82–3.

[32] L. Woodward, *Great Britain and the war*, p. xiii.

[33] Michael Howard, 'Europe on the eve of the first world war', in Evans and Pogge von Strandmann (eds.), *The coming*, 1.

at home, domestic crises grabbed the headlines. In Britain, Grey and Lloyd George emphasized the calm of the international scene: the real issue was Irish home rule and the possibility of Ulster loyalist opposition. French readers were engrossed in much more salacious fare. On 20 July the trial began of the wife of Joseph Caillaux. Madame Caillaux had shot the editor of *Le Figaro* in his office after he had published her love-letters to Caillaux. The affair did have serious diplomatic consequences, since *Le Figaro* was said to be in possession of deciphered German telegrams, and foreign embassies in Paris therefore changed their codes in July, thus shutting French cryptographers out from a most important intelligence source. But the Caillaux trial's popular appeal was of course as a *crime passionelle*.

The silence which Vienna had sought was thus relatively easily won. It was broken at 6 p.m. on 23 July with the delivery of the ultimatum to Serbia. Austria-Hungary cited Serbia's failure to suppress the terrorism emanating from within its borders as evidence that Serbia had failed to honour its undertaking of 31 March 1909 to sustain good relations with Austria-Hungary. It asked the Serbian government to condemn anti-Austrian propaganda, to dissolve *Narodna Odbrana*, to take action against those Serbians implicated in the plot, and to include Austro-Hungarian representation in the suppression of anti-Austrian activities within Serbia. Serbia was granted forty-eight hours within which to reply. In the capitals of the great powers German ambassadors had been in-structed on 21 July to be ready to give full support to the ultimatum on 24 July and to work to keep the efforts of the Austro-Serb quarrel localized. On the face of it the ultimatum, though severe, was not unreasonable, and the initial reactions received by the Germans were reassuring.

The ultimatum was hardly a surprise to Serbia. Probably alerted to Habsburg machinations by the Rome leak as early as 7 July, Pasic had confirmation of Austro-Hungarian troop movements by 18 July.[34] Out-wardly Serbia seemed self-confident and cocky. The tensions with the army and the imminence of elections meant that nobody could afford not to be nationalist, especially in a domestic context. Hartwig, Russia's ambassador to Belgrade, who had died on 10 July had been accorded a

---

[34] For what follows, see esp. Mark Cornwall, 'Serbia', in Wilson (ed.), *Decisions for war*. This revises the earlier literature which gives a more bellicose twist to Belgrade's position.

state funeral, which Pasic had turned into a paean for pan-Slavism. But militarily there was every reason for caution. The Balkan wars had left the army exhausted. Austria-Hungary's military attaché in Belgrade was of the opinion that it would take four years to recover (in itself an argument in favour of a quick Austrian strike while the opportunity offered), and the Serb ministry of war was planning a ten-year programme of reconstruction. In June Pasic had rejected a Greek request for an alliance against Turkey on the grounds that the army was not fit for another war. The assimilation of the new territories was far from complete, their populations proving resistant to military service. Revolt had resulted in the army being deployed overwhelmingly in the south, away from the axes of its mobilization in the event of war in the north.[35] Moreover, there were few obvious signs of support from Serbia's possible military allies. Above all, Russia—although it had promised military aid—had counselled restraint on 3 July, and had given no reassurances by 23 July.

On the evening of 23 July Pasic was electioneering in the south of the country. Prince Alexander immediately contacted the Tsar, expressing Serb willingness to go as far in meeting the Austro-Hungarian demands as was 'in keeping with the position of an independent country'.[36] This became the essence of the Serb reply to Vienna. Pasic returned to Belgrade on the following day. Despite his awareness of Serbia's vulnerability, he could not cave in to the Austrians without forfeiting his political position—in relation to both the electorate and the army. His aim, therefore, was to moderate the reactions of his colleagues, while playing for time in the hope that international responses, and particularly Russia's position, would become more emphatic. In the circumstances, the Serb reply was brilliant. By accepting most of the terms but not all—Pasic refused to allow Austro-Hungarian representation in Serbia's internal investigations—Serbia appeared the injured party and won widespread support. The European climate, so apparently favourable to Austria-Hungary up to 23 July, turned distinctly frosty after 25 July.

By then the Serb cabinet had given the order for mobilization. This can be seen as a show of bravado, an indication that Belgrade was confident of Russian support, and a response to the fear that its reply to Vienna would

[35] Stevenson, *Armaments and the coming of war*, 276–7, 353–5; Lyon, *Journal of Military History*, LXI (1997), 481–502.

[36] Petrovich, *Modern Serbia*, 615.

otherwise be seen as too weak by the Serb army. In practice, it was an act of desperation. Although the decision was taken on the afternoon of 25 July, before the Serb note was in Austrian hands, it was not put into effect until midnight. Even then Serbia had received only vague indications as to Russia's position: at least for the moment Serbia seemed to be on its own. It mobilized because it reckoned that Austria-Hungary would resort to military action the moment the ultimatum expired.

Its judgement was sound. The diplomatic solution, to which Belgrade had at least technically opened the path, was of no interest in Vienna. Within fifteen minutes of receiving the Serb reply the Austrian ambassador in Belgrade announced that it was unsatisfactory and that diplomatic relations between the two states were at an end. On the following day the Austro-Hungarian army began to mobilize against Serbia, and on 28 July Berchtold—still trying to push Conrad into a speedier response— secured Austria-Hungary's declaration of war on Serbia.

Sazonov received the news of the Austrian démarche in the morning of 24 July. The Tsar summoned a meeting of the Council of Ministers that afternoon. Bethmann Hollweg and Berchtold rested any hopes they entertained that Russia would stand back on three assumptions: that the Austro-Serb quarrel could be isolated, that the Tsar's fear that war would lead to revolution would keep Russia out, and that—with Poincaré and Viviani at sea on their return to France—French support for Russia would not be forthcoming. On all three counts they were proved wrong.

Austro-Hungarian action against Serbia could not be localized because nobody in the Triple Entente, and certainly neither Sazonov nor Grey, saw Austria-Hungary as an independent actor. The irony of Vienna's position was that uncertainty about the strength of German support had prompted a firm line, when to the opposition that very firmness seemed indicative of Austro-German solidarity. Austria-Hungary was therefore saddled with the bellicose image of Germany. By July 1914 Germany, in the light of the 1911 Moroccan crisis and, for Russia in particular, of the Liman von Sanders affair, was judged as moving progressively towards war. Neither crisis was interpreted as a self-contained attempt to use the threat of war as a diplomatic instrument. The German attitude to preventive war, the German fear that by 1917 Russia would be too strong and would be able to mobilize too fast, had been faithfully reported by the Russian military attaché in Berlin. 'Germany', he opined in 1912, 'is strenuously preparing for war in the immediate future.'[37] Although contact between the Foreign Ministry and the War Ministry was minimal, Sazonov's immediate reaction on 24 July was to link the Austrian ultimatum to this wider, preconceived view. Germany, he was convinced, was behind Austria-Hungary; he was also sure that Germany wished to use the crisis to launch a preventive war.

Tsar Nicholas was more cautious, not least because—as Bethmann Hollweg rightly judged—he did fear that war would lead to revolution. In February 1914 P. N. Durnovo, the minister of the interior responsible for suppressing the 1905 revolution, had written a memorandum for Nicholas in which he anticipated that a future European war would be long, that it would therefore generate great economic and domestic political strain, and that the efforts to compensate for Russian industrial backwardness would lead to a social crisis and to revolution.[38] Nicholas brought this insight to his deliberations on 24 July: 'war', he said, 'would be disastrous for the world and once it had broken out it would be difficult to stop.'[39]

In 1910 it might have been possible to argue that Durnovo's prognostications owed too much to the past, to the memory of 1905; in 1914 they looked more far-seeing. Russia suffered only 222 strikes in 1910, and the police reckoned all but eight of these were prompted by economic rather than political factors. In 1913 2,404 strikes took place, and 1,034 were classified as political; in 1914, of 3,534 strikes fully 2,565 were deemed political. Furthermore, workers' discontent had reached a peak during the French state visit in July.[40] However, a year previously the police, looking back over a decade of domestic strife, had been confident that the position was improving: they reported that the general mood of the population was calm, expressing the view that there was no danger of revolution in the near future, and that they could control such problems as did arise without the aid of the army.[41] Since the bulk of the population still worked on the land the police were probably justified in these

---

[37] William C. Fuller, 'Russian empire', in E. May (ed.), *Knowing one's enemies*, 109–10; also 122–3.

[38] Lieven, *Russia and the origins*, 77–80.

[39] Ibid. 66.

[40] Siegelbaum, *Politics of industrial mobilization*, 17–18; Linke, *Militärgeschichtliche Mitteilungen*, 32 (1982), 15.

[41] William C. Fuller, *Civil–military conflict in Imperial Russia*, 256–7.

opinions: urban strikes were not representative of society as a whole; the situation was not revolutionary in the sense that 1905 had been. In July 1914 N. A. Maklakov, the minister of the interior, reflected the police view. War, he thought, would rally the nation, and mobilization specifically would pre-empt industrial disturbance.

In discounting the fears of revolution, in seeing war as a unifying, not a divisive, agent in Russian society, ministers were also embracing the liberal imperialists' support for the Entente. Much of the weakness of Durnovo's case resided not in the arguments themselves, which were not simply perspicacious but also accurate reflections of recent Russian experience, but in his conviction that Russia's main concerns were Asiatic, that its principal rival was therefore Britain, and that by engaging in a European war against Germany Russia would be fighting as Britain's proxy. Such arguments were *passé* in St Petersburg in July 1914. Crucially, they were not ones which the Tsar was prepared to endorse. The naval talks with France and Britain had convinced Sazonov that the Entente was close to becoming a formal alliance. Poincaré's and Viviani's visit had brought Franco-Russian relations to a new high. More specifically, there are grounds for believing that during the French visit—despite Vienna's precautions—the Russians and French did know of Austria-Hungary's intentions with regard to Serbia. Again the German leak in Rome was the culprit, as the Russians had broken the Italian codes.[42] Even without this specific opportunity to concert their responses to the ultimatum, the Franco-Russian alliance was in little danger of fracturing under German pressure in late July. Izvolsky, as Russia's ambassador in Paris, and Paléologue, his French counterpart in St Petersburg, were firmly committed to the Entente and were not loath to exploit, or even exceed, the powers vouchsafed them.

Therefore, given that all three Austro-German assumptions about the Russian response proved to be wishful thinking, the conclusions of the Council of Ministers at their meeting on 24 July become less surprising.[43] Its chairman, I. L. Goremykin, was a nonentity by comparison with his predecessor V. N. Kokovtsov, who had acted as a restraining influence in

[42] Williamson, *Journal of Interdisciplinary History*, XVIII (1988), 811–12; Keiger, *France and the origins*, 150.
[43] D. W. Spring, 'Russia and the coming of the war', in Evans and Pogge von Strandmann (eds.), *The Coming*, 57–86, provides a full and instructive account.

both the November 1912 and January 1914 crises. The important voices were those of Sazonov, whose views have already been outlined, A. V. Krivoshein, the minister of agriculture, and the two ministers for the armed forces, V. A. Sukhomlinov for the army and I. K. Grigorovich for the navy. Krivoshein, like Sazonov, was a man of more liberal disposition than many in the council, and recognized the need to co-operate with the Duma in order to achieve some measure of popular participation in government. The key factor for Krivoshein was not just, as it was for many Russians in the wake of the Bosnian crisis, Russia's status as a great power. It was the relationship between humiliation abroad and the loss of governmental authority at home. In Krivoshein's hands the fear of revolution, which had constrained Russia since 1905, was no longer a justification for international inaction, but a reason for assertiveness and an answer to the increasing manifestations of workers' discontent.[44] War was not a prospect to be relished, given Russia's relative backwardness, but a threat sufficiently strong to suggest its use was the only way out of Russia's dilemma. Neither Sukhomlinov nor Grigorovich was prepared to say that such a policy was mistaken. The rearmament programme of neither the army nor the navy was complete, but both armed forces were in better shape than they had been for a decade. It is easy, and perhaps right, to see Sukhomlinov's assertion that the army was ready as a braggart's self-defence, a reluctance to be deemed cowardly. However, the army was no longer so weak that it was unable to support Russia's foreign policy, as had happened in 1909, and Germany's fears of its potential were mirrored by the high estimates formed by French and British observers. The council concluded by agreeing to ask Vienna to postpone its deadline by forty-eight hours, by urging Belgrade to be conciliatory, and by giving permission for four military districts, Kiev, Odessa, Moscow, and Kazan, to prepare for mobilization. The Tsar ratified these decisions at a further meeting of the council on 25 July. Thus, from the very outset Russia included a military element in its response to the crisis. On 26 July Russia began to recall its reservists, in a phase preliminary to mobilization itself. On 28 July, in response to Austria-Hungary's mobilization against Serbia, the four districts already alerted were ordered to mobilize.

---

[44] McDonald, *United government*, 204–6, 218; Leslie, *Wiener Beiträge*, XX (1993), 341–7, 381.

Sazonov saw the steps taken up to 28 July as a buttress to his diplomacy, not as an inevitable progression to war itself. Partial mobilization had not, in November 1912, led to hostilities. The delay between the order for the Russian army's mobilization and its ability to commence hostilities would be a minimum of fifteen days at the very best, and full Russian mobilization would take nearer a month. Thus, there was ample opportunity for further negotiation. But such calculations were naive. First, the Russian decision preceded the Serb reply to Austria-Hungary: it had the effect of giving Serbia a 'blank cheque' of its own, and it generated a pressure for acceleration comparable to that for which Austria-Hungary and Germany were striving from the other side. To be effective in aiding Serbia, and to seize the advantage of operating against the Austrians' rear while they were embroiled to the south-east, Russia had to mobilize fast. But Germany's own war plan, aiming first to concentrate against France and then turn against Russia, rested on that very delay in Russian mobilization which the decisions of 24 and 25 July were calculated to eliminate. If the Germans allowed the Russians time to mobilize without themselves doing so, and without actually beginning operations against France, they would risk defeat in the east before they had won in the west.

Sazonov was sufficiently sensitive to this last consideration to insist on partial, not general, Russian mobilization. In particular, the Council of Ministers' decision did not include the pivotal military district in Russia's western defences, whether the enemy was Austria-Hungary or Germany or both—that of Warsaw. The Russian chief of the general staff, Yanushkevitch, was a weak character, both newly appointed and unfamiliar with the details of Russia's military plans. But Dobrovsky, the head of the mobilization division, immediately objected, and on 26 July received strong support from the quartermaster-general, Yuri Danilov, on his return from manoeuvres in the Caucasus. Danilov was convinced that the main threat to Russia came from Germany, not Austria-Hungary. In any case, from a technical point of view partial mobilization was a nonsense. Active units were stationed in peacetime in the regions from where they drew their reserves, not in their concentration areas, so as to minimize the number of train movements. Thus, each corps area drew on resources and reserves from adjacent districts, and the railway movements which mobilization involved embraced all Russia. Partial mobilization would throw the army into chaos. Operationally, the exclusion of Warsaw meant that Russia would forfeit the opportunity to envelop Austria-Hungary—should that power indeed fight alone—and would fight with unnecessarily limited forces.[45] Danilov's concerns over partial mobilization were shared by the French. Sufficiently aware of the German plan to know that they would be the initial target, the French had been pressing the Russians to increase the speed of their mobilization so that the latter could commence operations in East Prussia within fifteen days and thus provide indirect support in the crucial opening stages of the battle in the west. Neither partial mobilization nor operations against Austria-Hungary would assist the French cause: what the alliance required was a rapid Russian advance on East Prussia—a point which Joseph Joffre, the French chief of the general staff, did not hesitate to make to the Russians on 27 July.

Thus the step taken on 28 July, to mobilize four districts only, was of a piece with the mobilizations in earlier Balkan crises—it was designed as an instrument of diplomatic utility. Militarily it was unsustainable. The idea that mobilization was not a peaceful act but 'the most decisive act of war' had been present in the thought of Russian officers since 1892. In 1912 the European military districts were told to regard mobilization as the opening of hostilities.[46] On the morning of 29 July Sazonov responded to military advice and pressed the Tsar into approving general mobilization. The Russian decision for general mobilization therefore preceded any reaction from Germany. Indeed, the developments of that day—the opening of Austrian hostilities against Serbia with the bombardment of Belgrade, and a warning from Bethmann Hollweg that Russian mobilization would force German mobilization and that for Germany mobilization meant war—although they confirmed Sazonov in his decision, produced an apparent weakening, rather than a strengthening, of Russian resolve. The Tsar, prompted by a cousinly telegram from the Kaiser, reverted to partial mobilization at midnight on 29 July. The Russian general staff was appalled, and by 30 July knew that Germany

[45] L. C. F. Turner, 'Russian mobilisation in 1914', in Kennedy (ed.), *War plans*, 252–68, takes a different view; Lieven, *Russia and the origins*, 148–50, has some effective criticisms of Turner. See also Danilov, *Russie dans la guerre mondiale*, 30–8.

[46] Fuller, *Strategy and power*, 355; Suchomlinow, *Erinnerungen*, 343; Tunstall, *Planning for war*, 113.

had begun its military preparations. Sazonov believed that a secret German mobilization was possible; he was also aware of German pressure for preventive action. Therefore he renewed his advocacy of general mobilization. On the afternoon of 30 July the Tsar capitulated. On 31 July Russia began general mobilization. The German ultimatum arrived the same day.

In retrospect Russian prevarication over the pattern of its mobilization had little effect on the outcome of the July crisis. The crucial decisions, given the nature of Germany's war plan, were taken on 24 July. Any military preparations by Russia, even if designed to counter Austria-Hungary alone, would have been sufficient to prompt German mobilization. This is obviously true if Germany is seen as an aggressive power, already committed to European war, and certainly not disposed to pass up the opportunity of having its eastern frontier protected by Austrian operations against the Russians and so being freed to concentrate in the west. But it is also applicable in the context of a more reactive interpretation, of Germany's self-imposed image as the tragic victim: the sense of being in a corner, the preoccupation with time which not only the mobilization timetable but also the political management of the crisis generated, combined with the fear of Russia and the obligation to Austria-Hungary to make Russia's partial mobilization as intolerable to Germany as general mobilization.

Bethmann Hollweg was nonetheless slow to realize the gravity of the crisis which confronted him. On 25 July Germany's ambassador in St Petersburg had reported that Russia was not likely to be held back by fear of domestic disorder. Despite this clear indication that the strategy of a short, sharp Austro-Serbian war would misfire, the German chancellor continued to pursue that objective. His policy up until 28 July was guided, as it had been before the Austrian ultimatum, by the desire to limit and to localize. On 26 July Grey, buoyed up by the apparent success of the conference system in 1913, proposed an international conference, again casting Britain and Germany as the restraining influences within their respective alliance systems. But Germany's experience of such conferences, after the two Moroccan crises, was—as it had been for its ally—one of humiliation. On 27 July the Germans rejected the British proposal, on the grounds that the affair was Austria-Hungary's alone. And by the time that Bethmann Hollweg had apprised Austria-Hungary of Britain's view (which he took pains to point out he did not share)—that the Serb reply was acceptable—Vienna had already rebuffed the Serbs and was preparing for war. From 24 July onwards Grey warned Germany's ambassador in London that war, if it came, would not be localized. But for Bethmann, politically isolated at home and with his foreign policy apparently bankrupt abroad, the lure of a quick Balkan coup was not yet gainsaid. Sazonov's policy up until 28 July could be seen as conciliatory; France—with Poincaré and Viviani not returned until 29 July—was in no position to give clear signals; even Grey's conference proposal betokened a preference for negotiation rather than belligerence. The determination to stick by the policy of 5 and 6 July put blinkers on Bethmann Hollweg and at the same time hardened the reactions of the other participants in the crisis. By the time he was alerted to the certainty of Russian involvement, and to the implications for German policy of Russian mobilization, he had lost the opportunity to manage events. Before 28 July the message from Britain above all, but also from France and Russia, was clear: the local war must be avoided in order to prevent a major war. Bethmann Hollweg did not attempt to avoid a major war until after the local war had been initiated.

The first indication of a change of tack came on 28 July. Wilhelm had returned from his cruise the preceding day. When he read the Serb reply to the Austrian ultimatum, its moderation convinced him that war was now no longer required; instead, the Austrians should halt in Belgrade and occupy it until terms were agreed. Bethmann Hollweg passed the proposal on to Vienna, but specifically disavowed any wish to hold Austria-Hungary back from the task of achieving its aims in relation to Serbia. Berchtold postponed replying. The messages being received from Berlin were contradictory; only the day before British proposals of mediation had been passed on without German endorsement, and by the night of 28/9 July Berchtold might reasonably argue that Austria's dwindling prestige in the Balkans would not survive any retraction from the military solution now under way. Speed and decisiveness were still Berchtold's objectives, as they had hitherto been those of Bethmann Hollweg.

On 29 July the alteration in Bethmann's approach became more evident. Grey must be held responsible for completing the change. Fritz Fischer, Imanuel Geiss, and others have seen Germany's policy in July as the denouement and continuation of its previous foreign policy.[47] Both Fischer and Geiss contend that the German chancellor accepted the possibility of a European war from the outset of the crisis but hoped that Britain would remain neutral. Therefore, for them, the Anglo-German naval negotiations of 1912 had had as their objective not détente per se, but the neutralization of Britain in the event of war. Undeniably Bethmann Hollweg worked for the maintenance of Anglo-German diplomatic links during July. But this, rather than evidence of continuity, is yet again an indication of Bethmann's wishful thinking and self-delusion in the three weeks up until 28 July. Over the previous decade the German general staff had entertained little doubt that, in the event of war in the west, the British would stand by the French. Clear statements to that effect had been made to Germany by Haldane in 1911 and by Grey in 1912: the implications were there in the Anglo-French staff talks and in Lloyd George's Mansion House speech. Bethmann had not shared the Anglophobia of Tirpitz, but the British naval talks with the Russians had convinced him of the rightness of the assumption that Britain would not be neutral in the event of a European war. Bethmann's hopes for Britain in July 1914 were therefore a reflection of his desire for a localized war. Obviously, if the local war became a general war it would serve Germany's interests if Britain espoused neutrality, but Bethmann Hollweg appreciated that in reality such an outcome was improbable. Where realism failed Bethmann was in his slowness to interpret Grey's warnings that an Austro-Serb war could not be localized as evidence that Britain would not long sustain the position of international arbitrator. On the afternoon of 29 July Grey made clear to the German ambassador that Britain would not remain neutral in the event of a continental war. Talk of mediation had given way to an explicit threat. Bethmann Hollweg's despair arose from the final realization that the policy of localization had failed.

By 30 July, therefore, the change in the chancellor's policy was complete. At 2.55 in the morning he dispatched an urgent telegram to the German ambassador in Vienna, calling on the Austrians to attempt mediation on the basis of 'the halt in Belgrade'. Faced with the immediate prospect of European war, neither the Kaiser nor Bethmann Hollweg wanted it.

[47] Geiss, *Journal of Contemporary History*, I (1966), 82; see also Geiss, *July 1914.*

The Austrian reaction was, predictably, one of confusion and frustration. The withdrawal of German support, feared and anticipated from the outset, had now come to pass. However, hostilities with Serbia had already commenced. The advice of Conrad von Hötzendorff from the beginning was that war could not be fought with limited means and limited objectives: given the size of the Serb army by 1914, Austria-Hungary would have to undergo a general mobilization to commence hostilities. A quick *coup de main* against Belgrade was therefore impossible, as well as being inappropriate. When Austria-Hungary's ministers discussed Bethmann's proposal on 31 July they could only endorse on political grounds the position adopted by Conrad on military: the last London conference was described as 'a frightful memory', and it made little sense for Vienna now to desist without a guarantee from Russia.[48]

The desire in Austria-Hungary to settle the Serb problem once and for all was supported by the attitude of Moltke. By 30/1 July the pressure from Berlin for swift Austrian action had not diminished; it simply came from a different quarter. Although Jagow had indicated to the Russians that partial mobilization would not trigger German mobilization, Moltke was of a different view. If the Austro-Hungarian army was fully committed to the war with Serbia, it would be unable to take an active role in operations against Russia, and yet this was the premiss upon which the German war plan rested. Unless a reasonable proportion of Franz Joseph's army tied down comparable Russian forces, Germany would not be able to deal with the dangers of a two-front war by concentrating the bulk of its divisions first against France. Time therefore pressed on Moltke in two ways. First, he could not afford to let the German mobilization fall behind that of Russia. But secondly, and more immediately, he could not allow the general war to follow so long after the outset of Austro-Serb hostilities that the Habsburg army could not concentrate against Russia rather than Serbia. Thus, on the afternoon of 30 July Moltke bypassed Bethmann Hollweg and urged Conrad to mobilize against Russia, not Serbia, and assured him that Germany would follow suit. Berchtold's response to Moltke's intervention was to ask, rhetorically, who ruled in Berlin: Moltke's message in itself did little more than confirm to Vienna the wisdom of its own continuing resolve.

[48] Regele, *Conrad*, 242–5, also 122.

The pressure Moltke put on Vienna, although seemingly fraught in its implications for civil–military relations, was no more than a response—and a somewhat belated one at that—to the circumstances in which Germany now found itself. German military intelligence had picked up an exchange of signals between Russia and France concerning mobilization on 24 and 25 July, but as late as 26 July was still anticipating a crisis that would carry on for several weeks.[49] Not until Falkenhayn's return to work on the 27th had the army's somewhat dilatory approach been challenged. Falkenhayn was appalled by the lack of resolution displayed by both the Kaiser and by Moltke. He was clear that the responsibility for policy was Bethmann Hollweg's, but argued that the chancellor's obligation to put to one side military advice for political reasons no longer held good when 'a crucial military interest was at stake'. On 29 July Falkenhayn felt that that point had been reached. He called for the declaration, *Zustandes drohender Kriegsgefahr*, the preliminary steps to mobilization. Moltke, aware that for Germany mobilization meant war, and fearful of its implications for Europe as a whole, would not endorse the minister of war's request, and Bethmann Hollweg took his cue from the chief of the general staff.[50] The chancellor emphasized his wish to leave the initiation of hostilities to Russia. But at the same time his acknowledgement that, if European war came it would include a German attack on Belgium and France, was contained in his request for British neutrality in exchange for German respect for Belgian and French territorial integrity, and confirmed by the preparation of an ultimatum to Belgium demanding its acceptance of the transit of German troops through its territory: the former in particular was a diplomatic gaffe that made the possibility of restraint yet more remote, but which reflected the pressure that Bethmann Hollweg was now under from the army. On 30 July Moltke's respect for Bethmann's wish to await the Russian response had—as his message to Conrad testified—evaporated. That evening he got the chancellor to agree that a decision on general mobilization would be made by noon on 31 July. Moltke was quite clear that the Tsar's equivocation over general or partial mobilization could make no difference to the German decision. Five minutes before their self-imposed deadline, Moltke and

[49] Showalter, *Tannenberg*, 95; Stevenson, *Armaments and the coming of war*, 400.
[50] Afflerbach, *Falkenhayn*, 153–9; see more generally Trachtenberg, *History and strategy*, 88–92.

Bethmann Hollweg heard that the Russians had finally decided on general mobilization. Germany issued the declaration of *Kriegsgefahr* that day, and ordered general mobilization on 1 August. Ultimatums were dispatched to St Petersburg and Paris on the night of 31 July; on the following morning Germany declared war on Russia.

The lack of either continuity or clarity in German policy was in itself a reflection of the absence of a guiding authority. Supreme command was in name vested in the Kaiser, but by 1914 Wilhelm no longer commanded the respect which his titles demanded: the monarchy was venerated as an institution rather than in the personality of its incumbent. Technically, the reconciliation of the views of the chancellor and of the chief of the general staff in late July was Wilhelm's responsibility. In practice, the management of the crisis reflected the dominance of first one personality, Bethmann Hollweg, and then another, Moltke. Bethmann had guided events up until 28 July by acting in isolation: he had encouraged the Kaiser to put to sea and Moltke to continue his cure. When the Kaiser returned, the belligerence he had expressed to Hoyos on 5 July had softened. Wilhelm, however, was caught by his own self-image, that of the steely warrior, and thus his reluctance to fight was compromised by his relationship with his military entourage and, above all, with Moltke. Wilhelm saw himself as the victim of an Entente conspiracy, initiated by his despised English uncle Edward VII, and the latter's Francophile ways. His capacity so to reduce the crisis of late July 1914 to the level of his own personal animosities cut across any possibility of drawing out the full implications of each step which Germany took.

The most striking illustration of the consequent absence of any German grand design was the confusion between German diplomacy, which aimed to limit war as far as possible, and German war plans, which rested on a worst-case analysis, that of a two-front war against France and Russia simultaneously. After the December 1912 Balkan crisis Moltke had concluded that the Franco-Russian alliance was sufficiently strong to mean that Germany could not fight one without having to reckon with the other. Therefore the plans for war against Russia alone, which in the normal course of events were updated by the general staff each year, were abandoned in April 1913. The army thus committed itself to a two-front war. However, the timing of the Austrian ultimatum in July 1914 was dictated by the wish to minimize the chances of a two-front war, to increase the possibility that if Russia acted in support of Serbia it would do so without France's aid. Of course, neither Bethmann Hollweg nor the Kaiser was blind to the realization that war with Russia would probably lead to war with the Entente as a whole: hence Bethmann's crassly provocative communication to Britain on 29 July. But they had not appreciated that in the general staff's view war in the east had inevitably to be preceded by war in the west. On the afternoon of 1 August Germany's ambassador in London reported that Grey had guaranteed that France would not fight Germany if Germany did not attack France. The report was false, and the elation which it produced in the Kaiser and in Bethmann Hollweg short-lived. But their jubilation was in marked contrast to the despair the report engendered in Moltke. 'If His Majesty', the latter recounted himself as saying, 'were to insist on directing the whole army to the east, he would not have an army prepared for the attack but a barren heap of armed men disorganised and without supplies.'[51]

The confusion in Germany as to how France would react was in considerable measure a self-inflicted wound. On 27 and 28 July the Germans jammed wireless transmissions between France and Russia, and between both places and the presidential cruiser. Thereafter the two allies routed their signals traffic through Scandinavia, so generating further delays in communication. Poincaré and Viviani did not return to Paris until 29 July. By deliberately trying to silence France's leaders, the Central Powers were left free to project on to France their own hopes. In practice French policy was remarkably consistent and predictable: more than that of any other great power, it reflected the developments of 1911–14 rather than the pressures and confusion of the July crisis itself.[52]

The doggedness of Poincaré's efforts to cement the Triple Entente had by 1914 achieved a momentum of their own. The original objective of his visit to St Petersburg was to promote better relations between Russia and Britain, and the crisis in the Balkans did not in itself bulk large. This was in part a reflection of ignorance: the French ambassador in Belgrade was ill, and the Quai d'Orsay received no information from Serbia between 14 and 25 July. Intelligence from Berlin was not much better, not least because Jules Cambon was home on leave until 23 July. But the comparative

---

[51] Quoted in Barnett, *Swordbearers*, 18.
[52] The discussion that follows draws on John Keiger, 'France', in Wilson (ed.), *Decisions for war*, esp. 121–30, and Hayne, *French foreign office*, esp. 269–301.

neglect of the Balkans in the St Petersburg talks was also an indication that, once the situation did become clear, the French would not be disposed to see the crisis in isolation. In Paris only the caretaker foreign minister, Bienvenu-Martin, sustained the hope that an Austro-Serb war could be localized. He was rapidly disabused of this notion by the ministry's senior officials, convinced that behind Austria-Hungary stood Germany, and determined that the preservation of the Entente was a more important objective in French foreign policy than the avoidance of war.

The principal problem confronting Poincaré was how to achieve the former without appearing so uncaring about the latter that France prejudiced either its international credibility or its domestic unity. The memory of France's entry to the war of 1870, when it had forfeited both, loomed large in his calculations. Military considerations were therefore consistently subordinated to diplomatic in order that France's defensive posture should be unmistakable. The war minister, Messimy, was kept in ignorance for much of July; the distinction between mobilization and a declaration of war was emphasized; and as late as 1 August the order for the army to keep 10 kilometres back from the Franco-Belgian frontier—thus making clear France's respect for Belgian neutrality—was reaffirmed. But Poincaré knew as well as Messimy and Joffre that France's security was bound to that of Russia, and that if Russia mobilized so would Germany. Thus, the tension created by affirming the Entente while asserting French defensiveness was played out in the relationship with Russia.

Pivotal to this dialogue, particularly during the periods of enforced silence and delayed communication, was France's ambassador in St Petersburg, Maurice Paléologue. Paléologue's early career had left him well versed in the Franco-Russian relationship, and particularly in its military dimensions. Furthermore, he had been at school with Poincaré, and shared the president's belief in the centrality of the Entente. Lunching with Sazonov on 24 July, he responded to Sazonov's conviction that the Austrian ultimatum required a robust response by averring that the Entente should stand up to the Central Powers. As a result of this exchange and, more explicitly, of delays in his reporting the steps taken by Russia on its route to general mobilization, Paléologue has been accused of deliberately stoking Russian aggression while at the same time endorsing Paris's conviction that Sazonov's policy was essentially pacific. Consequently Paris saw Germany's decision to mobilize as unprovoked, and felt its task to be the stiffening of Russian resolve. This interpretation, quite apart from its discounting of the practical difficulties in St Petersburg–Paris communications, elevates Paléologue's role while downgrading those of Sazonov and Poincaré. It overlooks the striking fact that Russian decision-making was remarkably little influenced by France. It also neglects the similarity between the policy which Paléologue pursued and that which Poincaré would have espoused had he been free to do so. To that extent Paléologue was a more than adequate stopgap when communications were broken. Once they were restored the delays in transmission on 30 and 31 July, whether contrived or not, buttressed Poincaré's position by stilling any suggestion that Russia had initiated hostilities and had thus invalidated the defensive basis of the alliance.

As a result, even if obscured from Germany, and overshadowed in the French press by Madame Caillaux's trial (the all-male jury gallantly acquitted her on 28 July), Poincaré's affirmation of the alliance continued unimpeded by its author's enforced silence. Indeed, it is worth remembering that on board ship with Poincaré was Viviani, who as a radical prime minister was much more disposed to soften France's support for Russia. By the time that he was able to do so, advising the Russians not to offer Germany a pretext for general mobilization, it was effectively too late.

Viviani's views, and the need to muzzle them, were a reflection of the domestic imperatives under which Poincaré increasingly felt himself to be operating. The elections of April/May 1914, and the shift to the left which they had produced, although in practice no block to nationalist sentiment, did point to a continuing threat to the three-year military service law. During July itself Messimy was working on a revision of the law, and Poincaré expected its amendment in autumn 1914. The military strength of the Franco-Russian alliance was thus likely to be challenged from within France, as well as by Austro-Germany policy without. The improvements in the French army since 1911, combined with growing evidence of Russian military strength, contributed by 1914 to greater optimism within the French general staff about its prospects in a war with Germany. As in the latter, therefore, so in the former: there was a sense that if war was to come to Europe, better now, with the French army profiting from the three-year law, and with Russian support guaranteed by a Balkan crisis, than later.[53]

The French president's resolve was heightened by the ecstatic welcome which he and Viviani were accorded on their arrival in Paris on 29 July. Four days previously the *Echo de Paris* had published an account of the visit of Germany's ambassador to the Quai d'Orsay: he had been seeking France's co-operation in localizing the conflict, but the version leaked by the foreign ministry to the French press carried a somewhat different spin. The call confirmed that Germany was prodding Austria-Hungary, and that its purpose was to carry on the policy of the second Moroccan crisis and split the Entente. Furthermore, the implications of such a policy were not simply diplomatic. The three-year-law agitation, and its centrality to recent domestic politics, had accustomed the French public to the idea of a surprise German attack. The fact that among the cries of 'Vive la France' Poincaré could also hear 'Vive l'armée' left him in no doubt of the prevailing mood.[54]

France's sense of now or never was contributed to by an inflated expectation of the likely British response. Paul Cambon, France's ambassador in London, had listened to those British friendly to the Entente rather than those who were not: his dispatches reflected the expectation generated by the Anglo-French naval agreement of 1912, that in the event of war with Germany the Entente would become a definitive alliance. On 1 August the mobilization orders to the French fleet assumed that the joint Anglo-French operational plans would be put into effect: in practice Britain had neither committed itself on this point nor yet sent an ultimatum to Germany.

It is tempting to see Britain's strategic imperative, the need to prevent any great power dominating the further coast of the English Channel and so providing a direct threat to Britain's sea-power, as creating an inevitability about Britain's entry to the First World War. Grey's foreign policy, combined with both naval and military staff talks, had established—so this argument would add—a continental commitment. A minority of the cabinet, as well as general-staff officers like Henry Wilson, did think like

[53] Krumeich, *Armaments*, 214–29; also C. M. Andrew, 'France and the German menace', in E. May (ed.), *Knowing one's enemies*, 146–8.

[54] Raithel, *Das 'Wunder' der inneren Einheit*, 192–9, 252–5.

this in July 1914. But they did not represent the sort of widespread consensus which would justify hostilities. Britain was the only great power to debate its entry to the war in parliament; it was also the only state that did not see its own territorial integrity under direct threat. The decision to fight, therefore, had to be justified to more people than was the case in other countries, but itself rested on a more indirect danger. The reluctance of the Foreign Office to treat foreign policy in an open way, Grey's own tendency to keep diplomacy from the cabinet—both these factors meant that British opinion had to be educated, coaxed, given time to develop, in late July.[55]

Indeed, as has already been seen, until 29 July Grey's approach to the crisis was one of caution. Liberalism's affection for the rights of small nations did not extend to Serbia. The *Manchester Guardian* was of the view that, 'if it were physically possible for Serbia to be towed out to sea and sunk there, the air of Europe would at once seem cleaner'.[56] Grey told the Austro-Hungarian ambassador that, if his country could fight Serbia without provoking Russia, he could 'take a holiday tomorrow'.[57] On 24 July Asquith, the prime minister, recognized the implications of the Austrian ultimatum for European relations and the possibility of a 'real Armageddon', but still reckoned that the British could be 'spectators'.[58] He could not at first see why a German victory would upset the balance of power in Europe, on the grounds that it had not done so in 1871, and as much as a week later he told the archbishop of Canterbury that the Serbs deserved a 'thorough thrashing'.[59] His major concern in July was Irish home rule. If his government did not carry a bill it would lose the support of the Irish members of parliament on whom it depended for an overall majority; if it did, Ulster loyalists threatened civil war. In the event the problems of yet a third small nation, Belgium, subsumed those of Serbia and allowed the Liberals to shelve those of Ireland.

Grey's self-appointed role as mediator between 24 and 29 July was not, therefore, adopted for the benefit of Germany. Domestically, he both had

[55] On Britain in the July crisis, see Michael Brock, 'Britain enters the war', in Evans and Pogge von Strandmann (eds.), *The coming*, 145–78; Hazlehurst, *Politicians at war*, 1–116; Wilson, *Policy of the entente*, esp. 135–47.

[56] A. May, *Hapsburg monarchy*, 52.

[57] Bridge, *From Sadowa*, 381.

[58] Brock and Brock (eds.), *Asquith*, 124–5.

[59] Cassar, *Asquith*, 13–15, 18–19.

to create time for a public awareness of the crisis to grow and had to have tried a diplomatic solution before he could hope to argue for the commencement of hostilities. Abroad, his purpose was to restrain Russia and France: he feared that by openly affirming the solidarity of the Entente he would encourage both powers to precipitate action. His allies, on the other hand, contended that a united front could have deterred Germany. Certainly the consequence of Grey's ambivalence was apparent failure: his efforts at negotiation did not moderate Austro-German behaviour, but they did alarm the Russians and the French. Grey could not afford to follow an independent line indefinitely. He had recognized in 1911 that Britain's own interests were too closely intertwined with those of the Entente for neutrality to be a genuinely viable option. By allying with France, Britain was better able to manage its own relationship with Germany, and to give itself the sort of continental military clout which its diminutive army could not. Even more important was the link with Russia: Russia's membership of the Entente committed it to rivalry with Germany, gave its policy a European twist, and so relieved the British of the challenge of its main rival in Central Asia. If Britain had failed to support France and Russia in 1914, its links with them would have been forfeit, and the reopening and deepening of those old and more traditional rivalries would have driven Britain into the only alternative, an Anglo-German alliance. For all Asquith's hope, isolation from Europe was no longer possible, not least because of its imperial consequences.

The events of late July went faster than Grey's diplomatic machinations. For some sections of the press, notably *The Times*, the Foreign Office's reactions were dilatory. But this did not mean that it had lost its sense of direction. As early as 26 July Grey used the decision of the First Sea Lord, Prince Louis of Battenberg, to keep the naval reserve at its stations as a signal to Germany. On 27 July the army and the navy were put on precautionary alert. The cabinet approved these steps on 29 July. On 31 July Eyre Crowe, head of the eastern and western departments at the Foreign Office and a well-established harbinger of the German menace, wrote that 'if England cannot engage in a big war [it] means her abdication as an independent State'.[60]

---

[60] Neilson, *Britian and the last Tsar*, 35.

But the British government was still not in a situation where it could adopt an unequivocal position. Grey made his commitment to the Entente clear to Germany, and was justified in doing so by Germany's own confirmation that it intended to march through France and Belgium. Yet at the same time he had to tell Paul Cambon that a clash between Austria-Hungary and Serbia did not constitute a direct threat to France, and that Britain was therefore free from any engagement. He had no other choice: on 31 July the cabinet continued to emphasize Britain's free hand, and as late as 1 August two of its members wanted a declaration that Britain would in no circumstances fight Germany.

The possibility of a split within the cabinet was the single most compelling argument for not forcing the pace of Britain's internal debate. In 1911 the radicals within British Liberalism had been weakened by the willingness of Lloyd George and Churchill to support Grey. But in 1914 Lloyd George wavered, responding to the anti-war sentiments of the Liberal press more than to the blandishments of Churchill.[61] The chancellor of the exchequer could be confident that a principled stand against entry to the war would be assured of major backbench support. Even on 2 August Asquith thought three-quarters of the Liberal party's members were opposed to war. If Asquith's cabinet did split over entry to the war, the Conservatives would gain power. The dread of such an outcome was a force for Liberal unity, even for the radicals. But its importance did not lie only in its ramifications for a single political party: a united Liberal government would be able to lead a united Britain into war, a divided party would betoken a divided country. The Labour party had discussed the possibility of a general strike in the event of war. Such a danger was real enough for a nation where the railwaymen, the dockers, and the seamen had all staged national strikes since 1911, and where trade-union membership had almost doubled since 1909. The possibility of social upheaval as a result of the economic strains of war was as threatening to Grey, who referred to the 1848 revolutions, as to other European leaders. In the City of London commercial opinion warned that war would lead to the collapse of credit. In such circumstances a Conservative-led entry to war would make the war itself a party issue; the Liberals, on the other

---

[61] Keith Wilson, 'Britain', in Wilson (ed.), *Decisions for war*, 176–8; David (ed.), *Inside Asquith's cabinet*, 179.

hand, not least by virtue of the electoral pact which they had struck with the Labour party in 1903, had a greater claim to represent the national interest.

Such arguments were not lost on the Conservatives themselves. The fear of Grey's replacement as foreign secretary by somebody of a more radical disposition was their corollary to the radicals' fear of a Conservative government. Although no nearer consensus on the issue than the rest of the country in late July, on 2 August the Conservatives' leader, Bonar Law, was able to write to Asquith pledging his party's support for the war. The issues for which the Conservatives were prepared to fight were Britain's status as a great power and the balance of power in Europe: Law was affirming Grey's commitment to the Entente.

Henceforth the attentions of Asquith and Grey could be focused firmly on the need to convince the radicals, and they could back up their blandishments with the implicit threat of being able to form a coalition government with the Conservatives should the radicals not follow Grey in his determination that Britain must support France. Nonetheless, the outcome of the cabinet held on the morning of 2 August was ambiguous. Grey informed the meeting of the French naval mobilization the previous day, and of France's dependence on Britain for the defence of its northern coast. The direct danger to British maritime interests posed by a German naval presence in the Channel and the North Sea was not a divisive issue. For some in the cabinet the decision to affirm Britain's naval obligations was therefore a step to deter Germany, not a step towards war itself. Their interpretation was confirmed when Germany promptly offered to remain out of the Channel.

Nonetheless, the cabinet's decision affirmed the 1912 Anglo-French naval talks. It had, at least in small degree, recognized that Britain could not enjoy a 'free hand' *sine die*. Furthermore, Germany's willingness to limit its naval activity was not matched in regard to its army. During the course of Sunday 2 August the key question became less Britain's support for France and more Britain's commitment to the maintenance of Belgian neutrality. Although the German threat to Belgium was not a new element in British calculations, it had been assumed that the Germans would advance south of the River Meuse, and might thus avoid a major irruption through Belgium, so encouraging the Belgian army itself to stand aside. In these circumstances Britain, although a guarantor of Belgium under the terms of the 1839 treaty, might reasonably regard itself as freed of any obligation to act. However, on 1 August the Belgian government stated its intention to defend its neutrality. Indications of German violation of that neutrality were evident the following day, and on the evening of 2 August the Germans delivered to Britain an ultimatum, demanding unimpeded passage through all Belgium. In reality the obligation to defend Belgian neutrality was incumbent on all the signatories to the 1839 treaty acting collectively, and this had been the view adopted by the cabinet only a few days previously. But now Britain presented itself as Belgium's sole guarantor. Its neutrality became the symbol around which Asquith could rally the majority of his cabinet, including Lloyd George. Gladstonian liberalism might abhor the instincts of Grey and Haldane, but it was committed to the defence of small nations: that commitment became the bridge which allowed *Realpolitik* and liberalism to join forces.

By the morning of 3 August the cabinet and the country were at last effectively united. The cabinet approved the mobilization of the army and the navy. On the same day Germany declared war on France, and on 4 August Britain—its ultimatum to Germany having expired—declared war on Germany. In the event only two ministers resigned: Britain's wavering may have muddied the European scene, but it clarified the domestic position. In the afternoon of 3 August Grey spoke in the House of Commons. It was a long speech, delivered in a conversational style, but its effect was extraordinarily powerful. Its appeal was to Britain's moral obligation; its attention was to the left; it eschewed specifically strategic arguments.

The war in which Britain thought it was about to engage was above all a war for British interests. Grey argued that, as a sea-power and as a trading nation, Britain would be almost as directly affected by the war if it remained neutral. The fact that Britain was a sea-power meant that the war would be limited because it would be naval; he told the House of Commons on 4 August that, by engaging in war, 'we shall suffer but little more than we shall suffer if we stand aside'.[62] If any pre-war commitments had effected British entry to the war, it had been the 1912 Anglo-French naval talks. The staff conversations, and the 1911 resolution of the

[62] Steiner, *Britain and the origins*, 210.

Committee of Imperial Defence to send an expeditionary force to the continent, formed no part of Britain's decision to fight. One of the reasons why the cabinet had been able to accept British belligerence had been its implicit assumption that the country was engaging in a naval war. Neither it nor the House of Commons made a specific decision in favour of a continental strategy; on 2 August the prime minister himself saw the dispatch of an expeditionary force to France as serving no purpose.

Thus, Britain's thinking on the sort of war in which it was embarking was as muddled as that of the other belligerents. Naval pressure on Germany would be of value only over the long term. The needs of France and Belgium were more immediate; there was a danger that Germany would be master of both long before British sea-power would be effective. Furthermore, the navy's strategy would itself become vulnerable if the European coastline was dominated by a hostile power. The 'moral' obligation therefore carried with it a continental commitment. In addition, Grey's public presentation of the war as limited did not conform to his gloomier prognostications with regard to the economic and social consequences; this contradiction was present even if the war did remain purely maritime, because the application of sea-power and of commercial pressure implied a war that would achieve its objects slowly and by directing its efforts against the German nation as a whole, rather than exclusively against its armed forces.

Insufficient clarity about the nature of the war on which they were embarking is a feature common to all the belligerents in 1914. Such a criticism, moreover, is not simply the product of hindsight. Between 1871 and 1914 the serious study of war was transformed; the success of the German general staff in the planning and execution of the wars of unification, and the need to respond tactically to the technological transformation wrought on the battlefield by quick-firing, long-range weaponry, prompted four decades of reform and analysis. Many professional soldiers recognized, in their plans for future war, individual elements which would prove characteristic of the battlefield of 1914–18. But, perhaps partly because of the increasingly demanding nature of their own specialist concerns, their overall outlook was narrowed. Specialist and technical concerns could prompt political lobbying in order to advance specifically military interests. Generals, however, were not on the whole involved in politics per se. The army may have been the focus of much attention from the radical right in France before 1914; soldiers themselves, however, identified with the nation as a whole and tended to accept republicanism as a general concept. The Dreyfus affair was a product, not of a politicized army, but of a professional army, over-zealous in the protection of its own identity from outside intervention. In Germany, Schlieffen might advise whether or not the opportunity was right for war in 1905, but he did not see it as his task to direct foreign policy by actively and vociferously advocating preventive war; in 1914 Moltke had no role at all in the management of the bulk of the July crisis. Ironically, therefore, for all the suspicions harboured by the left, soldiers were in some respects insufficiently political. Many of them did antici-pate tactical conditions in which stalemate and attrition would come to dominate warfare. But they too readily accepted, because it was the received wisdom in an area outside their specialist knowledge, that such conditions could not be long sustained because domestic economic and social collapse would follow.

The soldiers' narrow political vision was matched by the remarkable military ignorance of the civilian leaders. A century previously the tasks of military and political leadership were only just ceasing to be combined in a single individual; the First World War itself would prompt the creation of collective bodies designed to fuse the wisdom of soldiers, sailors, and politicians. But in July 1914 either there were no such com-mittees, or where they did exist, as in Britain and France, they were not consulted. Thus, statesmen like Bethmann Hollweg and Berchtold could evoke an image of war that implied quick and decisive battlefield success, when even a limited acquaintance with the changes in warfare since 1870 might have suggested a somewhat different scenario. Furthermore, the notion of war as a major catastrophe for Europe was a common one in July 1914, and yet it was not one which was necessarily related to military conditions in themselves, but was derived from assumptions about economic factors. The year 1870 once again provided a historical but superficial analogy. The Franco-Prussian War had prompted revolution in France; yet the revolution was seen as a phenomenon separate from the conditions of the war itself.

Military factors did, therefore, play a role in the origins of the war, but more in the shaping of general assumptions than in the mechanics of the crisis of late July. This is not to deny that the war plans of the powers affected the tempo of events in late July. Mobilization for Germany did mean war; less directly it probably also meant war for France—at least that was what General Boisdeffre had told the Russians on behalf of France in 1892.[63] But the staff plans were not called into operation until events had already made the implementation of military measures probable. In the Bosnian and Balkan crises mobilizations had been effected without war. At a much earlier stage in the July crisis images of war were being employed in the manipulation of events. Bethmann Hollweg relied on an apocalyptic view of European war and on the assumption (which was widely shared) that war would bring domestic political change, and even revolution, to persuade the powers not to fight. He saw the possibility of a limited war between Austria-Hungary and Serbia, reckoning that the other states would (in the language of contemporary strategic studies) be self-deterred. He was wrong: war was preferable to diplomatic defeat. The popular image of war proved insufficiently awful for deterrence to operate.

Furthermore, other powers applied deterrence in different ways. Poincaré reckoned that strong alliance blocs, backed up by military preparations and firm agreements, would keep the peace. The plans which the general staffs prepared, therefore, confirmed the alliances rather than ran counter to them. Poincaré and Sazonov both argued that, if Grey had been able to pledge British support earlier, the threat of a united Entente would have forced Germany to climb down. If they were right, theirs is an argument for clarity of intention—not uncertainty—as a keynote in deterrence. However, Britain, whose uncertainty was prompted not by the needs of foreign policy, nor by the argument that the creation of doubt as to its intentions in the mind of its opponent made for more effective deterrence, but by genuine domestic division, could defend its position by replying that the likelihood of its intervention was at least sufficient to have deterred Germany if Germany had had a mind to be deterred. Germany and Austria-Hungary calculated that the alliances would encourage the Entente powers to restrain each other from intervention, but for some reason would not have the same effect on the Triple Alliance.

[63] D. Jones, *Military–naval encyclopaedia*, i. 3.

The accusation levelled against the alliance system before 1914 is, however, more serious than that it failed to prevent war; it is that it actually provoked war. Kurt Riezler, writing before the outbreak of war, reckoned that one ally would restrain another; a vital interest for one would not be a vital interest for another. The military context was in part responsible for transforming a system of great-power management that was designed to be defensive into one of offence. The emphasis on speed of mobilization, the interaction of war plans, and Germany's central geographical position meant that a chain reaction became possible. But the interlocking sequence of mobilizations can be exaggerated; Serbia decided to mobilize ahead of Austria-Hungary; Austria-Hungary settled for general mobilization before Russia's position was known; Russia's move to mobilization preceded Germany's and yet Germany's decision was made before it was aware of the Russian position; Britain responded to Germany before it had decided to honour any commitment to France. The imperative of the alliance system was not one of altruism, but of brutal self-interest: Germany needed Austria-Hungary; France's military position was dependent on Russian support; British diplomacy was unsustainable if it allowed the Entente to shatter.

By 1914, therefore, the alliances had become a major vehicle for the expression of a great power's status. This was the context into which Germany's *Weltpolitik* fitted. By 1914 Germany simultaneously sought affirmation as a world power and as a continental power. Furthermore, it did so in a way calculated to infuriate. Bethmann Hollweg put a large share of the blame for the war on his own country: 'the earlier errors of a Turkish policy against Russia, a Moroccan against France, fleet against England, irritating everyone, blocking everybody's way and yet not really weakening anyone.'[64] By July 1914 each power, conscious in a self-absorbed way of its own potential weaknesses, felt it was on its mettle, that its status as a great power would be forfeit if it failed to act.

Such a view, however nebulous and unsatisfactory, helps to explain why the July crisis cannot stand in isolation. To a certain extent, and particularly in the final week of that month, the crisis did generate its own momentum. The speed of events outstripped the speed of communications. Insufficient time elapsed for reflection and calculation. But the

---

[64] Herwig, 'Imperial Germany', in E. May (ed.), *Knowing one's enemies*, 93.

postures which the powers adopted in that week were themselves reflections of the previous crises, and the decisions taken earlier narrowed the options available later. Russia had to support Serbia because it had not done so in 1909; Germany had to support Austria-Hungary because it had backed down in 1913; France had to honour the commitments to Russia Poincaré had repeated since 1912; Britain's apparent success in mediation in 1913 encouraged a renewed effort in 1914. Thus, too, the fluidity which had characterized the international scene in the first of the major crises, that over Morocco in 1905, and which had particularly revolved around the attitudes of Britain, Russia, and Italy, had given way to considerable rigidity.

Such explanations are unfashionably political and diplomatic. Economic and imperial rivalries, the longer-range factors, help explain the growth of international tension in the decade before 1914. Economic depression encouraged the promotion of economic competition in nationalist terms. But trade was international in its orientation; economic interpenetration was a potent commercial argument against war. Imperialism, as Bethmann Hollweg tried to show in his pursuit of détente, could be made to cut across the alliance blocs. Furthermore, even if economic factors are helpful in explaining the long-range causes, it is hard to see how they fit into the precise mechanics of the July crisis itself. Commercial circles in July were appalled at the prospect of war and anticipated the collapse of credit; Bethmann Hollweg, the Tsar, and Grey envisaged economic dislocation and social collapse. In the short term, the Leninist interpretation of the war as a final stage in the decline of capitalism and imperialism, of war as a way of regulating external economic imbalance and of resolving internal crises, cannot be appropriate as an explanation of the causes of the First World War.

Indeed, what remains striking about those hot July weeks is the role, not of collective forces nor of long-range factors, but of the individual. Negatively put, such an argument concludes that the statesmen of 1914 were pygmies, that Bethmann Hollweg was no Bismarck. Nobody, with the possible exception—and for a few days only—of Grey, was prepared to fight wholeheartedly for peace as an end in itself. Domestically Berchtold, Sazonov, and Bethmann Hollweg had acquired reputations for diplomatic weakness, which they now felt the need to counter by appearing strong. But even this interpretation fuses the individual with wider national pressures. More bizarre is the conjunction of the individual with accident—the wrong turn of Archduke Franz Ferdinand's driver, and the fortuitous positioning of Princip who had already assumed that his assassination attempt had failed. If Bethmann Hollweg's wife had not died in May would he—it seems reasonable to ask—have been less fatalistic, less resigned in his mood in July? And Conrad von Hötzendorff, whose advocacy of preventive war proved so important to Austrian calculations at the beginning of July—were his motives patriotic or personal? He calculated that, as a war hero, he would be free to marry his beloved Gina von Reininghaus, already the wife of another.[65] Conrad's infatuation cannot, obviously, explain the outbreak of the First World War. But it remains a reminder that the most banal and maudlin emotions, as well as the most deeply felt, interacted with the wider context.

[65] Williamson, *Journal of Interdisciplinary History*, XVIII (1988), 816.

PART II

WILLINGLY TO WAR

4

WAR ENTHUSIASM

'My darling One & beautiful—', Winston Churchill wrote to his wife on 28 July 1914, 'Everything tends towards catastrophe, & collapse. I am interested, geared-up & happy.'[1] The intensity of the July crisis released the adrenalin of the cabinets of Europe. But the statesmen knew that, if war was its outcome, the emotion which fired them would need also to be shared by their electorates. Bülow in 1909 and Bethmann Hollweg in 1912 each expressed the view that wars were caused not by the ambitions of princes and politicians, but by the action of the press on public opinion.[2] The evidence to support their belief was sparse. Public opinion had certainly played its part in railroading the British cabinet into war in the Crimea in 1854. However, in Germany's case Bismarck's wars had been cabinet wars, at least in their causation. What was true was that the outbreak of hostilities had in turn prompted public demonstrations, both in Prussia and France.[3] Popular enthusiasm might not cause war, but it certainly needed to condone it.

The distinction between the feelings of the masses in the lead-up to war and their reactions when the war broke out was particularly important in 1914. It is one which recent historiography has done much to explore. But the historian's knowledge of what is to come, not only in the war itself but also in the rest of the twentieth century, can make any analysis of the sentiments of 1914 mawkish and maudlin. The contrast, however

[1] Soames, *Speaking for themselves*, 96.
[2] Rosenberger, *Zeitungen als Kriegstreiber?*, 33.
[3] Rohkrämer, *Militarismus der kleinen Leute*, 89–92, moderates this view; for a comparison between 1870 and 1914, see Meinecke, *Strassburg/Freiburg/Berlin*, 138.

metaphorical, between a sun-dappled and cultured civilization and a mud-streaked and brutish battlefield can too easily suggest that, if the peoples of Europe were enthusiastic about the war, then they were, at least momentarily but also collectively, mad. It is perhaps more comforting, but equally simplistic, to conclude that war enthusiasm was a 'myth', that the cameramen caught images that were unrepresentative or were posed, fulfilling briefs that were themselves directed from on high.

The outbreak of the war has become one of the most unassailable divisions in the compartmentalization of the past. It marks the end of the 'long' nineteenth century, which began with the French Revolution in 1789, and it inaugurated the 'short' twentieth century, which closed with the end of the Cold War. This sense that 1914 was a break in continuity is not simply a product of hindsight, a manipulation of historians. It was one frequently expressed at the time. Adolf Hitler later recalled that 'I sank to my knees and thanked heaven from an overflowing heart that it had granted me the good fortune to be alive at such a time'.[4] Many people joined the crowds precisely because they felt that history was being made. Indeed, the historians of the day told them that this was the case. Friedrich Meinecke, then in Freiburg, described 1 August 1914 as 'a new historical epoch for the world'.[5] Writing thirty years later, in 1944, and aware not only of what the First World War, but also the Second had meant for Germany, he could still affirm that 3 August 1914 was 'one of the most beautiful moments of my life, which even now pours into my soul with a surprising suddenness the deepest trust in our nation and the highest joy'.[6]

What had so moved Meinecke was not the war in the Balkans but the news that all the Reichstag parties would approve war credits. Max Weber too, although hostile to the war in a political sense, welcomed the national effusion which it generated, and which gave the war meaning regardless of its outcome.[7] Popular demand may not have caused the war, but once it came, the sublimation of distinctions of class, of politics, and of profession which were the people's response to it generated its own euphoria. The Austrian writer Stefan Zweig, who was a Jew and would become an exile from Nazism, but who, like Hitler,

---

[4] Eksteins, *Rites of spring*, 306.   [5] Kruse, 'Kriegsbegeisterung', 85.
[6] Meinecke, *Strassburg/Freiburg/Berlin*, 137.   [7] Mommsen, *Weber*, 190–1.

joined the crowds, albeit in Vienna rather than Munich, wrote of 'a rushing feeling of fraternity'.

Strangers spoke to one another in the streets, people who had avoided each other for years shook hands, everywhere one saw excited faces. Each individual experienced an exaltation of his ego, he was no longer the isolated person of former times, he had been incorporated into the mass, he was part of the people, and his person, his hitherto unnoticed person, had been given meaning.[8]

Zweig was a middle-class intellectual and Vienna a capital city. But the sensations which he experienced were not confined to such orbits. Louis Barthas, a cooper in Peyriac-Minervois, a socialist and a non-practising Catholic, a father and a reservist, described the response of his village to France's general mobilization in very similar terms. Brothers who had fallen out were reconciled; mothers-in-law and sons and daughters-in-law, who only the evening before had been at blows, exchanged kisses; neighbours who had ceased all neighbourly relations became the best of friends. Barthas espoused the anti-militarism of his political convictions. But he acknowledged that party divisions were forgotten. The first effect of the war was, paradoxically, to bring peace.[9]

Nor was hatred of the enemy a primary element in this bonding. The crowds passed by the embassies of enemy powers. While personal encounters remained recent and therefore vivid, the foe could still be an individual. Britons caught in Leipzig at the outbreak of hostilities experienced no personal unpleasantness.[10] The first French prisoners of war to arrive in Germany were warmly received by German women, and plied with wine and chocolate.[11] The *East London Observer* on 8 August praised the local German community and reminded its readers that, 'in the indignation of the moment one must not forget to behave oneself justly, and like a gentleman and a friend'.[12] The general feeling in Paris was that the Germans were mad, not bad.[13] And in some instances official policy endorsed this restraint. In Berlin films which might arouse violence against foreign residents were censored.[14] In Vienna

[8] Zweig, *World of yesterday*, 173–4.   [9] Barthas, *Carnets de guerre*, 14.
[10] Cooper, *Behind the lines*, 22; see also Plaut, 'Psychologie des Kriegers', 11–15.
[11] Daniel, *War from within*, 23.
[12] Panayi, *Enemy in our midst*, 275; see also D. Winter, *Death's men*, 23–4.
[13] Raithel, *Das 'Wunder' der inneren Einheit*, 444–5.
[14] Gary Stark, 'All quiet on the home front: popular entertainment, censorship and civilian morale in Germany, 1914–1918', in Coetzee and Shevin-Coetzee (eds.), *Authority, identity*, 75.

the Entente monarchs even retained their colonelcies of Austro-Hungarian regiments.[15]

This is not to say that xenophobia did not play its part in the popular response to the war. Indeed, at a passive level it was a powerful force for national integration. Rumour was 'the oldest means of mass communication in the world'. In the absence of news, gossip was preferable to silence; it was both a cause of communal feeling and its consequence.[16] In the towns the press could feed off such chatter and then propagate it. In the countryside things were quieter, and the press less evident and less influential. Traditionally, the peasant's distrust of outsiders embraced his fellow nationals from other districts. On the outbreak of war such suspicions could be readily subsumed within the hatred of foreigners whipped up by the chauvinism of the urban press.

Widespread migration and European cosmopolitanism meant that the opportunities for active, and frequently misdirected, enmity were numerous. In France Alsatians and Lorrainers were assaulted because of their accents. In Germany a Bavarian woman found herself under suspicion in Cologne, and in Nuremberg Prussian officers were attacked on the presumption that they were Russian.[17]

The search was not so much for the enemy without as the enemy within: this was the obverse of the solidarity which the war generated. Spies were everywhere. In Germany the scare was officially promoted. On 2 August 1914 the public was asked to assist in the detection of the large numbers of Russian agents alleged to be active in the rear, and especially in the vicinity of railway lines. By the following day sixty-four 'spies' had been exposed in the railway stations of Berlin alone. All were entirely innocent and the suspects included two army officers. Any form of uniform was deemed to be a disguise, a presumption which proved particularly vexatious for priests and nuns. The report that Frenchmen were driving cars through Germany to deliver gold to Russia stoked the enthusiasm of local governments, which set up their own patrols and roadblocks: a total of twenty-eight people were killed as a consequence.[18] The Stuttgart police became more exasperated than most.

---

[15] Rauchensteiner, *Tod des Doppeladlers*, 189.

[16] Geinitz, *Kriegsfurcht und Kampfbereitschaft*, 161–3; also 167–8.

[17] Gerd Krumeich, 'L'Entrée en guerre en Allemagne', in Becker and Audoin-Rouzeau (eds.), *Sociétés européennes*, 69.

[18] Verhey, 'Spirit of 1914', 175–81; Raithel, *Das 'Wunder' der inneren Einheit*, 447–54.

Clouds were being mistaken for aeroplanes, stars for airships, and bicycle handlebars for bombs. Their director complained that: 'Our streets are filled with old women of both sexes in pursuit of unworthy activities. Everyone sees in his neighbour a Russian or a French spy and believes himself duty-bound to beat him up—and also to beat up the policeman who comes to his rescue.'[19]

The German general staff asked the public to scale down its efforts on 7 August. But spy hysteria was not simply a response to official prompt-ings. The suggestibility of the British public had already been primed by the novels of Erskine Childers and William Le Queux. These fictions received apparently authoritative corroboration from the British army's last commander-in-chief and most famous living icon, Lord Roberts, who had said that there were 80,000 trained German soldiers in the country, many of them working in station hotels. By the beginning of September the Metropolitan Police alone had received between 8,000 and 9,000 reports of suspected espionage. Although they deemed ninety of these worthy of further investigation, none was proved to have any foundation.[20]

In France, where spy mania also developed without government promotion, xenophobia became fused with economic self-interest. As in Britain, the pre-war press had carried stories of German espionage. Léon Daudet of the *Action française* had accused Maggi, an inter-national dairy-products firm with its headquarters in Switzerland, of being a front for a German spy network. Maggi was also a major competitor for smaller French businesses. Maggi's outlets were pillaged on 2 August, while the police stood by: the action was legitimated on the grounds that the firm was German.[21] Such a speedy conversion of enthusiasm into hostility, and of hostility into economic self-interest, required press manipulation. In Britain, although there were isolated attacks on shops owned by enemy aliens in August, there was no major outbreak of violence until 17 October, when it was directly provoked by the arrival of Belgian refugees. Within two days 400 police had to be deployed to keep order in Deptford, and the following weekend com-parable demonstrations broke out in Crewe.[22]

[19] Ulrich und Ziemann, *Frontalltag im ersten Weltkrieg*, 29; Liang, *Rise of modern police*, 190.
[20] Panayi, *Enemy in our midst*, 33–8, 153–4.   [21] Weber, *Action française*, 89–90.
[22] Panayi, *Enemy in our midst*, 72–3, 224–8, 283.

An example of economic opportunism masquerading as war enthusiasm is provided by the small businesses competing in the international market for ladies' underwear. A Leipzig firm declared in its advertising that Paris corsets were un-German and a danger to the health of German women. Any lady who felt truly German, and in particular those concerned for future generations of Germans, would use only the 'Thalysia-Büstenhalter' and the 'Thalysia-Edelformer'. Wolsey, a British manufacturer, warned the country's womenfolk that there was 'a great deal of "unmarked" German made underwear about', and J.-B. Side Spring Corsets thanked them 'for their hearty response to an appeal to support the All-British corset movement'.[23]

With her hygienic German foundation garments in place, the German woman had still to resist the temptation to don the latest Paris fashions. She was warned that shameless French dresses rendered their wearer 'a caricature of human nature'. By appealing to women to resist what was implicitly a male interest in sexual exploitation, the advertisers were fusing feminism with nationalism. They were also incorporating women in a fight in which they were unlikely to participate directly, but to which their spending power could nonetheless contribute. As the Sunlight Seifenfabrik announced in its promotion of soap in the *Neukölner Tageblatt* on 4 September 1914, the transfer of its British capital to German ownership was 'not an insignificant victory in the realm of German economic life'.[24]

Etymology, so often abused by advertisers, became part of the campaign. The Leipzig corset-makers reminded their readers that clothes were no longer *chic* but *pfiff*. In a climate in which German shoppers rejected marmalade as being English and camembert as French, it made business sense to replace cosmopolitanism with nationalism. In Hamburg the Cafe Belvedere was retitled the Kaffehaus Vaterland and the Moulin Rouge the Jungmühle. Customers ate *Hühnerragu* rather than fricassée, even if they were unsure about its ingredients.[25]

The changing of names could be more than a pragmatic response to market conditions; it might also be prudent. By the autumn 500 German residents in Britain had discarded their Teutonic surnames

---

[23] Ibid. 135–7; Hirschfeld und Gaspar, *Sittengeschichte des Weltkrieges*, i. 76–7.
[24] Berliner Geschichtswerkstatt, *August 1914*, 248, 274.
[25] Berliner Geschichtswerkstatt, *August 1914*, 275; Ullrich, *Kriegsalltag*, 16, 23.

for something more Anglicized.[26] They included the royal family, who in 1917 became Windsors rather than Saxe-Coburgs, and the First Sea Lord, who in due course ceased to be Battenberg in favour of Mountbatten, and Santa Claus, who was dubbed Father Christmas. Even the capital of Russia was no longer St Petersburg but Petrograd.

Those contemporaries who were able to stand back from such reactions turned to psychology for explanations and rationalizations. Some found it in crowd theory. Gustav Le Bon, who had postulated the existence of a hysterical mass mind in the 1890s, found proof for his arguments in the outbreak of the war. 'The mentality of men in crowds', he argued in 1916, 'is absolutely unlike that which they possess when isolated.' Beliefs 'derived from collective, affective, and mystic sources' swamped the critical faculties of even the most intelligent men. They shaped what Le Bon called the 'unconscious will', which, partly because it was inherited and partly because it was common to the nation as a whole, generated illusions which had the force of truth. Some found much of this reasoning persuasive. In 1921 Freud traced the 'coercive character of group formation' back to his theory of the primal horde, first developed in 1913.[27]

Others looked to sex for an answer. War made permissible acts which were in peace considered immoral. Sadism and brutality were part of the individual's unconscious, now legitimated and given free rein. Herein was the sense of liberation to which the crowds gave vent. The processes of mobilization and recruitment carried the implication that women were only available to soldiers, when in reality they were not available to anyone because the soldiers had to depart for the front. Thus, the lack of sublimation heightened the sexual potency of the situation. The attractions of uniform played their part. Into this mix of fetishism and sexual exploitation the psychologists also injected romance. Wives fell 'in love with their partner all over again in his new personality, the personality he assumes with his smart uniform, and this pride and love communicate themselves to the man, who departs for the carnage with a light heart'.[28]

---

[26] Panayi, *Enemy in our midst*, 53–4.

[27] Le Bon, *Psychology of the Great War*, esp. 31–46, 169–73, 266–8; Pick, *War machine*, 96, 224.

[28] Fischer and Dubois, *Sexual life during the World War*, 64; also Hirschfeld und Gaspar, *Sittengeschichte des Weltkrieges*, esp. x, 31–5, 48–9, 53–69. Fischer and Dubois seem to have used Hirschfeld and Gaspar, which is much fuller.

The employment of private emotions for state purposes was exposed by an Austrian, Andreas Latzko, in his collection of short stories *Menschen im Krieg* (*Men in battle*), published in 1918. In 'Off to war' a shell-shocked officer, a composer in civilian life, refuses to respond to the solicitude of his visiting wife. After she has left he tells the other convalescents of a fellow officer's young wife, commended by the colonel for her pluckiness, her patriotism, and above all her restraint when the regiment departed for the front. 'My wife was in the fashion too, you know,' the composer fulminates. 'Not a tear! I kept waiting and waiting for her to begin to scream and beg me at least to get out of the train, and not go with the others—beg me to be a coward for her sake. Not one of them had the courage to. They just wanted to be in the fashion.' Thus the greatest disillusionment of the war was not the war itself but the discovery 'that the women are horrible'. They sent men to war 'because every one of them would have been ashamed to stand there without a hero... No general could have made us go if the women hadn't allowed us to be stacked on the trains, if they had screamed out they would never look at us again if we turned into murderers.'

Latzko's sarcasm is vented on a major's wife who has become a nurse, a role which has given her the opportunity to flirt with lightly wounded officers while raising 'her high above herself'.[29] The ambivalence of the nurse's position is central in understanding this interpretation of the role of women in promoting war enthusiasm. She was urged to be patriotic rather than compassionate, disciplined rather than emotional. Her task was to return men to the firing line, fit to fight; to harden their resolve, not to undermine it. *Das Rote Kreuz*, the journal of the German nursing movement, told its readers in March 1914 that the most important attribute of mothers in war was the willingness to sacrifice their sons for their country, while that of Red Cross sisters was obedience. The largest German nursing movement, the *Vaterlandische Frauenverein*, known as 'the Kaiserin's army', had 3,000 branches and 800,000 members in 1914, and in all there were over 6,300 bodies of nurses with 1.1 million members. Even in Britain the Voluntary Aid Detachments, formed under the auspices of the Territorial Army, had 50,000 members by 1914. Many women were being 'militarized' before the war:

[29] Latzko, *Men in battle*, 20–1, 36–7.

the distinction between the private and the public spheres was already eroded.[30]

The ability of all the belligerents to interpret the war defensively covered over the contradictions which were implicit in the nurse's vocation and of which Latzko complained. Women as a whole may have been much more dubious about the war than men, and certainly more so than allowed for by Latzko. But the soldier sallied forth to protect his wife and children. Thus a primitive and basic response could be rolled into the patriotism demanded of the modern state. Those women who could rationalized their readiness to let their husbands go as a sacrifice for 'God and fatherland'; those who could not saw it as an act of self-protection and of maternal responsibility. 'It is a thousand times better', wrote a contributor to a German magazine on pastoral theology, 'to [fight for home and hearth] on the frontier and in enemy territory, than to have the enemy enter the homeland and take everything.'[31]

Most contemporary explanations for war enthusiasm tended to rest on the rationalization of emotions rather than on logic itself. What they reflected above all was surprise—on two counts. The first was surprise that the war had broken out at all. Freud expressed this with his customary clarity in the spring of 1915:

We were prepared to find that wars between the primitive and civilized peoples, between the races who are divided by the colour of their skin—wars, even, against and among the nationalities of Europe whose civilization is little developed or has been lost—would occupy mankind for some time to come. But we permitted ourselves other hopes. We had expected the great world-dominating nations of white race upon whom the leadership of the human species has fallen, who are known to have world-wide interests as their concern, to whose creative powers were due not only our technical advances towards the control of nature but the artistic and scientific standards of civilization—we had expected these peoples to succeed in discovering another way of settling misunderstandings and conflicts of interest.[32]

The second source of surprise was that the populations of Europe embraced the war as they did. The picture of widespread enthusiasm

[30] Henrick Stahr, 'Liebesgaben für den Ernstfall. Das Rote Kreuz in Deutschland zu Beginn des Ersten Weltkriegs', in Berliner Geschichtswerkstatt, *August 1914*, 83–9; Summers, *Angels and citizens*, 237, 247–8, 253–60, 272–3, 278.

[31] Geinitz, *Kriegsfurcht und Kampfbereitschaft*, 157.

[32] Freud, 'Thoughts for the times', 276.

does stand in need of modification and of amplification. But its fundamental message remains unequivocal. The belligerent peoples of Europe
accepted the onset of war; they did not reject it. And yet the anticipation
that there could be opposition, that mobilization could be sabotaged,
that the workers in key war industries would strike, that reservists
would not report for duty, was widely held. Part of the apocalyptic
vision of war entertained by Bethmann Hollweg, by the Tsar, and by
Grey rested on the assumption that war would not be accepted by the
working class.

5

SOCIALISM AND THE INTERNATIONAL

The strength of socialism provided good grounds for the fears of government. After 1912 the German socialists, the SPD, constituted the largest single party in the Reichstag; the 1914 French elections gave the socialists almost thirty more seats than they had held in 1910, and their gains represented an increase of half a million votes since 1906. The rate of growth outstripped the pace of the economic and social change which underpinned it. In 1910, the socialist parties of the world claimed 2.4 million party members; by 1914 this figure had swollen to 4.2 million.[1]

A major plank of socialism for many, but not all, of its adherents was pacifism. In 1889, to mark the centenary of the French Revolution, the Second International was formed to link the socialist parties of the world. But the first Moroccan crisis revealed how little had been done by 1905 to co-ordinate the responses of its members in the face of war. The German trade unions, asked by the French syndicalist organization, the Confedération Générale du Travail (CGT), to co-operate in anti-war demonstrations, responded that such an initiative should come not from them but from the SPD, as it was the German workers' political organization. The SPD was of the view that the French socialist party should take the lead, and the latter consequently accused the former of interfering in France's domestic arrangements.[2] Prompted by this fiasco, the International

---

[1] Haupt, *Socialism and the Great War*, 132. For what follows, see Haupt; Joll, *Second International*; Kirby, *War, peace and revolution*, 1–40.

[2] Milner, *Dilemmas of Internationalism*, 134–8.

debated its response to war at its 1907 conference in Stuttgart. The French socialists Jean Jaurès and Edouard Vaillant proposed that war should be hindered by measures ranging from parliamentary intervention through mass strikes to revolution. But others feared that strikes and revolutions, particularly at times of national danger, were calculated to invite govern-mental repression and so threaten rather than advance the cause of socialism. August Bebel, the leader of the German socialists, proposed a formula that was less precise and consequently less provocative: workers and their parliamentary representatives should hinder the outbreak of war by the most effective means available; if war broke out nonetheless, they should work for its rapid conclusion. Although Bebel's resolution was adopted, it was given a revolutionary rider by three more-radical figures, Rosa Luxemburg, V. I. Lenin, and Y. O. Martov: in the event of war socialists were to use the opportunity to hasten the demise of class rule.[3]

Thus, the Stuttgart resolution was a compromise, long on strategy and short on tactics. In 1910, at Copenhagen, Vaillant, this time in conjunction with a Briton, Keir Hardie, tried to give it precision. They proposed a general strike as the means to avert war. The German socialists opposed, and rather than split over the issue the congress agreed that further consideration should be postponed until its next meeting, due to be held in Vienna in 1913. In the event, however, the outbreak of the first Balkan war disrupted the timings. An emergency meeting was held in Basle at the end of 1912. Rather than debate the Vaillant–Hardie proposal, the Basle meeting opted for a more general appeal to all pacifist elements, including the middle class. Convening in Basle cathedral, the Second International clothed its pacifism with a moral and even religious fervour which still lacked precision but now seemed to be effective. Anti-war demonstrations coincided with the conference, and the pressure for restraint put on governments was apparently reflected in their pursuit of peaceful solutions in 1913. The congress due to be held that year was postponed until September 1914, when a definitive decision on whether or not socialists would counter war with a general strike would be taken.

Governmental fears of socialist strength, and specifically of the International's pursuit of pacifism, were reflected in the optimism

---

[3] Miller, *Burgfrieden und Klassenkampf*, 34–5.

which overtook socialists themselves in 1913. The fact that the principal European crises of the previous decade had been settled without a major war confirmed their belief in the effectiveness of their own influence and in the argument, espoused especially by the German socialists, that premature alarm in the event of a crisis would only bring discredit on the International. Even Jean Jaurès, the great French socialist, whose primary goal became the pursuit of peace and who urged the International into a more active and interventionist policy, succumbed to the general euphoria. In July 1914, therefore, socialists everywhere were slow to respond. Their ignorance of secret diplomatic exchanges ensured that they could do no more than follow events, until—like everybody else—they were overtaken by the speed of developments in the last few days.

On 29 July 1914 the committee of the International Socialist Bureau, the permanent secretariat of the International, convened in Brussels to discuss the timing and location of the congress scheduled to be held in Vienna that autumn. First to speak was the leader of the Austrian socialists, Viktor Adler. His mood was despondent. He saw war between Austria-Hungary and Serbia as unavoidable, and regarded his most important task as the preservation of his party and its institutions: he told his international colleagues that 'the ideas of a strike and so on are only fantasies'.[4] Adler's defeatism was roundly criticized by Hugo Haase, Bebel's successor as leader of the SPD in the Reichstag. Haase called for action to uphold the peace, and was supported by the two other Germans present, Karl Kautsky (the party's principal Marxist theoretician) and Rosa Luxemburg (who represented Poland). But Haase himself was labouring under an illusion. He thought that one of the principal upholders of European peace was the German government. Misled, the mood of the meeting recovered its optimism. On Jaurès's suggestion the committee decided that the best approach would be for the national parties not to approve war credits; it did not, however, regard the situation as sufficiently urgent for it to pre-empt the deliberations of the congress itself, which were to be brought forward to 9 August and held in Paris. 'It will be like Agadir,' Jaurès remarked, to Vandervelde, the Belgian socialist, on 30 July. 'There will be ups and

---

[4] Miller, *Burgfrieden und Klassenkampf*, 44.

downs. But it is impossible that things won't turn out all right.'[5] On the same day Jaurès found time to visit the Flemish primitives at the Musée des Beaux Arts before he returned to France. The following evening he was dead, the victim of an assassin's bullet.

There is no reason to believe that, even had the International been made aware of the implications of the July crisis, it could have mounted a more effective response to the danger which confronted it. Its view of war was conditioned by its view of imperialism: its stock image was a war of territorial acquisitiveness generated by economic competition, not a war of self-defence. By concentrating on the abstract, by treating peacetime militarism as the immediate danger, and by construing the threat of war within Europe itself as remote, it avoided exposing latent splits in its own body.

Within the International the revolutionary left did not share the majority's abhorrence of war. They argued that imperialism was the last stage of capitalism, that the arms race which colonial rivalry generated increased the exploitation and consequently the class-consciousness of the workers, and that the result of war would be the opportunity to create class revolution. Some rigid theorists contended that, far from moderating militarism and imperialism, and their accompanying threat of war, true revolutionaries should be fostering them. The rhetoric of Internationalism continued to give expression to at least some of these ideas. But the success in averting war shown by capitalist society led many German socialists, including Bebel, Haase, and Kautsky, to reckon that capitalism recognized the dangers attendant on war for itself and would moderate its behaviour accordingly. Such thinking acted as a bridge to the majority of socialists, who were increasingly of a reformist rather than a revolutionary disposition. The pre-war expansion of socialism owed much to its fusion with the trades-union movement, whose objectives were less theoretical and political, more pragmatic and economic. Rosa Luxemburg's conviction in January 1913 that capitalism was breaking down, that imperialism was in its last stages, and that the moment was ripe for a socialist offensive did not reflect the dominant view. Co-operation and collaboration with capitalism at home went hand in hand with moderation in Internationalism, an emphasis on

5 Joll, *Second International*, 168.

arbitration, and a call for arms reductions. Even if the 1914 International congress had debated the Vaillant–Hardie proposal, the majority would have rejected the use of a general strike to counter war, and the only outcome would have been a bitter split.

Not the least of the difficulties that would have confronted the International if it had embraced the idea of a general strike was its uneasy relationship with trade unionism. The International was an organization of socialist parties. Anxious in its early days to exclude anarchists, it had focused on the primacy of political action and rejected the weaponry of mass strikes. Such an approach made life uncomfortable for trade unionism, but found its rationalization in a division of labour. The economic problems of the working class were taken up internationally by the International Secretariat of Trade Unions, formally established in 1901. Dominated by the German Free Trade Unions, in the hands of Carl Legien, its focus was practical and its priority to support the development of strong national organizations rather than to promote international activity per se. French syndicalists were unhappy with this approach: they were at once both more international and more anarchist, but they found that none of abstention, confrontation, or co-operation could make the Germans change their position. France was far from being alone in its stance, but German trades unions had their way by dint of superior organization and superior numbers. In 1909 the entry of the United States to the International Secretariat of Trade Unions consolidated its approach. By 1913, when the International Secretariat changed its name to the International Federation and elected Legien its president, revolutionary syndicalism was on the defensive and the division between German and French trade unionism even more evident than that between German and French socialism. When, at the Belgian national congress of trades unions in Brussels on 27 July 1914, Léon Jouhaux, the general secretary of the CGT, asked Legien for a meeting, he was reluctantly accorded a five-minute conversation over a cup of coffee on the afternoon of the final session.[6]

Legien's pragmatism was realistic. Trade unionism had to be stronger nationally before it could exercise international influence. In France only 9 per cent of workers were members of trades unions in 1914.

---

[6] Milner, *Dilemmas of Internationalism*, esp. 48–59, 71–83, 193–9.

Even in Germany, as Haase pointed out in 1912, the two industrial sectors most vital to the conduct of the war, the railway and munitions workers, were not unionized. The country with a well-organized proletariat, where the trades unions could call an effective general strike, would be overrun by the country that was less well-developed in socialist terms. In the latter nascent trades unionism, if the workers opposed war, would be crushed by a state rendered more powerful by its need to respond to the onset of hostilities.

The solution which Haase therefore advocated in 1912 was for each country to follow its own course. Thus the International showed itself to be no more than a federation of national bodies, within which the idea of Internationalism itself retreated as socialism within individual states advanced. In particular, the pacifist impetus in 1913 itself came not from the International but from joint Franco-German collaboration. It was left to the initiative of the socialist parties of each of these countries, and particularly of France, to fill the gap left by the inability of the International to agree on the means with which it would oppose war. And yet, although putting itself in the hands of national forces, socialism's view of nationalism remained too ambivalent for it to be able to harness its appeal to the ends of internationalism. Rosa Luxemburg saw the class struggle as an international undertaking which national self-determination could only undermine; Marx and Engels had been more pragmatic, recognizing that nationalism might be a means to the revolutionary end, but confining their support of it to the so-called 'historic' nations, and thus excluding many of the ethnic groups within the Austrian and Russian empires. In 1912 the Balkan socialists were amazed to discover that Jaurès's enthusiasm for peace extended to support for Turkey rather than his accepting the justice of a war of national liberation. Thus, by 1914 socialist theory remained undecided about the role of nationalism, while socialist practice was determined by national circumstances.

An additional paradox was that the success of socialism in each country increased its adaptation to national circumstances, and so weakened its internationalism. Thus, in those countries where internationalism remained strongest in the face of war, socialism as a whole was weak and the protest therefore relatively ineffectual. Both socialist members of parliament in Serbia opposed the approval of war credits. In Russia on 8 August all three socialist groupings in the Duma, the

Bolsheviks, Mensheviks, and Trudoviks, proved sufficiently loyal to principles of the Second International to abstain from the approval of war credits. But the Russian socialists had no effective organizations at the local level. In Moscow there were neither Social Democrat nor Socialist Revolutionary committees functioning. In St Petersburg the socialist underground networks had been smashed by the secret police, and control of the legal organizations was the subject of fierce competition between Mensheviks and Bolsheviks. Furthermore, the parties of the left were divided not only against each other, but also internally, those in exile tending to be more *dirigiste* and less pragmatic than those still in Russia.[7]

Responses to the war did not resolve the differences of Russian socialism. At both the Stuttgart and the Copenhagen congresses the Socialist Revolutionaries had been amongst the foremost supporters of resolutions against war. But the imprecision of the Stuttgart resolution—as revolutionary leaders found out when they tried to implement it at the end of July in Vyborg[8]—made it an inadequate guide. Arguably Lenin remained truest to the fundamental principles of the International, even if in practice he rejected its authority. In the 'seven theses', written at the end of August 1914, he described the war as a consequence of a crisis in capitalism, and concluded that 'the correct slogan is the conversion of the present imperialist war into a civil war'.

If Germany won, the Russian people would be handed over to the exploitation of a foreign ruling class; if Germany was defeated, Russia could help activate a revolution within Germany itself. These arguments meant that the appeal made to the Russian socialists by Vandervelde, that they support the Entente, had some unlikely supporters, including the exiled anarchist Kropotkin, and Georgii Plekhanov, Russian social democracy's leading theorist.

Lenin's fiercely independent line from abroad was moderated by the Bolsheviks still in St Petersburg. In the Duma they joined with the Mensheviks to declare that 'the proletariat...will at all times defend the cultural wealth of the nation against any attack from whatever quarter', and their reply to Vandervelde—although it rejected defencism

---

[7] McKean, *St Petersburg*, 126–9; Melancon, *Socialist Revolutionaries*, 67.
[8] McKean, *St Petersburg*, 356–7.

per se—accepted the possibility of their defending a new democratic Russia.[9] Kerensky, the Trudovik leader, revealed how very similar considerations, especially when conditioned by pragmatism, could produce a radically different outcome. He declared that the war would not have happened if the governments of Russia and of the other belligerents had been democratic. But now that it had begun, the threat to the people of Russia—as opposed to their rulers—required that they be defended: 'Peasants and workers, all who desire the happiness and welfare of Russia... harden your spirits, collect all forces, and when you have defended the country, liberate it.'[10] Here was a statement that was at once both defencist and revolutionary—a paradoxical realism which left open the path to inter-socialist party co-operation within Russia but which could only undermine the immediate effectiveness of its wider appeal. Thus, to equate 'defencism' with reformism does not do justice to the revolutionary ambitions of many, if not most, of its advocates. Whereas the 'defeatists' saw the war as the opportunity for revolution, the 'defencists' saw it as the precursor to revolution: the former stood for action as soon as possible, the latter for preparation for action later.

Even if the socialists within Russia were more united than Lenin's rhetoric suggested, and even if they were collectively more loyal to the spirit of the International than socialists elsewhere, the fact remains that they lacked the power to influence their country's policies. The strongest and most successful socialist party in the world was that of Germany. Its ability to moderate the behaviour of its government promised not merely domestic repercussions but also direct benefits to Internationalism. The argument voiced by Kerensky and others— that the Russian people had to defend themselves—would cease to operate if Germany was not, or did not appear to be, the aggressor.

Socialists in France and Russia looked to Germany for a lead, but it was in Austria above all that the SPD could have exercised a direct effect. Austrian social democracy was reconstituted in 1897 in six autonomous national groupings. In 1910 the Czechs broke away completely, and in 1912 they were prepared to reject the war service law which made every citizen liable for war-related service and suspended the rights of

---

[9] Longley, *English Historical Review*, CII (1987), 599–621; McKean, *St Petersburg*, 358–61, also 350–4.

[10] Melancon, *Socialist Revolutionaries*, 65–6, also 22–6.

workers' organizations. The Austro-German socialists, on the other hand, accepted the primacy of national defence. Viktor Adler, the leader of the Austrian party, had been virtually alone in his pessimism about the prospects for Internationalism both at Basle in 1912 and in Brussels on 29 July 1914. When war came he embodied his decision to support his country's actions with a statement of the dilemma: 'An incomprehensible German to have done anything else. An incomprehensible Social Democrat to have done it without being racked with pain.'[11] He then resigned his party responsibilities. If Germany's socialists had been able to take a strong stand against the war those of Austria might well have followed their lead. In the event the socialist party of neither of the Central Powers opposed the war: thus was Internationalism forfeit to national priorities.

The decision of the German socialists to support the war was both more confused and more hectic than the development of the SPD in the previous decade suggested would be likely. However, the success of the party made it revisionist rather than revolutionary, and to that extent its decision in 1914 was of a piece with its earlier development. Between 1878 and 1890 socialist activity in Germany was banned, except within the Reichstag. The ending of the anti-socialist law was marked in 1891 by the adoption at Erfurt of a party programme whose objectives, while ultimately Marxist, were in the short term compatible with liberalism and were to be achieved by parliamentary means and not by revolution. This confusion between ideals and reality was confirmed in 1903: formally speaking, the party rejected the notion that working-class conditions were improving under capitalism and that therefore the socialist objective should be to work with the existing state so as to transform it from within. The rejection of this argument threw up two problems: first, it denied the truth, which was that the material position of workers in Germany was improving; and secondly, it was not accompanied by a credible alternative policy, since revolution was seen as the consequence of an inevitable collapse of capitalism, not something to be actively sought. The bulk of the socialists' votes came from urban workers. The trades union influence within the party was strong: at least forty-five of the 110 socialist deputies in the Reichstag in 1914 had

---

[11] Joll, *Second International*, 181; also, Rauchensteiner, *Tod des Doppeladlers*, 35, 139.

arrived there by way of the trades unions.[12] Therefore, although the
party's leaders showed their desire in 1891 and in 1903 to reflect Marxist
nostrums, the practical need to attend to the economic position of its
constituents, and the obvious growth and success of the party while it
did so, made it more collaborationist than its overt stance allowed.
Indeed, the appearance in the years after the 1905 Russian revolution
of an activist left wing, whose most vociferous campaigner was Rosa
Luxemburg, was evidence of the revisionist trend of the majority of the
party. As the party grew in size and success, so its bureaucracy grew too:
the executive authorities of the party tried to follow a position which
was neutral in terms of policy but which, in practice, acknowledged the
party's reliance on the trades unions, at least as a counterweight to the
left. The party's declaratory status, isolating itself from the activities of
the state and awaiting its opportunity to succeed when Kaiserism
collapsed, was impossible to sustain after its success in the 1912 elections. The Reichstag socialist delegation had perforce to take a part in
the Reichstag's (admittedly limited) role in Germany's government.
Although the socialists did not form a link with the Progressives or
the Centre in 1912, the possibility of such a bloc within the Reichstag was
beginning to enter the realm of practical politics.

Symptomatic of the SPD's reformism was its attitude to the army. In
1904 Bebel declared that the party was a determined defender of the
principle of universal military service, which it saw as an honourable
obligation for all men of military age.[13] But implicit within this apparent acceptance of the principal embodiment of the state's power was a
challenge to the army's function as an instrument of monarchical
authority, and to its possible role in suppressing the workers. Bebel
wanted a fuller form of conscription in order to create a true nation in
arms, defensive in its capabilities and, more importantly, democratic in
its organization. The party was anti-militarist but not anti-military; its
goals were domestic and its interest in international relations periph-
eral. Pacifism was not integral to its identity.

[12] Snell, *American Historical Review*, LIX (1953), 66–7. On German socialism generally in
this period, see Nettl, *Past and Present*, 30 (1965); Schorske, *German social democracy*; Ryder,
German revolution, chs. 1 and 2; Calkins, *Haase*, chs. 3 and 4; Groh, *Journal of Contemporary
History*, I (1966), 4, 151–77; Miller, *Burgfrieden und Klassenkampf*; Kruse, *Krieg und nationale
Integration*.
[13] Vogel, *Nationene im Gleichschritt*, 223.

But by 1907 the SPD's neglect of overseas affairs was unsustainable. Bülow's espousal of *Weltpolitik* exploited international issues for domestic ends. German expansion promised full employment and better standards of living, so luring workers from socialism to his centre-right coalition. The SPD, therefore, chose to fight the 1907 elections on German policy in South West Africa. The Herero rebellion had been crushed with brutality, but its horrors failed to move German workers. The SPD lost thirty-six seats. If there was a case for continuity from Bülow's *Weltpolitik* to the origins of the war and from there to the development of German war aims, then there is also a case for saying that the workers, having embraced *Weltpolitik* in 1907 out of economic self-interest, had to support the war in 1914 for the same reason.[14]

The case against such a continuity is that, at one level, the result of the 1907 election galvanized the SPD into finding a foreign policy that was both more coherent and more distinctively socialist. To that extent the Stuttgart resolution, also of 1907, was well timed. In 1911, during the second Moroccan crisis, the party organized demonstrations in favour of peace: 100,000 people attended a rally in Berlin on 20 August, and 250,000 on 3 September. But at another level the so-called 'Hottentot' election was also a reminder of the unwisdom of challenging nationalism. Even at Stuttgart Bebel stressed that the International should be concentrating on the conditions of the working class, not on the issues of war and peace. Foreign policy was the prerogative of the Kaiser: to trespass into such territory might invite a setback comparable with the earlier anti-socialist laws, and so undermine the obvious achievements of German socialism. The SPD fought to keep foreign policy out of the 1912 election, and thereafter the pacifism of German socialism waned. The Balkan wars suggested both that détente and limitation were possible, and that capitalism itself recognized the dangers inherent in anything else. In 1913 the SPD's handling of the Zabern affair revolved once again around the domestic implications of militarism, not the external security of the Reich.

Indications that German socialists would not resort to strike action to disrupt mobilization multiplied. For the SPD mass strikes were a way to

---

[14] Gunther Mai, ' "Verteidigungskrieg" und "Volksgemeinschaft". Staatliche Selbstbehauptung, nationale Solidarität und social Befreiung in Deutschland in der Zeit des Ersten Weltkrieges (1900–1925)', in Michalka (ed.), *Erste Weltkrieg*, 585–6.

respond to repression from above, not to avert hostilities between states. Even in the midst of the pacifist euphoria of 1911 Karl Kautsky described the policy of the Vaillant–Hardie proposal as 'heroic folly', more likely to shatter the party than to prevent war. In December 1913 the general commission of trades unions rejected the Vaillant–Hardie recommendation, and in May 1914 Haase, entrusted with the formulation of the German response, urged its authors to withdraw it.[15]

The split which the SPD feared the issue of war might generate was not simply one between the socialist party and the German state but also (and perhaps inevitably, given the first danger) one within the party itself. Pacifism in 1911–12 revealed a first set of fissures; it attracted middle-class supporters who were not necessarily socialists, while at the same time antagonizing those on the left of the party who saw war as the final crisis of capitalism. The decline of pacifism in 1913 produced another set. In June a majority of the party (fifty-two members) voted for the increases in the German army: it justified its policy on the grounds that the army's growth was to be funded by a progressive tax on property, and on the promise therein of a fundamental restructuring of Germany's taxation system. But thirty-seven party members opposed, and seven abstained.

For the protagonists of the International, buoyed up by the prevalent optimism of 1913, the significance of the vote on the army law lay not in its result, an indication that most German socialists rated the defence of the nation more highly than the advancement of peace, but rather in the division, which suggested that radicalism was re-emergent within the German party following the death of Bebel in August. This uncertainty about the future direction of the German socialist party was reflected within its leadership. Friedrich Ebert, Bebel's successor as party leader, had been the party's secretary and put the priority on party unity; Haase, the new leader within the Reichstag, found himself torn between party loyalty and his own personal opposition to the growth of the regular army.

These problems were compounded by the French socialists. In emphasizing the problems of war and peace rather than the condition of

---

[15] Stargardt, *German idea of militarism*, 93, 128–37, 140, 155; Verhey, 'Spirit of 1914', 27–30; Milner, *Dilemmas of internationalism*, 199.

the working class, they shifted the International's focus from the area of their own weakness to that of the Germans, and so were able to challenge the Germans for primacy in world socialism. A joint meeting of French and German parliamentary delegations at Berne in May 1913 illustrated the Germans' confusion. It resolved to call for limits in arms spending and the enforcement of international arbitration. At the time Jaurès and his fellow internationalists might have been encouraged by such indications. But in hindsight the message seemed different: the French provided 121 delegates, of whom only thirty-eight were socialists, while the Germans could muster a mere thirty-four, all but six of whom were socialists.

In the event, the dilemma between radical pacifism and revisionist nationalism was sufficiently genuine for both currents to find expression in the response of German socialism to the July crisis itself. The radical phase lasted from 25 July to 30 July. Ebert was on his honeymoon, and did not return to Berlin till 28 July. Of the party's parliamentary leaders, Hermann Molkenbuhr and Philipp Schiedemann were also on holiday, one at Cuxhaven and the other in the Dolomites. Haase's authority was thus unchallenged. He was unequivocal: on 25 July he issued a proclamation on behalf of the party, condemning Austria-Hungary's actions, opposing German support for its ally, and declaring the working class's resistance to war. The party's newspaper, *Vorwärts*, took a similar line.

Over the next four days mass demonstrations against war occurred all over Germany. Although none individually was on the scale of the largest held in 1911, that in Berlin on 28 July attracted 100,000 people and prompted the police, who at first had underestimated attendance at the rallies, to ban further meetings in the interests of traffic control. By 31 July 288 anti-war demonstrations had taken place in 163 cities and communes, involving up to three-quarters of a million people.[16]

These protests were designed to uphold the peace: in that sense they were not directed against the German government, nor necessarily against any ultimate decision to go to war which it might take. Haase was convinced that Austria-Hungary was at fault and that Germany was

---

[16] Kruse, *Krieg und nationale Integration*, 30–41; recent historians have played up the scale of these demonstrations, in contrast to earlier interpretations. See also Raithel, *Das 'Wunder' der inneren Einheit*, 244–7; Stargardt, *German idea of militarism*, 142.

working to restrain its ally. The government itself did not feel
threatened. As early as 25 July the Prussian minister of war, Falkenhayn,
told the deputy commanding generals in each corps area that there was
no need to take action against the SPD. On the following day Haase saw
Clemens von Delbrück, the Prussian minister of the interior, who
reassured him that the SPD's demonstrations would be tolerated.
Thus did Bethmann Hollweg's policy of the 'diagonal' reap the reward
prefigured by the 1913 army law debate. In its anxiety to avoid a clash
with the government over foreign policy, the SPD put the best possible
interpretation on the chancellor's actions. On 30 July *Vorwärts* praised
even the Kaiser 'as a sincere friend of the people's peace'.[17] By then the
immediate objectives of both the SPD and Wilhelm were the same, to
localize a Balkan war. To all intents and purposes Haase and Bethmann
Hollweg were working together, the actions of the former confirming
the irenic public image pursued by the latter.

The replacement of pacifism with nationalism was more the product
of external events than of machinations on the part of the SPD's
revisionists. Socialists could remain united in their opposition to an
Austrian war of aggression and to a local crisis that did not appear as an
immediate danger to Germany itself. But as the crisis developed Russia's
mobilization presented a direct threat, not only to Germany but also to
socialism both within Germany and throughout the world. By 30 July
the socialist leaders accepted that a war was inevitable, and that defence
against Russia was its justification.

The possibility that the SPD would embrace war against Tsarism was
ingrained long before 1914.[18] The socialist press was able to tap a vein of
xenophobic rhetoric that was not only spiteful but also spontaneous.
'We do not want our wives and children to be sacrificed to the bestial-
ities of the Cossacks', wrote Friedrich Stampfer at the end of July.[19] He
was not the dupe of Bethmann Hollweg but a spokesman for German
workers. In the following weeks the SPD leadership would continue to
link defencism with Russophobia. Reports of atrocities from East Prussia not only justified the SPD's rationalization of the war, but also
cemented the links between it and the rest of Germany. Distant from

---

[17] Quoted in Raithel, *Das 'Wunder' der inneren Einheit*, 186.
[18] Stargardt, *German idea of militarism*, 138–9, 147.
[19] Miller, *Burgfrieden und Klassenkampf*, 54.

the industrial heartlands of German socialism, the peasants of the rural marchlands were portrayed as pastoralists defending order and progress against the nomads of the Asiatic steppe. This was an interpretation with which the right could be as content as the left.[20]

If the party's leaders had been slow to grasp the gravity of the crisis in early July, they were under no illusions as to what confronted them by the end of the month. But their very sense of urgency helped exacerbate the weaknesses in party leadership already consequent on Bebel's death. On 28 July Haase, Kautsky, and Luxemburg left for the meeting of the International's executive in Brussels: at a stroke the most forceful exponents of radicalism were removed from centre-stage. On the following day Bethmann Hollweg asked to see Haase. In his stead, the party was represented by Albert Südekum. Südekum was not a member of the party's committee nor of the parliamentary party's committee, but he nonetheless assured the chancellor that the SPD had no plans for strike action. On the same day Ludwig Frank, a Reichstag deputy who believed that the moment for protest was past, said that socialist soldiers must do their duty for Germany: it is possible that he went further, and began to organize a group on the right wing of the party ready to vote in favour of war credits.[21] On 30 July the rump leadership present in Berlin convened. It anticipated the resumption of the persecution endured by socialism under Bismarck, and sent Ebert to Switzerland with the party funds; he did not get back until 3 August.

Haase returned to Berlin on 31 July, and at a meeting of the party committee held on the same day called for the rejection of war credits. The choice which the committee debated was essentially that between Haase's line and abstention: only Eduard David was ready to put the case for the approval of war credits. Thus far, therefore, German socialism seemed likely to follow the policy proposed in Brussels by Jaurès. Hermann Müller was dispatched to France to convey this message.

Formally speaking, both now and later, the SPD took little account of the trades unions. But on 1 August the free trades unions and the

---

[20] Peter Jahn, '"Zarendreck, Barabarendreck—peitscht sie." Die russische Besetzung Ostpreussens 1914 in der deutschen Offentlichkeit', in Berliner Geschichtswerkstatt, *August 1914*, 150.

[21] Miller, *Burgfrieden und Klassenkampf*, 42–3, 46–8; Kruse, *Krieg und nationale Integration*, 49–52.

government struck a bargain whereby the former agreed not to strike in the event of war in exchange for a government undertaking not to ban them. Next day the trades unions endorsed the deal. Following Legien's emphasis on the economic functions of the trades unions, they put their priority on protecting the interests of their members against the ravages of the unemployment which it was expected war would bring—a task they could not fulfil if they were prevented from functioning. Technically the trades unions had steered clear of politics; in practice they had restricted the range of options open to the SPD.

Even more important, however, than the decision of the trades unions was the fact that Germany was now at war. Pacifism and nationalism were no longer compatible. When the parliamentary party met on 3 August to concert its position before the Reichstag session of the following day, the choice which it confronted was no longer that debated on 31 July; it was whether or not the SPD would accord the German people the means with which to defend themselves. In the circumstances the previously preferred position of the majority—abstention—was no longer a serious option. Four out of six on the parliamentary committee were in favour of approving war credits, and seem to have been better organized than the two who were opposed, Haase and Lebedour. Seventy-eight members of the parliamentary party wanted to vote in favour of war credits, and only fourteen against. The majority argued that opposition invited defeat, and with defeat would come the extinction of the party, either at the hands of the enemy or at those of disillusioned German workers. On 4 August the socialist party, reflecting its inner discipline and led by Haase, voted as a bloc in favour of war credits. Its vote was unconditional. The party's position was unaffected either by the growing awareness of Germany's possible guilt in causing the war or by the realization that Germany's intended strategy was not defensive.

The SPD would later argue that its ultimate decision was pre-empted by the will of the people. The decision of the trades unions provided backing for that view. So too did some of the evidence of party feeling at the local level. But working-class sentiment more generally was much more equivocal, and to that extent the SPD's claim was disingenuous.[22]

---

[22] Verhey, 'Spirit of 1914', 238–40, 246–7; Mai, *Ende des Kaiserreichs*, 19; Kruse, *Krieg und nationale Integration*, 54–61.

The leadership was not as passive a victim of events as it liked to pretend. When Wilhelm II declared on 4 August, 'I no longer recognize parties; I recognize only Germans', he was expressing a sentiment with which most socialists agreed. Their relief at no longer having to maintain the effort to isolate themselves, at having to set at odds their own nationality and their political convictions, was genuine. But they did not feel that, in accepting the *Burgfrieden*, the expression of German unity, they were abandoning the class struggle. Those socialists who embraced the war did so because they saw it as a means by which to achieve their political objectives. The reward for collaboration, they believed, would be constitutional and social reform. At its meeting of 3 August the parliamentary party specified as one quid pro quo the democratization of the Prussian suffrage. But it also saw on the horizon economic change, as war industry compelled the state to intervene in the management of the processes of production.

Thus, those who in 1914 wanted, by denying war credits, to obey the letter of the party's 1903 decision to reject revisionism found themselves isolated, at loggerheads not only with Germany as a whole but also with the party specifically. On the other hand, those who overturned the 1903 decision, and in doing so reflected the trends implicit in German socialism over the previous decade, found that their position was little better. In practice *Burgfrieden* did not inaugurate reform but confirmed the status quo. The price which the socialists paid for ending their battle with the German state was the transference of that division into the party itself.

In some ways French working-class politics before 1914 were a mirror image of the Germans'. The split between the socialist party and the trades-union movement, the Confédération Générale du Travail (CGT), was open; the differences between the workers and the state, a republic and the heir of the French Revolution, had less practical justification than in Germany; and Internationalism, rather than widen these two divisions, had the effect of narrowing them. It was this last point, the vitality of French support for Internationalism, expressed above all in the rhetoric and personal commitment of Jean Jaurès, which gave French socialism a significance in July 1914 that its other weaknesses might have appeared to have denied it.

From its formation in 1895 the CGT rejected parliamentary methods and political parties as means by which to free the working class.

Instead, the latter was to liberate itself through strike action. This faith in revolutionary syndicalism was reaffirmed at the CGT conference in Amiens in 1906. But in repelling the more intellectual, theoretical, and bourgeois approaches of political socialism, the CGT increased its dependence on its own resources which were—both in money and in members—slender. Its dilemmas were compounded by its faith in Internationalism. Working-class solidarity across national frontiers might have provided revolutionary syndicalism with the strength that it lacked in any one country. In practice, the CGT had to reckon with the domination of the German trades unions, committed to reformism and to an economic rather than a political programme. Furthermore, in one respect at least France grew more like Germany. Although the CGT did not forget the international aspects of armed force, its anti-militarism focused increasingly on the use of the army to break strikes. These threads—revolutionary action, internationalism, and anti-militarism— were pulled together by the resolution at the CGT congress in Marseilles in 1908: 'it is necessary, on an international level, to educate workers so that in the event of war between nations the workers will respond to the declaration of war with a declaration of the revolutionary general strike.' Léon Jouhaux, appointed general secretary of the CGT in the following year, used the occasion of the peace demonstration on 28 July 1911 to affirm this policy.[23]

As the rhetoric waxed, effectiveness waned. The call of the 1908 resolution was for education. The 1911 demonstrations encouraged the CGT to believe the working class had indeed been alerted to the dangers of war. Thus, the task of the CGT was to continue its proselytism so that the workers would react spontaneously to the threat of war. Responsibility for the signal for the general strike was passed from the CGT itself to its local branches and to the workers in general. Its own statements on tactics became vague. Instead, it aimed to create a broad front in favour of peace, designed to inhibit the actions of government. On 16 December 1912 it called a general strike as a warning to the state: it claimed 600,000 supporters, but in practice only 30,000 responded in Paris, and a further 50,000 in the rest of France. Furthermore, its continuing international isolation made a mockery of its strategy, as

---

[23] Milner, *Dilemmas of Internationalism*, 146–7, 176–80; see also 8–11, 60–3, 116–19.

well as tempting it into the sort of attacks on German socialists and trades unionists which were not suggestive of transnational solidarity.

Its anti-militarism meant that the CGT loomed large in the demonology of the right. The growth in military absenteeism, which accounted for the equivalent of two army corps between 1902 and 1912, was attributed to its influence.[24] In 1913 it was blamed for what were largely spontaneous demonstrations within the army against the three-year service law. Its response to these attacks was not greater militancy, but moderation. Revisionism and reformism, already gaining ground from 1908–9, grew in strength as CGT membership fell—by more than half between 1911 and 1914. In the latter year it embraced only about 6 per cent of all employees, and no more than 14 per cent of industrial workers.[25] Even those unions still committed to revolution were divided over tactics: Merrheim, the leader of the militant metalworkers' federation, felt that the CGT's anti-militarism was weakening it, and that it should focus on economic issues—views which prompted a clash with the hard-line Seine syndicate. The CGT in 1914 might still maintain the semblance of revolutionary anti-militarism, not least thanks to the attacks of its opponents, but beneath that veneer genuine anti-patriotism had declined.

The retreat of the CGT did not betoken a setback for French working-class politics as a whole. The gradual replacement of anti-patriotic pacifism by anti-militarist defencism opened the way to greater co-operation between it and the French socialist party. The leaders of both organizations, Jouhaux and Jaurès, were anxious to mark out common ground, and the former recognized full well the greater European influence exercised by the latter through the International. The two staged a joint demonstration against war on 24 September 1911. Thereafter, the campaign against the three-year law gave them a common domestic platform. The possibility of collaboration was already evident before July 1914.[26]

From 14 to 16 July 1914 the socialist party held an extraordinary meeting in Paris to decide on its attitude to the Vaillant–Hardie proposal. Jules Guesde wished to defuse the issue of pacifism, seeing it as an

---

[24] Porch, *March to the Marne*, 111.   [25] Renouvin, *La Crise européenne*, 73.

[26] Milner, *Dilemmas of Internationalism*, 179–80, 204–5.

obstruction to, and distraction from, the broader tasks of socialism in France, and recognizing the practical impossibility of effecting a general strike in the event of war. Opposed to him was Jean Jaurès. Jaurès's anti-militarism did not constitute anti-patriotism. His objection to the three-year law was the specific one of opposition to a regular, professional army: in *L'Armée nouvelle* (1911) he presented the classic case for a citizen militia committed to the defence of its own territorial integrity. Jaurès, for all his fervent Internationalism, was a French patriot, fired by an idealized interpretation of the legacy of the French Revolution, and convinced that in 1793 and again in 1871 citizen soldiers had rallied to save republican France from foreign invasion. His support of the Vaillant–Hardie proposal at the Paris congress was not, therefore, a reflection of the CGT's 1908 resolution: the purpose of a general strike would not be to disrupt mobilization, to sabotage France's defence. Jaurès wanted a preventive strike, called before the crisis turned to war, internationally organized so that the workers would pressurize their governments into arbitration and away from hostilities. The fact that his support of a general strike as an instrument against war bore a superficial relationship to CGT policy was also not without its attractions. Because such a strike depended on being international, Jaurès believed that a clear decision by the French patriots in Paris would send a signal to socialists elsewhere, and above all in Germany, whose Internationalism he thought to be waxing. Jaurès's policy was visionary rather than pragmatic: he was seeking a target for the International, not dictating immediate tactics for socialism in France. However, Jaurès's calculations were not without an element of realism: it found its expression in his conviction that if the strike failed, if arbitration did not lead to conciliation and war was declared, then the proletariat must defend its nation's independence. The Paris conference approved Jaurès's motion by the convincing, but significantly not overwhelming, majority of 1,690 to 1,174.[27]

Both the CGT and the socialists in France had, therefore, provided sufficient grounds to justify the belief that they would encourage opposition to the war. Their public declarations obscured the fact that they

---

[27] On Jaurès specifically, see Kriegel, *Le Pain et les roses*, 81, and 107–24. On French socialism generally in this period, see Becker, *1914: comment les français sont entrés dans la guerre*, pt. 1, ch. 3 and pt 2, ch. 3; Kriegel and Becker, *1914: la guerre et le mouvement ouvrier français*.

lacked any tactics for immediate implementation—that the CGT would not itself call a strike, and that the socialists needed the CGT's co-operation to be able to carry a strike through—and also that for neither body did anti-militarism constitute anti-patriotism. Both groups shared the widespread failure to appreciate the gravity of the July crisis. On 26 July, when *La Bataille syndicaliste*, the CGT's newspaper, announced that the workers must respond to the declaration of war by striking, Jouhaux was away in Brussels; the summons was that of the paper's editors rather than of the CGT itself. When the CGT committee did meet, on 28 July, and Jouhaux reported on his disappointing conversa-tion with Legien, it rapidly became clear that most syndicalists were fearful of arrest and of being seen as traitors to France. On 29 July the CGT abandoned first the call for a strike and then Internationalism, blaming Austria-Hungary rather than capitalism for the crisis. In the areas outside Paris a total of ninety-four meetings and demonstrations against the coming war were arranged by both syndicalists and social-ists; seventy-nine of them took place, and they peaked between 28 and 31 July. In Paris, a big demonstration was held by the syndicalists on the evening of 27 July, but the majority of protests thereafter (of the total of sixty-seven) were organized by the socialists and, as in the provinces, intensified at the end of the month. In general the protests were calm, and the government's response—although firmer with syndicalists than socialists—restrained. Indeed, the greater danger of violence could be from neither socialists nor gendarmes but from patriotic crowds in-censed by anti-militarism and bent on taking matters into their own hands.[28]

Socialist behaviour in late July reflected the lack of urgency felt by Jaurès. His attention was on the efforts of the International; his belief was that the crisis would be protracted. Furthermore, when he met Viviani on 30 July he was convinced that the French government was doing everything possible to maintain peace, and that in the circumstances strike action was not appropriate. Jaurès's greatest achievement in these last hours of his life was to convince the CGT of his point of view, and so manage the fusion between the two major working-class political groups. A joint socialist and syndicalist demonstration in favour of peace was

---

[28] Becker, *1914*, 149–88; Pourcher, *Les Jours de guerre*, 21.

planned for 9 August. Jouhaux was persuaded by Jaurès that the date should not be brought forward to 2 August, that the emphasis on calm and deliberation should be maintained. So the CGT was persuaded to put a higher premium on the unity of French socialism than on its opposition to war. Thus, while socialism in Germany—despite its apparent unity—began to fragment under the threat of war, in France it coalesced.

However, the CGT's abandonment of a revolutionary strike in the event of mobilization, and its espousal of pacifist demonstrations preceding war, were also the product of necessity. On 30 July *La Bataille syndicaliste* reported the remark to the Council of Ministers of Adolphe Messimy, the minister of war: 'Laissez-moi la guillotine, et je garantis la victoire.'[29] In the following days working-class leaders were to sound the tocsin of 1793, 'la patrie en danger': they therefore needed little reminding that the defence of revolutionary France had been accompanied by the drastic domestic measures of the Terror.

The consequent fear, that outright opposition to mobilization—which the syndicalist press had openly discussed in the past—would invite such government measures as would threaten the survival of the CGT itself, was totally justified. The Ministry of War's preparatory measures for mobilization included provision for the arrest of spies and, increasingly before 1914, anti-militarists. About 2,500 names figured on the list, *carnet B*, of whom 710 were associated with anti-militarism and 1,500 were French: thus, the majority of those listed were representative figures of the French working class associated with anti-militarism. The implementation of the arrests was in the hands of the minister of the interior Louis Malvy, a radical. On 30 July Malvy told the departmental prefects that they should act firmly against any syndicalist or anarchist summons to a general strike, but that otherwise they could tolerate socialist meetings in support of peace provided they were well ordered and posed no threat to mobilization. On the following day Malvy suggested to the council of ministers that he need not arrest the militant syndicalists named in *carnet B*, and the council, on the advice of the director of the Sûreté Générale, agreed. However, before Malvy acted on the council's decision he was visited by Miguel Almereyda, the editor of *Le Bonnet rouge*, a newspaper of the militant left, who was himself listed in *carnet B*.

---

[29] Kriegel and Becker, *1914*, 99.

Almereyda, it was subsequently argued, appealed to Malvy's desire for political support from the left, and urged him to exempt anarchists from arrest. On the evening of 1 August Malvy instructed the prefects of departments that no arrests at all should be made under the provisions of *carnet B*. In practice a few individuals had already been arrested in response to the earlier order to mobilize. Particularly in the departments of the Nord and Pas-de-Calais the detention of suspected anarchists and anti-militarists was more frequent and more extended. The police, the prefects, and the army, admittedly in a region conscious of its immediate vulnerability to invasion, combined to thwart the government's wishes. Malvy's interpretation of his fellow ministers' views was perhaps more relaxed than they intended. But in the circumstances of 1914, given the position adopted by the CGT, the use of conciliation rather than coercion was totally justified. The threat of the implementation of *carnet B* had been sufficient to support the syndicalist conversion to the Jaurèsian approach.[30]

The realization that the government was not disposed to use repressive measures helped give the CGT committee greater confidence when it met on the evening of 31 July. It resolved to take all possible steps to prevent war, albeit now limited to pacifist demonstrations and short of a general strike. It was too late. Jaurès, the pivot of the French peace movement and hence of the now-united working-class parties, was reported dead as they deliberated. Mobilization was declared a few hours later. On 2 August the CGT could do no more than appeal to the workers of France for co-operation with the government. Revolutionary syndicalism rejected its traditional hostility to the state. On 4 August Jouhaux, standing in front of Jaurès's coffin, affirmed his faith in the justice of the French cause.

Thus, when later the same day Poincaré called on the chamber of deputies for a *union sacrée*, he was formalizing what was already a *fait accompli*. Indeed, Poincaré's speech was simply read out on his behalf, as the constitution forbade the president from directly addressing the chamber. All ninety-eight socialist deputies supported the vote for war credits. The decision not to implement *carnet B* had sent the first signal

---

[30] On *carnet B*, see Becker, *1914*, 379–400; Kriegel, *Le Pain et les roses*, 96–104; Pourcher, *Les Jours de guerre*, 24–6; in English, Watt, *Dare call it treason*, 42–7; Liang, *Rise of modern police*, 205–6.

for fusion, and it had been reciprocated in the CGT's acceptance of collaboration rather than segregation. But the really potent symbol of national unity was the death of Jaurès.

In mid-July, after the socialists' meeting in Paris, journalists on the right had threatened to shoot Jaurès: Jaurès, 'C'est l'Allemagne', wrote Charles Maurras in *Action française*.[31] The left could therefore easily have held the right responsible for Jaurès's death, and so made it the flashpoint for the divisions of the Third Republic. Instead, the man who had symbolized internationalism and pacifism before the war became the focus for defencism and patriotism at its outbreak. The betrayal of his hopes of socialist solidarity by the vote of the SDP in Germany consolidated and deepened this mood, but did not initiate it. Gustav Hervé, who had initially favoured revolution as the proper response to war, had already begun to moderate his position by 1912. On 1 August 1914 he wrote in *La Guerre sociale*: 'They have assasinated Jaurès; we shall not assassinate France.'[32] He enlisted the next day. More importantly, the grief of the left was affirmed by the outrage of the right: recognition of the man's worth embraced the entire political spectrum. Therefore the *union sacrée* reflected not a nationalism that suppressed political divergences, but one that embraced the full range of a liberal society. Many Frenchmen went to war specifically for Jaurès's ideals: they were fighting a war of defence, the successful conclusion to which would lay the foundation for truly lasting Internationalism and even for a republican Germany. On the right the war was a vindication of their virulent nationalism and of the three-year law. The *union sacrée* was thus an entirely utilitarian formulation, with the single objective of defending France. Only as the war lengthened would the ideological differences underpinning it become evident.[33]

Efforts to give immediate political expression to the *union sacrée* showed that in practice, as in Germany, the war gave strength to the political status quo rather than to change. However, in France, as opposed to Germany, the existing government rested on the radicals and on the centre-right, and thus represented a wider cross-section of

---

[31] Becker, *La France en guerre*, 11.

[32] Duroselle, *La Grande Guerre des français*, 54–5.

[33] On the meaning of *union sacrée*, see Becker in *Revue historique* CCLXIV (1980), 65–74; *Vingtième siècle revue d'histoire*, 5 (1985), 111–21; *La France en guerre*, 11–38.

opinion. On the most vital issue before the war, the three-year law, the 1914 elections had produced no clear mandate. Viviani's cabinet contained only five ministers opposed to the law and ten who favoured it. When Viviani reshuffled his ministry on 26 August he continued to exclude the clerical and nationalist right, and the two socialists who now entered the government (Guesde and Sembat) were balanced by the inclusion of Delcassé (foreign office), Millerand (war ministry), Briand, and Ribot. These four appointments were justified—and generally accepted—by the wartime need for energy and expertise, but they also signified a consolidation of the centre and of the influence of the president, Poincaré, rather than that of the prime minister, Viviani. Even radical socialism, which provided four ministers, and which in 1913 had threatened to form a left-wing bloc with the socialists in opposition to the three-year law, was subsumed by this drift to the right. Its leader, Caillaux, his credit forfeit to his pursuit of détente in 1911, found no place. Clemenceau, the maverick but Germanophobe spokesman of radicalism, refused to serve.[34] Political opposition was recognized, not by the formation of a true coalition, but by the creation of innumerable committees, which gave parliamentary figures a role in the war effort without entrusting them with ministerial responsibility. Viviani's governmental reshuffle was, therefore, among the most tardy and incomplete reflections of the *union sacrée*. More symbolic was the committee of national security, formed on 6 August to undertake relief work, and which included a cardinal, a Protestant pastor, the chief rabbi, a freethinker, a royalist, a bourgeois, a socialist, and a syndicalist.

The hopes of Jaurès and his fellow Internationalists on 29 July rested in large measure on Grey's offer of arbitration. The fact that the British government had so obviously agonized over its decision for war, and had in the process made the only significant bid for peace, is perhaps a major contribution in understanding what is otherwise a somewhat bizarre phenomenon. In both France and Germany the left justified its eventual support of the war by the need for national defence against a reactionary enemy. Britain faced no direct danger to its territorial integrity or to its domestic political institutions; and yet not only was

---

[34] On the fate of the radical socialists, see S. Bernstein in Fridenson, *1914–1918*, 65–77.

the left effectively unanimous in its support of the war, it also gave that support with barely a whimper.

British society was openly fragmented in 1914. The activities of the suffragettes, the succession of major strikes between 1911 and 1914 (40 million working days were lost in 1912), the opposition of the Ulster Unionists to Irish home rule, were all challenges not only to the Liberal government but to liberalism. Extra-parliamentary agitation had become a major means of political expression. Even more worrying were the efforts on the right to undermine parliamentary sovereignty: in 1909–10 the Conservatives used the House of Lords to block a Commons-approved budget, and in 1914 they condoned Ulster loyalism to the point of backing the para-military Ulster Volunteer Force and supporting the so-called 'Curragh mutiny', the refusal of the officers of the 3rd cavalry brigade to enforce Irish home rule in Ulster.

Yet, despite these manifestations of class and regional division, the emotion generated by the war in Britain did not contain that element of relief at new-found unanimity across the classes which so characterized the fusion of left and right in France and Germany. The nation was united when it voted for war credits, and yet it did not give that moment of unity a title—the English language coined no equivalent to the *union sacrée* or the *Burgfrieden*. The acceptance of the war without the agonizing to be found across the Channel is perhaps the best negative indicator of how little either liberalism or parliamentary sovereignty was genuinely under threat—despite all the overt divisions—in 1914. An elected Liberal government had genuinely and conscientiously grappled with the issues that confronted it, and had then decided that war was the only possible step: both the Conservative and Labour parties supported that decision.

To the underlying faith in parliament and the constitution must be added another element—in itself a product of the first—in explaining the weakness of anti-war sentiment in Britain. Intellectual socialism lacked the strength that it had acquired in France and Germany. Indications of this were already evident in 1911, during the second Moroccan crisis, when Lloyd George managed to settle the railway strike by an appeal to the national interest. On 2 August 1914 the British section of the International staged a major demonstration against the war, and in particular against a war on behalf of tsarist Russia. Ramsay MacDonald, the Labour party's chairman, distinguished between the behaviour of the German government and his sympathy for the German people. That the war was a product of the arms race and of covert diplomacy was a theme expressed by him and, on 5 August, by a majority of the national executive of the party. But the themes in all this were not the revolutionary ones of international working-class solidarity or of an absolute opposition to war in itself. Indeed, although MacDonald resigned the party chairmanship when it became clear that the party as a whole was more enthusiastic about the war than he was, his views were not very different from those of his successor, Arthur Henderson, and both were agreed that the war should be fought until Germany was defeated. MacDonald's resignation led to his rapprochement with the more Marxist and pacifist Independent Labour Party. The Labour party itself was dominated by the trades unions: it followed that its concerns were revisionist and economic, its priorities domestic, and its general sentiment patriotic. The Trades Union Congress had withdrawn from the Second International after 1896, and resisted Legien's suggestions that it become involved in the work of the International Secretariat.[35] Working-class culture, at least in London, was determined less by socialism and more by recreation, by football, by the music hall. Middle-class intellectuals had little influence, and the Labour party itself was shown, during the pre-war strikes, to be lacking in a clear, alternative political programme. On 29 August the party executive decided to support the army's recruiting campaign.[36]

Part of the explanation for the weakness of Internationalism within the Labour party was that pacifism was not its exclusive prerogative, but was shared with elements of the Liberal party. The Gladstonian and nonconformist heritage of nineteenth-century Liberalism, plus the addition of social reforming elements in the 1890s, meant that Grey's major worry in the domestic accounting for his foreign policy was over the reactions of radicals within his own party. Their principal journal, the *Manchester Guardian*, was particularly vociferous: 'Englishmen', it fulminated on 30 July 1914, 'are not the guardians of Servian well-being, or

[35] Milner, *Dilemmas of internationalism*, 7, 76–8.

[36] On Labour's response to the war, see McKibbin, *Evolution of the Labour party*, ch. 5; Marquand, *Ramsay MacDonald*, ch. 9; also Stedman Jones, *Journal of Social History*, VII (1974), 460–508.

even of the peace of Europe. Their first duty is to England and to the peace of England.' On that same day the parliamentary Liberal party resolved that 'on no account will this country be dragged into the conflict'.[37] But the strength of their case resided in their emphasis on Serbia and on their rejection of such constructions as the balance of power. When France was threatened, so was the security of Britain. Moreover, the demands of self-preservation and of anti-war instincts were no longer incompatible, but were rationalized by the claim that Britain fought to defend Belgian neutrality and to uphold international law. Not fighting in 1914 could, therefore, be interpreted as as great an affront to Liberal ideals as fighting. Thus, no immediately effective opposition to the declaration of war emerged from this quarter either. The two ministers who resigned from Asquith's cabinet retired from politics. Charles Trevelyan, a backbench MP, abandoned junior office to oppose the war, and organized a group of about thirty Liberal MPs committed to securing peace as soon as possible. On 17 November Trevelyan's initiative resulted in the creation—with the support of the Independent Labour Party—of the Union of Democratic Control: the four major objectives of the union embraced a more open conduct of diplomacy, greater parliamentary accountability, national self-determination, and measures for disarmament. Implicit within it was an acceptance of the current war.

The argument that the outbreak of the First World War somehow constituted a failure on the part of socialism is a point of view that only a minority of socialists in 1914 would have accepted. 'War', the British socialist historian, R. H. Tawney, wrote on 28 November 1914, 'is not the reversal of the habits and ideals we cultivate in peace. It is their concentration by a whole nation with all the resources on an end as to which a whole nation can agree.'[38] The emphasis of Jaurèsian Internationalism was on the better management of foreign policy, on the use of arbitration in the event of a crisis, rather than on outright pacifism. *In extremis* war could be justified. And most socialists in Europe, presented with the imminence of war, and enamoured of doctrinal debate and intellectual clarity as ends in themselves, found little difficulty in producing a

---

[37] J. F. V. Keiger, 'Britain's "union sacrée" in 1914', in Becker and Audoin-Rouzeau, *Les Sociétés européennes et la guerre*, 42, 44.
[38] J. M. Winter, *Socialism and the challenge of war*, 155.

cogent case for involving themselves in the events which overtook them. The willingness to defend carried with it the expectation that the nation itself could become a better society, and that the war might be the means to achieve that. The *union sacrée* and the *Burgfrieden* could be interpreted as expressions of socialist fraternity; the war—it was widely believed—would be an agent for domestic social reform. But, on the plane of Internationalism, this was also the last war, the war to end wars, the vehicle for establishing a lasting international order. Through the war, French socialists argued, republicanism would be introduced to the Central Powers; through the war, Kurt Renner of the Austrian social democrats contended, imperialism and monopoly capitalism, which were embodied in Britain, would be overcome. The First World War was therefore not the sort of war against which socialism had aligned itself: it was a war for justice and liberty, not of imperial aggrandizement.

6

THE IMAGININGS
OF THE
INTELLECTUALS

Some socialists at least shared the view, common elsewhere across the political spectrum, that war between nations was inevitable. Nothing in Marx suggested that this was not true; a similar determination led the Italian philosopher Benedetto Croce to respond to war as part of the historical process. Many of the leading statesmen in 1914, as part I of this book has shown, were led to comparable conclusions by their acceptance of social Darwinism. Thus, Bülow considered that: 'In the struggle between nationalities, one nation is the hammer and the other the anvil; one is the victor and the other vanquished ... it is a law of life and development in history that where two national civilizations meet they fight for ascendancy.'[1]

The difference between the Marxists' approach and Bülow's was one of outcomes: socialist determinism posited a better and war-less world as an ultimate conclusion. Present in Bülow's picture was a double pessimism: first, that one of two nations would be forced into irretrievable decline by the outcome of war; and second, that war was part of a recurrent and eternal process.

---

[1] Quoted in Stephen van Evera, 'The cult of the offensive', in Steven Miller, *Military strategy*, 63.

Such negativity was not a necessary response to Darwinism.[2] True, Darwin had used an emotive and Hobbesian vocabulary to describe evolution. He had observed that tribes with superior martial qualities prevailed. But he would not conclude that society was becoming more military as time passed. Instead, he saw war as an evolutionary phase: culture and education, liberalism and industrialization would in due course moderate the genetic inheritance of struggle and violence. This positivist strain was explored by Darwin's contemporaries and successors, notably Herbert Spencer and T. H. Huxley. By 1914 many biologists were using their discipline to predict the evolution of a war-less world.

The impact of this optimistic version of social Darwinism was muted. First, the pacifist movement, under the influence of Norman Angell's *The great illusion* (1910), was in the thrall more of economics than of biology: states would not fight because war did not pay. Even reformist socialists, for all the continuing conviction of those on the left that the crisis of capitalism could only be resolved through war, found Angell's arguments persuasive. The problem was that these very themes—the triumph of capitalism and of economic self-interest—fed fears which were deemed to have biological implications. Prosperity was not merely softening people, rendering them decadent and ultimately unfit; it was also—through social reform—keeping alive the weak who in harsher times would have died. Therefore a world in which military competition was replaced by economic rivalry was likely to be racially degenerate.

Thus, the popular and fashionable impact of biology before the outbreak of the First World War was less in social Darwinism per se and more in the field of eugenics. Some students of heredity contended that humanity could only advance by improving its genetic endowment, and that future generations should therefore be fathered not by the weak, propped up by the nascent welfare state, but by the strong. The latter would be forged in war, itself a parent to innovation as well as to the advancement of the great civilizing empires. Those who opposed this line of thought did so because they disagreed not with its basic assumptions, but with its belief that the effects of war were eugenic. The unfit were exempted from military service: consequently war eliminated the strong while protecting the weak. Pessimism was inherent in both

---

[2] The discussion which follows is heavily dependent on Crook, *Darwinism, war and history.*

camps. Those who saw war as eugenically favourable had to accept war as a biological necessity; those who concluded that war was dysgenic reckoned that war would be biologically disastrous.

Any solutions to this dilemma were long term and fanciful rather than immediate. The American philosopher William James called in 1910 for 'the moral equivalent of war'. He wanted to hone military ideals, but in a more constructive and pacific environment than combat. Graham Wallas of the London School of Economics was influenced by James and worried about the 'baulked disposition' of young men endowed with warlike qualities but unable to find alternative outlets for them. His solution, a change in the quality of life interspersed with challenges, was vague. His conclusion was pessimistic. Fear of 'the blind forces to which we used so willingly to surrender ourselves' had replaced the liberals' faith in progress. 'An internecine European war', Wallas wrote in *The great society*, which appeared in the spring of 1914, 'is the one enormous disaster which over-hangs our time.'[3]

Therefore the debates surrounding Darwinism by 1914, for all the positivism of many of their proponents, were couched in apocalyptic terms. In this they reflected what was perhaps a general trend: the subordination of science to art, the triumph of Romanticism over the Enlightenment. From physics to psychology, science was being moulded less by the dictates of its own empirical reasoning amd more by a total conception in which art, and the emotional experience which it conveyed, as well as history were central to the overall vision.[4]

Pre-1914 art—using the word in its broadest sense—abounds with images of the apocalypse, of the world's end and of Christ's second coming. For the religious, like Vasily Kandinsky, the message of the Resurrection was ultimately optimistic, devastation and despair were the path to renewal and regeneration. Kandinsky's less abstract imagery used mounted figures, knightly riders with military overtones. But many artists portrayed the apocalypse in terms that were not exclusively associated with the inevitability of destructive war. Thomas Mann's novella *Death in Venice*, published in 1913, employs the metaphor of plague, not war. The series of paintings executed by Ludwig Meidner in 1912 and 1913, with their bombed cities, storm-laden skies, and piles of corpses,

[3] Wallace, *War and the image of Germany*, 16–19.   [4] Eksteins, *Rites of spring*, 31–2.

undeniably gave forceful and visual expression to the anticipated terrors of modern war; in conception, however, they were as much a response to the frenzied pace of industrialization and urbanization (and particularly, in this case, of Berlin).[5] Where the references to war are more direct, as in Franz von Stuck's allegorical painting of war completed in 1894 or Arnold Böcklin's rendering of the four horsemen of the apocalypse painted two years later, they may be as much a reflection of the *fin de siècle* as anticipations of imminent European conflict.

Stuck's picture portrays war as a handsome young man, his head crowned with the laurels of victory, while corpses are piled at his feet. But with the new century these associations of beauty and heroism gave way to decadence and decay: the painters Walter Sickert and Egon Schiele may have explored murder, prostitution, and disease rather than war, but the apocalyptic undertow is still present. War became part of the vocabulary of fatalism.[6] Oswald Spengler started writing his book *Decline of the West* in 1911; Andrei Belyi's novel *Petersburg*, published in 1914, used the somewhat hackneyed metaphor of a time-bomb to illustrate the condition of Europe; Gustav Holst spent the summer of 1914 composing the *Planets*, beginning with Mars. Such prefigurings were not uncommon.

The apocalyptic view of war was not primarily concerned with the causes of war in the same way as either Marxism or social Darwinism. Many artists, for all their anticipations of war, were still surprised by its outbreak. Much of the intellectual and artistic attention to war before 1914 was devoted to war as a phenomenon in itself, with battle not as a means but as an end. For a generation younger than that directly influenced by social Darwinism,[7] war was a test of the individual rather than of the nation. It was Friedrich Nietzsche who appealed to the student, to the radical, and to the romantic. 'You say it is the good cause that hallows war?', he had written in *Thus spake Zarathustra*; 'I tell you: it is the good war that hallows every cause.' Nietzsche's metaphors, the superman, the will to power, were replete with martial images. Marking what would have been the philosopher's seventieth birthday on 15 October 1914 in the *Strassburger Post*, Theodor Kappstein

    [5] Cork, *A bitter truth*, 13–14.
    [6] Klaus Vondung, 'Visions de mort et de fin de monde: attente et désir de la guerre dans la litterature allemande avant 1914', in Vandenrath *et al.* (eds.), *1914*, 221–8.
    [7] Stromberg, *Redemption by war*, 78–9.

celebrated his summons to 'a life-endangering honesty, towards a contempt for death ... to a sacrifice on the altar of the whole, towards heroism and quiet, joyful greatness'.[8] For the Kaiserreich Nietzsche's influence was subversive. Only after the war broke out was he appropriated as a patriotic icon, a process in which the radical right and enemy propaganda colluded. After all, Nietzsche himself was a self-confessed European, scathing about the nationalist preoccupations of Bismarckian Germany. Intellectuals influenced by him did not reflect the national limitations of politicians: in 1910 Rupert Brooke, to be seen in 1914 as representing something essentially English in British letters, found his inspiration abroad, writing: 'Nietzsche is our Bible, Van Gogh our idol.'[9] What Brooke and his contemporaries expected to find in war was, therefore, more immediate and more personal than the serving of patriotism. Indeed, if they had viewed the war primarily as one fought for national objectives they might have found it far harder to accept. Another British poet, Charles Sorley, recognized the irony in his fighting for England, which embodied 'that deliberate hypocrisy, that terrible middle-class sloth of outlook', against Germany, which was doing 'what every brave man ought to do and making experiments in morality'.[10]

Brooke has been castigated as the embodiment of British public-school idealism, gulled into enthusiasm for the war by false ideals and vain hopes. This misses the point. Brooke was scared. The war was therefore a test of his courage, a personal challenge to which he had to respond or think less of himself: 'Now God be thanked,' he wrote, 'who has matched us with this hour.' By embracing the war in spite of his fears the individual became a hero. He also gained the means to live life more intensely: soldiers, a Hungarian, Aladar Schöpflin, said in late August 1914, 'are going into the totality of life',[11] and Walter Bloem, a novelist and German reserve officer, felt that war service had made his novels 'my own living present'.[12]

The notion that modern society was too safe, that boredom and enervation were the consequences, was propagated by popular British

   [8] Aschheim, *Nietzsche legacy*, 143; see also Joll, '1914: the unspoken assumptions', in Koch (ed.), *Origins*, 1972 edn., 323.

   [9] Stromberg, *Redemption by war*, 38.

   [10] Jay Luvaas, 'A unique army', in Kann *et al.* (eds.), *Habsburg empire*, 100–1.

   [11] Eva Balogh, 'The turning of the world' in Kann *et al.* (eds.), *Habsburg empire*, 188.

   [12] Bloem, *Advance from Mons*, 21.

writers like John Buchan and H. Rider Haggard. In France Charles Péguy and Ernest Psichari, both killed in the opening weeks of the war, had written successful books venerating the glory of war and the asceticism of military service. In Germany A. W. Heymel penned a poem in 1911 that longed for war as an end to the 'opulence of peace', and in the winter of 1912–13 Johannes R. Becker portrayed his generation as rotting, seated at their desks, as they waited for the trumpet call to a 'great world war'.[13]

Much of this was self-consciously an attack on rationalism. The development of psychoanalysis in the years before the war had emphasized that balancing man's intellect were his subconscious and his emotions. Sigmund Freud above all had criticized the intellectual tendency to suppress or ignore feelings. But even Freud was unprepared for the emotional force of the war's outbreak. To his surprise he found that his 'libido' was mobilized for Austria-Hungary. The war revealed to him how thin was the veneer of culture: he was appalled to discover that civilized states committed horrors and barbarities against each other which they would never have condoned in their own citizens. He could only conclude that many men observed social norms in defiance of their true natures: 'we are misled', he wrote in the spring of 1915, 'into regarding men as "better" than they actually are.'[14]

In emphasizing the need to integrate both intellect and emotion by being more aware of the latter, psychoanalysis legitimized a preoccupation with the mystic, the inexplicable. Something of what psychoanalysis was saying had been anticipated by Romanticism, by its emphasis on the worth of the individual and his own creativity, and Nietzsche could be employed as a link between the two. By forsaking his desk for action, the writer gathered those experiences which were essential to his creativity. Thus, the seemingly irrational search for danger was rendered rational as a means for emotional and intellectual self-discovery.

Although the willingness to wage war for many was, therefore, a personal test rather than a national one, the response of the intellectuals went on to emphasize the collective social good which would follow from war's conduct. Indeed, for men whose inclinations and callings tended to render them solitary, not the least of war's attractions was its

[13] Vondung, 'Visions de mort', in Vandenrath (ed.), *1914*, 231–2.
[14] Freud, 'Thoughts for the times', 283; see also Falzeder and Brabant (eds.), *Correspondence of Freud and Ferenczi*, 13.

effect in integrating their individual aspirations with those of society as a whole. The idea that the destructive effects of war were beneficial, that war cleansed and renewed society, was one familiar to social Darwinists. Both they and the younger generation of intellectuals were ready to welcome war as driving out decadence: 'Today's man', Dezso Kosztolanyi wrote on 4 October 1914,—'grown up in a hothouse, pale and sipping tea—greets this healthy brutality enthusiastically. Let the storm come and sweep out our salons.'[15] Jettisoned were the bourgeois values of the commercial classes: war trampled on their financial calculations, and in clothing their sons in uniform rendered null the niceties of social rank. The individual found fulfilment, not in pursuit of personal profit, but in the altruism and hardness of military service. The causes of war lay, at least indirectly, in the softness and self-indulgence of pre-1914 Europe. 'This is not a war against an external enemy' opined the painter Franz Marc, 'it is a *European civil war*, a war against the inner invisible enemy of the European spirit.'[16] Brooke's famous description of recruits remains remarkably evocative of the mood—'as swimmers with cleanness leaping, glad from a world grown old and cold and weary'.

Less pleasing to the elder statesmen of social Darwinism was the reversal of the traditional hierarchy implicit in this rejection of bourgeois society. Front-line service was a young man's activity; the middle-aged struggled to be accepted by the army, and in doing so denied the seniority and maturity of their years in pursuit of the fashion for youth. War enthusiasm was an assertion of the values of the younger generation against those of the older. Max Scheler, the German philosopher, declared that the war had rendered the nostrums of the older generation *passé*, while for their successors it was neither a nightmare nor a burden but 'an almost metaphysical awakening from the empty existence of a leaden sleep'.[17] In France in 1913 Henri Massis and Alfred de Tarde, under the pseudonym of 'Agathon', had published a study of the student generation of 1912: they had depicted their calling to action, to absolutes, to things of the spirit, to order and hierarchy, and their turning away from introspection and relativism.[18] The French generation of 1914

---

[15] Balogh, in Kann *et al.* (eds.), *Habsburg empire*, 187.

[16] Quoted in Ecksteins, *Rites of spring*, 94; see also Hynes, *A war imagined*, 3–4, 19.

[17] Scheler, *Genius des Krieges*, 12.

[18] Wohl, *The generation of 1914*, 5–10; also Cruickshank, *Variations on catastrophe*, 18–23.

was thus given an identity that was specifically opposed to that of their republican and anticlerical fathers.

However, the conflict of ideas was not one simply between generations but also one between different views of the values which wartime society would elevate. For some the liberation from materialism and from bourgeois nostrums was to be accomplished by a return to a pastoral idyll. Western Europe had still not come to terms with its increasingly urban existence; G. D. H. Cole, Maurice Barrès, Émile Durkheim, Max Weber—all saw city life, with its destruction of community and its erosion of family, as undermining social cohesion. The war, by calling men to a life that demanded physical fitness, to a career spent outside, that tested the individual against the natural elements as much as against the enemy, was consonant with a return to nature. It is striking that writers from Britain, the country that had been most industrialized for longer, were the most expressive of this aspect of war enthusiasm. Officers in autumn 1914 proved acute observers of the countryside through which they were passing, and readily fell back on the terminology and analogies of field sports. B. F. Cummings, whose multiple sclerosis prevented any such escape, used more turbulent imagery in his diary on 30 June 1914: 'Civilization and top hats bore me. My own life is like a tame rabbit's. If only I had a long tail to lash it in feline rage! I would return to Nature—I could almost return to Chaos.'[19]

Cummings's threat of violence provides a bridge to a very different vision of society, and one embraced particularly by artists. The avant-garde had already declared war on the existing order before July 1914. The opening manifesto of the Futurists, published in 1909, began with the lines: 'There is no more beauty except in strife.' In this and subsequent declamations the Futurists replaced romanticism with industrialism. 'Let's kill the moonlight,' F. T. Marinetti announced; 'the first lines of the great Futurist aesthetic' lay in the locomotive, the factory, the products of heavy industry; 'a roaring motor car, which seems to run on shrapnel, is more beautiful than the Victory of Samothrace'.[20] Marinetti lived out his elevation of violence by going to Tripoli in 1911, to the Balkans in 1912, and joining the Italian army in 1915. Although Marinetti

[19] W. N. P. Barbellion [B. F. Cummings], *Journal of a disappointed man*, 129.
[20] Northern Arts and Scottish Arts Council, *Futurismo 1909–1919: exhibition of Italian Futurism*, 25–6, 33.

claimed that Futurism was an Italian movement, he had published the first manifesto in Paris, and its appeals were to find echoes in German Expressionism and in British Vorticism.

The Vorticists' publication *Blast*, the first number of which was published on 20 June 1914, and whose prime movers were Wyndham Lewis and Ezra Pound, emphasized the unconscious, the 'crude energy' of the primitive world, but derived from Futurism its use of machines for subject-matter, and its belief that war's violence and destruction would be liberating influences. 'Killing somebody', Wyndham Lewis wrote, 'must be the greatest pleasure in existence: either like killing yourself without being interfered with by the instinct of self-preservation—or exterminating the instinct of self-preservation itself.'[21]

The paradox was that war, with its bringing of death, was the end of dead life: for Rilke war was 'a deadly enlivening'.[22] It meant the end of art for art's sake. 'The fight over words and programmes is over,' declared Julius Meier-Graefe in the opening issue of an avant-garde publication *Kriegszeit*, on 31 August 1914; 'What we were missing was meaning—and that brothers, the times now give us...The war has given us unity. All parties are agreed on the goal. May art follow!'[23] Thomas Mann had struggled to come to terms with the war; for all his anticipations of catastrophe, he had not reckoned with his imaginings becoming reality. But by September he had identified with the German nation and its people, and in October his 'Thoughts on the war' likened the artist to the soldier: both live life with intensity and thrive on danger. The artist—the soldier in the artist—should, he declared, thank God for the collapse of a peaceful world; victory was immaterial; war was a moral necessity, both 'a purging and a liberation'.[24] Nor was this determination to put the war to the service of art simply a manifestation of German *Kultur*. Across the Channel the elder statesmen of literature, painting, and music, including Edmund Gosse and Charles Stanford, made similar points.[25]

---

[21] Quoted by Hynes, *A war imagined*, 9–10.

[22] Bernhard Boschert, '"Eine Utopie des Unglückes stieg auf"'. Zum literarischen und publizistichen Engagement deutscher Schriftsteller für den Ersten Weltkrieg', in Berliner Geschichtswerkstatt, *August 1914*, 130–1.

[23] Cork, *A bitter truth*, 46.

[24] Mann, 'Gedanken im Kriege', 9–11; see also Wysling (ed.), *Letters of Heinrich and Thomas Mann*, 120–3.

[25] Hynes, *A war imagined*, 10–19.

Too often conscious of their isolation, intellectuals welcomed the opportunity for incorporation. 'We were no longer what we had been for so long: alone!', wrote Max Scheler. 'The gaps which had opened up, breaking contacts between life's elements—individual, people, nation, world, God—were closed again in an instant.'[26] For Scheler, as for his fellow sociologist Georg Simmel, the war united the demands of the day with the direction of ideas. Poetry, philosophy, prayers, and culture were fused. A new form of society was forged.[27] Friedrich Meinecke wrote: 'Every immeasurable division of labour and distinction of talents and interests, which hitherto had threatened to tear apart our common life and to contract our lives as individuals, brought forth in us benedictions.'[28]

The Expressionist painter Max Beckmann, who in 1909 anticipated that war would be a force for regeneration and social reunification, found what he was looking for in the opening stages of the campaign in the east (where he was a medical orderly). Exhilarated by the mood of universal enthusiasm, he concluded on 24 September 1914 that 'I have in this short time lived more than I have done for years'.[29]

Most writers, intellectuals, and artists therefore not only embraced the popular enthusiasm for war but actively promoted it. Stefan Zweig revealed that 'poems poured forth that rhymed *Krieg* [war] with *Sieg* [victory] and *Not* [necessity] with *Tod* [death]'.[30] The satirist Frank Wedekind, the immorality of whose plays (including *Pandora's Box*) had roused official disapproval, delivered a speech in the Munich playhouse on 18 September 1914 vaunting 'the loyal brotherhood of arms', the unity of Germany, social democracy, and the imperial high command.[31] Those who opposed the war, who resisted the nationalization of culture, the German condemnation of Shakespeare, or the British rejection of Goethe, were few, and most even of them were temporarily carried away by the exuberance of the moment.

[26] Scheler, *Genius des Krieges*, 11.
[27] Michael Reiter, 'Deutschlands innere Wandlung: Georg Simmel zum Krieg', in Berliner Geschichtswerkstatt, *August 1914*, 215–16; see also 132–3.
[28] Raithel, *Das 'Wunder' der inneren Einheit*, 478–9.
[29] Beckmann, *Briefe im Kriege*, 10; see also Cork, *A bitter truth*, 37.
[30] Zweig, *World of yesterday*, 178.
[31] Sackett, *Popular entertainment*, 70.

7

POPULAR
RESPONSES

Historians can too easily fall victim to the testimony of their own kind. The written word, particularly when conveyed with power and elegance, provides accessible and seductive evidence. The temptation is all the greater in relation to 1914, when intellectuals themselves wished to imagine that their ideas shaped the popular mood. Because the young, the students, the educated, the articulate—in sum, Agathon's subject-matter—staged demonstrations supporting the war, the phenomenon of war enthusiasm can become overblown, with the result that the high-falutin ideas of a minority are projected on to the majority.

This caveat is important. Genuine enthusiasm was more frequent in towns and among white-collar workers. The largest single occupational group in most armies was the peasantry, and the reactions of agricultural communities to mobilization were less positive. These differences can be exaggerated. Compulsory primary education meant that the populations of at least Britain, France, and Germany, rural as much as urban, were broadly speaking literate. Words were a way of giving the emotions of the individual a common currency. The 'over-production' (to use the description of one contemporary commentator) of diaries, letters, and poetry in 1914 is characterized by a shared vocabulary, an approved style, which is itself evidence of the ability of language to pervade, externalize, and universalize the emotions which war generated.[1]

[1] Plaut, 'Psychographie des Kriegers', 2–3, 8.

Education was also a potent means of creating national identity. Germany's victory in the Franco-Prussian War was widely interpreted as a triumph of more than battlefield prowess. It was also seen as a reward for modernization, in which educational excellence had played a major part. The effect was not only to promote reform in schools but also to nationalize the curriculum. 'I seek soldiers,' the Kaiser told the Berlin schools conference in 1890; 'we should educate young Germans, and not young Greeks and Romans.'[2] Between 1870 and 1914 the pedagogues of Europe began to give instruction in their own national histories as well as in those of the ancient world.

For France, its recent past—a mixture of revolutions and defeats—was the stuff of continuing political debate. In 1880 the Third Republic signalled its determination to inculcate patriotism through the conceptual legacy of the Revolution. Unable to identify a recent French victory that was the product of a politically safe regime, it settled on 14 July and the storming of the Bastille as an annual celebration of nationhood. An example of domestic strife, in which the army had turned against the government, was not the happiest of precedents. Furthermore, the use of the classroom for the dissemination of the same message aroused the ire of the monarchical and clerical right. But with the passage of time the Bastille Day parade became a vehicle for the integration of the army with the republic. Soldiers found that their values of discipline, order, and devotion to duty were trumpeted as models for emulation by the citizens of the republic. In 1912 the veterans of the Franco-Prussian War, hitherto neglected as the servants of an imperial regime and the victims of defeat, were invited by Poincaré to take part in the 14 July festivities. Ernest Lavisse set about defusing the divisiveness of France's recent past by constructing a national history which integrated the legacies of both royal and republican regimes. On 28 June 1914 France celebrated the 700th anniversary of the battle of Bouvines.[3]

Other states had less difficulty in finding victories which could become the focus of national commemoration. In 1912 Russia honoured the centenary of Napoleon's defeat with éclat.[4] In Germany the anniversary

    [2] Schubert-Weller, *Kein schönrer Tod*, 54–5.
    [3] Hanna, *Mobilization of the intellect*, 5–6, 28–35; Raithel, *Das 'Wunder' der inneren Einheit*, 19; Mitchell *Victors and vanquished*, 143–57; Becker, *France en guerre*, 19–20; Vogel, *Nationen im Gleichschritt*, 39, 98–9, 125–6, 178–88, 196–9, 208–9, 228.
    [4] Suchomlinow, *Erinnerungen*, 349.

of Sedan could combine the army's homage to the veterans of 1870 with its celebration of the Reich's foundation. But after the twenty-fifth anniversary in 1895, Sedan Day declined in significance, and in 1913 was superseded by the unveiling of the massive memorial on the battlefield of Leipzig, significant less for the defeat of Napoleon and more for its part in the evolution of a populist German nationalism. War, argued the most politicized figure in German historical writing, Heinrich von Treitschke, was the key to the creation of the state, and the state was what gave society its shape.[5]

Songs, speeches, sermons, parades, and public festivals—these were the means by which words, and the ideas behind them, permeated the consciousness of the illiterate. But it was the printed word which in 1914 possessed a power which it had never had before, and of which the cinema, the radio, and the television would deprive it in the future. The proliferation of schools, which created a market, and the advent of the railway, with its ease of delivery, stimulated the growth of a national press. In Britain Lord Northcliffe's *Daily Mail*, which anticipated the war and stoked fears of German militarism, claimed a circulation in 1910 of 900,000.[6] *The Times*, bought by Northcliffe in 1909, followed a similar editorial line, and by reducing its price tripled its circulation early in 1914, and then doubled it again with the outbreak of war.[7] In France the leading Paris dailies had national distribution networks. *Le Petit Parisien* enjoyed a circulation of 1.5 million, and *Le Matin* and *Le Journal* 1 million each. Although about 3,000 daily newspapers were published in France, the mass-circulation papers, with their headlines, photographs, and sensationalism, accounted for about 40 per cent of the market. In Germany, by contrast, readerships remained regional or, at best, clearly defined in party and religious terms. Thus, *Vorwärts*, the SPD's paper, spoke for the party as a whole, but was only one of ninety-one socialist dailies with a combined readership of 1.5 million. About eighty newspapers were published in greater Berlin, and 4,221—as well as 6,421 periodicals—throughout Germany.[8] Russia in 1900 had 125 daily papers; in 1913 it had 856, and those

[5] Pick, *War machine*, 90–2; Vogel, *Nationen im Gleichschritt*, 144–5, 170–8.

[6] McEwen, *Journal of Contemporary History*, XVII (1982), 466.

[7] Morris, *The scaremongers*, 346.

[8] Kriegel and Becker, *1914*, 22; Raithel, *Das 'Wunder' der inneren Einheit*, 11, 35–7; Verhey, 'The spirit of 1914', 55–7. Rosenberger, *Zeitungen als Kriegstreiber?*, 71, is the source for German newspaper totals; Verhey says there were 3,600 and Raithel over 2,000.

that flourished were overtly nationalistic in tone.[9] By 1912 Serbia had 199 newspapers and magazines, and they claimed a total circulation of 50 million copies.[10]

In the case of the German press a symptomatic change occurred between the first Moroccan crisis and the events of July 1914. It became increasingly self-referential, with newspapers reporting as news opinions voiced by other publications. Those views were themselves more often the comments of other journalists than of the principal political actors. The press was therefore creating its own reality. The mediation of the newspapers and the gloss which they gave to events themselves helped shape outcomes.

Although more German papers opposed war than advocated it between 1905 and 1914, significant shifts occurred within that pattern. Less often was war portrayed as an extreme and unique solution to a foreign crisis; hostility to the Entente meant that the nature of the anticipated conflict moved from being a bilateral engagement to a multilateral *Weltkrieg*. In 1905–6 four major German papers from across the political spectrum advocated peace. In 1911 they had split, both collectively and individually, with the SPD's *Vorwärts* opposing war most consistently but even then not continually. By July 1914 the dominant mood was fatalism, a belief that the peaceful conduct of international relations had failed and that war was the sole untested solution. Only 25 per cent of articles published by the four advocated war, but roughly 66 per cent expected that war would be the outcome of the crisis; and although 46 per cent reckoned that the war would be a local Austro-Serb clash, 30 per cent anticipated a major war. Furthermore, these were opinions derived more from the experience of the previous international crises than from the events of July 1914. In the last week, between 26 July and 2 August, an unsurprising 44 per cent of articles regarded war as probable; exactly the same percentage had taken a similar stance from the outset of the crisis, in the week beginning 5 July.[11]

At least indirectly, therefore, the societies of Europe imbibed some of the more rarefied thinking about war and nationalism. Furthermore, the campaign for military preparedness was not conducted by the press

---

[9] Lieven, *Russia and the origins*, 119, 130–2.
[10] Petrovich, *Modern Serbia*, 585–7.
[11] Rosenberger, *Zeitungen als Kriegstreiber?*, esp. 163–4, 200–5, 263–72, 283–300, 325–6.

alone. The significance of the leading German extra-parliamentary groups rose steadily before 1914, and in the latter year the Navy League boasted 331,000 members and 776,000 affiliated members. The claim that these organizations were new in two senses—in that they appealed to the petty bourgeois and that they signalled a form of radical nationalism which ultimately would lead to the Nazis—has been disputed. The combined membership of all these groups, about 1 million in 1914, undoubtedly includes a large measure of double-counting. The Pan-German League, which acted as a sort of holding organization for the others, peaked at 22,000 members in 1901. Moreover, the leadership of the Army League was not petty bourgeois but solidly professional—as well as middle-aged. Its membership rose in step with the agitation for the 1912 and 1913 army bills, and declined thereafter. Nonetheless, such efforts to downplay the significance of the nationalist organizations in Germany neglect the fact that their primary purpose was to mould opinion beyond their own memberships through the instrument of propaganda. *Die Flotte*, the Navy League's monthly magazine, had 360,000 readers in 1912, and *Die Wehr*, the Army League's equivalent publication, 90,000 in 1913. Furthermore, the message of these journals was deeply uncomfortable for traditional conservatism. Increased armaments carried as their corollary tax reform and genuinely universal service. If the membership of the veterans' organizations, many of whose values stood comparison with those of the extra-parliamentary pressure groups, is added, perhaps 15 per cent of voters were involved, including a large proportion of industrial workers, peasants, and smallholders.[12]

The weaknesses in party politics made pressure groups a more significant feature of debate in Germany than elsewhere. Nonetheless, Britain established its own Navy League in 1893, and it had 100,000 members in 1914. The National Service League was formed in 1902 to lobby for conscription and claimed 270,000 members, including associate members, in 1914.[13] Much of the effectiveness of the British groups

---

[12] Shevin-Coetzee, *German Army League*, esp. 4–12, 17, 59–60, 78–97, 122; Thomas Rohkrämer, 'Der Gesinnungs-militarismus der "kleinen Leute" im Deutschen Kaiserreich', in Wette (ed.), *Krieg des kleinen Mannes*, 95–6; Rohkrämer, 'August 1914—Kriegsmentalität und ihre Voraussetzungen', in Michalka (ed.), *Erste Weltkrieg*, 762.

[13] Kennedy, *Anglo-German antagonism*, 370–3. Membership figures given for the British National Service League fluctuate; these are from Adams and Poirier, *Conscription controversy*, 17.

rested on the fears of a German invasion, preceded by a swarm of German spies and fifth-columnists. Erskine Childers's *Riddle of the sands* (1903) has been one of the few lasting works of this genre, but more famous at the time was William Le Queux's *The Invasion of 1910*, serialized by the *Daily Mail* in 1911. The best-known of the French nationalist organizations, *Action française*, indicates the perils of judging influence in terms of circulation. *Action française's* eponymous newspaper, characterized by *Vorwärts* as offering 'the most bizarre mixture of intelligence, vulgarity, science, and stupidity', increased its circulation immediately before the war, but still sold only 31,000 copies in 1914.[14] *Action française* and the others were not without significance, but in explaining war enthusiasm their importance resides in their being part of a much greater whole.

Alongside them must be placed the youth organizations, frequently paramilitary in nature, which cultivated physical fitness and group loyalty, and so prepared their members for military service. Baden Powell, the founder of the Boy Scouts, declared that every boy 'ought to learn how to shoot and obey orders, else he is no more good when war breaks out than an old woman'.[15] Formally speaking, the features that are most striking about these youth movements are the opposite of those of the extra-parliamentary organizations—those of the liberal societies were founded first and even tended to be more openly military.

In this respect Britain's principal contribution in international terms, the Boy Scouts, was somewhat misleading. First, they were founded comparatively late, in 1908. Secondly, Baden Powell, himself the hero of the siege of Mafeking in the Boer War, averred that their aims were imperial, to be 'the frontiersmen of our Empire', and not military. Plenty of the precepts promulgated in *Scouting for boys* had warlike applications, but the core activity was what the founder called 'wood craft', essentially survival skills for life in the wild. The scouts themselves were organized into small patrols and encouraged to be self-reliant; they were not formed into large groups and drilled in the execution of the tactics of fire and movement.

Much more overtly militarist, with drum and bugle bands and pill-box hats, were the members of an evangelical organization dating from the

---

[14] Becker, *1914*, 24–7.   [15] De Groot, *Blighty*, 38.

1880s, the Boys' Brigade. William Smith, its founder, was not only a member of the Free Church of Scotland but also an officer in the Volunteers. The Volunteers were part-time soldiers, organized for home defence, and in 1903 about 8 per cent of British males—including an increasing number of the working class—had gained military experience through service with them.[16] When in 1907 Haldane set about the reorganization of the Volunteers to form the Territorial Army, he included provision for the establishment of an Officers Training Corps in schools and universities: accused of fostering militarism in British educational establishments, he replied by saying that militarism already ran high. The evidence generated by the Boer War, both nationally in the demonstrations after the relief of Mafeking, and specifically in the willingness of the Volunteers to serve overseas, suggests that this was fair comment. The recreational appeal of part-time service became the means by which a Nietzschean anxiety to test one's courage was transmitted into action. On the outbreak of hostilities Herbert Read, a member of Leeds University Officers Training Corps, applied for a Territorial Army commission despite his pacifism; and John Reith, who had joined a Territorial infantry battalion from Glasgow University Officers Training Corps, excitedly greeted the war as 'an entirely personal affair'.[17] By 1914 possibly 41 per cent of all male adolescents in Britain belonged to a youth organization, one in three Oxford undergraduates was a member of the Officers Training Corps, and Cambridge was debating whether service in the corps should be a condition of graduation.

Increasingly, therefore, concerns about the lack of compulsory military service in Britain came to underpin public support for the more militant youth movements. Unlike Britain, France had conscription, but still feared that it did not have enough men to hold the line against Germany. Therefore, alone of the major powers, it developed its 5,500 societies for the promotion of gymnastics and shooting among the young specifically as a preparation for military service. The army supported the groups from 1895, and in 1905 the government accorded them formal approval as a corollary of two-year service. In 1912 the minister for war, Alexandre Millerand, told France's schools that, 'You

---

[16] Anne Summers, *History Workshop*, 2 (1976), 104–23.
[17] Stryker, 'Languages of sacrifice', 149; Reith, *Wearing spurs*, 13.

prepare their minds as well as their bodies with the patriotic duty to love France, to place it above all else, to be ready to sacrifice even their lives'.[18] In that year the scheme claimed 650,000 members, but in doing so exaggerated its influence: at best only about 14 per cent of all conscripts underwent pre-service training, and in some areas the figure dropped as low as 1 per cent.

By contrast, Germany's initial reasons for embracing comparable schemes were domestic. The worries about urbanization, that it was corrupting the young, undermining their health, and drawing them into a world of alcohol, tobacco, and pulp fiction, were ones shared in Britain. But significantly, the first fruits of this fear of decadence and degeneration, a movement to promote gymnastics, were manifest in 1889, the year in which the Second International was founded. The real danger was socialism. In the following year the rehabilitation of the SPD created direct competition for the hearts and minds of Germany's working-class youth. Karl Liebknecht reckoned that socialism's window of opportunity was the gap between leaving school at 14 and being called up for military service at 18. The German gymnastics association set out to counter socialism, claiming 400,000 members in 1889, 625,000 in 1899, and 945,000 in 1910. However, some of the members went further, seeing in it a device by which to prepare for and maximize the benefits from military service.

The military imperative did not assume parity with, let alone primacy over, the political until 1911. The scouting movement, propagated through a bastardized translation of Baden Powell's book in 1909, emphasized health and hygiene, and had only 14,000 members by the end of 1911. It was more overtly military than its British equivalent, concentrating on marching and group activities rather than the individual and his return to nature, but the indirect effect was to promote these attributes in its rival organization, the *Wandervogel*. In January 1911 the Prussian minister of public worship and instruction allocated a million marks from the state budget to fund the youth movements. His aims were still domestic, but the response he elicited linked *Volkskraft* to *Wehrkraft*. General Colmar von der Goltz established an umbrella

---

[18] Farrar, *Principled pragmatist*, 147. Farrar says there were 8,500 clubs; the figure of 5,500 is from Storz, *Kriegsbild und Rüstung*, 314. See also Jules Maurin and Jean-Charles Jauffret, 'L'Appel aux armes 1872–1914', in Pedroncini (ed.), *Histoire militaire de la France*, iii. 93.

organization, the *Jungdeutschlandbund*. It built on regional intitiatives, particularly in Bavaria, where officers had already begun to involve themselves in the training of Germany's adolescents. The *Jungdeutschlandbund* had access to the army's barracks and exercise areas. Unlike the Boy Scouts, it made clear to parents that their offspring were being prepared to serve Germany in the next war. The movement took its members away most weekends, so rupturing the bonds of family and community (and upsetting the churches). Its marching songs spoke of combat and death on the battlefield. By 1914 the *Jungdeutschlandbund* claimed 700,000 members. In reality, the active membership may have been as little as 10 per cent of that. Falkenhayn, as Prussian minister of war, was worried that the organization was not getting to those German male youths particularly at risk from anti-militarism. Prompted by the French three-year service law, he proposed to Bethmann Hollweg that, if voluntary enlistment failed, compulsion should follow.[19]

Falkenhayn's desire to extend conscription to Germany's teenagers in 1913–14 coincided with his ministry's increasing acceptance that conscription for adults should be truly universal rather than selective. The manpower needs of its war plans had caused the general staff to lobby for a true nation in arms since Schlieffen. The Ministry of War feared the radicalizing effects both for the army, not least in the composition of its officer corps, and for society. After all, the classic corollary of military obligations was civic rights. In 1904 it was the SPD's leader, August Bebel, who declared that his party favoured the full enforcement of universal military service.[20] But by 1913 Falkenhayn, smarting from the Zabern affair, saw that conscription could enable the army to strike back; it could militarize society.

The success of the German armies in 1870 had hallowed a form of conscription which emphasized the principle of universal military service, not as part of a defensive citizen army but within the context of a professional regular army. Military service aimed to internalize values which linked the government, the people, and the nation, and which

[19] Schubert-Weller, *Kein schönrer Tod*, is full; see also Stargardt, *German idea of militarism*, 98–103, 130; Storz, *Kriegsbild und Rüstung*, 314; Shevin-Coetzee, *German Army League*, 53–4; Thomas Rohkrämer, 'August 1914—Kriegsmentalität und ihre Voraussetzungen', in Michalka (ed.), *Erste Weltkrieg*, 769–70.
[20] Vogel, *Nationen im Gleichschritt*, 222–3.

made the army the school for the nation. Furthermore, the preferred recruit remained the peasant. Thus, that very occupational group least likely to be affected by the other nationalist currents was directly involved in this, the most pronounced form of the subordination of the individual to the state.

The call-up was a rite of passage, the moment when, probably for the first time, the young man left his family and village to step into the wider world. He departed an adolescent and returned an adult. The sphere which he entered contained comradeship and sexual opportunity; but in forsaking the constraints of parental authority the soldier submitted to the state in its most obvious manifestations. Many remained within the army's thrall for the rest of their lives. The veterans' organizations established in Germany to commemorate the dead and to honour the victors of 1870 in due course also accepted those who had completed their service after the Franco-Prussian War and had never seen combat. By 1914 these organizations claimed 2.83 million members. They kept alive the virtues of crown and nation originally inculcated by military service itself. They were opposed to membership of the SPD or of trades unions. They also promoted tension between the generations. First as sons and then as soldiers, those too young to have served in 1870 heard the stories of the heroes of Sedan. They saw the medals on their chests and paid homage at the memorials to their fallen comrades. On the one hand the experience created a social Darwinian fear, that Germany had reached its apogee in 1871 and was therefore in decline. On the other, it fostered rivalry—a need for the young men to prove themselves as valiant in battle as their fathers. Both responses could only, it seemed, be resolved by the next war.[21]

The widespread experience of military service already possessed by those mobilized in 1914 is perhaps the single best explanation for the mood of acceptance which predominated throughout Europe. Those passing through the countryside of Germany, France, or Russia in late July 1914 commented not on the enthusiasm of the population but on its calm and quietness. Hysterical crowds, anxious to fight, were phenomena of Berlin, Paris, and Moscow, not of the hinterlands. They were

[21] Rohkrämer, *Militarismus der kleinen Leute*, esp. 27, 34–41, 49–50, 56, 72–3, 148–9, 182–3, 258, 270.

responses to events rather than their precipitants. The very first assemblies in Germany and France, on 24 July, were in Strasbourg and Nancy, both border towns liable to be invaded at the outset of hostilities. Panic buying of food generated long queues; anxiety about savings produced runs on the banks. The time of year helped. Although the weather became cooler after 22 July, the long summer evenings encouraged people seeking mutual reassurance to congregate outside. Above all, crowds were formed by the appetite for news as the crisis unfolded. In Berlin people assembled along the Unter den Linden and the Potsdamer Platz, close to government buildings; in Paris they congregated in the northern boulevards, especially between the Madeleine and the Place de la République, where the main press offices were situated. Another focus were the cafés and bars in which newspapers could be scanned and information exchanged and dissected. The press and the people formed a symbiotic relationship, the latter gathering to buy the latest editions and the former reporting those gatherings and interpreting them as evidence of enthusiasm.[22] The reports of the metropolitan papers were then propagated by the local press, so encouraging smaller towns to emulate what was believed to be the example of the capital.[23]

Domestically, governments were aware that if the crisis ended in war they needed to be able to command the consent of their populations. Internationally, they were using the responses of the public in their management of the crisis. At the very least, therefore, the crowds were tolerated rather than dispersed. Suggestions that governments went even further and orchestrated them have been made in relation to Russia and Germany, but have not been corroborated by firm evidence.[24] That there was manipulation by other bodies is not in doubt. In Vienna its promoters were army officers and in Berlin youth groups, student societies, and the media themselves.[25]

[22] The fullest comparison of the July 1914 crowds is that for France and Germany in Raithel, *Das 'Wunder' der inneren Einheit*, esp. 222–64. For Germany alone, see Verhey, 'The spirit of 1914', 85–157, and more briefly Fritsche, *Germans into Nazis*, 13–36.

[23] Geinitz, *Kriegsfurcht und Kampfbereitschaft*, 70–8, 132.

[24] Dittmar Dahlmann, 'Russia at the outbreak of the First World War', in Becker and Audoin-Rouzeau (eds.), *Les Sociétés européennes*, 59; Röhl, 'Germany', in Wilson (ed.), *Decisions for war*, 32—but see Wolff, *Tagebücher*, i. 65–6.

[25] Michel, *Guerres mondiales et conflits contemporains*, 179 (1995), 7.

The first patriotic demonstrations in Berlin occurred on the evening of 25 July, as the Serb response to the Austro-Hungarian ultimatum brought extra editions of the newspapers on to the streets. Crowds of between 2,000 and 10,000 people formed, making perhaps 30,000 demonstrators in all. Many of them were drunk. They gathered at sites of national commemoration and moved between the embassies of the major powers, singing patriotic songs. Two aspects of this phenomenon were new. In the past street demonstrations were the method of political protest preferred by the urban working class; workers were absent from these crowds, which were made up of students and young members of the middle classes. Secondly, the police, instead of breaking them up, let the demonstrations run their course, the last not dispersing until 3.45 a.m.

The next day was a Sunday, and as such provided the freedom from work which allowed fresh crowds to form. The other major cities of Germany, some of which witnessed demonstrations on a much smaller scale than those of Berlin on the 25th, saw larger assemblies on the 26th. But most consisted of no more than 200 people, and there was still little feeling evident in the towns and countryside. The crowds were airing their support for Austria-Hungary in its struggle with Serbia rather than seriously contemplating the imminent advent of European war. In France, on the other hand, an awareness of the implications of what was happening was evident from the outset. In 1900 the cry of 'vive l'armée' had been deemed anti-Dreyfusard, anti-republican, and indeed—in the view of one newspaper—positively Jesuitical.[26] As major crowds formed in Paris for the first time on the night of the 26th, the shout that came up was not 'vive la République' but 'vive l'armée'.

Although demonstrations persisted throughout the week, the resumption of work and the hope that the conflict would be localized at first diminished their scale and promoted their orderliness. On 27 July the *Berliner Tageblatt* said that it was now time for the rowdy young men who had been on the streets for the past two days to go to bed.[27] On Wednesday 29 July Poincaré and Viviani returned to Paris, proceeding in state from the Gare du Nord surrounded by crowds shouting 'vive la France'. On the same day the report of Russia's partial mobilization alerted the German

---

[26] Vogel, *Nationen im Gleichschritt*, 240.
[27] Berliner Geschichtswerkstatt, *August 1914*, 16.

people to the dangers of war. The crowds which assembled on the following day were very different from those of 25/6 July. They were drawn from all classes; they were older and less noisy. Although *Vorwärts* called the idea of war enthusiasm an 'absurd fraud',[28] enthusiasm was not entirely absent from the major assemblies of 31 July. The Kaiser returned to Berlin to a welcome comparable with that vouchsafed Poincaré two days before. Nonetheless, the mood was no longer buoyed up by the elements of student frivolity that had characterized the first demonstrations. Seriousness was now the keynote. Hoarding was evidence of anxiety, not enthusiasm. In Hamburg, according to Wilhelm Heberlein of the SPD, 'most people were depressed, as if they were to be beheaded the next day'.[29]

The following day, 1 August, crowds assembled throughout Germany, not out of enthusiasm but in nervous anticipation of general mobilization. Indeed, Theodor Wolff, looking back on the anniversary of 1 August in 1919, was persuaded that when the order came what followed was not 'what one calls mass enthusiasm' but 'the release of an enormous inner tension'.[30] Some got drunk to dull their pain; others sang hymns; almost all bowed to the inevitable and accepted their patriotic duty. When Hans Peter Hanssen, an SPD deputy, travelled from Schleswig to Hamburg and thence to Berlin on 2 August, the mood of resignation had deepened. Class distinctions evaporated as people went out of their way to be kind to one another, but he was emphatic that there was no rejoicing and no enthusiasm: 'over all hung that same heavy, sad, and depressed atmosphere.'[31]

In Germany those units that departed first did so in subdued spirits. Many were worried about the economic implications of their absence. Would their jobs remain open? How would their families survive? Would the withdrawal of so much labour from the workforce result in the collapse of businesses and widespread unemployment for those who stayed behind? By late August many of these fears would seem warranted, as urban unemployment rose from 2.8 per cent in June to

[28] Kruse, 'Kriegsbegeisterung', 174.
[29] Quoted by Verhey, 'The spirit of 1914', 153; also by Kruse, *Krieg und nationale integration*, 59.
[30] Verhey, 'The spirit of 1914', 162; see also Ullrich, *Kriegsalltag*, 13; Gerd Krumeich, 'L'Entrée en guerre en Allemagne', in Becker and Audoin-Rouzeau (eds), *Les Sociétés européennes*, 67–71.
[31] Hanssen, *Diary of a dying empire*, 11–14.

23 per cent.[32] In rural areas the economic problems were even more immediate. The harvest was still not complete, and the problems of gathering it were compounded by the army's requisitioning of horses. Regions close to frontiers anticipated invasion, with further depredations likely to be the least of its consequences. The defensive nature of the war seemed all too obvious in south-west Germany, where the sounds of fighting in Alsace were soon followed by the visible evidence of wounded and prisoners of war. Fears in Freiburg, fed by the memory of fighting in the region in 1870–1, dwelt on the atrocities likely to be committed by French African troops. In southern Bavaria some wives committed suicide rather than confront these problems on their own.[33]

The most striking evidence of an alternative picture, indeed of genuine enthusiasm, was the rush of volunteers to the German colours. Propaganda spoke of at least 1.3 million voluntary enlistments by mid-August: in reality 260,672 men had attempted to join up by 11 August, and 143,922 had been accepted. By the beginning of 1915 308,000 Germans had enlisted voluntarily. The response was most sluggish in Bavaria and Württemberg. Although the real figure for enlistments was significantly lower than was claimed, it remains high for a country with conscription. Germany did, of course, exempt nearly half of its elegible male population from service in peacetime, and it was in part these men on whom voluntary enlistment depended. Not to go was to court social rejection; to go might be the only alternative to short-term unemployment.[34] But many were under-age, the youthful students celebrated in wartime propaganda and post-war literature. The schools returned from their holidays between 3 and 12 August. Teachers were amazed by the 'self-sacrificing love of the fatherland' shown by pupils they had come to see as materialistic and peace-loving. In all three Berlin schools subject to one annual report the entire top forms, those aged 17 or over, volunteered. The *Wandervogel* produced disproportionate numbers, and for those rejected on account of their age special 'youth companies'

[32] Kruse, *Krieg und nationale Integration*, 160–1; Raithel, *Das 'Wunder' der inneren Einheit*, 420–1.

[33] Geinitz, *Kriegsfurcht und Kampfbereitschaft*, 104, 135, 314–29, 330–4; Ziemann, *Front und Heimat*, 44–6.

[34] Bernd Ulrich, 'Des Desillusionierung der Kriegsfreiwilligen von 1914', in Wette (ed.), *Krieg des kleinen Mannes*, 114; Ulrich, 'Kriegsfreiwillige. Motivationen-Erfahrungen-Wirkungen', in Berliner Geschichtswerkstatt, *August 1914*, 233–7; Verhey, 'The spirit of 1914', 206–10.

were formed.[35] Others were of their fathers' generation, too old to be liable for immediate call-up and too young to have served in 1870. Many of the latter confronted what Paul Plaut, an applied psychologist who gathered evidence at the time, reckoned to be a 'psychic crisis': the war shattered the normal tenor of their lives and created a new focus. The positive reaction was to embrace the war. Many of his respondents cited the importance of patriotism, but all of them discounted the phenomenon of war enthusiasm. The most common thread was a sense of duty.[36]

War enthusiasm in Germany developed during the course of August: it followed the war's outbreak rather than preceded it. As the enemy took shape, the idea of pure defence on which the war's immediate acceptance was grounded was moderated. The aims of the war gained in definition, and included objectives which could be defined as offensive and even annexationist.

The sense that the war was a new departure for Germany internally now became common currency for both right and left. Johann Plenge, writing in 1915, said that if there were to be a public festival to commemorate the war, it should be the celebration of mobilization of 2 August—'the celebration of inner victory'. Thomas Mann described this triumph in paradoxes in November 1914, speaking of 'the brotherly co-operation of social democracy and military authority', and citing a radical writer to the effect that 'under the military dictatorship Germany has become free'.[37]

The SPD was less cynical with regard to such contrivances than might have been expected. Ludwig Frank, who had lobbied for his party's support for war credits, wrote to a lady friend on 23 August, 'I am happy: it is not difficult to let blood flow for the fatherland, and to surround it with romanticism and heroism.'[38] Frank, a Jew as well as a socialist, was killed in action on 3 September, one of only two Reichstag deputies to fall in the war.

---

[35] Ingeborg Rürup, ' "Es entspricht nicht den Ernste der Zeit, dass die Jugend müssig gehe". Kriegsbegeisterung, Schulalltag und Bürokratie in den höheren Lehranstalten Preussens 1914', in Berliner Geschichtswerkstatt, *August 1914*, 181–2; Schubert-Weller, *Kein schönrer Tod*, 214, 229.

[36] Plaut, 'Psychographie des Kriegers', 4–16.

[37] Rürup, 'Der "Geist von 1914" ', 17; Mann, 'Gedanken im Kriege', 9.

[38] Kruse, *Krieg und nationale Integration*, 101.

Socialists of middle-class backgrounds may have been more responsive to the opportunity which the war presented for reintegration in German society. But during August the working classes became increasingly proud of their own reaction to the hostilities. Reports of victories began with the (premature) news of the fall of Liège on 7 August; the battles of the frontiers after 20 August produced a sequence of celebrations that climaxed on 2 September, the anniversary of Sedan. Flags, hitherto rarely flown in Germany, and associated in any case with the monarchy, appeared in growing profusion in working-class areas. *Deutschland über alles* gained in popularity, as did evangelical hymns linking Protestantism with nationality.[39] By late August the police in Berlin reported that, despite the worries about unemployment, the mood of the workers was good.[40]

Feelings in France evolved in not dissimilar ways. Boarding a train in St Étienne on 28 July, Daniel Halévy had watched a young officer taking leave of his parents: he had seen expressions such as theirs only in cemeteries, at gravesides. Regular soldiers were being deployed on the frontiers, but Halévy's own hopes of peace only evaporated on 30 and 31 July, the days of waiting, which he described as 'like one endless evening'.[41] He called 1 August the end of hope. On the same day *Le Temps* said the mood in Paris was serious but not sad. Patriotic crowds, mostly of young men and numbered in hundreds rather than thousands, formed in the city's streets that evening.[42] Halévy arrived in the capital on the following day. He observed a man in tears, supported by his friend, a sergeant, on the Pont Neuf. He described Paris as a scene from the Bible, but of a superhuman Bible which had never been committed to paper: 'this city of three million inhabitants had received a death blow.' He acknowledged the mood of resignation, but saw also despair.[43] Monsignor Alfred Baudrillart, the rector of the Institut Catholique in Paris, who arrived in the city on the same day, noticed the role that drink had in evoking overt enthusiasm. His verdict on the

[39] Raithel, *Das 'Wunder' der inneren Einheit*, 460–6; also 428–34, 440; Berliner Geschichtswerkstatt, *Aug. 1914*, 69, 124.

[40] Materna and Schreckenbach, *Dokumente aus geheimen Archiven*, 22 Aug. 1914.

[41] Halévy, *L'Europe brisée*, 25–7, 39.

[42] Raithel, *Das 'Wunder' der inneren Einheit*, 268–74.

[43] Halévy, *L'Europe brisée*, 31.

underlying mood reflected a more fixed resolve: an acceptance of the inevitable and a determination not to give in.[44]

France differed from Germany in being less industrialized, with fewer large regional cities. Thus, small rural communities were even less touched by the speculation of the press. In the Languedoc under half the population read the newspapers, and much of what it did read was concerned with local reporting.[45] When the church bells rang out late on the afternoon of 1 August the peasants were working in the fields, bringing in the harvest. Many assumed that there was a fire. They were put right by the local gendarme or the notice which he had posted—not by the press. As the realization broke, the strongest emotions were shock and consternation. In the villages of the Isère, according to the reports of the local authorities, only 5 per cent of people greeted the war with enthusiasm. This figure rose to 31 per cent in the towns of Grenoble and Vienne. But the key point was that, as in Paris, the general mood was one of resolution.[46] An analysis of six different rural departments suggests that 16 per cent of people received the news of mobilization with favour, 23 per cent with *sang froid*, and 61 per cent with reserve.[47] This may not have been the enthusiasm of legend, but nor was it rejection.

The French army had anticipated that 13 per cent of those mobilized would fail to appear. In the event 1.5 per cent were classed as deserters, and many of those proved to be vagrants, mentally deficient, or Bretons who could not read French. The numbers of genuine defaulters—perhaps 1,600 in all—were so few as to make generalizations fraught. Anti-militarism was not a significant factor; religion may have been, as Catholics in particular were alienated by the anticlericalism of the Third Republic, several to the point of seeking out missions overseas.[48]

Many reservists left for the front immediately. But for others there was more time to come to terms with what was happening. Women were vital in helping men accept their obligations. The search for

---

[44] *Carnets du Cardinal Baudrillart*, 26–7.

[45] Maurin, *Armée-guerre-société*, 566–7, 572.   [46] Flood, *France 1914–18*, 7–15.

[47] Becker, *1914*, 294, also generally 270–357; for a briefer survey see Becker, in Fridenson (ed.), *1914–1918*.

[48] Jules Maurin and Jean-Charles Jauffret, 'Sous les drapeaux', 113–15, and 'Les Combattants face à l'épreuve de 1914 à 1918', 272–5, in Pedroncini (ed.), *L'Histoire militaire de la France*, iii; Maurin, *Armée-guerre-société*, 383–5.

mutual reassurance drew communities together.[49] Even more important was the mood in the barracks themselves. Soldiers had been more aware of the preceding tension, and greeted the war with both relief and optimism: they found the sadness of civilians somewhat embarrassing. It was their positive outlook which swept up the more reluctant reservists.[50] By the time of departure enthusiasm was more in evidence: only 20 per cent now manifested reserve, whereas 30 per cent showed *sang froid*, and 50 per cent favour.[51] Étienne Tanty's company marched off in the early evening of 8 August, and most of his comrades used the afternoon to get drunk. By the time they fell in, two-thirds of them did not know where they were; they could not stand up straight and threw everything into chaos as they struggled to find their equipment. Maurice Maréchal, the cellist, left Rouen at 7 a.m. on the following morning, too early to satiate his anxiety with alcohol. His inner fear competed with the pride generated by the popular acclaim.[52] As units marched off to the strains of the *Marseillaise* and the *Chant du départ*, tricolours waving over their heads and flowers falling at their feet, public and private feelings were fused. Families who said farewell to their fathers, husbands, and sons were sustained by the sharing of the experience and by a sense of fellowship.

These public displays gave substance to the *union sacrée*, helping to transform what was initially a formula for national defence, a response to a temporary crisis and a term little used by newspapers, into a more sustained effort to put national divisions to one side. The *union sacrée* could not draw on France's immediate past: deeply divided by the Dreyfus affair, it nurtured at least two different conceptions of society, one libertarian and egalitarian, and the other hierarchical and authoritarian, the most potent manifestation of this division being the clash between republicanism and clericalism. Baudrillart was abused at the Gare St Lazare and in the street on 2 and 3 August. As August wore on he encountered more tolerance. The government itself, through its prefects and mayors, deliberately promoted the *union sacrée* at the local level. On public occasions teacher and priest—the representatives of the republic and of Rome—joined together on the same platform for the sake of France.

---

[49] Flood, *France 1914–18*, 7–15.   [50] Maurin, *Armée-guerre-société*, 573, 679.
[51] Becker, *1914*, 319.   [52] Guéno and Laplume (eds), *Paroles de poilus*, 13, 37.

The underlying tensions were not removed, but all sides recognized that the corollary of a war of national defence was a sustained effort to generate national unity: 'it is vital', wrote Baudrillart in his diary on 29 September, 'not to do anything to destroy a union which is so precarious.'[53]

In Austria-Hungary the army expected one in ten of those called up not to appear.[54] On the whole its fears proved unfounded. Some inducement was provided by the fact that mobilization orders were issued in the native tongues of the reservists. In the Austrian lands problems were greatest in Croatia and Slovenia, where between 600 and 700 men deserted. But figures were lower in the Italian-speaking areas of Tyrol and the Adriatic, and in Bohemia fell to only nine. Foreigners proved anxious to demonstrate their loyalty and enlisted voluntarily in large numbers. In Hungary the Magyars used the excuse of mobilization to arrest large numbers of non-Magyars on the basis of a secret list and on the grounds of suspicion alone.[55] The immediate effects were less damaging than might have been expected. Romanian peasants in Hungary responded without enthusiasm, but they nonetheless arrived at the depots earlier and in greater numbers than anticipated.[56] In Bosnia anti-Serb excesses in the aftermath of the Sarajevo assassinations cowed dissidents.

However, the opportunity to stress the solidarity of the state was not seized. The Reichsrat was not recalled, and the political parties thus evaded any pressure to commit themselves to the defence of the empire in formal terms.[57] Much of the evidence of real exuberance in late July derives solely from Vienna. As in other countries, it did not anticipate the war's outbreak but was a response to it. It therefore rested on the idea of a short, sharp war against Serbia alone, in the hope that it would resolve Austria-Hungary's internal problems. As the Balkan conflict gave way to a general European war, and as Austria-Hungary confronted conflict with Russia, the enthusiasm of its people ebbed. In Germany and France popular determination deepened during the course of

[53] Baudrillart, *Carnets du Cardinal Baudrillart*, 27–8, 31, 80, 85; also Flood, *France 1914–18*, 17–23; Robert Vandenbussche, 'Psychose de guerre dans le nord? 1910–14', in Vandenrath *et al.* (eds.), *1914*, 128–9, 138, 160–4; Jean-Jacques Becker, 'La Genèse de l'union sacrée', in ibid. 208–9, 214–15; Becker, *La France en guerre*, 13–15, 30–8.

[54] Glaise von Horstenau, *Ein General im Zwielicht*, i. 285.

[55] Herwig, *First World War*, 79, 127.

[56] Taslauanu, *With the Austrian army*, 6, 11.

[57] Michel, *Guerres mondiales et conflits contemporains*, 179 (1995), 7.

August; in Austria-Hungary it declined. Freud, having joined in the earlier euphoria, found that 'gradually a feeling of discomfort set in, as the strictures of the censorship and the exaggeration of the smallest successes' reminded him of the empire's underlying weaknesses. 'The only thing that remains real', he concluded on 23 August, 'is the hope that the high ally will hack us out.'[58]

But a war for Germany was not what the Czechs wanted. Many were at least passive supporters of Russia. The mood in Prague was more reserved than that in Vienna from the outset. Both the 1908 and 1912 mobilizations had triggered mutinies in Czech units. On 22 September two Czech Landwehr battalions left the city displaying their national colours and a red flag with the words 'we are marching against the Russians and we do not know why'. One of the battalions was disbanded in April 1915 after large-scale desertions to the enemy.[59] In Bohemia itself a railway strike and popular demonstrations meant that 121 Czech radicals were arrested within a few months, and eighteen of them condemned to death; by the year's end almost a thousand would be imprisoned.[60]

In Russia itself the belief that the war could be popular was an important element in sustaining the resolve both of the Tsar and of the council of ministers. The latter had convinced itself from the outset of the crisis, on 24 July, that a failure to support Serbia would foment the prevailing disorder rather than assuage it. When Nicholas II approved general mobilization his own determination, which—particularly in the light of Durnovo's telling memorandum—was shaky at best, was sustained by the thought that what he was doing commanded popular support.[61] Certainly the press across a wide political spectrum commended his actions, and called for national unity.

Superficially the incidence of strikes during July might have suggested that any opposition to mobilization would be focused in the cities. Workers and reservists in Riga paraded with banners saying 'Down with the war!' But in some senses socialist activity had exhausted itself by the time mobilization was declared. The responses among the workers of St Petersburg were resigned, if not enthusiastic. This was the mood caught

---

[58] Falzeder and Brabant (eds.), *Correspondence of Freud and Ferenczi*, 13.
[59] Deak, *Beyond nationalism*, 197; Zeman, *Break-up of the Habsburg empire*, 50–2, 55–7.
[60] Rauchensteiner, *Tod des Doppeladlers*, 178–80.
[61] Lieven, *Nicholas II*, 197, 204.

by Marc Chagall in a series of drawings depicting the troops' departure for the front.[62] Overt opposition was a rural more than an urban phenomenon. Surprise, the initial response as elsewhere, generated first stunned silence and then lamentation. But as the news was assimilated, communities were divided more than united by their reactions. In the wake of the 1905 defeat, military reformers had argued that effectiveness in modern war relied on a sense of nationalism. Two-thirds of pre-war conscripts were literate, and their period in uniform became an opportunity to inculcate a loyalty to Russia. On the other hand, an appeal to national unity, even if endorsed in varying degrees and for divergent reasons by the Duma, meant little to a population whose lives were regulated by regional loyalties. Although long used to the state's conscription of manpower, the peasants were particularly concerned by the economic dimensions of mobilization. On the one hand were their worries for the provision and sustenance of their families; on the other were the shortages of food and accommodation at the collection and redistribution centres for the troops themselves. Calculations as to the scale of the subsequent disorders vary: thirty-one districts in seventeen provinces were affected on mobilization, and a month later the police reckoned that forty-nine out of 101 provinces and oblasts in European and Asiatic Russia had suffered riots. In Barnaul, the authorities lost control of the city for a time, and over 100 died. In four provinces tens of thousands of reservists were involved, and one report put the numbers of dead and wounded at 505 in European Russia alone. On 13 August Maklakov, the minister of the interior, authorized the provincial governors to suppress any disturbances without mercy.[63]

In the circumstances, the fact that 96 per cent of those mobilized reported for duty represented a successful outcome. Provincial officials orchestrated patrotic demonstrations as units left for the front. And the mood, even if not as resilient as that of France or Germany, hardened as the weeks passed. The Duma's resolution to support war credits, however much it embraced even more divergent motives than did the

[62] McKean, *St Petersburg*, 357–8; Lobanov-Rostovsky, *Grinding mill*, 20; Cork, *A bitter truth*, 40–1.

[63] Dittmar Dahlmann, 'Russia at the outbreak of the First World War', in Becker and Audoin-Rouzeau (eds.), *Les Sociétés européennes*, 53–61; Wildman, *End of the Russian imperial army*, 77–9; Rogger, *Journal of Contemporary History*, I (1966) 105–6; Sanborn, *Slavic Review*, LIX (2000), 267–89 . See also Andolenko, *Histoire de l'armée russe*, 306, and Danilov, *Le Russie dans la grande guerre*, 155–6.

comparable votes in Germany and France, at least betokened a political armistice for the time being. Victories against the Austrians, despite the dire reports from East Prussia, fed these different interpretations of Russianness. Major patriotic demonstrations were reported by the police in October, and in the same month popular culture reflected national feeling through circuses, films, and puppet shows.[64]

Because of its comparatively underdeveloped economy Russia was less exposed to the currents of pre-war nationalism, but its people went to war nonetheless. Belgium was its mirror image; possessed of an advanced economy, its neutrality prevented it being subject to the full force of pre-war militancy. If surprise was a common response to the outbreak of war, then it reached its greatest intensity in Brussels. As late as 28 July the Catholic press supported Austria-Hungary's handling of Serbia as though the crisis was still localized. The German ultimatum to Belgium and its rejection produced a reaction whose spontaneity and scale amazed the gratified government. Belgians were outraged by the Germans' implication that their honour could be bought in return for financial compensation. Thus, it was the ultimatum rather than the invasion which produced integration. The king became its focus, appealing to a sense of nationhood and history in terms which were effectively novel in Belgian discourse. Belgium's socialists cleaved to these notions rather than to the International, and Albert reacted by appointing Emil Vandervelde a minister of state on 4 August. Up to 20,000 volunteers joined the army, most for reasons of patriotism rather than economic necessity, and mostly (as elsewhere) from urban rather than rural areas. As Belgium lost its territory it found an identity.[65]

It is Britain, however, that provides by far the best illustration of the development from war enthusiasm into fighting power. Britain saw its navy as its prime defence; it had no tradition of conscription, and its small army was drawn to a disproportionate extent from the lower end of the working class. Popular militarism embraced many forms before 1914, but they did not include that of being a regular soldier. The army needed 35,000 recruits each year, and yet only once between 1908 and

---

[64] Jahn, *Patriotic culture in Russia*, esp. 8–9, and n. 13.

[65] Jean Stengers, 'Belgium', in Wilson (ed), *Decisions for war*, 152, 157, 161–4; Stengers, *Guerres mondiales et conflits contemporains*, 179 (1995), 17–20; Stengers, 'La Belgique', in Becker and Audoin-Rouzeau (eds.), *Les Sociétés européennes*, 79–85.

1913 did it get more than 30,000. Nor was the Territorial Army, which Haldane had grandly portrayed as the nation in arms, committed to home defence, any more popular: in 1913 it was almost 67,000 men below its establishment of 300,000, and it had a 12.5 per-cent annual wastage rate.[66]

On 6 August 1914 the newly appointed secretary of state for war, Lord Kitchener, received parliamentary approval for an increase in the army of 500,000 men. This was the first of his 'New Armies'; by mid-August he was aiming for four such armies, giving him twenty-four divisions in addition to the six formed by the existing regular army. Between 4 and 8 August a total of 8,193 men enlisted; in the second week of the month 43,354 came forward, and in the third 49,982. With the news of the battle of Mons and the retreat to the Marne, and press reports of the exhaustion and disarray of the exiguous British Expeditionary Force, recruiting in the final week of August reached 63,000, and in the first week of September 174,901. By 12 September 478,893 men had joined the army since the war's outbreak, and 301,971 since 30 August. Of a total of 5.7 million who served with the British forces in the First World War, 2.46 million were to enlist voluntarily by the end of 1915.[67]

Two features are immediately striking in these figures. First, popular enthusiasm was clearly transformed into active service; secondly, the process by which it did so was delayed in its operation. All classes responded positively to Kitchener's appeal. However, the professional and commercial classes did so disproportionately: over 40 per cent of those eligible in both categories joined the army, thus suggesting that their exposure to the influences of the press, to the appeal to escape the office routine of bourgeois life, was not without its effect. By contrast, only 22 per cent of those in agriculture enlisted, and they constituted 8.4 per cent of all recruits. The agricultural workforce was older than many other occupations, and its contribution to the war effort was direct, but in addition it was cut off from many of the influences of popular nationalism. The methods of recruiting employed in rural areas were traditional and paternalist, relying on a sense of deference and obligation rather than on regional links and bonds of friendship. In Sussex such

---

[66] Simkins, *Kitchener's army*, 17–19.
[67] Simkins, *Kitchener's army*, xiii–xv, 39–40, 49–75.

techniques were insufficient.[68] In the Highlands of Scotland the sparse-
ness of the population underlined the impossibility of adhering to
strictly territorial recruiting. Cameron of Lochiel recalled emigrants
to Scotland. Macdonald of Clanranald appealed to the memory of the
1745 rebellion, citing the Hanoverian (i.e. British) army's treatment of the
Jacobites as evidence of German brutality.[69] Just under 30 per cent of
those employed in manufacturing industry enlisted. It is possible that
high working-class enlistment in August and September was related to
unemployment. The immediate effect of the war's declaration was an
increase in unemployment by 10 per cent: 78 per cent of Birmingham
recruits in August came from the same social classes as before the war, and
by September nine out of ten unemployed were reported as having
enlisted. As a general pattern, therefore, industrial and urban areas
produced more recruits than rural areas. By 4 November 1914 237 per
10,000 of the population had volunteered from southern Scotland, 196
from the Midlands, and 198 from Lancashire; by contrast the west of
England had mustered only eighty-eight per 10,000, the eastern counties
eighty, and southern Ireland thirty-two. Urban civic pride became a
powerful factor and was embodied in the idea of 'Pals' battalions, units
made of up friends, linked by professional, recreational, or educational
ties: 145 service battalions and seventy-nine reserve battalions were raised
locally. The 'Pals' movement was particularly strong on Merseyside,
and comparatively weak in Scotland. The big exception, Glasgow, raised
three battalions for the Highland Light Infantry, the 15th battalion from
the corporation's tram service, the 16th from the Boy's Brigade, and the
17th from the city's chamber of commerce. Typical of a community cut off
from such collective influences, from the excitement generated by the
press and the parades, was Gwynedd in north-west Wales. Perplexity at
the war, the lack of military traditions, the separateness from England, all
combined to produce low rates of recruiting.[70]

[68] Grieves, *Rural History*, IV (1993), 55–75.

[69] Ewen Cameron and Iain Robertson, 'Fighting and bleeding for the land: the Scottish
Highlands and the Great War', in C. M. M. Macdonald and E. Macfarland (eds.), *Scotland and
the Great War*.

[70] Parry, *Welsh History Review*, XIV (1988), 78–92; on voluntary recruiting in general, see
Simkins, *Kitchener's army*; Beckett and Simpson, *Nation in arms*, 7–12; Winter, *The Great War
and the British people*, 25–35; Douglas, *Journal of Modern History*, XLII (1970), 570–4; Dewey,
Historical Journal, XXVII (1984), 199–223.

Some of the factors experienced in Gwynedd were common to Britain as a whole, and help explain the slowness with which recruiting boomed in August. Ernest Jones wrote to his friend Sigmund Freud on 3 August that, 'London is absolutely quiet and indistinguishable from other times except for the newspapers'.[71] The Liberal press concluded, once war was declared, that it had no option but to support the national effort. With no immediate danger to Britain, the prevailing mood was one of obligation. Reservists reported for duty almost without exception. But others had to put their affairs in order; there were delays in sorting out separation allowances for their families; and their employers were reluctant to lose them.

Within a month many of these factors were operating in the other direction. Women distributed white feathers to those not yet in uniform; employers promised to keep jobs open for men on their return. Britain's delay was evidence of a general European phenomenon. The speed of the crisis had changed war from a remote contingency to an immediate actuality: people took time to adjust. The attempt by international socialism to prevent the war and the obvious manifestations of bellicosity were more sequential than they were simultaneous: the failure of the first created the opportunity for the second.

The enthusiasm with which Europe went to war was therefore composed of a wide range of differing responses. Its universality lay in their convergence and not in their component parts. Intellectuals welcomed war as an instrument with which to change pre-war society; many of those who joined up did so to defend it. For the latter, the foundations were as much psychological as ideological: community and conformity gave shape to lives disordered by the upheavals which the war caused.[72] The common denominator may more accurately be described as passive acceptance, a willingness to do one's duty; enthusiasm was the conspicuous froth, the surface element only.

The mood relied in large part on an ignorance of the conditions of modern war. The bulk of popular literature continued to portray war as a matter of individual courage and resource, to use imagery more appropriate to knights-errant and the days of chivalry. 'Where then are horse

---

[71] Paskauskas (ed.), *Correspondence of Freud and Jones*, 298.
[72] Geinitz, *Kriegsfurcht und Kampfbereitschaft*, 178–9.

and rider? Where is my sword?', Wilhelm Lamszus had asked ironically in
Das Menschenschlachthaus (the slaughterhouse of mankind), published
in 1912. Like H. G. Wells in Britain, Lamszus had recognized that the next
war would represent the triumph of the machine over human flesh.[73] But
the inherent optimism of the human condition, the belief that the best
will occur rather than the worst, the intimations of immortality to which
youth is subject, persuaded many that technical progress would make war
less lethal, not more so. The *Breisgauer Zeitung* assured its readers on
1 August that their chances of coming back in one piece from this war were
greater than in previous wars. The modern battlefield was much less
bloody because of the extended distances at which fighting occurred.
Moreover, high-velocity bullets were of smaller calibre and therefore
passed through the body with less damage. Such wounds as were inflicted
could be rapidly treated thanks to the advances of modern medicine.[74]
British regular soldiers who had served in South Africa did not share the
general exuberance; recent knowledge of war—in their case that with
Japan in 1904—may also have contributed to the reluctance of Russian
reservists.[75] But in France, Germany, and Austria-Hungary no such
experience of combat could clutter their idealized views.

Popular enthusiasm played no part in causing the First World War.
And yet without a popular willingness to go to war the world war could
not have taken place. The statesmen had projected internal collapse as a
consequence of prolonged fighting. Instead, the societies of all the
belligerents remained integrated until at least 1917, and in large part
into 1918. The underlying conviction of the war's necessity, of the duty
of patriotic defence, established in 1914, remained the bedrock of that
continuing commitment.

[73] Boschert, 'Eine Utopie des Unglücks stieg auf', in Berliner Geschichtswerkstatt, *August 1914*, 134.

[74] Geinitz, *Kriegsfurcht und Kampfbereitschaft*, 285–6.

[75] Meinertzhagen, *Army diary*, 78; Gordon-Duff, *With the Gordon Highlanders*, 343; Terraine (ed.), *General Jack's diary*, 22; Dunn, *The war the infantry knew*, 1; Wildman, *End of the Russian imperial army*, 82.

PART III

CONCLUSION

8

THE IDEAS OF 1914

Within three months the third Balkan war had embroiled the bulk of the world's three most populous continents, Europe, Africa, and Asia. It had, moreover, embraced two more, Australia and—via Canada—North America. 'The war', Alfred Baudrillart, wrote in his diary on 31 October 1914, 'is extending to the whole universe.'[1]

Baudrillart's hyperbole reflected the global status of the European powers. Africans found themselves fighting because they were the subjects of Britain, France, Germany, or Belgium, not because they were Africans. Furthermore, London's primacy as the world's financial capital and Paris's status as an international lender meant that even those nations that were formally independent could not remain untouched by the war's outbreak in 1914. Neutrality in the political sense did not result in immunity from the war's effects in every other sense. Neither the United States nor China became formal belligerents until 1917, but their domestic politics, their diplomacy, and their wealth were all contingent on the war from its very outset.

To contend that the war was truly global throughout its duration is, of course, not the same as also saying that its purposes were commensurate with its scale. Indeed, it has been the presumption of hindsight that they were not. The Great War has often been portrayed not as a world war but as a European civil war, a squabble between brothers, united—if only they had realized it—by more than divided them, a struggle where the means were massively disproportionate given the ends.

---

[1] Baudrillart, *Carnets*, 92.

The now-considerable literature on war aims reinforces this approach, because it states the objectives of each power in geographical or economic terms. Being drawn up as agendas for peace settlements, war aims—however extensive—rested on the presumption that negotiation would become possible. Their implication is some form of limitation, even if those limits tended to be set far beyond the bounds of acceptability for the enemy and, often, for allies. War aims were a retrospective effort to give shape to something bigger. They did not cause the war. Even those of Germany were developed during the conflict, not before it. The powers of Europe entered the war without clearly defined geographical objectives; if they had, the First World War might indeed have been nearer to the 'cabinet wars' of Bismarck or even of the eighteenth century than it was. When the war broke out, it was not a fight for the control of Alsace-Lorraine or Poland or Galicia. It was, as Bethmann Hollweg melodramatically anticipated in 1913, 'a battle for existence'.[2]

Big ideas, however rhetorical, shaped the war's purpose more immediately and completely than did more definable objectives. 'The War of 1914', an Oxford classics don, Alfred Zimmern, told an audience from the Workers' Educational Association at its summer school that year, 'is not simply a war between the Dual Alliance and the Triple Entente: it is ... a war of ideas—a conflict between two different and irreconcilable conceptions of government, society and progress.'[3] Later that year H. G. Wells published *The war that will end war*. 'We fight', he declared, 'not to destroy a nation, but to kill a nest of ideas ... Our business is to kill ideas. The ultimate purpose of this war is propaganda, the destruction of certain beliefs and the creation of others.'[4]

Wells was no more a militarist than Zimmern was a Germanophobe. For all Wells's use of the word 'propaganda', his book was not propaganda in the narrowly defined sense: neither he nor Zimmern held the views they did because they were mouthpieces for the British government. In due course the ideas with which they were concerned did indeed become the meat of official propaganda; but their emotional charge derived precisely from the personal conviction that underpinned them. The issues were moral and, ultimately, religious.

    [2] Schulte, *Vor dem Kriegsausbruch*, 116.
    [3] Seton-Watson *et al.*, *War and democracy*, 318.   [4] Marrin, *Last crusade*, 98.

In a sectarian sense, the Thirty Years War was the last great European war of religion. Thereafter notions of just war atrophied, and vindications for the recourse to arms were couched in political and national terms. In the First World War neither alliance was shaped by a clearly defined creed. Muslim and Christian, Catholic and Protestant, were to be found on both sides of the line. Germany stressed its Lutheran credentials within Europe, but became—by virtue of its pact with Turkey—the spokesman for Catholicism in the Holy Land. The same alliance also made it the protector of the Jews. In this case, however, the function was replicated rather than reversed within Europe itself: France, the persecutor of Dreyfus, and Russia, the architect of anti-Semitic pogroms, were Germany's enemies. Zionism, however, found its advocate in Britain. In confessional terms Britain and Germany should have been aligned. The fact that they were not shattered German theologians like Adolf von Harnack. Their disillusionment was deepened by Britain's readiness to ally with Shinto Japan and to deploy Hindu troops in Europe. Ernst Troeltsch described the consequences for international Christianity, 'the religion of the white race', as 'a downright catastrophe'.[5]

Troeltsch's despair went further. The destruction and hatred which the war unleashed seemed to make Christianity itself 'an alien message from an alien world'. This was not a new lament: its origins were both pre-war and domestic. Church–state relations in many of the belligerent countries were increasingly fraught. Societies had become sufficiently secularized in their pursuit of material progress for church leaders to be tempted to see the war's advent as divine retribution. For them, the war could be welcomed as a necessary and God-given process of cleansing and rejuvenation.

Paradoxically, therefore, optimism trod hard on the heels of pessimism. The response of many on mobilization was to turn to religion for guidance and comfort. In Hamburg church attendance rose 125 per cent in August. In Orcival, in France, 4,115 people received communion in 1913 but 14,480 did so in 1914.[6] Much of what moved congregations was spiritual and mystical. In a sermon delivered in October 1914

[5] Rubanowice, *Crisis in consciousness*, 101; also Pressel, *Kriegspredigt*, 128–30; Huber, *Kirche und Öffentlichkeit*, 171–3, 181–2.

[6] Hope, *German and Scandinavian protestantism*, 591; Becker, *Great War and the French people*, 188.

Pastor L. Jacobsköller saw the war as a new Whitsun, the coming of the Holy Ghost 'like a mighty, rushing wind'.[7] God acquired a fresh immediacy, awesome and judging as well as loving and compassionate. Ernst Barlach's lithograph for *Kriegszeit*, a weekly magazine, entitled *Holy War*, showed a robed figure, his identity obscured, with sword poised.[8] Its message was ambiguous. Was this a vengeful God, purging the world of decadence and unbelief, or could it be a more partial God, punishing only His chosen people's foes?

Much of the rhetoric of holy war delivered from the pulpits of Europe in 1914 opted for the second interpretation. The *Solingen Tageblatt* on 5 August declared that this is 'a holy war': 'Germany can and is not allowed to lose . . . if she loses so, too, does the world lose its light, its home of justice'.[9] In Britain, the bishop of London, Arthur Winnington-Ingram, was of the view that 'the Church can best help the nation first of all by making it realise that it is engaged in a Holy War, and not be afraid of saying so'.[10] The cellist Maurice Maréchal, then a 22-year-old music student, wrote to his mother on 2 August 1914 in terms that were more emotive and romantic. He had that day passed Rouen cathedral on his way back home: the building was saying, 'I am the Glory, I am the Faith, I am France. I love my children, who have given me life, and I protect them.'[11]

The crux of such pronouncements was their identification of church with state. Nowhere was this more evident than in the only formal declaration of holy war, that made in Constantinople on 14 November 1914 and issued in the name of a spiritual leader, the Caliph, who, as Sultan, was also a temporal ruler. In Russia the Orthodox church fused its own proselytization with the Russification of the empire's ethnic communities. Under the leadership of the minister of religion, the church used the opportunity of the war not only to intensify its persecution of Jews and Muslims but also to root out Lutherans in the Baltic states, Catholics in Poland, and, above all, Uniates (or Greek Catholics) in the Ukraine.[12] In a series of fourteen lithographs entitled *Mystical Images of War* Natalia

---

[7] Pressel, *Kriegspredigt*, 17–18; also 188–91.   [8] Cork, *Bitter truth*, 47.
[9] Verhey, 'The "spirit" of 1914', 273.   [10] Marrin, *Last crusade*, 139.
[11] Guéno and Laplume, *Paroles de poilus*, 11.
[12] Pares, *Fall of the Russian monarchy*, 64–5; Rauchensteiner, *Tod des Doppeladlers*, 29; Zeman, *Break-up of Habsburg empire*, 5–6.

Goncharova subscribed to this fusion of Russia's history with its religion, her final print showing the spirit of St Alexander Nevsky, who routed the Teutonic knights in 1242.[13] Significantly, the *lubok*, a traditional form of popular broadside, was revived in Russia in 1914–15. Although the *lubki* rarely referred to the church, they used iconic elements to emphasize the holiness of the struggle, with the Entente as the Trinity and Russia and the Russian soldier as mother and child.[14]

In western Europe the fact that Catholics were committed to both sides reduced the Vatican to virtual silence. But the German invasion of Belgium and northern France acquired the trappings of a holy war with almost immediate effect. The German army was heir to two traditions. The first, forged by the French army in the Vendée and in the Peninsular War, saw Catholic priests as the orchestrators of local guerrillas and resistance movements. The second was Bismarck's anti-Catholic *Kultur-kampf*. The stories of German atrocities often had priests and nuns as their victims. If they accepted the accusations, German soldiers excused their actions as responses to 'conspiratorial Catholicism';[15] if they denied them, their prosecutors cited as evidence the physical destruction suffered by churches, notably at Louvain and Reims.

For the Catholics themselves, their sufferings were an opportunity to re-establish the links between church and state. In Belgium Cardinal Mercier, archbishop of Malines, became a symbol of resistance. In his 1914 Christmas message he told his flock that, 'The religion of Christ makes patriotism a law: there is no perfect Christian who is not a perfect patriot.'[16] In occupied France the mobilization of teachers and then the severance from Paris could leave the curé as the most important local figure. Indeed, the Germans' victimization and even execution of the clergy may have reflected the latter's exercise of secular rather than spiritual leadership. The archbishop of Verdun told Baudrillart of one curé who had been stripped and flogged in front of his parishioners, and of another who had been clothed in his vestments and then forced to watch the rape of his maid.[17] However much exaggerated by French and British propaganda, such stories were not without

[13] Cork, *Bitter truth*, 48.   [14] Jahn, *Patriotic culture in Russia*, 24, 28.

[15] Horne and Kramer, *Journal of Modern History*, LXVI (1994), 24.

[16] Stengers, *Guerres mondiales et conflits contemporains*, 179 (July 1995), 31.

[17] Baudrillart, *Carnets*, 100.

foundation.[18] More importantly, they were believed at the time. Baudrillart established a Catholic committee to produce anti-German
propaganda, and in April 1915 it published *La Guerre allemande et le
catholicisme*. Thus the war provided the opportunity for France's Catholics both to challenge republican aspersions on their loyalty, and to win
back Frenchmen for Rome.

   In 1429 Joan of Arc had passed through Auxerre on her way to raise the
siege of Orléans. In 1914 the city's cathedral church of St Étienne commis-
sioned a stained glass depiction of the maid directing operations: it
carried the words attributed to Joan—'I have been sent by God the King
of Heaven to drive you out of all France.' The ambiguity as to whom her
words were addressed proved helpful. A declaration directed at the
English in 1429 could in 1914 be targeted at the Germans. Before the
First World War's outbreak the cult of Joan of Arc promoted political
division more than patriotic unity. The campaign for her canonization
and for her appropriation as a national symbol was orchestrated by the
Catholic right. But there existed another image of Joan, not of the church
militant or of martial success, of Joan clad not in armour but in a dress;
this was a peasant girl betrayed by the king whose coronation she had
achieved and burned at the stake by the church which she had served.
Both images carried patriotic overtones, even if the second was of a
revolutionary France rather than a royalist one. The outbreak of the
war, and particularly the bombardment of Reims cathedral, where
Charles VII had been crowned under a standard held aloft by Joan,
permitted these divergent interpretations to be integrated. At one level,
therefore, the iconography of Joan in late 1914 was simply further evidence
of the *union sacrée* and its capacity for reconciliation. But it carried a
further message. The posters and postcards bore a legend that was both a
reminder and a promise: 'Dieu protège la France.'[19]

   Catholicism was hardly the monopoly of the Entente. Austrian fealty
to the Vatican contrasted strongly with the anticlericalism of the Third
Republic. And the latter made France an even greater threat in the

---

   [18] The subject of atrocities and also of their relationship to propaganda will be dealt with in a
subsequent volume. Trevor Wilson challenged the evidence of atrocities in Belgium used by the
British, *Journal of Contemporary History*, XIV (1979), 369–83; but John Horne and Alan Kramer
have affirmed it—see *Journal of Modern History*, LXVI (1994), 1–33, and *German atrocities*.
   [19] The Auxerre window is by Edmond Socard, from a painting by Paul Louzier. See also
Krumeich, *Jeanne d'Arc*, esp. 10–12, 187–99, 216–18.

adjacent territories of Catholic south Germany. Efforts were made to render Freiburg's cathedral as symbolic as those of Reims or Louvain. *Illustrierte Zeitung*, a Leipzig journal, highlighted its vulnerability with a picture of a French air raid over the city on 13 December 1914. Alsatian priests were not martyrs but traitors; the number reported by the German press as having been executed for treason proved to be double the number actually in orders. Thus, the themes of allied propaganda and the accusations of Entente Catholics were turned. The fact that Germany's propaganda in neutral states was entrusted to the leader of the Catholic Centre party, Matthias Erzberger, reinforced the specifically Catholic dimension to the German riposte. The charges levelled by Baudrillart's committee received a point-by-point rebuttal in a volume written by A. J. Rosenberg at Erzberger's request, and Georg Pfeilschifter presided over a collaborative volume, *Deutsche Kultur, Katholizismus und Weltkrieg* (German culture, Catholicism, and world war). Significantly Pfeilschifter's contributors, like Rosenberg himself, were predominantly academic theologians rather than clerics. The Vatican had asked Erzberger to keep the episcopate out of the controversy.[20]

The Germans were portrayed not merely as anti-Catholic but frequently also as anti-Christian. The root of this second charge was liberal theology. In Germany biblical scholarship had neglected faith in favour of research, religion in favour of rationality, and so removed the moral force from Christian teaching. The invasion of Belgium was cited as evidence, the act of a society which denied the natural law of the civilized world. Adolf von Harnack and Ernst von Dryander, the primate of the German Evangelical church, rejected these allegations. In late August the first of a succession of manifestos was drawn up under their aegis, and addressed to Evangelical churches abroad—particularly in the United States. Its distribution was entrusted to the Deutsche Evangelische Missions-Hilfe, created in December 1913 to promote missionary work in the German colonies. The fusion of Evangelism and propaganda, the broadening in focus from Germany's own overseas possessions to the world as a whole, helped redefine the church's mission in political and cultural as well as religious terms.[21]

[20] Geinitz, *Kriegsfurcht und Kampfbereitschaft*, 280, 398; Epstein, *Erzberger*, 101–2; Erzberger, *Erlebnisse*, 11–18; Pfeilschifter (ed.), *Deutsche Kultur, Katholizismus und der Weltkrieg*.

[21] Andresen, *Dryander*, 313–16, 331–3, 346–8; Pressel, *Kriegspredigt*, 108–18.

The result was a new theology. The war enabled orthodox Lutherans and liberal theologians to converge. Both saw victory as the means to the application of the kingdom of God within an ethical community; Protestantism could be confirmed as the religious bedrock of the German cultural state.[22] The Lutheran church's evangelism, therefore, embraced the spirit of 1914 as an opportunity to relaunch itself not only in the wider world but also at home. Preachers did not move from their texts to contemporary life, but vice versa, addressing their parishioners' immediate experiences and using the Bible to reinforce the message. The Old Testament acquired a fresh relevance—evidence of God's use of war as judgement, and of his endorsement of a chosen people seeking a political and cultural independence.[23]

Luther himself became a hero—the fusion, like Joan of Arc in France, of religion, nationality, and historical identity. The Reformation joined the wars of unification in the historical foundations of the German state. The early Protestant church had relied on the secular powers for its survival, and was thus prey to state intervention from the outset of its existence.[24] Luther had recognized the dangers by propounding his doctrine of the two kingdoms. But, in seeking to separate the spiritual from the temporal, he had curtailed the church's role in national life while not preventing its appropriation for the purposes of nationalism. The Pan-German League and, particularly, the Army League were overwhelmingly Protestant in composition.[25]

God, therefore, became an active participant in the historical process. His nature in these circumstances was not determined by the needs of private morality but of public. The crowds on 1 August 1914 sang Luther's great hymn, 'Ein feste Burg ist unser Gott', a song that was at once both national and religious. Ernst Troeltsch moved under the impact of the war from theology to history, because the German form of Christianity was Lutheranism and the German state embodied the best form of Lutheranism in political practice. Patriotism, therefore, became both a source of faith and a Christian duty.[26]

---

[22] Huber, *Kirche und Öffentlichkeit*, 145, 168–9.
[23] Pressel, *Kriegspredigt*, 35–44; Doehring, *Ein feste Burg*, ii. 363–5.
[24] Marrin, *Last crusade*, 109–18.
[25] Ferguson, *Pity of war*, 18.
[26] Pressel, *Kriegspredigt*, 75–6, 176, 202–4; Rubanowice, *Crisis in consciousness*, 102–3, 107–9.

On the occasion of the opening of the Reichstag on 4 August 1914 Ernst von Dryander preached in Berlin cathedral. The Kaiser was in the congregation. Dryander was entirely persuaded of the significance of this marriage of church and state. As he was later to say, 'I owe the best that I have to my fatherland not *in spite* of, but *because* of, my being a Christian—the best not only in time, strength and wealth, but also in the marrow of my strength, my relationship to God and to my faith'.[27] His text on 4 August was St Paul's Epistle to the Romans, chapter 8, verse 3: 'If God be for us, who can be against us?' His assumptions were cultural, in his rejection of materialism and his hopes of national regeneration, and they were historical. He cited Treitschke, and he summoned up Luther and 'the old heroes of 1813'. 'We march to the fight for our culture against unculture, for German morality against barbarity, for the free, German, God-fearing person against the instincts of the uncontrolled mass ... We know that we fight not only for our existence but also for the existence of the most holy of possessions that we have to perpetuate.' The key issue, he concluded, was not 'whether God is with us, but whether we are with God'.[28]

Dryander explored themes which became central to Germany's sense of purpose, whether expressed by believers or agnostics. Bernhardi, the military publicist, wrote in *Internationale Monatsschrift* in November 1914: 'God reveals himself in victory by which He makes truth defeat appearance. It is God's law that condemns the vanquished, and it is, therefore, His will that the conqueror should dictate such peace terms as shall display his inner strength by his external power and greatness.'[29] The philosopher and, in due course, founding father of sociology Max Scheler, who was the son of a Protestant and a Jew, but who later converted to Catholicism, contended that the war was a holy war precisely because it was about fundamental issues associated with the existence of the nation. War was the moment when God passed judgement, and the mobilization of the state's resources as it put its fate in God's hands in itself made the war a just one.[30]

[27] Pressel, *Kriegspredigt*, 203.

[28] Doehring, *Ein feste Burg*, i. 14–18; see also Andresen, *Dryander*, 319–20.

[29] Verhey, 'The "spirit" of 1914', 289; see also Lange, *Marneschlacht und deutsche Öffentlichkeit*, 113–16.

[30] Scheler, *Der Genius des Krieges* (first published in article form in October 1914, and as a book in 1915), 55, 86–8.

For thinkers in France and Britain the Nietzschean spin in this sort of thought—'the religion of valour, the religion of might is right', in the words of *The Times* on 10 September 1914[31]—suggested not a reworked Christianity but a departure from it. Baudrillart's Institut Catholique saw the root of the problem as Kant, Nietzsche's logical predecessor. In asserting that God was beyond human comprehension and that man could know only himself, Kant had, in the eyes of French Catholics, elevated man and with him the law and the moral authority of the state. For republicans, socialists, and anti-Catholics in France, Kant's emphasis on rationality was of course right and Catholicism superstitious and wrong. Conveniently too, Kant had written about perpetual peace.[32]

The divisions in French approaches to Kant highlighted not only the split between church and state in the republic but also the pre-war French conviction that there were two Germanies. Kant personified the cerebral, spiritual, and reasoned Germany; Hegel the materialist, militarist, and nationalist. During the war itself this division would find another, more practical interpretation, that of a German people (presumably Kantian) being guided, gulled, and misled by a German leadership (presumably Hegelian). In due course much Entente propaganda came to rest on the conviction that the German masses were fundamentally liberal and rational. But the corollary of such a belief was that the allied purpose was itself revolutionary. Its task was not only to clear the Germans out of France and Belgium but also to overthrow the Kaiser and establish a German republic. Guided by their hopes of internationalism and perpetual peace, French socialists were as intellectually committed to the dismemberment of Germany—and therefore to a big war for big ideas—as were French Catholics and German Protestants.[33]

For many French intellectuals the notion of the two Germanies was scuppered by the manifesto of ninety-three German university teachers published by the *Berliner Tageblatt* and other major newspapers on 4 October 1914. Provocatively addressed 'An die Kulturwelt' (to the world of culture), it made clear that the unity of orthodox Lutherans and academic theologians which underpinned the August manifesto had now been extended. The ideas embraced by the church were endorsed by

[31] Martin, *Times Literary Supplement*, 5 Aug. 1994, 11–12.
[32] Hanna, *Mobilization of intellect*, 108–18, and for what follows 9–10.
[33] Robert, *Les Ouvriers*, 28–30; also Milner, *Dilemmas of Internationalism*, 214.

professors from throughout the Reich, of all religions and of all disciplines. Most claimed to be apolitical in the sense of being above party, but all parties bar the SPD were represented.

The signatories had international reputations as well as international contacts. Their pre-war assumptions were neither insular nor chauvinist. One of the most distinguished was the classicist Ulrich von Wilamowitz-Moellendorff. Wilamowitz orchestrated the preparation of a further manifesto published on 16 October 1914 in English, French, Italian, and Spanish as well as German. Thanks to the efforts of Dietrich Schäfer, professor of history, pupil of Treitschke, and pre-war stalwart of the Army League, virtually the entire German academic profession— over 4,000 names, including almost every professor at every German university—endorsed the declaration. Numbered among them were closet socialists, future pacifists, and sceptics, including Max Weber and Albert Einstein. The professors rejected the accusations that Germany had caused the war, had broken international law in its invasion of Belgium, and had committed atrocities against the civilian populations of that country and of France. Their list of denials concluded with two assertions: first, that the future of European culture rested on the victory of German so-called 'militarism'; and secondly, that in defining this militarism there was no distinction to be made between Prussia and the rest of Germany, or between the German army and the German nation: 'both are one.'[34]

A third manifesto, emanating from the University of Tübingen and entitled 'Appel au monde civilisé', was published on 17 October. In the long run their combined effects were counter-productive: they disseminated the charges against Germany by repeating them. But the immediate consequences arose from their association of German *Kultur* with German militarism.

The world of scholarship and the arts fragmented into national components. Sigmund Freud, writing in the spring of 1915, mourned science's loss of 'her passionless impartiality'.[35] The Institut de France dismissed

---

[34] Brocke, 'Wissenschaft und Militarismus', 649–64; Schwabe, *Wissenschaft und Kriegsmoral*, 22–4; I have not been able to consult Jürgen Ungern-Sternberg von Pürkel and Wolfgang von Ungern-Sternberg, *Der Aufruf an die Kulturwelt. Das Manifest der 93 und die Anfänge der Kriegspropaganda im Ersten Weltkrieg* (Stuttgart, 1996).

[35] Freud, 'Thoughts for the times', 275.

from its honorary membership all those German professors who had signed the manifesto, and on 3 November 100 members of the French literary and artistic world countered with their own declaration. The signatories, who included representatives of the left like Georges Clemenceau, and of the right like Maurice Barrès, as well as Debussy, Gide, Matisse, and Monet, declared that 'the intellectual and moral richness of humanity is created by the natural variety and independence of all nations' gifts'. The Académie des Sciences replied on the same day in terms which were both more chauvinistic and more questionable: 'Latin and Anglo-Saxon civilisations are those which have produced the majority of the great discoveries in the mathematical, physical and natural sciences in the last three centuries.' It was left to historians like Ernest Lavisse, director of the École Normale Supérieure, to explain the roots of pan-Germanism and to work out the implications of German culture for the German 'theory and practice of war'.[36]

On 12 December 1914 Henri Bergson, the doyen of French philosphy, delivered his presidential address to the Académie des Sciences Morales et Politiques. For Bergson the union of the two Germanies had been effected not in 1914 but in 1871. Germany had opted not for an organic, natural unification, but for a mechanical and artificial form derived from Prussia. The basis of Germany's victories was material prosperity, and the ideas that followed did so as an effect of unification, not as its cause. Germany's philosophy was 'a translation into intellectual terms of her brutality, her appetites, and her vices'. German atrocities, and the belief of German academics that the ends justitifed such means, were evidence of 'barbarism reinforced by civilisation'.[37]

For Bergson individually, and for French academics collectively, herein was the key to the war's purpose. The defence of France was transformed into the defence of civilization. Once again the Huns were at the gates, and this time the threat was far greater because they had harnessed to the cause of barbarity the machinery of the state and the material advantages of industrialization. For those on the left the civilization which they were protecting was the legacy of 1789, equality and fraternity, principles of universal application. For those on the right

---

[36] Hanna, *Mobilization of intellect*, 78–90; Brocke, 'Wissenschaft und Militarismus', 667–8.
[37] Bergson, *Meaning of war*, 18–20, 29–33.

the sources lay further back, with Charles Martel and Charlemagne. Common ground was a recovery of classicism. Athenian republicanism appealed to the left, the reinvigoration of Latin teaching favoured the church. Both saw in the classics an enduring and international definition of civilization which endorsed France's mission.[38]

Bergson's lecture on the meaning of the war was published in English in 1915, and reprinted several times. But British philosophers were hesitant about following his example, for two reasons. The first was the uncertainty of some about making the leap from academic to public life. The war promoted emotion and instinct to the detriment of reason and law, and herein lay the second difficulty. The former qualities were more characteristic of the European philosophical tradition, which included not only Nietzsche but also, as the liberal and would-be neutral, L. T. Hobhouse, pointed out, Bergson himself.[39]

More representative of the British academic profession as a whole than Hobhouse's doubts about public involvement was an initial reluctance to nationalize the world of learning. A group of nine scholars, mostly from Cambridge, wrote to *The Times* on 1 August 1914 to protest against a war with Germany, which was 'leading the way in Arts and Sciences', on behalf of Serbia and Russia, which most certainly were not. Six weeks later fifty-three writers, including G. K. Chesterton, Arthur Conan Doyle, Rudyard Kipling, and H. G. Wells, were prompted by the government to address the editor of the same newspaper in order to condemn Germany's appropriation of 'brute force to impose its culture upon other nations', but they still confessed their high regard for that same culture. Even on 21 October 1914 117 British academics prefaced their reply to the German professors' manifesto with an expression of their deep admiration for German scholarship and science, and an affirmation of their 'ties with Germany, ties of comradeship, of respect, and of affection'.[40]

The sequence of letters shows a conversion that marches in step with, but not ahead of, the pattern of popular recruiting. Its significance lies less

---

[38] Hanna, *Mobilization of intellect*, 142–5, 155–6, 166, 174; also Raithel, *Das 'Wunder' der inneren Einheit*, 379–80.

[39] Wallace, *War and the image of Germany*, 48.

[40] Brocke, 'Wissenschaft und Militarismus', 670; Wallace, *War and the image of Germany*, 24–5.

in the fact that British intellectuals, like those of Germany, came to endorse the government line, and more in their determination, again as in Germany, to forsake reflection and research for action. The Oxford History School produced a succession of pamphlets concerning the causes of the war from mid-September 1914. Like the manifestos of the German professors, these publications became the foundation for more officially directed propaganda. But the dons insisted that their reaction was spontaneous: the initiative was their own.

Like those of France, the scholars of Britain were clear that the cause on which their country had embarked was a universal one. The assumption of this burden was a consequence of empire because, in the words of Alfred Zimmern, 'Of the Great Powers which between them control the destinies of civilisation Great Britain is at once the freest, the largest, and most various'.[41] Britain, therefore, supported France not because it now finally felt able to endorse the claim of the ideas of the French Revolution to universality, but out of respect for France's own evolution to democracy: France, as another Oxford man, the historian Ernest Barker, said, is 'one of the great seed-beds of liberal thought and ideas'.[42]

Civilization, a key word in France, was also a central concept in Britain. However, Alfred Zimmern was clear that its meaning was different in Britain: 'it stands for something moral and social and political. It means, in the first place, the establishment and enforcement of the Rule of Law...and, secondly...the task of making men fit for free institutions.' Britain was fighting for 'Law, Justice, Responsibility, Liberty, Citizenship', concepts which 'belong to civilised humanity as a whole'.[43] The Oxford historians agreed. In their first pamphlet, *Why we are at war: Great Britain's case*, they said that Britain was fighting for 'the public law of Europe'.[44]

Law in this case meant the natural law to which the church too subscribed, and which Christianity had appropriated from the Greeks. It meant less international law in a legal sense and more a common morality; it implied that treaties had a sanctity which derived not merely from the honour of those who signed them but also from a

---

[41] Seton-Watson *et al.*, *War and democracy*, 371.
[42] Wallace, *War and the image of Germany*, 62.
[43] Seton-Watson *et al.*, *War and democracy*, 363–4.
[44] Oxford Faculty of Modern History, *Why we are at war*, 115–16.

Christian world order. 'If', G. W. Prothero wrote, 'international morality is regarded as of no account, a heavy blow is dealt at commercial and
private morality as well. The Reign of Law, the greatest mark of civilization, is maintained in all its parts.' Law was, therefore, indivisible: the
law which regulated international relations was in principle the same as
that which upheld the rights of property, the sanctity of marriage, and
the workings of credit.[45]

The problem was that of giving such academic concepts immediacy.
The Oxford historians tried: 'We are a people in whose blood the cause
of law is the vital element.' Alfred Zimmern went further. As the author
of *The Greek commonwealth*, he was appalled that Wilamowitz-Moellendorff, whose scholarship he admired, could regard Prussia as superior to Athens because Prussia was a monarchy. Zimmern therefore
spurned any constitutional definitions of democracy for something
much more organic: 'Democracy is a spirit and an atmosphere, and
its essence is trust in the moral instincts of the people.' He sidestepped
the troubling issues of empire, crown, and franchise to emphasize the
responsibility which British democracy cast on the individual citizen.[46]

Bethmann-Hollweg helped. His contemptuous reference to the Belgian guarantee as 'a scrap of paper' gave a force to what was otherwise in
danger of being either theory or rhetoric. The Belgians became the
personification of ideas. Hensley Henson, the dean of Durham, likened
them to the Israelites in their sufferings under the tyrannies of Egypt
and Babylon.[47] 'A democracy armed with faith is not merely strong,'
Zimmern explained: 'it is invincible; for its cause will live on, in defeat
and disaster, in the breast of every one of its citizens. Belgium is a living
testimony to that great truth.'[48] Walter Sickert gave these words visual
expression. His own opposition to violence was first undermined by the
emotional jingoism of the music halls which he painted so well. But it
was Belgium that rationalized the shift: in October 1914 he painted *The
soldiers of King Albert the Ready*, based on the defence of Liège, and in
January 1915 he exhibited *The integrity of Belgium*.[49]

---

[45] Gullace, *American Historical Review*, CII (1997), 722–3.
[46] Seton-Watson *et al.*, *War and democracy*, 1–2.
[47] Marrin, *Last crusade*, 129.   [48] Seton-Watson *et al.*, *War and democracy*, 2.
[49] Cork, *Bitter truth*, 54–7; also *The Times Review*, 14 Nov. 1992, pp. 38–9.

Thanks to Belgium, the Asquith cabinet had been able to rally round the rights of small nations and the sovereignty of international law. Thereafter Asquith was able to invert the sequence. Britain fought not for Belgium, but for what Belgium represented. In a speech on 19 September the prime minister defined Britain's reasons for entering the war as threefold: first, to uphold 'the public law of Europe'; secondly, 'to enforce the independence of free states'; and thirdly, 'to withstand...the arrogant claim of a single Power to dominate the development of the destinies of Europe'.[50] By elevating the principles over the principality, Asquith evaded the knotty issues of Belgium's pre-war record as a colonial power. The good ousted the bad. For Germany the opposite was the case. Monolithic and militarist, its crime was the assumption that its culture, a product of the state, was appropriate to peoples whose languages and traditions were different. In the circumstances, the notion of there being two Germanies was a difficult one to sustain.

Surprisingly, Lloyd George tried to do so. In a speech in Bangor on 28 February 1915 he expressed his admiration for German music, German science, and 'the Germany of a virile philosophy that helped to break the shackles of superstition in Europe'. Even now he saw the issue of which Germany would dominate as unresolved, comparing it to a Wagnerian struggle 'between the good and the evil spirit for the possession of the man's soul'. The outcome would depend on who won the war. If Germany was victorious, then 'we shall be vassals, not to the best Germans', but 'to a Germany that talks through the vacuous voice of Krupp's artillery'.[51]

A few others could still see the distinction. Dean Inge took Nietzsche on his own terms, highlighting his praise of individualism and stressing that his writings justified neither militarism nor racism.[52] Alfred Zimmern resisted the temptation to cull extracts from 'Treitschke's brilliant and careful work', or to forget that 'Nietzsche, like many other prophets, wrote in allegory'.[53] But they were increasingly isolated, Zimmern even within his own university. Sir Walter Raleigh, Oxford's professor of English literature, was delighted to have the excuse 'to be rid of the

[50] Seton-Watson *et al.*, *War and democracy*, 239.
[51] Grigg, *Lloyd George*, 216; also 161–6.   [52] Marrin, *Last crusade*, 103.
[53] Seton-Watson *et al.*, *War and democracy*, 350.

German incubus...It has done no good, for many years, to scholarship;—indeed, it has produced a kind of slave-scholarship'.[54] Even
Zimmern's fellow classicist Gilbert Murray, a Liberal, a would-be neutral
before the war and an ardent internationalist after it, saw the opportunity to reassert a specifically British approach to learning, based on
'feeling and understanding' rather than research for its own sake: 'we are
always aiming at culture in Arnold's sense not Bernhardi's.'[55]

Whether Murray read Bernhardi may be doubted; unlike some other
British academics, he had never studied at a German university. Ignorance, not least of the German language, underpinned many of the
portrayals of German ideology. In France, Bergson's idea that German
philosophy had become the pawn of an alliance between militarism and
industrialism was vital to his optimism concerning the war's outcome:
material resources could be exhausted, those of the spirit could not. But
Bergson's interpretation was flawed. It rested on his memories of 1870,
and of France's awareness ever since of its growing inferiority, both
demographically and economically. In 1914 Britain's entry into the war
ensured that collectively the Entente had a combined national income
60 per cent greater than that of the Central Powers.[56] Not Germany but
France now stood to gain from a war of materialism.

Germany's awareness of its economic inferiority directed its thinking
on war along routes very different from those which Bergson—or for
that matter Murray—imagined. Despite his place in Entente demonology, Bernhardi perhaps matters least as an indicator of military
thought, since he was at odds with much of the prevailing ethos in
the general staff. But it is nonetheless worth pointing out that,
according to *Germany and the next war*, war was not to be undertaken
lightly, it should be fought according to moral conventions, and it
should be limited in its objectives.[57] Effectively, Bernhardi gave himself
little choice, since he was highly critical of 'material prosperity, commerce and money-making',[58] the very means which would enable the
war to be fought at greater intensity and for more grandiose aims. In

---

[54] Wallace, *War and the image of Germany*, 36.   [55] Ibid. 38; see also 105.

[56] Ferguson, *Pity of war*, 248.

[57] Marrin, *Last crusade*, 108 (citing Bernhardi, *Germany and the next war*, 18–19, 45, 48, 79,
85–7).

[58] Offer, *Politics and society*, XXIII (1995), 216.

this respect at least, Bernhardi aligned himself with the German army collectively. It feared economic progress as a threat to its warlike and warrior qualities.[59] Material and demographic inferiority in 1914 confirmed its predisposition to trust in alternative strengths. As the year ebbed away, Moltke pinned his hopes of ultimate German victory not on superior armament or even on greater military efficiency but on 'the high idealism of the German people'.[60]

Things of the spirit were the key: *Geist* was the catchword. Moltke himself was an anthroposophist; in private he admitted, 'I live entirely in the arts'.[61] On the eastern front one of his army commanders, August von Mackensen, put his faith in 'our inner strength'.[62] This was not the vocabulary of professionalism or modernism, let alone materialism. Moreover, these soldiers were expressing themselves in terms similar to those used by academics. In *Die Nationen und ihre Philosophie* (1915), Wilhelm Wundt rejected the British idea that individual progress was linked to industrial development. He condemned British ethics, which harnessed economic growth to utilitarianism and materialism to positivism, as the path to shallowness and mediocrity.[63] The sociologist Werner Sombart produced the most extreme version of this thesis. In *Händler und Helden* (Traders and heroes) (1915) he described man as living two lives on earth, one superficial and the other spiritual: life itself was a continuing effort to pass from one to the other. The struggle was essentially a personal one, but war gave it transcendant qualities. In these circumstances the free response to duty's call and the willingness to sacrifice self characterized Sombart's 'hero'. Therefore, the significance of war for the state lay not in social Darwinism, not in terms of the state's standing in relation to its neighbours, but in the nation's ability to elevate the spirit and will of its people. War found the state at its acme. 'The sword and the spirit', Max Scheler wrote, 'can create a beautiful, worthy marriage.' Its fertility was proved for him by the link between the Persian wars and Greek philosophy and between the Napoleonic wars and Hegel. 'The war of 1914', Sombart concluded, 'is the war of Nietzsche.'[64]

[59] Echevarria, *War & Society*, XIII (1995), 23–40.   [60] Verhey, 'The "spirit" of 1914', 311.
[61] Eksteins, *Rites of spring*, 89.   [62] Schwarzmüller, *Zwischen Kaiser und 'Führer'*, 98.
[63] Ringer, *Decline of German mandarins*, 185.
[64] Sombart, *Händler und Helden*, 53, 61–5; Scheler, *Genius des Krieges*, 34–5, 94–5.

Both Sombart and Scheler, born in 1863 and 1874 respectively, belonged to that younger generation which had come to maturity in
Wilhelmine Germany after Bismarck's fall. By contrast, Rudolf Eucken
was already 20 when 1866 had inaugurated a promise that he felt had not
yet been fulfilled. Before unification Germany had found its identity not
in politics but in philosophy, literature, and music. Since then Germans
had worked hard to improve their material lot, but in so doing had lost
their vocation. Eucken, a Nobel prizewinner and the dominant figure in
German philosophy, particularly in spiritual existentialism, hankered for
his subject's return to the centre of national life. The outbreak of the First
World War provided him with the opportunity to fulfil his aspirations.
Like Sombart, Scheler, and the leaders of the church, he celebrated war's
power to reinvigorate the moral health of the individual. And he went as
far or even further in pursuing its collective implications. His 1914
publication, on 'the world historical significance of the German spirit',
asserted that Germany could not be defeated while it remained truly
united and stood fast in its inner strength.[65]

If *Geist* was a word that concerned the feelings of the individual but
could be extended to the community, *Kultur* embraced concepts that
began with the community but were defined nationally. Sombart
quoted Novalis to the effect that 'all culture derives from the relationship of a man with the state'.[66] *Kultur* was shaped by language and
history, but its vitality rested also on the civic virtues to which *Geist*
gave rise—idealism, heroism, subordination to the community.[67] Thus,
the German professors declared in their October manifesto that 'Our
belief is that the salvation of all European culture depends on the
victory for which German "militarism" is fighting, the discipline, the
loyalty, the spirit of sacrifice of the united free German people'.[68]

Kultur's opponent was 'civilization'. There was, of course, a paradox
here. Germany was civilized, in the sense that it had benefited as much
as any state from the advances in science and technology so fundamental to Europe's primacy in the world at the beginning of the twentieth

---

[65] Lübbe, *Politische Philosophie*, 176–84; see, in English, Mommsen, *Imperial Germany*,
206–14.
[66] Sombart, *Händler und Helden*, 74–7.
[67] Chickering, *Imperial Germany*, 135.
[68] Kruse, 'Kriegsbegeisterung', 85.

century. Even Eucken acknowledged this: the distinction of Germans as technicians, traders, and industrialists meant that 'today people are in the habit of calling us the Americans of Europe'.[69] But the civilization which Thomas Mann saw as the opposite of *Kultur* was itself more cultural than technological.[70] In part it was materialistic, and hence damaging to the heroic spirit; in part it was egalitarian, a fruit of 1789. Civilization, according to another philosopher, Paul Natorp, was the culture of society, and that meant a levelling down of the best to conform with the average. It could make a man a slave. *Kultur*, on the other hand, was liberating. The contrast was Kant's, but the context in 1914 was no longer moral but political.[71]

The clash between civilization and culture took German thought back to its late-eighteenth-century roots. In condemning civilization, the philosophers of 1914 were reflecting the rationality of the Enlightenment and the consequences of the French Revolution. They argued that, following what was essentially an alien, French track, philosophy had elevated the rule of law and the rights of the individual, and so had promoted selfishness and materialism. At one level, therefore, the summons of 1914 was a call to rediscover the ideas of the *Aufklärung* and to refurbish the memory of 1813. More important even than Kant or Hegel in the nationalist context was Fichte. Fichte's *Reden an die deutsche Nation* (Speeches to the German nation) (1808) symbolized the engagement of the philosopher with the life of the state, and his endowment of the nation with its own identity and his subordination of the individual to the nation connected the themes of the war of liberation with those of 1914. Between 1890 and 1900 Fichte's philosophy was the subject of only ten noteworthy studies; between 1900 and 1920 over 200 appeared. The context of Fichte's writing, the defeat at Jena in 1806, and the long path from there to liberation, ensured that his relevance did not dwindle as the adversities of the war multiplied.[72]

Although France was home to the Enlightenment and to the alleged triumph of its ideas in politics, France was not, in 1914, Germany's principal ideological foe. As Paul Natorp was prepared to concede,

---

[69] Sieferle, 'Der deutsch–englische Gegensatz', 159.
[70] Mann, 'Gedanken im Kriege', 7.
[71] Lübbe, *Politische Philosophie*, 190–1; Scheler, *Genius des Krieges*, 50.
[72] Lübbe, *Politische Philosophie*, 194–201.

Germany had derived from revolutionary France both its sense of nationalism and the idea of the nation in arms.[73] For writers like Sombart
and Scheler, the clashes between Germany and France, or even
between Germany and Russia, were second-order issues tacked onto the
war of real significance for world history, that between Germany and
Britain. The enemy was capitalism, because this was the true threat to
the spirit.

Sombart, like Wundt, characterized British philosophy as preoccupied with economics. It had neglected matters of the spirit for practical
problems, and the consequences had permeated British life. The elevation of trade resulted in the pursuit of economic self-interest and the
subordination of the state. The latter was seen as no more than a
necessary evil. War, which for Scheler found the state in its highest
form, was for the British superfluous. In their ideal world it would not
exist, and when they did fight they did so for economic objectives and,
very often, by economic means. The aristocracy was motivated by
commerce rather than by honour, and the army and navy were no
more than instruments for armed trade and colonial plunder. But the
British practised cultural as well as economic imperialism. Their empire
swamped alternative languages and traditions. Its aim, J. A. Cramb was
quoted as saying, was 'to give all men within its bounds an English
mind'. The ideal of gentlemanly self-restraint curbed the dynamic effects
of personality and character. Even in international relations Britain, by
the use of balance-of-power theory, elevated weak powers at the expense
of the strong. Its own credentials as a democracy were doubtful: it was a
colonial power abroad and a centralized state (rather than a federal one,
like Germany) at home. Britain nonetheless was bent on persuading the
rest of the world that freedom should be defined solely in political
terms. The fear, above all, was that the 'cant' of capitalism and its
political expression, liberalism, was sapping even German culture of
its own identity.[74] The greatest danger to Germany, in the view of Max
Weber's brother Alfred, was 'Anglicization'.[75]

---

[73] Ibid. 188.

[74] Sombart, *Händler und Helden*, esp. 4–43; Scheler, *Genius des Krieges*, 25–31, 53–4; Kjellen,
Politischen Probleme, 130–4.

[75] Sieferle, 'Der deutsch–englische Gegensatz', 142.

Implicit in Weber's formulation was his recognition that the threat was insidious. Even in late July 1914 Germany had preferred to see itself as the guardian of the civilization of western Europe against Russia. Animosity towards Britain was moderated by the common inheritance of Protestantism. But by the same token, Britain's decision to side with the enemy required more explanation. Its entry into the war was construed as a massive betrayal. Within days, Britain had replaced Russia as the focus for German hatred. Friedrich-Wilhelm Foerster rationalized Britain's behaviour in terms of a dualism not unlike that used by British commentators in regard to Germany. In 1914 the evil, imperialist side of Britain had triumphed over its better, peace-loving aspect. Others were less forgiving: Britain's decision was selfish and exploitative. The war did not confront Britain itself with any direct threat, and its effects could not be morally uplifting when Britain had no intention of committing itself wholeheartedly to its conduct. War, by definition, could not be a source of spiritual elevation when its motivation was economic gain. The clash of philosophies was rendered in popular terms. Britain's decision to side with France and Russia was evidence of its perfidy, and its determination to do so was driven by its pursuit of mammon. Neither honour nor spirit was part of its conceptual vocabulary.[76]

Thus, the outbreak of the war itself marked a change in patterns of thought. Ernst Troeltsch saw it as evidence that ideas stemmed from events, not events from ideas.[77] The reworking of the legacies of the Enlightenment and the French Revolution was not simply a means by which Germany rediscovered its cultural roots; it also helped put a shape on time. The long nineteenth century, which began in 1789, had ended in 1914. If the first date marked the French Revolution, the second marked the German one. The 'ideas of 1914', however much they tapped into the thought of Kant, Hegel, or Fichte, were essentially a new departure. In *Die Ideen von 1914* (The ideas of 1914) (1915), Rudolf Kjellen, a Swedish economist, associated the French Revolution with freedom and the ongoing German revolution with its replacement by

[76] Schwabe, *Wissenschaft und Kriegsmoral*, 27–8; Pressel, *Kriegspredigt*, 128–30; Raithel, *Das 'Wunder' der inneren Einheit*, 102–4, 215; Horn (ed.), *Stumpf*, 26–7; Kennedy, *Anglo-German antagonism*, does of course trace deeper roots.

[77] Pressel, *Kriegspredigt*, 20.

order and responsibility. Johann Plenge picked up these points in 1916 with *1789 und 1914. Die symbolischen Jahre in der Geschichte des politischen Geistes* (1789 and 1914. The symbolic years in the history of the political spirit).

Germany's mission, according to Kjellen, was 'leadership without domination'. World powers had followed one of two models—the Roman, with its tendency to centralize and dominate in a political sense, and the Greek, with its patriarchal presumption of superior values. Britain had veered to the latter, but had not abandoned the former. Germany's task was to promote a third way.[78] 'German freedom', Ernst Troeltsch explained, 'has no craving for world domination, either materially or spiritually. Germany wants freedom of coexistence for various peoples and not the extermination of different possibilities of development nor stereotyping in the name of some alleged law.'[79] Herein were the intellectual foundations for the national liberation movements which Germany sponsored for India, Persia, Tunisia, Egypt, Ireland, and elsewhere. The challenge was to relate means to ends. To beat the British, it had first to join them. Germany's ability to implement the new order was predicated on its achieving world-power status through victory on the battlefield.[80]

Britain was a declining power, as Gerhart von Schulz-Gaevernitz had argued in 1906.[81] It therefore had a vested interest in the status quo, because only thus could it buttress a position which it could no longer sustain by other means. Germany, on the other hand, was in the ascendant, a young nation with a young Kaiser, prepared to embrace innovation in the sciences and the arts. The world's need to advance forced it to fight: progress was impossible without Germany's acceptance of its role as a revisionist power. The idea that Germany went to war as an escape from its domestic dilemma, as a way of resolving the challenge to its conservative elites and of evading pressure for constitutional change, assumes a mood of cultural despair. But many of the Kaiser's own generation saw doors opening, not closing. Adolf von Harnack, the first president of the Kaiser Wilhelm Society, expected

[78] Kjellen, *Politischen Probleme*, 134.   [79] Rubanowice, *Crisis in consciousness*, 112.

[80] Ringer, *Decline of the German mandarins*, 186; Huber, *Kirche und Öffentlichkeit*, 151; Schwabe, *Wissenschaft und Kriegsmoral*, 112.

[81] Sieferle, 'Der deutsch–englische Gegensatz', 144.

the marriage of traditionalism and modernism to lead 'to an unprecedented increase in the vitality of the German organism'.[82] Karl Helfferich, banker not Junker, born in 1872, likened Wilhelm's reign to the Renaissance. In *Deutschlands Volkswohlstand 1888–1913* (Germany's national wealth, 1888–1913), published in 1913, he believed that Germany's economic development was proving Marxism wrong.[83] For many Germans the example of France suggested that full-blown parliamentary government implied atrophy, decay, and disorder. The war intensified Germany's responsibility for renewal. 'The German eagle', Paul Natorp wrote in *Krieg und Friede* (War and peace) in 1915, 'is not like the bird of Minerva, which, according to Hegel, first begins its flight at dusk. We signify the morning chorus of a new day not only for Germany, but also for mankind.'[84]

The so-called failure of German liberals and social democrats to remain true to their beliefs in 1914 becomes more comprehensible when set against the rhetoric of reform rather than reaction. During August 1914 the SPD press was ready to redirect its ire from Russian tsarism to the British bourgeoisie.[85] In *Die Sozialdemokratie* (1915) Paul Lensch used Hegel to argue that Britain had fulfilled its world-historical role, that individualism and liberalism, the British way, had been absorbed, and that now it was Germany's turn to pioneer the nationalization of social democracy.[86] For the liberals, national survival and national identity were sufficiently central to make the appeals of 1914 not uncongenial. Friedrich Naumann argued that British liberalism was inappropriate to Germany, with its different traditions and its greater deference to order and authority. Neither he nor Max Weber could embrace full-blooded parliamentary government with the enthusiasm of a Gladstonian. While their suspicions of the popular will would not have been unfamiliar to mid-nineteenth-century British liberals, their articulation of the alternatives carried collectivist overtones that sprang from very different roots. The people and the state should be united in terms which clearly tapped into the ideas of *Kultur*. The state itself would implement social reform on the worker's behalf but without itself being fully democratic. Instead, a dualism of

---

[82] Johnson, *Kaiser's chemists*, 16.   [83] Williamson, *Helfferich*, pp. v–vi, 111–14.
[84] Lübbe, *Politische Philosophie*, 186.
[85] Kruse, *Krieg und nationale Integration*, 70–6, 92–3, 124–30.
[86] Sieferle, 'Der deutsch–englische Gegensatz', 149–55.

democracy and monarchy, *das soziale Volkskaisertum*, would represent a new synthesis.[87]

The immediate effect of the war was to solidify the intellectual under-pinnings of the monarchy rather than undermine them. The balance of the Bismarckian constitution provided a security against the irrational excesses of the masses, while the unity provided by the crown eliminated the divisions and instability characteristic of republican France. 'We Germans', Kalweit, the chairman of the Danzig church consistory ex-plained, 'are born monarchists.' That did not mean blind allegiance to princes, but that they saw the value in the embodiment of the idea of the state's unity and will in a living person. The words 'monarchy' and 'democracy' too easily suggested an antithesis, Kalweit argued. He pre-ferred to use *Kaiserherrlichkeit* and *Volksmacht*, which not only linked abstractions to people but also—more debatably—implied conver-gence.[88]

Therefore, for many liberals and even some socialists German free-dom was distinct from the freedoms of revolutionary France or liberal Britain. In December 1915 Kurt Riezler tried to define these opposing conceptions of freedom. The west European powers practised 'freedom without regulation, with the fewest possible concessions by the individ-ual to the state, freedom through equality, the formula of the French Revolution'. German freedom, on the other hand, had evolved out of its reaction to the ideas of 1789, and had been defined by Fichte as freedom through the state, an organization set above the individual. The latter was 'ready to concede to the state in all respects, as the state's strengths should be the function of a freedom in which every man is ranked according to his own strengths, but not valued equally'.[89] One gain for the individual was the sense of meaning which arose from sharing in a common endeavour. But more important was the freedom for the spirit which order bestowed. Ernst Troeltsch, who before the war had written on the significance of Protestantism for the modern world, was the key figure in linking this balance between public duty and inner life to Lutheranism. In *Die deutsche Freiheit* (The German freedom) (1915) he

[87] Sheehan, *German liberalism*, 267–78; also Naumann, 'Deutscher Liberalismus', in *Werke*, iv. 316–20; Mai, *Ende des Kaiserreichs*, 33; Struve, *Elites against democracy*.

[88] Doehring, *Ein feste Burg*, ii. 370.

[89] Diary entry, 4 Dec. 1915, Riezler, *Tagebücher*, 317–18; see also 325.

emphasized that the 'progress in the idea of freedom' which 1914 sign-ified 'in the first place must be a thing of feeling and life style, but then also the clearly recognisable spirit of our public arrangements'.[90]

The war, therefore, conferred on Germany the opportunity to propa-gate 'a third way' in political thought as well as in international rela-tions, a path between capitalism and Marxism, individualism and collectivism. Johann Plenge's celebration of the 'ideas of 1914' argued that 'under the necessity of war socialist ideas have been driven into German economic life, its organization has grown together into a new spirit, and so the assertion of our nation for mankind has given birth to the idea of 1914, the idea of German organization, the national unity of state socialism'.[91] Walther Rathenau, who through the Kriegsrohstoff-samt (war raw materials office), set up on 13 August 1914, had tried to apply the principles of corporatism to public life, was therefore both putting the *Burgfrieden* into practice and testing the principles of 'the new economy' for possible post-war application. Reflecting later in the war on what had been achieved, he was more hesitant than Plenge in referring to socialism. 'The new economy' was not so much a creation of the state as an organic growth, established through the resolve of citizens, enabled by the intermediary of the state freely to unite to overcome rivalry between themselves and to co-ordinate their different achievements and qualities. The key words were rationalization and responsibility rather than self-interest and profit: the result would be—and here Rathenau used the title of Wichard von Moellendorff's 1916 publication—a *Gemeinwirtschaft*.[92]

For Paul Lensch, one of the advocates of state socialism, it was the primacy of the community which defined Germany as a modern state, just as it was the principle of individualism which now characterized Britain as backward. Lensch saw Germany's lead over Britain as mani-fested in three fundamental attributes—universal compulsory education, universal suffrage, and universal military service.[93] Militarism and social-ism were therefore not in tension, but were supporting attributes of the

[90] Lübbe, *Politische Philosophie*, 227–30.

[91] Michalka, 'Kriegsrohstoffbewirtschaftung, Walther Rathenau, und die "kommende Wirtschaft"', in id. *Der Erste Weltkrieg*, 497.

[92] Ibid. 494–5; also Michalka, 'Kriegswirtschaft und Wirtschaftskrieg', in Böhme and Kallenberg (eds.), *Deutschland und der Erste Weltkrieg*, 189–90.

[93] Sieferle, 'Der deutsch–englische Gegensatz', 153.

new state. The pre-war argument of the right, that the army was the school of the nation by virtue of its ability to inculcate subordination and service to the community, was now assimilated further to the left. Scheler saw militarism in the sense of conscription as evidence not of barbarism but of a form of higher state development. This admiration for the close links between army and society in Germany was increasingly couched not in the Rousseauesque vocabulary of the nation in arms or of the citizen soldier, but in metaphysical exuberance. For Troeltsch, the *Volksheer,* 'an army of the people', was 'flesh from our flesh and spirit from our spirit'.[94] For Scheler, war was a manly activity which elevated honour and nobility, while subordinating the individual to the state. The experience of war made the collective personalities of nations self-aware: it realized the nation as a 'spiritual total person'.[95] Militarism in this sense not only gave meaning to the community, it also elevated *Kultur* over civilization. Nachum Goldmann, in *Der Geist des Militarismus* (The spirit of militarism) (1915), described the military spirit as the means to human progress because it combined equality of opportunity with the virtues of a meritocracy.[96] A state which honoured the achievements of soldiers over all others also rewarded obedience, courage, self-confidence, and discipline: 'order inside and order outside', as Sombart put it. But in linking militarism back to spirit and to culture Sombart was moved to some of his more excessive statements. Militarism was 'the manifestation of German heroism', the union of Potsdam and Weimar: 'It is *Faust* and *Zarathustra* and Beethoven scores in the trenches. Then the Eroica and the Egmont overture are also the most real militarism.'[97]

Sombart's hyperbole, its reference to Goethe as well as Nietzsche, encapsulated the core of Entente objections to the German ideologies of 1914. Both Goethe and Nietzsche described themselves as Europeans who happened to be Germans. The presumption in Sombart's writing was the opposite, that the rest of Europe needed to be Germanized. He saw the German people as the chosen people of the twentieth century; they were as much an elect as the Greeks and the Jews had been. Such a status imposed on Germany hard obligations.[98] Ultimately it might have to fight

---

[94] Rubanowice, *Crisis in consciousness*, 103.
[95] Scheler, *Genius des Krieges*, 34, 81, 91.
[96] Sieferle, 'Der deutsch–englische Gegensatz', 146.
[97] Sombart, *Händler und Helden*, 84–6.   [98] Ibid. 136–43.

the world to save the world. The messianic implications—and Gotthilf
Herzog likened Germany's burden to that of Christ[99]—incorporated the
sense of mission developed by the war theology of the Lutheran church.
Religion and nation became indistinguishable. In a sermon delivered in
1915 in celebration of the Reformation, Friedrich Rittelmeyer asserted
that, 'The German ability for understanding makes us particularly suited
to be the nation to bring other, non-Christian nations to Christendom,
the German capacity for honesty makes us especially suited to fight the
fight between religion and natural science, and the German spiritual sense
makes us particularly fitted to fight today's battle against superficiality
and shallowness, against the entire culture of materialist ostentation,
which will invade mankind'.[100]

One German soldier wrote in August 1914: 'Our victory enables
Europe's survival with an infusion into German culture of fresh blood.
The victory will not come easily for us. But if there is any sense of right and
of God's direction in history... then the victory must be ours, sooner or
later.'[101] Eucken argued that it was this sense of mission which made
Germany invincible.[102] Germany *could* not lose, because 'the defeat of
Germanness would signify the collapse of mankind',[103] and it *would* not
lose because defeat was impossible for a nation of believers. The longer
the war lasted, the more Dryander and others harped on these aims. The
very duration of the conflict became a test of faith and of spiritual
resolve.[104]

Sombart was at pains to stress that the aim was not German expansion in a territorial sense: 'we have more important things to do. We
have our own spiritual existence to unfold, the German soul to keep
pure.'[105] For some commentators, including Paul Lensch on the left and
Oswald Spengler on the right, it was this very characteristic of the First
World War—that it was about ideas and principles, and their claims to
universality—which likened it to a civil war. And that carried for them
not the pejorative connotations of later generations, of brother fighting
brother, but the devastation, intensity, and length of the Thirty Years
War. Such conflicts were about the issues that really mattered, not about

[99] Pressel, *Kriegspredigt*, 165.   [100] Ibid. 117.   [101] Rürup, 'Der "Geist" von 1914', 4.
[102] Lübbe, *Politische Philosophie*, 183.   [103] Pressel, *Kriegspredigt*, 120.
[104] Ibid. 217–19; Andresen, *Dryander*, 328–9, 341.
[105] Sombart, *Händler und Helden*, 143.

territory or treasury. The difference between civil war as traditionally defined and the world war as they defined it was that now nations rather than classes or social groups appropriated the monopolies in ideas, social structures, and economic organization. In this sense the *Weltkrieg* was a *Weltbürgerkrieg*.[106]

For Scheler, what determined whether a war was just was the commitment of those fighting it to the ideas that were at stake. The quality of those beliefs mattered less than the depth of conviction itself.[107] Many of the 'ideas of 1914' were as subjective as Scheler's definition implied; they represented sloppy thinking by academics anxious to integrate their disciplines with the currents of the day. Lumping was more important than splitting, connections more significant than divisions. The results were unscientific. Historians were happy to collude in history as spirit rather than as objective reality; philosophers sought to make politics moral, but instead politicized morality. By late 1915 some, not least in Germany, began to have second thoughts. A minority of German academics, including Troeltsch, recognized the need for an eventual accommodation, particularly with liberalism and the west. Max Weber and Hans Delbrück were both patriots, but were contemptuous of patriotic emotion. Delbrück was one of the few professors who had refused to sign the manifestos of October 1914, and he continued to emphasize more traditional definitions of militarism, with the consequent need for the army and the conduct of war to be subordinated to political direction.[108] In 1917 the historian Friedrich Meinecke, who charted a course from enthusiasm to moderation, called for the demobilization of the intellect as a precondition for peace.[109] But for most the war's very nature confirmed and deepened the ideas first hatched in 1914. Its duration and intensity, its geographical extension, its effects on the state and its relationship with its citizens, endorsed rather than undermined the idea that 'the war', as the Kaiser wrote to Houston Stewart Chamberlain on 15 January 1917, 'is the battle between two world views'.[110]

[106] Sieferle, 'Der deutsch–englische Gegensatz', 153–4, 160.

[107] Scheler, *Genius des Krieges*, 101.

[108] Brocke, 'Wissenschaft und Militarismus', 682–3; Ringer, *Decline of the German mandarins*, 193–7; Schwabe, *Wissenschaft und Kriegsmoral*, 24–5, 32–3, 49, 55; Huber, *Kirche und Öffentlichkeit*, 179.

[109] Verhey, 'The "spirit" of 1914', 301.

[110] Hartmut Zelinsky, 'Kaiser Wilhelm II, die Werk-Idee Richard Wagners und der Weltkampf', in Röhl (ed.), *Der Ort Kaiser Wilhelms II*, 303.

The Kaiser's conclusion was that such polarities could never be resolved by reconciliation or negotiation: 'One must *win*, the other must *go down*!' On his enemy's side, J. W. Carliol saw the war in very similar terms, albeit much closer to its outbreak: 'Underneath, and at the root of this Titanic conflict, antagonistic principles and powers, irreconcilable ideas and ideals, the ideals of faith and the ideals of force are contending. These are the sap of the contention: the very breath of its nostrils and the source of its vigour. But for them this war, with its world-encompassing issues, would never have come into being; and until one of them has been utterly vanquished it cannot reach its end.'[111]

Of course, an assessment of the impact of the 'ideas of 1914' requires some quantification of the transfer from published page to public thought. How successful were the intellectuals in shaping their contemporaries' views of the war? By September 1915 the eighty-seven pamphlets so far published as a result of the initiative of the Oxford History School had a total print-run of 500,000 copies.[112] Most of the German pamphlets appeared in a comparable series, *Der deutsche Krieg*. The absorption of this output in officially directed propaganda confirms at one level that what these economists, historians, and sociologists were doing was no more than saying what their governments wanted them to say. On the other hand, the effectiveness of propaganda is measured not by the nature of its message but by the degree of receptivity it encounters. On this reckoning, the determination of the belligerent states to appropriate the 'ideas of 1914' suggests that they were also what the people wanted to hear. Soldiers' letters, not only of 1914 but later in the war, frequently mouthed the phrases and ambitions of the academics' outpourings.[113]

This should not be surprising, for many of the ideas flowed in the opposite direction from that which normally preoccupies historians. Anxious to illustrate the influence, or lack of it, of intellectuals, they labour over inadequate evidence in order to show transfers from high culture to popular thought. But in 1914 the experiences of August prompted the intellectuals to assimilate the pre-war nostrums of the populists. Many of the ideas embraced and developed by Troeltsch,

---

[111] Pick, *War machine*, 141–2.   [112] Ferguson, *Pity of war*, 235–6.

[113] See, for Germany, Witkop, *Kriegsbriefe gefallener Studenten*; for Britain, Hynes, *War imagined*, 119; for France, Hanna, *Mobilization of intellect*, 24, 211–16, and Audoin-Rouzeau, *À travers leurs journaux*, 203.

Scheler, Sombart, and others in Germany were already common currency in the publications directed at, and produced on behalf of, the veterans' organizations before the war.[114] The responses of the intellectuals were frequently uninhibited and altruistic. But their openness to ideas from below was also a recognition of the opportunity which the war conferred for internal reintegration. Britain became the vehicle for Germany's worries about its own culture; internal threats were externalized, and so could be attacked; the process of unification from below could be completed by defence against the danger from without. The maintenance of the *Burgfrieden*, or of the *union sacrée*, itself became a condition for victory. In this sense war aims were domestic: Troeltsch told his readers 'to become more German than we were'.[115]

The assimilation of the 'ideas of 1914' had two consequences. First, it removed any effective limits on the objectives of the war very soon after its onset. The ideas applied a vocabulary of absolutes which justified all that followed. Indeed, they could rationalize even defeat, both because it was only material and because its consequences need only be temporary. Secondly, it meant that final victory could not be achieved until one side had reversed the process, most probably by absorbing the ideas of the other. The advocates of 'state socialism' in Germany, like Lensch and Plenge, saw constitutional reform and the abolition of the Prussian three-class franchise as the most important step required of Germany in its role as modernizer. But that was also an objective of the Entente, not because liberals wished to install state socialism in Germany but because they saw democratization as a check to militarism. Thus, for a general like August von Mackensen the enemy was parliamentary government, whether without or within.[116]

The effect of enshrining the war as a conflict between liberalism and militarism, between individualism and community, between anarchy and order, between capitalism and state socialism, was to make its immediate focus the Anglo-German antagonism. But the values which Britain claimed to defend in 1914 were as deeply, or more deeply, etched in the United States of America. Furthermore, as the exigencies of the

---

[114] Rohkrämer, *Militarismus der 'kleinen Leute'*, 178–258.
[115] Rubanowice, *Crisis in consciousness*, 107; see also Schwabe, *Wissenschaft und Kriegsmoral*, 13; Ringer, *Decline of the German mandarins*, 187; Pressel, *Kriegspredigt*, 23.
[116] Schwarzmüller, *Zwischen Kaiser und 'Führer'*, 150.

war forced Britain to modify its liberalism in the pursuit of greater
military effectiveness—to conscript, to curb free trade, to control
profits—so its ideological differences seemed much less striking to
Germans than did those of the United States. The Entente's ease of
access to American markets, and America's condoning of the blockade
which denied Germany comparable status, confirmed that the sin of
perfidy and the pursuit of mammon were even more firmly entrenched
across the Atlantic than across the Channel. The consequence of the
'ideas of 1914' was the extension of the war, not only ideologically but
ultimately geographically.

FURTHER READING

In the guide to further reading, which follows, as far as possible works are given by the names of their author only. Where this has created ambiguity, an abbreviated title of the work itself follows. Further details of title, and place and date of publication are to be found in the bibliography, which lists the principal books and articles used in the writing of this book. The opportunity has been taken to update it with publications that have appeared since the chapters were first completed.

Langdon is a good introduction to the development of the debate on the war's origins, and can therefore also serve as a historiographical guide. Mombauer, *Origins of World War I*, goes over similar ground, but is more up to date. Herwig's article in *International Security* describes what happened to the German historians in the 1920s, and Keith Wilson's collection, *Forging the collective memory*, deals with other nations and their approaches to publication. The involvement of the foreign ministries resulted in serried ranks of volumes of documents.

These were quarried by Luigi Albertini, who completed the definitive history of the war's origins, published in Italian during the Second World War, and in English in three volumes in 1957. This replaced the accounts which appeared in the inter-war period, and it has not been surpassed, despite the work of Fritz Fischer. For those daunted by the scale of Albertini, there are many brief surveys of the issues. The best, by James Joll, is organised thematically, reflecting his own article (to be found in Koch) on the 'unspoken assumptions' which underpinned the war's origins; it can therefore be hard to follow for those who need first to read a narrative account. Many textbooks, including Bridge and Bullen, provide that.

For Germany, Fischer's position can be followed both through his own writings and through the work of Geiss. The two of them were included in the first edition of the volume of essays edited by Koch, although by the time of the second edition this book had become more obviously representative of those who were opposed to Fischer. Berghahn's book, *Germany and the Approach of War*, puts the case for the interrelationship between domestic and foreign policy. Fischer's most distinguished critic was Gerhard Ritter, whose four-volume treatment of German militarism from Frederick the Great to Ludendorff still justifies the epithet magisterial.

Austria-Hungary is served by two outstanding books in English. Bridge takes the long view on the Dual Monarchy's foreign policy; Williamson closes in on July 1914 itself. The articles by Leslie provide detail. Afflerbach's *Der Dreibund* is definitive on the Triple Alliance.

Nothing comparable exists for the Entente, but Williamson, *The Politics of Grand Strategy*, is outstanding on the Anglo-French relationship, particularly its military aspects, and Neilson looks at Britain and Russia. On Russia, read Lieven and McDonald. Bitsch plugs a big gap on Belgium, and can be filled out with Stengers's articles. Keiger deals with France and can be supplemented by Hayne; it is striking how little on this aspect of the war has been written recently in France itself, particularly given the wisdom of what Renouvin and Droz achieved in the inter-war years. Britain is covered by Steiner, whose book has been updated in collaboration with Neilson. Keith Wilson's collection of his own essays, *The Policy of the Entente*, cumulatively puts a more politicised view.

Two contrasting collections of documents, both excellent, deal with the July crisis. Geiss is strong for Germany, is fuller in the German edition than the English, and has a powerful introduction. Williamson and Van Wyk move further east in focus. The Brocks' edition of Asquith's letters to Venetia Stanley are gripping as well as enlightening. Evans's and Pogge von Strandmann's volume of essays allow Michael Brock to use his work to good effect, and in the same volume Spring is helpful on Russia. Keith Wilson's book in a similar genre, *Decisions for War*, is particularly good, with Mark Cornwall putting a new perspective on Serbia and Stengers writing on Belgium. Both volumes have chapters on Germany (by Röhl in Wilson, and by Pogge von Strandmann in his own and Evans's book), which take a Fischerite line; Kaiser's article does not.

Many good articles on war planning were collated by Kennedy in another edited collection. Snyder's book, which tried to embrace the war plans in a general thesis, although exciting at the time, now looks rather tired and over-stated. Recent scholars have been more attracted to the idea of a land arms race: Stevenson, *Armaments and the Coming of War*, is the key text here. Herrmann, despite a title which suggests that he is doing the same thing as Stevenson, is not: his focus is more on comparative tactical development, as is that of Storz. The Schlieffen 'plan' was published by Ritter, but it is now easier to put it in context, with Foley's collection of Schlieffen's writings, and Zuber's book of documents on war planning. The debate on German plans needs to take account of Bucholz and Mombauer, *Moltke*, on the one hand, and Förster and Zuber on the other. Zuber's article generated a healthy debate with Holmes and Foley in *War in History*. French war plans can be followed through Contamine, as well as Williamson's *Politics of Grand Strategy*, and the British through Gooch and Philpott.

On the navies, Berghahn, *Der Tirpitz-Plan*, has now been largely overtaken by Epkenhans. In English, Herwig deals with the main issues regarding the German navy, and Steinberg remains a gem. The Royal Navy was for long dominated by the legacy of Marder, but Sumida and Lambert have revised him in fundamental ways.

The failure of international socialism to stop the war is the subject of two books—Haupt and, especially, Joll. Kirby gives a full account of European socialism in the war itself. The German socialists were treated in a seminal work by Schorske but for readers of German Miller and Kruse are better on the outbreak of the war itself. Stargardt considers the German socialists' ambivalence in relationship to militarism in particular. Kriegel and Becker cover French socialism, and Milner is very helpful on workers not just in France but also elsewhere. McKean, Melancon and Longley confront the divisions in Russia.

Becker pioneered approaches to the issue of popular responses to the outbreak of war in 1914. A brief summary of his conclusions is to be found in English in Fridenson. It may be argued that quantification is not a sensible way to understand emotions, and others have eschewed approaches that are so schematic. Raithel compares France with Germany, and Verhey deals with Germany alone. Geinitz is an excellent case study for Freiburg. These works expose how deficient is our picture for the other belligerents. Sanborn and Lohr have begun to fill the gap for Russia, but Austria-Hungary and Britain remain largely untreated. British voluntary recruiting provides some answers—on which see Simkins and Dewey—and Panayi considers anti-German sentiment.

Works on intellectuals in 1914 fall into two groups—those that deal with their prefigurings of war, and those that treat their rationalisations of it once it had been declared. Wohl, Stromberg and Pick are pre-eminent in the first group. Crook and Lindemann stand out on social Darwinism. On reactions to the war see Wallace for Britain, Hanna for France, and Mommsen, Flasch and Lübbe for Germany. Eksteins straddles the divide in a work that is as engaging as it is stimulating. This, however, is one aspect of the war where sampling the publications of 1914 itself is probably the best way forward.

BIBLIOGRAPHY

Adams, R. J. Q., and Philip P. Poirier, *The conscription controversy in Great Britain, 1900–18* (London, 1987).

Addington, Larry H., *The Blitzkrieg era and the German general staff* (New Brunswick, 1971).

Addison, Christopher, *Four and a half years: a personal diary from June 1914 to January 1919*, 2 vols. (London, 1934).

Afflerbach, Holger, *Der Dreibund: europäische Grossmacht- und Allianzpolitik vor dem Ersten Wertking* (Vienna, 2002).

—— *Falkenhayn. Politisches Denken und Handeln im Kaiserreich* (Munich, 1994).

—— 'Wilhelm II as supreme warlord in the First World War', *War in History*, V (1998), 427–49.

Ageron, Charles-Robert, *Les Algériens musulmans et la France (1871–1919)*, 2 vols. (Paris, 1968).

Ahmad, Feroz, *The Young Turks: the Committee of Union and Progress in Turkish politics 1908–1914* (Oxford, 1969).

—— 'Ottoman armed neutrality and intervention August-November 1914', *Studies in Ottoman Diplomatic History*, IV (1990), 41–69.

—— 'War and society under the Young Turks, 1908–1918', in Albert Hourani, Philip S. Khoury, and Mary C. Wilson (eds.), *The modern Middle East: a reader* (London, 1993).

Albertini, Luigi, *The origins of the war of 1914*, 3 vols. (London, 1957).

Andolenko, C. R., *Histoire de l'armée russe* (Paris, 1967).

Andresen, Bernd, *Ernst von Dryander: eine biographische Studie* (Berlin, 1995).

Andrew, Christopher, *Secret service: the making of the British intelligence community* (London, 1985).

—— *Théophile Delcassé and the making of the Entente Cordiale* (London, 1968).

—— and A. S. Kanya-Forstner, *France overseas: the Great War and the climax of French imperial expansion* (London, 1981).

—— and ——, 'France, Africa, and the First World War', *Journal of African History*, XIX (1978), 11–23.

—— and ——, 'The French colonial party and French colonial war aims 1914–1918', *Historical Journal*, XVII (1974), 79–106.

Ascher, Abraham, 'Radical imperialists within German social democracy 1912–1918', *Political Science Quarterly*, LXXVI (1961), 555–75.

Aschheim, Steven E., *The Nietzsche legacy in Germany 1890–1990* (Berkeley, 1992).

Assmann, Kurt, *Deutsche Seestrategie in zwei Weltkriegen,* (Heidelberg, 1957).

Baer, Alexander, 'The Anglo-German antagonism and trade with Holland, with special reference to foodstuffs, during the First World War', Cambridge University Ph.D. thesis, 1997.

Baker, Paul, *King and country call: New Zealanders, conscription and the Great War* (Auckland, 1998).

Balfour, Michael, *The Kaiser and his times* (London, 1964).

Barbellion, W. N. P., [B. F. Cummings], *The journal of a disappointed man and a last diary* (London, 1984; first published 1919 and 1920).

Barnett, Correlli, *The swordbearers* (London, 1963).

Barooah, Nirode Kumar, *India and the official Germany 1886–1914* (Frankfurt, 1971).

Barthas, Louis, *Les Carnets de guerre de Louis Barthas, tonnelier, 1914–1918*, ed. Rémy Cazals (Paris, 1997; first published 1978).

Bartholdy, Albrecht Mendelssohn, *The war and German society: the testament of a liberal* (New Haven, 1937).

Baudrillart, Alfred, *Les Carnets du Cardinal Baudrillart (1914–1918)*, ed. Paul Christophe (Paris, 1994).

Bauer, Max, *Der grosse Krieg in Feld und Heimat* (Tübingen, 1921).

Becker, Jean-Jacques, *1914: comment les français sont entrés dans la guerre* (Paris, 1977).

—— 'Union sacrée et idéologie bourgeoise', *Revue historique*, CCLXIV, (1980), 65–74.

—— *The Great War and the French people* (Leamington Spa, 1985; first published 1983).

—— 'L'Union sacrée: l'exception qui confirme la régle', *Vingtième siècle revue d'histoire*, 5 (1985), 111–20.

—— *La France en guerre 1914–1918: la grande mutation* (Brussels, 1988).

—— and Stéphane Audoin-Rouzeau, *Les Societés européennes et la guerre de 1914–1918* (Paris, 1990).

Beckett, Ian F. W., and Keith Simpson, *A nation in arms: a social study of the British army in the First World War* (Manchester, 1985).

Beckmann, Max, *Briefe im Kriege* (Munich, 1984; first published 1916).

Bell, A. C., *A history of the blockade of Germany and of the countries associated with her in the Great War, Austria-Hungary, Bulgaria, and Turkey* (London, 1937; actually published 1961).

Bellon, Bernard P., *Mercedes in peace and war: German automobile workers, 1903–1945* (New York, 1990).

Berghahn, V. R., *Germany and the approach of war 1914* (London, 1973).

Berghahn, V. R., *Modern Germany: society, economy and politics in the twentieth century*, 2nd edn. (Cambridge, 1987).

Berghahn, Volker, *Der Tirpitz-Plan. Genesis und Verfall einer innen politischen Krisenstrategie unter Wihelm II* (Düsseldorf, 1971).

—— and Martin Kitchen (eds.), *Germany in the age of total war* (London, 1981).

Bergson, Henri, *The meaning of the war: life and matter in conflict* (London, 1915).

Berliner Geschichtswerkstatt (ed.), *August 1914: ein Volk zieht in den Krieg* (Berlin, 1989).

Bernard, Philippe, and Henri Dubief, *The decline of the Third Republic 1914–1938* (Cambridge, 1985; first published 1975–6).

Bernhardi, Friedrich von, *Germany and the next war* (London, 1914).

Bernstorff, Johann-Heinrich, *Deutschland und Amerika. Erinnerungen aus dem fünfjährigen Kriege* (Berlin, 1920).

Beztuzhev, I. V., 'Russian foreign policy February–June 1914', *Journal of Contemporary History*, I (1966), 93–112.

Binding, Rudolf, *A fatalist at war* (London, 1929).

Bitsch, Marie-Thérèse, *La Belgique entre La France et l'Allemagne 1905–1914* (Paris, 1994).

Blake, Robert *The unknown prime minister: the life and times of Andrew Bonar Law 1858–1923* (London, 1955).

—— (ed.), *The private papers of Douglas Haig 1914–1919* (London, 1952).

Bloch, I. S., *Modern weapons and modern war* (London, 1900).

Bloch, Jean de [i.e. I. S.], *La guerre*, 6 vols. (Paris, 1898).

Boemeke, Manfred F., Roger Chickering, and Stig Förster (eds.), *Anticipating total war: the German and American experiences 1871–1914* (Cambridge, 1999).

Bogacz, Ted, '"A tyranny of words": language, poetry, and anti-modernism in England in the First World War', *Journal of Modern History*, LVIII (1986), 643–68.

Böhme, Helmut, and Fritz Kallenberg (eds.), *Deutschland und der erste Weltkrieg* (Darmstadt, 1987).

Borgert, Heinz-Ludger, 'Grundzüge der Landkriegführung von Schlieffen bis Guderian', in Militärgeschichtliche Forschungsamt, *Handbuch zur deutschen Militärgeschichte 1648–1939*, vol. IX (Munich, 1979).

Bosworth, Richard, *Italy and the approach of the First World War* (London, 1983).

Bourne, J. M., *Britain and the Great War 1914–1918* (London, 1989).

Bourne, K., and D. C. Watt (eds.), *Studies in international history* (London, 1967).

Brécard, Général, *En Belgique auprès du Roi Albert: souvenirs de 1914* (Paris, 1934).

Bridge, F. R., *From Sadowa to Sarajevo: the foreign policy of Austria-Hungary 1866–1914* (London, 1972).

—— and Roger Bullen, *The great powers and the European states system 1815–1914* (London, 1980).

Brock, Michael, and Eleanor Brock (eds.), *H. H. Asquith: letters to Venetia Stanley*, (Oxford, 1985; first published 1982).

Brocke, Bernhard vom, ' "Wissenschaft und Militarismus". Der Aufruf der 93 "an der Kulturwelt!" und der Zusammenbruch der internationalen Gelehrten-republik im Ersten Weltkrieg', in Wm. M. Calder III, Hellmut Flashar, and Theodor Linken (eds.), *Wilamowitz nach 50 Jahren* (Darmstadt, 1985).

Brodie, Bernard, *Sea power in the machine age*, 2nd edn. (Princeton, 1943).

Brown, Judith, *Gandhi's rise to power: Indian politics 1915–1922* (Cambridge, 1972).

—— *Modern India: the origins of an Asian democracy* (Delhi, 1985).

Bruendel, Steffen, *Volksgemeinschaft oder Volkstaat: die 'Ideen von 1914' und die Neuordnung Deutschlands im Ersten Weitkrieg* (Berlin, 2003).

Brusilov, A. A., *A soldier's note-book 1914–1918* (London, 1930).

Bucholz, Arden, *Hans Delbrück and the German military establishment: war images in conflict* (Iowa City, 1985).

—— (ed.), *Delbrück's modern military history* (Lincoln, Nebr., 1997).

—— *Moltke, Schlieffen, and Prussian war planning* (New York, 1991).

Bunselmeyer, Robert E., *The cost of the war 1914–1919: British economic war aims and the origins of reparation* (Hamden, Conn., 1975).

Burchardt, Lothar, *Friedenswirtschaft und Kriegsvorsorge. Deutschlands wirtschaf-tliche Rüstungsbestrebungen vor 1914* (Boppard am Rhein, 1968).

—— 'Walther Rathenau und die Anfänge der deutschen Rohstoffbewirtschaf-tung im Ersten Weltkrieg', *Tradition*, XV (1970), 169–96.

—— 'Zwischen Kriegsgewinnen und Kriegskosten: Krupp im Ersten Weltkrieg', *Zeitschrift für Unternehmensgeschichte*, XXXII (1987), 71–123.

Burk, Kathleen, 'The diplomacy of finance: British financial missions to the United States 1914–1918', *Historical Journal*, XXII (1979), 351–72.

—— Britain, *America and the sinews of war, 1914–1918* (Boston, 1985).

—— (ed.), *War and the state: the transformation of British government, 1914–1919* (London, 1982).

Buse, D. K., 'Ebert and the coming of World War I: a month from his diary', *International Review of Social History*, XIII (1968), 430–48.

Busch, Briton Cooper, *Britain, India, and the Arabs, 1914–1921* (Berkeley, 1971).

Bussy, Carvel de (ed.), *Count Stephen Tisza, prime minister of Hungary: letters (1914–1916)* (New York, 1991).

Cain, P. J., and A. G. Hopkins, *British imperialism: crisis and deconstruction 1914–90* (London, 1993).

Cairns, John C., 'Intellectuals, war, and transcendence before 1914', *Historical Reflections*, X (1983), 1–17.

Calkins, Kenneth R., *Hugo Haase: democrat and revolutionary* (Durham, NC, 1979).

Callwell, C. E., *Experiences of a dug-out 1914–1918* (London, 1920).

Camena d'Almeida, P., *L'Armée allemande avant et pendant la guerre de 1914–1918* (Nancy, 1919).

Cassar, George H., *Kitchener: architect of victory* (London, 1977).

—— *The tragedy of Sir John French* (Newark, 1985).

—— *Asquith as war leader* (London, 1994).

Castex, Raoul, *Théories stratégiques*, 5 vols. (Paris, 1927–35).

Cecil, Hugh, and Peter Liddle (eds.), *Facing Armageddon: the First World War experienced* (London, 1996).

Charmley, John, *Splendid Isolation? Britain, the balance of power and the origins of the First World War* (London, 1999).

Chickering, Roger, *Imperial Germany and the Great War 1914–1918* (Cambridge, 1998).

Churchill, Winston S., *The unknown war: the eastern front 1914–1917* (London, 1941; first published 1931).

Cimbala, Stephen J., 'Steering through rapids: Russian mobilization and World War I', *Journal of Slavic Military Studies* IX (1996), 376–98.

Claus, Rudolf, *Die Kriegswirtschaft Russlands bis zur bolschewistischen Revolution* (Bonn, 1922).

Clayton, Anthony, *France, soldiers and Africa* (London, 1988).

Cochenhausen, Friedrich von, *Conrad von Hoetzendorf: eine Studie über seine Persönlichkeit* (Berlin., 1934).

Coetzee, Frans, and Marilyn Shevin-Coetzee (eds.), *Authority, identity and the social history of the Great War* (Providence, 1995).

Cohen, Stuart A., *British policy in Mesopotamia 1903–1914* (London, 1976).

—— 'The genesis of the British campaign in Mesopotamia, 1914', *Middle Eastern Studies*, XII (1976), 119–32.

Conrad von Hötzendorf, Franz, *Aus meiner Dienstzeit 1906–1918*, 5 vols. (Vienna, 1921–5).

Contamine, Henri, *La Révanche 1871–1914* (Paris, 1957).

Cork, Richard, *A bitter truth: avant-garde art and the Great War* (New Haven, 1994).

Cornwall, Mark (ed.), *The last years of Austria-Hungary: essays in political and military history 1908–1918* (Exeter, 1990).

Corrigan, H. S. W., 'German–Turkish relations and the outbreak of war in 1914: a reassessment', *Past and present*, 36, (1967), 144–52.

Craig, Gordon, *The politics of the Prussian army 1640–1945* (London, 1955).

—— *Germany 1866–1945* (Oxford, 1981; first published 1978).

—— 'The Kaiser and the Kritik', *New York Review of Books*, 18 Feb. 1988.

Crampton, Richard J., *Bulgaria 1875–1918: a history* (Boulder, Col., 1983).

Crampton, Richard J., *The hollow détente: Anglo-German relations in the Balkans 1911–1914* (London, 1979).

Cron, Hermann, *Geschichte des deutschen Heeres im Weltkriege 1914–1918* (Osnabrück, 1990; first published 1937).

Crook, Paul, *Darwinism, war and history: the debate over the biology of war from the 'Origin of the Species' to the First World War* (Cambridge, 1994).

Crouzet, François, 'Recherches sur la production d'armements en France (1815–1913)', *Revue historique*, CCLI (1974), 45–84.

Crow, Duncan, *A man of push and go: the life of George Macaulay Booth* (London, 1965).

Cruickshank, John, *Variations on catastrophe: some French responses to the Great War* (Oxford, 1982).

Cruttwell, C. R. M. F., *A history of the Great War 1914–1918*, 2nd edn. (Oxford, 1936).

—— *The role of British strategy in the Great War* (Cambridge, 1936).

Dahlhaus, Friedrich, *Möglichkeiten und Grenzen auswärtiger Kultur-und Pressepolitik dargestellt am Beispiel der deutschen–türkischen Beziehungen 1914–1918* (Frankfurt am Main, 1990).

Dallin, Alexander *et al.*, *Russian diplomacy and eastern Europe 1914–1917* (New York, 1963).

Daniel, Ute, *The war from within: German working-class women in the First World War* (Oxford, 1997; first published 1989).

Danilov, Youri, *La Russie dans la guerre mondiale (1914–1917)* (Paris, 1927).

David, Edward (ed.), *Inside Asquith's cabinet: from the diaries of Charles Hobhouse* (London, 1977).

Davis, Lance E., and Robert A. Huttenback, *Mammon and the pursuit of empire: the political economy of British imperialism 1860–1912* (Cambridge, 1986).

Deák, István, *Beyond nationalism: a social and political history of the Habsburg officer corps, 1848–1918* (New York, 1990).

Dedijer, Vladimir, *The road to Sarajevo* (London, 1967).

De Groot, Gerard J., 'Educated soldier or cavalry officer? Contradictions in the pre–1914 career of Douglas Haig', *War & Society*, IV (1986), 51–69.

—— *Douglas Haig, 1861–1928* (London, 1988).

—— *Blighty: British society in the era of the Great War* (London, 1996).

Deist, Wilhelm (ed.), *The German military in the age of total war* (Leamington Spa, 1985).

Delbrück, Clemens von, *Die wirtschaftliche Mobilmachung in Deutschland 1914* (Munich, 1924).

Delbrück, Hans, *Krieg und Politik 1914–1916* (Berlin, 1918).

Dewey, P. E., 'Military recruiting and the British labour force during the First World War', *Historical Journal*, XXVII (1984), 199–223.

Dignan, Don, *The Indian revolutionary problem in British diplomacy 1914–1919* (New Delhi, 1983).

Dix, Arthur, *Wirtschaftskrieg und Kriegswirtschaft: zur Geschichte des deutschen Zusammenbruchs* (Berlin, 1920).

Djemal Pasha, *Memoirs of a Turkish statesman 1913–1919* (London, [1922]).

Djordjovic, Dimitrije, ' "Vojovda" Radomir Putnik', in Bela K. Király and Albert A. Nofi (eds.), *East central European war leaders: civilian and military* (Boulder, Col., 1988).

Dockrill, Michael, and David French (eds.), *Strategy and intelligence: British policy and intelligence during the First World War* (London, 1996).

Doehring, Bruno (ed.), *Ein feste Burg: Predigten und Reden aus eiserner Zeit*, 2 vols. (Berlin, 1915).

Doerries, Reinhard R., *Washington–Berlin 1908/1917: die Tätigkeit des Botschafters Johann Heinrich Graf von Bernstorff in Washington vor dem Eintritt der Vereingten Staaten von Amerika in den Ersten Weltkrieg* (Dusseldorf, 1975); English edition, *Imperial challenge: Ambassador Count Bernstorff and German–American relations, 1908–1917* (Chapel Hill, 1989).

Doise, Jean, and Maurice Vaïsse, *Diplomatie et outil militaire 1871–1969* (Paris, 1987).

d'Ombrain, Nicholas, *War machinery and high policy: defence administration in peacetime Britain 1902–1914* (Oxford, 1973).

Douglas, Roy, 'Voluntary enlistment in the First World War and the work of the Parliamentary Recruiting Committee', *Journal of Modern History*, XLII (1970), 564–85.

Droz, Jacques, *Les Causes de la première guerre mondiale* (Paris, 1973).

Dua, R. P., *Anglo-Japanese relations during the First World War* (New Delhi, 1972).

Ducasse, André, Jacques Meyer, and Gabriel Perreux, *Vie et mort des français 1914–1918* (Paris, 1959).

Dülffer, Jost, 'Limitations on naval warfare and Germany's future as a world power: a German debate 1904–1906', *War & Society*, III (1985), 23–43.

Dunn, J. C., *The war the infantry knew 1914–1919: a chronicle of service in France and Belgium* (London, 1987; first published 1938).

Duroselle, Jean-Baptiste, *La France et les français 1914–1920* (Paris, 1972).

—— *La Grande Guerre des français: l'incomprehensible* (Paris, 1994).

Duus, Peter (ed.), *The Cambridge History of Japan*, 6 vols. (Cambridge, 1988–99).

—— Ramon H. Myers, and Mark R. Peattie (eds.), *The Japanese informal empire in China, 1895–1937* (Princeton, 1980).

Dyer, Gwynne, 'The origins of the 'nationalist' group of officers in Turkey 1908–18', *Journal of Contemporary History*, VIII (1973), 121–64.

Echenberg, Myron, *Colonial conscripts: the 'tirailleurs sénégalais' in French West Africa, 1857–1960* (Portsmouth, NH, 1991).

Echevarria, Antulio J., II, 'On the brink of the abyss: the warrior identity and German military thought before the Great War', *War & Society*, XII (1995), 23–40.

—— 'A crisis in warfighting: German tactical discussions in the late nineteenth century', *Militärgeschichtliches Mitteilungen*, 55, (1996), 51–68.

—— 'General staff historian Hugo Freiherr von Freytag-Loringhoven and the dialectics of German military thought', *Journal of Military History*, LX (1996), 471–94.

Eley, Geoff, 'The view from the throne: the personal rule of Kaiser Wilhelm II', *Historical Journal*, XXVIII (1985), 469–85.

Ekoko, Elango, 'British war plans against Germany in West Africa, 1903–14', *Journal of Strategic Studies*, IV (1984), 440–56.

Eksteins, Modris, *Rites of spring: the Great War and the birth of the modern age* (London, 1989).

Elze, Walter, *Tannenberg. Das deutsche Heer von 1914. Seine Grundzüge und deren Auswirkungen im Sieg an der Ostfront* (Breslau, 1928).

—— *Der strategische Aufbau des Weltkrieges 1914–1918* (Berlin, 1933).

Epkenhans, Michael, *Die wilhelminische Flottenrüstung 1908–1914. Weltmachtstreben, industrieller Fortschritt, soziale Integration* (Munich, 1991).

—— 'Military–industrial relations in Imperial Germany, 1870–1914', *War in History*, X (2003), 1–26.

Epstein, Klaus, *Matthias Erzberger and the dilemma of German democracy* (New York, 1971).

Erzberger, Matthias, *Die Rüstungsausgaben des Deutschen Reiches* (Stuttgart, 1914).

—— *Erlebnisse im Weltkrieg* (Stuttgart, 1920).

Evans, David C., and Mark R. Peattie, *Kaigun: strategy, tactics, and technology in the Imperial Japanese Navy, 1887–1941* (Annapolis, 1997).

Evans, R. J. W., and Hartmut Pogge von Strandmann (eds.), *The coming of the First World War* (Oxford, 1988).

Fairbanks, Charles H., jr, 'The origins of the Dreadnought revolution: an historiographical essay', *International History Review*, XIII (1991), 246–72.

Falkenhayn, Erich von, *General headquarters 1914–1916 and its critical decisions* (London, [1919]).

Falls, Cyril, *The First World War* (London, 1960).

Falzeder, Ernst, and Eva Brabant, *The correspondence of Sigmund Freud and Sándor Ferenczi*, vol. II, *1914–1919*, (Cambridge, Mass. 1996).

Farrar, L. L., jr, *The short-war illusion: German policy, strategy and domestic affairs, August–December 1914* (Santa Barbara, 1973).

—— *Divide and conquer: German efforts to conclude a separate peace, 1914–1918* (Boulder, Col. 1978).

Farrar, Marjorie Millbank, 'Politics versus patriotism: Alexandre Millerand as French minister of war', *French Historical Studies*, XI (1980), 577–609.

—— *Principled pragmatist: the political career of Alexandre Millerand* (New York, 1991).

Fay, Sidney Bradshaw, *The origins of the world war* (New York, 1934).

Feldman, Gerald D., *Army, industry and labor in Germany 1914–1918* (Princeton, 1966).

—— 'The political and social foundations of Germany's economic mobilization, 1914–1916', *Armed Forces and Society*, III (1976), 121–45.

—— *The great disorder: politics, economics and society in the German inflation 1914–1924* (New York, 1993).

—— *Hugo Stinnes. Biographie eines Industriellen 1870–1924* (Munich, 1998).

Ferguson, Niall, 'Germany and the origins of the First World War: new perspectives', *Historical Journal*, XXXV (1992), 725–52.

—— 'Public finance and national security: the domestic origins of the First World War revisited', *Past and Present*, 142 (1994), 141–68.

—— *Paper and iron: Hamburg business and German politics in the era of inflation, 1897–1927* (Cambridge, 1995).

—— *The pity of war* (London, 1998).

Ferro, Marc, *The Great War 1914–1918* (London, 1973).

Ferry, Abel (ed.), *Les Carnets secrets (1914–1918)* (Paris, 1957).

Fischer, Fritz, *Germany's aims in the First World War* (London, 1967; first published 1961).

—— *World power or decline: the controversy over Germany's aims in the First World War* (London, 1974; first published 1965).

—— *War of illusions: German policies from 1911 to 1914* (London, 1975; first published 1969).

Fischer, H. C., and E. X. Dubois, *Sexual life during the world war* (London, 1937).

Kurt Flasch, *Die geistige Mobilmachung. Die deutsche Intellektuellen und der erste Weltkrieg* (Berlin, 2000).

Flood, P. J., *France 1914–1918: public opinion and the war effort* (Basingstoke, 1990).

Florinsky, Michael T., *The end of the Russian empire* (New Haven, 1931).

Foch, Ferdinand, *The memoirs of Marshal Foch* (London, 1931).

Foerster, Wolfgang, *Le comte Schlieffen et la guerre mondiale: la stratégie allemande pendant la guerre de 1914–1918* (Paris, 1929; first published 1921); English edition, *Count Schlieffen and the world war* (US Army War College, 1983).

Foley, Robert T. (ed.), *Alfred von Schlieffen's military writings* (London, 2003).

—— 'Schlieffen's last Kriegsspiel', *War Studies Journal*, III (1998), 117–33; IV (1999), 97–115.

Fontaine, Arthur, *French industry during the war* (New Haven, 1926).

Fontana, Jacques, *Les Catholiques français pendant la grande guerre* (Paris, 1990).

Förster, Stig, *Der doppelte Militarismus. Die deutsche Heeresrüstungspolitik zwischen Status-quo-Sicherung und Aggression, 1890–1913* (Stuttgart, 1985).

—— 'Der deutsche Generalstab und die Illusion des kurzen Krieges, 1871–1914. Metakritik eines Mythos', *Militärgeschichtliche Mitteilungen*, 54 (1995), 61–95.

—— 'Im Reich des Absurden. Die Ursachen des Ersten Weltkrieges', in Bernd Wegner (ed.), *Wie Kriege entstehen* (Padersorn, 2000).

Forsyth, Douglas J., *The crisis of Liberal Italy: monetary and financial policy, 1914–1922* (Cambridge, 1993).

France—see Ministère de la Guerre

Frantz, Gunther (ed.), *Russland auf dem Wege zur Katastrophe. Tagebücher des Grossfürsten Andrej und des Kriegsministers Poliwanow. Briefe der Grossfürsten an den Zaren* (Berlin, 1926).

Fraser, T. G., 'Germany and Indian revolution', *Journal of Contemporary History*, XII (1977), 255–72.

—— 'India in Anglo-Japanese relations during the First World War', *History*, LXIII (1978), 366–82.

Freedman, Lawrence, Paul Hayes, and Robert O'Neill (eds.), *War, strategy and international politics: essays in honour of Sir Michael Howard* (Oxford, 1992).

French, David, *British economic and strategic planning 1905–1915* (London, 1982).

—— *British strategy and war aims 1914–1916* (London, 1986).

Freud, Sigmund, 'Thoughts for the times on war and death' (1915), in James Strachey (ed.), *The standard edition of the complete psychological works of Sigmund Freud*, vol. XIV (London, 1957).

Fridenson, Patrick, *1914–1918: l'autre front* (Paris, 1977); English edition, *The French home front 1914–1918* (Providence, RI, 1992).

Friedman, Isaiah, *Germany, Turkey, and Zionism 1897–1918* (Oxford, 1977).

Fritzsche, Peter, *Germans into Nazis* (Cambridge, Mass, 1998).

Fuller, William C., jr, *Civil–military conflict in imperial Russia 1881–1914* (Princeton, 1985).

—— *Strategy and power in Russia 1600–1914* (New York, 1992).

Galet, Émile Joseph, *Albert king of the Belgians in the Great War* (London, 1931).

Galbraith, John S., 'British war aims in World War I: a commentary on statesmanship', *Journal of Commonwealth and Imperial History*, XIII (1984), 25–45.

Gall, Lothar, Gerald Feldman, Harold James, Carl-Ludwig Holtfrerich, and Hans E. Büschger, *The Deutsche Bank 1870–1995* (London, 1995).

Ganz, A. Harding, 'Colonial policy and the imperial German navy', *Militärgeschichtliche Mitteilungen*, 21 (1977), 35–52.

Gat, Azar, *The development of military thought: the nineteenth century* (Oxford, 1992).

Gatrell, Peter, 'After Tsushima: economic and administrative aspects of Russian naval rearmament, 1905–1913', *Economic History Review*, 2nd series, XLIII (1990), 255–70.

—— *Government, industry and rearmament in Russia, 1900–1914: the last argument of tsarism* (Cambridge, 1994).

—— and Mark Harrison, 'The Russian and Soviet economies in two world wars: a comparative view', *Economic History Review*, 2nd series, XLVI (1993), 425–52.

Gatzke, Hans W., *Germany's drive to the west (Drang nach Westen): a study of Germany's western war aims during the First World War* (Baltimore, 1950).

Geinitz, Christian, *Kriegsfurcht und Kampfbereitschaft. Das Augusterlebnis in Freiburg. Eine Studie zum Kriegsbeginn 1914* (Essen, 1998).

Geiss, Imanuel, 'The outbreak of the First World War and German war aims', *Journal of Contemporary History*, I (1966), 75–91.

—— *July 1914: the outbreak of the First World War: selected documents* (London, 1967 ; German edition, 2 vols, Hannover, 1964).

Gemzell, Carl-Axel, *Organization, conflict, and innovation: a study of German naval strategic planning 1888–1940* (Lund, 1973).

Genevoix, Maurice, *Neath Verdun, August–October 1914* (London, 1916).

George, Mark, 'Liberal opposition in wartime Russia: a case study of the Town and Zemstvo Unions, 1914–1917', *Slavonic and East European Review*, LXV (1987), 371–90.

Germains, Victor Wallace, *The Kitchener armies: the story of a national achievement* (London, 1930).

Geyer, Dietrich, *Russian imperialism: the interaction of domestic and foreign policy 1860–1914* (Leamington Spa, 1987).

Geyer, Michael, *Deutsche Rüstungspolitik 1860–1980* (Frankfurt am Main, 1984).

Gifford, Prosser, and Wm. Roger Louis (eds.), *Britain and Germany in Africa: imperial rivalry and colonial rule* (New Haven, 1967).

Gilbert, Bentley Brinkerhoff, 'Pacifist to interventionist: David Lloyd George in 1911 and 1914. Was Belgium an issue?', *Historical Journal*, XXVIII (1985), 863–85.

—— *David Lloyd George: a political life. The organizer of victory 1912–1916* (London, 1992).

Gilbert, Charles, *American financing of World War I* (Westport, Conn., 1970).

Gilbert, Martin, *Winston S. Churchill*, vol. III, *1914–1916*, and companion volume (London 1971–2).

—— *First World War* (London, 1994).

Glaise von Horstenau, Edmund, *Ein General im Zwielicht. Die Erinnerungen Edmund Glaises von Horstenau. Band 1. K. u. k. Generalstabsoffizier und Historiker* (Vienna, 1980).

Gleason, William, 'The all-Russian Union of Zemstvos and World War I', in Terence Emmons and Wayne S. Vucinich (eds.), *The Zemstvo in Russia: an experiment in local self-government* (Cambridge, 1982).

Goldrick, James, 'The battleship fleet: the test of war, 1895–1919', in J. R. Hill (ed.), *The Oxford Illustrated History of the Royal Navy* (Oxford, 1995).

Golvine, N., *The Russian army in the world war* (New Haven, 1931).

—— *The Russian campaign of 1914: the beginning of the war and operations in East Prussia* (Fort Leavenworth, 1933).

—— 'La Bataille de Galicie', *Revue militaire française*, 158 (août 1934), 220–50; 159 (sept. 1934), 281–301.

Goltz, Colmar von der, *Denkwürdigkeiten* (Berlin, 1932).

Gooch, John, *The plans of war: the general staff and British military strategy c1900–1916* (London, 1974).

—— *The prospect of war: studies in British defence policy 1847–1942* (London, 1981).

Gordon, Andrew, 'The crowd and politics in imperial Japan: Tokyo 1905–1918', *Past and Present*, 21 (1988), 141–70.

Gordon, Donald C., *The dominion partnership in imperial defense, 1870–1914* (Baltimore, 1965).

Gordon, Michael, 'Domestic conflict and the origins of the First World War: the British and German cases', *Journal of Modern History*, XLIV (1974), 191–226.

Gordon-Duff, Lachlan, *With the Gordon Highlanders to the Boer War and beyond* (Macclesfield, 1998).

Görlitz, Walter (ed.), *The Kaiser and his court: the diaries, note books and letters of Admiral Georg von Müller, Chief of the Naval Cabinet, 1914–1918* (London, 1961; first published 1959).

Gottlieb, W. W., *Studies in secret diplomacy during the First World War* (London, 1957).

Gourko, Basil, *Memories and impressions of war and revolution in Russia 1914–1917* (London, 1918).

Graf, Daniel W., 'Military rule behind the Russian front 1914–1917: the political ramifications', *Jahrbücher für Geschichte Osteuropas*, XXII (1974), 390–411.

Granier, Gerhard, 'Deutsche Rüstungspolitik vor dem Ersten Weltkrieg. General Franz Wandels Tagebuchaufzeichnungen aus dem preussischen Kriegsministerium', *Militärgeschichtliche Mitteilungen*, 38 (1985), 123–62.

Gratz, Gustav, and Richard Schüller, *Der wirtschaftliche Zusammenbruch Österreich-Ungarns* (Vienna, 1930).

Gray, Colin, *The leverage of sea power: the strategic advantages of navies in war* (New York, 1992).

Grebler, Leo, and Wilhelm Winkler, *The cost of the world war to Germany and Austria-Hungary* (New Haven, 1940).

Grieves, Keith, ' "Lowther's Lambs": rural paternalism and voluntary recruitment in the First World War', *Rural History*, IV (1993), 55–75.

Griffiths, Richard, *Marshal Pétain* (London, 1970).

Grigg, John, *Lloyd George: from peace to war 1912–1916* (London, 1985).

Groener, Wilhelm, *Der Feldherr wider Willen. Operative Studien über den Weltkrieg* (Berlin, 1930).

—— *Lebenserinnerungen. Jugend, Generalstab, Weltkrieg*, ed. Hiller von Gaertringen (Göttingen, 1957).

Groh, Dieter, 'The "unpatriotic socialists" and the state', *Journal of Contemporary History*, I (1966), 151–77.

Grove, Mark, 'The development of Japanese amphibious warfare, 1874 to 1942', in Strategic and Combat Studies Institute, *Occasional Paper*, 31 (1997).

Guillen, P. (ed.), *La France et l'Italie pendant la première guerre mondiale* (Grenoble, 1976).

Guéno, Jean-Pierre, and Yves Laplume, *Paroles de poilus: lettres et carnets du front (1914–1918)* (Paris, 1998).

Guinn, Paul, *British strategy and politics 1914 to 1918* (Oxford, 1965).

Gullace, Nicoletta F., 'Sexual violence and family honor: British propaganda and international law during the First World War', *American Historical Review*, CII (1997), 714–47.

Güth, Rolf, 'Die Organisation der deutschen Marine in Krieg und Frieden 1913–1933', in Militärgeschichtliches Forschungsamt, *Handbuch zur deutschen Militärgeschichte 1684–1939. VIII. Deutsche Marinegeschichte der Neuzeit* (Munich, 1977).

Gutsche, Willibald, 'Die Entstehung des Kriegausschusses der deutschen Industrie und seine Rolle zu Beginn des ersten Weltkrieges', *Zeitschrift für Geschichtwissenschaft*, XVIII (1970), 877–98.

Hadley, Michael L., and Roger Sarty, *Tin-pots and pirate ships: Canadian naval forces and German sea raiders 1880–1918* (Montreal, 1991).

Halévy, Daniel, *L'Europe brisée; journal et lettres 1914–1918*, ed. Sébastien Laurent (Paris, 1998).

Haley, Charles D., 'The desperate Ottoman: Enver Pasha and the German empire', *Middle Eastern Studies*, XXX (1994), 1–51, 224–51.

Halpern, Paul, *The naval war in the Mediterranean 1914–1918* (London, 1987).

—— *A naval history of World War I* (London, 1994).

—— *Anton Haus: Österreich-Ungarns Grossadmiral* (Graz, 1998).

Hamilton-Grace, R. S., *Finance and war* (London, 1910).

Hamm, Michael F., 'Liberal politics in wartime Russia: an analysis of the progressive bloc', *Slavic Review*, XXXIII (1974), 453–68.

Hancock, W. K., *Smuts: the sanguine years 1870–1919* (Cambridge, 1962).

—— and Jean van der Poel (eds.), *Selections from the Smuts papers*, vol. III, *June 1910–November 1918* (Cambridge, 1966).

Handel, Michael I. (ed.), *Clausewitz and modern strategy* (London, 1986).

Hankey, Maurice, Lord, *Government control in war* (Cambridge, 1945).

—— *The supreme command 1914–1918*, 2 vols. (London, 1961).

Hanna, Martha, *The mobilization of intellect: French scholars and writers during the Great War* (Cambridge, Mass., 1996).

Hanssen, Hans Peter, *Diary of a dying empire*, ed. R. H. Lutz, M. Schofield, and O. O. Winther (Port Washington, NY, 1973; first published 1955).

Hardach, Gerd, *The First World War 1914–1918* (London, 1977; first published 1970).

Harvey, A. D., *Collision of empires: Britain in three world wars, 1793–1945* (London, 1992).

Haste, Cate, *Keep the home fires burning: propaganda in the First World War* (London, 1977).

Haupt, Georges, *Socialism and the Great War: the collapse of the Second International* (Oxford, 1972).

Hayashima, Akira, *Die Illusion des Sonderfriedens. Deutsche Verständigungspolitik mit Japan im ersten Weltkrieg* (Munich, 1982).

Haycock, Ronald, and Keith Neilson, *Men, machines, and war* (Waterloo, Ont., 1988).

Hayne, M. B., *The French foreign office and the origins of the First World War 1898–1914* (Oxford, 1993).

Hazlehurst, Cameron, 'Asquith as prime minister, 1908–1916', *English Historical Review*, LXXXV (1970), 502–31.

—— *Politicians at war, July 1914 to May 1915: a prologue to the triumph of Lloyd George* (London, 1971).

Hecker, Gerhard, *Walther Rathenau und sein Verhältnis zu Militär und Krieg* (Boppard am Rhein, 1983).

Helfferich, Karl, *Der Weltkrieg* (Karlsruhe, 1925; first published 1919).

—— *Money* (New York, 1969; from the German edn. of 1923).

Heller, Joseph, *British policy towards the Ottoman empire 1908–1914* (London, 1983).

Henderson, W. O., *Studies in German colonial history* (London, 1962).

Hendrick, Burton J., *The life and letters of Walter A. Page* (London, 1930).

Herrmann, David, *The arming of Europe and the making of the First World War* (Princeton, 1996).

Herwig, Holger H., 'Admirals versus generals: the war aims of the imperial German navy, 1914–1918', *Central European History*, V (1972), 208–33.

—— 'Clio deceived: patriotic self-censorship in Germany after the Great War', *International Security*, XII (1972), 5–44.

—— *The German naval officer corps: a social and political history 1890–1918* (Oxford, 1973).

—— *'Luxury' fleet: the imperial German navy 1888–1918* (London, 1980).

—— 'From Tirpitz plan to Schlieffen plan: some observations on German military planning', *Journal of Strategic Studies*, IX (1986), 53–63.

—— 'The failure of German sea power, 1914–1945: Mahan, Tirpitz and Raeder reconsidered', *International History Review*, X (1988), 68–105.

—— 'Disjointed allies: coalition warfare in Berlin and Vienna, 1914', *Journal of Military History*, LIV (1990), 265–80.

—— 'The German reaction to the *Dreadnought* revolution', *International History Review*, XIII (1991), 273–83.

—— *The First World War: Germany and Austria-Hungary 1914–1918* (London, 1997).

Herzfeld, Hans, *Der Erste Weltkrieg*, 7th edn. (Munich, 1985; first published 1968).

Hewins, W. A. S., *Apolgia of an imperialist: forty years of empire policy*, 2 vols. (London, 1929).

Hiley, Nicholas, 'The failure of British espionage against Germany 1907–1914', *Historical Journal*, XXVI (1983), 867–89.

—— 'The failure of British counter-espionage against Germany, 1907–1914', *Historical Journal*, XXVIII (1985), 835–62.

—— 'Counter-espionage and security in Great Britain during the First World War', *English Historical Review*, CI (1986), 635–70.

Hindenburg, Paul von, *Out of my life* (London, 1920).

Hinsley, F. H., (ed.), *British foreign policy under Sir Edward Grey* (Cambridge, 1977).

Hirschfeld, Gerhard, '1986 regional conference: war and society in modern German history', *German History*, IV (1987), 64–91.

—— Gerd Krumeich, Dieter Langewiesche, and Hans-Peter Ullmann, *Kriegserfahrungen. Studien zur Sozial- und Mentalitätsgeschichte des Ersten Weltkriegs* (Essen, 1997).

Hirschfeld, Magnus, and Andreas Gaspar, *Sittensgeschichte des Weltkrieges*, 2 vols. (Leipzig, 1930).

L'Histoire, 14–18: mourir pour la patrie (Paris, 1992).

Hobson, J. M., 'The military-extraction gap and the wary Titan: the fiscal sociology of British defence policy 1870–1913', *Journal of European Economic History*, XXII (1993), 461–506.

Holmes, Terence M., 'The reluctant March on Paris: a reply to Terence Zuber's 'The Schlieffen plan reconsidered', *War in History*, VIII (2001), 208–32.

Hope, Nicholas, *German and Scandinavian protestantism 1700 to 1918* (Oxford, 1995).

Hörich, Gerhard, *Die deutsche Seekriegführung im ersten Weltkriegshalbjahr* (Berlin, 1936).

Horne, John, (ed.), *State, society and mobilization in Europe during the First World War* (Cambridge, 1997).

Horne, John, and Alan Kramer, 'German "atrocities" and Franco-German opinion, 1914: the evidence of German soldiers' diaries', *Journal of Modern History*, LXVI (1994), 1–33.

—— and——, *German atrocities 1914: a history of denial* (London, 2001).

House, Jonathan M., 'The decisive attack: a new look at French infantry tactics on the eve of World War I', *Military Affairs*, XXX (1976), 164–9.

Hovanissian, Richard G., *Armenia on the road to independence 1918* (Berkeley, 1967).

Howard, Harry N., *The partition of Turkey: a diplomatic history 1913–1923* (New York, 1966; first published 1931).

Howard, Michael, *The continental commitment: the dilemma of British defence policy in two world wars* (Harmondsworth, 1974; first published 1972).

Huber, Wolfgang, *Kirche und Öffentlichkeit* (Stuttgart, 1973).

Hughes, Daniel J., 'Schlichting, Schlieffen, and the Prussian theory of war in 1914', *Journal of Military History*, LIX (1995), 257–78.

Huguet, Victor, *Britain and the war: a French indictment* (London, 1928).

Hull, Isobel V., *The entourage of Kaiser Wilhelm II 1888–1918* (Cambridge, 1982).

Hunt, Barry S., and Adrian Preston (eds.), *War aims and strategic policy in the Great War 1914–1918* (London, 1977).

Hüppauf, Bernd, 'Langemarck, Verdun and the myth of a "new man" in Germany after the First World War', *War & Society*, VI (1988), 70–103.

Hynes, Samuel, *A war imagined: the First World War and English culture* (London, 1990).

Ingram, Edward (ed.), *National and international politics in the Middle East: essays in honour of Elie Kedourie* (London, 1986).

Jahn, Hubertus F., *Patriotic culture in Russia during World War I* (Ithaca, 1995).

Janssen, Karl-Heinz, *Der Kanzler und der General. Die Führungskrise um Bethmann Hollweg und Falkenhayn (1914–1916)* (Göttingen, 1967).

Jarausch, Konrad H., 'The illusion of limited war: Chancellor Bethmann Hollweg's calculated risk, July 1914', *Central European History*, II (1969), 48–76.

—— *The enigmatic chancellor: Bethmann Hollweg and the hubris of imperial Germany* (New Haven, 1973).

Jauffret, Jean-Charles, 'L'Organisation de la réserve à l'époque de la révanche, 1871–1914', *Revue historique des armées*, 174 (1989), 27–37.

Jeffery, Keith, *The British army and the crisis of empire 1918–22* (Manchester, 1984).

Jenkins, Roy, *Asquith* (London, 1964).

Jerabek, Rudolf, *Potiorek. General im Schatten von Sarajevo* (Graz, 1991).

Joffre, J., *Mémoires du Maréchal Joffre (1910–1917)*, 2 vols. (Paris, 1932).

Johnson, Franklyn Arthur, *Defence by committee: the British Committee of Imperial Defence 1885–1959* (London, 1960).

Johnson, Jeffrey Allan, *The Kaiser's chemists: science and modernization in imperial Germany* (Chapel Hill, 1990).

Joll, James, *The Second International 1889–1914* (London, 1975).

—— *The origins of the First World War* (London, 1984; 2nd edn. 1992).

Jones, Archer, and Andrew J. Keogh, 'The Dreadnought revolution: another look', *Military Affairs*, XLIV (1985), 124–31.

Jones, David, 'Nicholas II and the supreme command: an investigation of motives', *Sbornik*, XI (1985), 47–83.

—— (ed.), *The military-naval encyclopedia of Russia and the Soviet Union* (Gulf Breeze, 1978–).

Jones, Gareth Stedman, 'Working-class culture and working-class politics in London, 1870–1900: notes on the remaking of a working class', *Journal of Social History*, VII (1973–4), 460–508.

Jones, G. Gareth, 'The British government and the oil companies, 1912–1924: the search for an oil policy', *Historical Journal*, XX (1977), 647–72.

Jordan, Gerald (ed.), *Naval warfare in the twentieth century 1900–1945: essays in honour of Arthur Marder* (London, 1977).

Kaiser, David, 'Germany and the origins of the First World War', *Journal of Modern History*, LV (1983), 442–74.

Kann, Robert, Bela K. Kiraly, and Paula S. Fichtner (eds.), *The Habsburg empire in World War I: essays on the intellectual, military, political and economic aspects of the Habsburg war effort* (New York, 1977).

Kaspi, André, 'French war aims in Africa, 1914–1919', in Prosser Gifford and Wm. Roger Louis (eds.), *France and Britain in Africa: imperial rivalry and colonial rule* (New Haven, 1971).

Kautsky, Karl (ed.), *Die deutschen Dokumente zum Kriegsausbruch 1914*, 4 vols. (Berlin, 1922).

Kedourie, Elie, *England and the middle east: the destruction of the Ottoman empire 1914–1921* (London, 1956).

Keiger, John F. V., *France and the origins of the First World War* (London, 1983).

—— 'Jules Cambon and Franco-German détente, 1907–1914', *Historical Journal*, XXVI (1983), 641–59.

Keithly, David M., 'Did Russia also have war aims in 1914?', *East European Quarterly*, XXI (1987), 137–45.

Kenez, Peter, 'A profile of the prerevolutionary officer corps', *California Slavic Studies*, VII (1973), 121–58.

Kennedy, Greg, and Keith Neilson (eds.), *Far-flung lines: essays on imperial defence in honour of Donald Mackenzie Schurman* (London, 1997).

Kennedy, Paul, *The rise of the Anglo-German antagonism 1860–1914* (London, 1980).

Kennedy, Paul, *The rise and fall of the great powers: economic change and military conflict from 1500 to 2000* (London, 1988).

—— (ed.), *The war plans of the great powers 1880–1914* (London, 1979).

Kent, Marian (ed.), *The great powers and the end of the Ottoman empire* (London, 1984).

Kielmansegg, Peter Graf, *Deutschland und der Erste Weltkrieg*, 2nd edn. (Stuttgart, 1980).

King, Jere Clemens, *Generals and politicians: conflict between France's high command, parliament and government, 1914–1918* (Berkeley, 1951).

Kiraly, Bela, Nandor F. Dreisziger, and Albert A. Nofi (eds.), *East Central European society in World War I* (Boulder, Col., 1985).

Kirby, David, *War, peace and revolution: international socialism at the crossroads 1914–1918* (Aldershot, 1986).

Kitchen, Martin, *The German officer corps 1890–1914* (Oxford, 1968).

Kiszling, Rudolf, *Österreich-Ungarns Anteil am Ersten Weltkrieg* (Graz, 1958).

Kjellen, Rudolf, *Die politischen Probleme des Weltkrieges* (Leipzig, 1916).

Klein, Fritz, *Deutschland im ersten Weltkrieg*, 3 vols. (Berlin, 1968).

Klotz, L.-L., *De la guerre à la paix* (Paris, 1924).

Knauss, Robert, *Die deutsche, englische und französische Kriegsfinanzierung* (Berlin, 1923).

Knox, Alfred, *With the Russian army 1914–1917, being chiefly extracts from the diary of a military attaché*, 2 vols. (London, 1921).

Koch, H. W., (ed.), *The origins of the First World War: great power rivalry and German war aims* (London, 1972); 2nd edn. (1984).

Kocka, Jürgen, *Facing total war: German society 1914–1918* (Leamington Spa, 1984; first published 1973).

Koss, Stephen, *Asquith* (London, 1976).

Krauss, Alfred, *Die Ursachen unserer Niederlage. Erinnerungen und Urteile aus dem Weltkrieg*, 3rd edn. (Munich, 1923).

Kriegel, Annie, *Le Pain et les roses: jalons pour une histoire des socialismes* (Paris, 1968).

—— and Jean-Jacques Becker, *1914: la patrie et le mouvement ouvrier français* (Paris, 1964).

Krieger, Leonard, and Fritz Stern (eds.), *The responsibility of power: historical essays in honor of Hajo Holborn* (London, 1968).

Kroboth, Rudolf, *Die Finanzpolitik des deutschen Reiches während der Reichskanzlerschaft Bethmann Hollwegs und die Geld und Kapitalmarktverhältnisse (1909–1913/14)* (Frankfurt am Main, 1986).

Krohn, Claus-Dieter, 'Geldtheorien in Deutschland während der Inflation 1914 bis 1924', in Gerald D. Feldman, Carl-Ludwig Holtfrerich, Gerhard A. Ritter, and Peter-Christian Witt (eds.), *Die Anpassung an die Inflation* (Berlin, 1986).

Kronenbitter, Günther, *"Krieg im Frieden". Die Führung der k.u.k. Armeé und die Großmachtpolitik Österreichs-Ungarns 1906–1914* (Munich, 2003)

—— 'Die Macht der Illusionen. Julikrise und Kriegsausbruch 1914 aus der Sicht des deutschen Militärattachés in Wien', *Militärgeschichtliche Mitteilungen*, 57 (1998), 519–50.

Krumeich, Gerd, *Armaments and politics in France on the eve of the First World War: the introduction of three-year conscription 1913–1914* (Leamington Spa, 1984; first published 1980).

—— *Jeanne d'Arc in der Geschichte. Historiographie—Politik—Kultur* (Sigmaringen, 1989)

Kruse, Wolfgang, 'Die Kriegsbegeisterung im deutschen Reich zu Beginn des Ersten Weltkrieges', in Marcel van der Linden and Gottfried Mergner (eds.), *Kriegsbegeisterung und mentale Kriegsvorbereitung* (Berlin, 1991).

—— *Krieg und nationale Integration: eine Neuinterpretation des sozialdemokratischen Burgfriedensschlusses 1914/15* (Essen, 1993).

—— (ed.), *Eine Welt von Feinden. Der Grosse Krieg 1914–1918* (Frankfurt am Main, 1997).

Kuhl, Hermann, *Le Grand état-major allemand*, ed. Général Douchy (Paris, 1922; first published 1920).

Kühlmann, Richard von, *Erinnerungen* (Heidelberg, 1948).

Lackey, Scott W., *The rebirth of the Habsburg army: Friedrich Beck and the rise of the general staff* (Westport, Conn., 1995).

La Gorce, Paul-Marie de (ed.), *La Première Guerre Mondiale*, 2 vols. (Paris, 1991).

Laloy, Émile, 'French military theory 1871–1914', *The Military Historian and Economist*, II (1917), 267–86.

Lambert, Nicholas A., 'Admiral Sir John Fisher and the concept of flotilla defence, 1904–1909', *Journal of Military History*, LIX (1995), 639–60.

—— 'British naval policy, 1913–1914: financial limitation and strategic revolution', *Journal of Modern History*, LXVII (1995), 595–626.

—— '"Our bloody ships" or "our bloody system"? Jutland and the loss of the battle cruisers, 1916', *Journal of Military History*, LXII (1998), 29–55.

—— *Sir John fisher's Naval revolution* (Columbia, South Carolina, c 1999).

Lambi, Ivo Nikolai, *The navy and German power politics, 1862–1914* (Boston, 1984).

Landau, Jacob M., *Pan-Turkism in Turkey: a study of irridentism* (London, 1981).

—— *The politics of pan-Islam: ideology and organization* (Oxford, 1990).

Langdon, John W., *July 1914: the long debate, 1918–1990* (New York, 1991).

Lange, Karl, *Marneschlacht und deutsche Öffentlichkeit 1914–1939. Eine verdrängte Niederlage und ihre Folgen* (Dusseldorf, 1974).

Lange, Sven, *Hans Delbrück und der 'Strategiestreit': Kriegführung und Kriegsgeschichte in der Kontroverse 1879– 1914* (Freiburg, 1995).

Laqueur, Walter, *Young Germany: a history of the German youth movement* (London, 1962).

Latzko, Andreas, *Men in battle* (London, 1930; first published 1918).

Lautenschlager, Karl, 'Technology and the evolution of naval warfare', *International security*, VII (1983), 3–51.

Le Bon, Gustave, *The psychology of the Great War* (London, 1916).

Le Révérend, André, *Lyautey* (Paris, 1983).

Leslie, John Duncan, 'Austria-Hungary's eastern policy in the First World War, August 1914 to August 1915', Cambridge University Ph.D. thesis, 1975.

——— 'Österreich-Ungarn vor dem Kriegsausbruch. Der Ballhausplatz in Wien im Juli 1914 aus der Sicht eines österreicher-ungarischen Diplomaten', in Ralph Melville, Claus Scharf, Martin Vogt, and Ulrich Wengenroth (eds.), *Deutschland und Europa in der Neuzeit 2. Halbband* (Stuttgart, 1988).

——— 'The antecedents of Austria-Hungary's war aims: policies and policy-makers in Vienna and Budapest before and during 1914', *Wiener Beiträge zur Geschichte der Neuzeit*, XX (1993), 307–94.

Liang, Hsi-Huey, *The rise of modern police and the European state system from Metternich to the Second World War* (Cambridge, 1992).

Lieven, D. C. B., *Russia and the origins of the First World War* (London, 1983).

——— *Nicholas II: emperor of all the Russias* (London, 1993).

Lincoln, W. Bruce, *Passage through Armageddon: the Russians in war and revolution 1914–1918* (New York, 1986).

Lindemann, Thomas, *Les doctrines darwiniennes et la guerre de 1914* (Paris, 2001).

Linke, Horst Günther, 'Russlands Weg in den Ersten Weltkrieg und seine Kriegsziele 1914–1917', *Militärgeschichtliche Mitteilungen*, 32 (1982), 9–34.

Lohr, Eric, *Nationalizing the Russian empire: the Campaign against enemy aliens during World War I* (Cambridge, Mass., 2003).

Longley, D. A., 'The Russian Social Democrats' statement to the Duma on 26 July (8 August) 1914: a new look at the evidence', *English Historical Review*, CII (1987), 599–621.

Lübbe, Hermann, *Politische Philosophie in Deutschland. Studien zu ihrer Geschichte* (Munich, 1974; first published 1963).

Lucas, Charles (ed.), *The empire at war*, 5 vols. (Oxford, 1921–6).

Ludendorff, Erich, *My war memories 1914–1918*, 2 vols. (London, 1919).

——— *Urkunden der obersten Heeresleitung über ihre Tätigkeit 1916–18* (Berlin, 1920).

Lumby, E. W. R. (ed.), *Policy and operations in the Mediterranean 1912–14* (London, 1970).

Lutz, Ralph Haswell (ed.), *Documents of the German revolution: fall of the German empire 1914–1918*, 2 vols. (Stanford, 1932).

Luvaas, Jay, *The education of an army: British military thought, 1815–1940* (London, 1965).

Lyon, James M. B., ' "A peasant mob": the Serbian army on the eve of the Great War', *Journal of Military History*, LXI (1997), 481–502.

Macdonald, Catriona M. M., and E. W. McFarland (eds.), *Scotland and the Great War* (East Linton, 1999).

McDonald, David MacLaren, *United government and foreign policy in Russia 1900–1914* (Cambridge Mass., 1992).

McEwen, John M., 'The national press during the First World War: ownership and circulation', *Journal of Contemporary History*, XVII (1982), 459–86.

Macfie, A. L., *The end of the Ottoman empire 1908–1923* (London, 1998).

McGibbon, Ian, *The path to Gallipoli: defending New Zealand 1840–1915* (Wellington, 1991).

McKale, Donald M., ' "The Kaiser's spy": Max von Oppenheim and the Anglo-German rivalry before and during the First World War', *European History Quarterly*, XXVII (1997), 199–219.

—— *War by revolution: Germany and Great Britain in the Middle East in the era of World War I* (Kent, Ohio, 1998).

McKean, Robert B., *St Petersburg between the revolutions: workers and revolutionaries, June 1907–February 1917* (New Haven, 1990).

McKibbin, Ross, *The evolution of the Labour party 1910–1924* (Oxford, 1974).

—— 'Why was there no Marxism in Great Britain?', *English Historical Review*, XCIX (1984), 297–331.

McLaughlin, Peter, *Ragtime soldiers: the Rhodesian experience in the First World War* (Bulawayo, 1980).

McNeill, William H., *The pursuit of power: technology, armed force, and society since A.D. 1000* (Oxford, 1983).

Mai, Gunther, *Das Ende des Kaiserreichs. Politik und Kriegführung im Ersten Weltkrieg* (Munich, 1987).

Maier, Charles S., 'Wargames: 1914–1919', *Journal of Interdisciplinary History*, XVIII (1988), 819–49.

Mann, Thomas, 'Gedanken im Kriege', *Politische Schriften und Reden*, vol. II (Frankfurt am Main, 1960; first published November 1914).

Marder, Arthur J., (ed.), *Fear God and dread nought: the correspondence of Admiral of the Fleet Lord Fisher of Kilverstone*, 3 vols. (London, 1952–9).

Marder, Arthur J., *From the Dreadnought to Scapa Flow: the Royal Navy in the Fisher era, 1904–1919*, 5 vols. (London, 1961–70).

Marquand, David, *Ramsay MacDonald* (London, 1977).

Marquis, Alice Goldfarb, 'Words as weapons: propaganda in Britain and Germany during the First World War', *Journal of Contemporary History*, XIII (1978), 467–98.

Marrin, Albert, *The last crusade: the Church of England in the First World War* (Durham, NC, 1974).

Martin, Nicholas, 'Nietzsche under fire', *Times Literary Supplement*, 5 Aug. 1996.

Marwick, Arthur, *The deluge: British society and the First World War* (London, 1965).

Materna, Ingo, and Hans-Joachim Schreckenbach, with Bärbel Holtz, *Dokumente aus geheimen Archiven*. Band 4 *1914–1918*. *Berichte des Berliner Polizeipräsidenten zur Stimmung und Lage der Bevölkerung in Berlin 1914–18* (Weimar, 1987).

Matuschka, Edgar Graf von, 'Organisationsgeschichte des Heeres 1890–1918', in Militärgeschichtliche Forschungsamt, *Handbuch zur deutschen Militärgeschichte*, vol. V (Frankfurt am Main, 1968).

Maurer, John H., *The outbreak of the First World War: strategic planning, crisis decision making, and deterrence failure* (Westport, Conn., 1995).

Maurin, Jules, *Armée-Guerre-Société: soldats languedociens (1889–1919)* (Paris, 1982).

May, Arthur J., *The passing of the Hapsburg monarchy 1914– 1918*, 2 vols. (Philadelphia, 1966).

May, Ernest R., 'American policy and Japan's entrance into World War I', *Mississippi Valley Historical Review*, XL (1953–4), 279–90.

—— (ed.), *Knowing one's enemies: intelligence assessment before the two world wars* (Princeton, 1984).

Meaney, Neville, *The search for security in the Pacific, 1901–14* (Sydney, 1976).

Meinecke, Friedrich, *Strassburg/Freiburg/Berlin 1901–1919: Erinnerungen* (Stuttgart, 1949).

Meinertzhagen, R., *Army diary 1899–1926* (Edinburgh, 1960).

Meintjes, Johannes, *General Louis Botha: a biography* (London, 1970).

Melancon, Michael, *The Socialist Revolutionaries and the Russian anti-war movement, 1914–1917* (Columbus, Ohio, 1990).

Menning, Bruce W., *Bayonets before bullets: the imperial Russian army, 1861–1914* (Bloomington, 1992).

Messimy, Adolphe, *Mes souvenirs* (Paris, 1937).

Meynier, Gilbert, *L'Algérie révelée: la guerre de 1914–1918 et le premier quart du XXe siècle* (Genève, 1981).

Michalka, Wolfgang, (ed.), *Der Erste Weltkrieg. Wirkung, Warnehmung, Analyse* (Munich, 1994).

Michel, Bernard, 'L'Autriche et l'entrée dans la guerre en 1914', *Guerres mondiales et conflits contemporains*, 179 (juillet 1995), 5–11.

Michel, Marc, *Gallieni* (Paris, 1989).

Michelson, Alexander M., Paul N. Apostol, and Michael W. Bernatzky, *Russian public finance during the war* (New Haven, 1928).

Miller, Geoffrey, *Superior force: the conspiracy behind the escape of 'Goeben' and 'Breslau'* (Hull, 1996).

—— *Straits: British policy towards the Ottoman empire and the origins of the Dardanelles campaign* (Hull, 1997).

Miller, Steven E. (ed.), *Military strategy and the origins of the First World War* (Princeton, 1985).

Miller, Susanne, *Burgfrieden und Klassenkampf: die deutsche Sozialdemokratie im Ersten Weltkrieg* (Dusseldorf, 1974).

Millett, Allan R., and Williamson Murray (eds.), *Military effectiveness*, vol. I, *The First World War* (Boston, 1988).

Milner, Susan, *The dilemmas of internationalism: French syndicalism and the international labour movement, 1900–1914* (New York, 1990).

Ministère de la Guerre, État-Major de l'Armée—Service Historique, *Les Armées françaises dans la grande guerre*, 11 vols. (Paris, 1922–37).

Miquel, Pierre, *La Grande Guerre* (Paris, 1983).

Mitchell, Allan, *Victors and vanquished: the German influence on army and church in France after 1870* (Chapel Hill, 1984).

Mitchell, Donald W., *A history of Russian and Soviet sea power* (London, 1974).

Mollin, Volker, *Auf dem Wege zur 'Materialschlacht'. Vorgeschichte und Funktionen des Artillerie-Industrie-Komplexes im deutschen Kaiserreich* (Pfaffenweiler, 1986).

Mombauer, Annika, 'Helmuth von Moltke and the German general staff—military and political decision-making in imperial Germany, 1906–1916', Sussex University D. Phil thesis, 1997 ; published as *Helmuth von Moltke and the orgins of the First World War* (Cambridge, 2001).

—— *The origins of World War I: controversies and consensus* (London, 2002).

—— 'A reluctant military leader? Helmuth von Moltke and the July crisis of 1914', *War in History*, VI (1999), 417–46.

Mommsen, Wolfgang, 'Domestic factors in German foreign policy before 1914', *Central European History*, VI (1973), 3–43.

—— 'Society and war: two new analyses of the First World War', *Journal of Modern History*, XLVII (1975), 530–8.

—— *Max Weber and German politics 1890–1920* (Chicago, 1984; first published 1959).

—— *Imperial Germany 1867–1918: politics, culture, and society in an authoritarian state* (London, 1995).

Mommsen, Wolfgang (ed.), *Kultur und Krieg. Die Rolle der intellektuellen, Künstler und Schriftsteller im Ersten Weltkrieg* (Munich, 1996).

Le Monde, La Trés Grande Guerre (Paris, 1994).

Morgan, Kenneth O., *Lloyd George* (London, 1974).

Morgenthau, Henry, *Ambassador Morgenthau's story,* (New York, 1919).

Morris, A. J. A., *The scaremongers: the advocacy of war and rearmament 1896–1914* (London, 1984).

Moses, John A., 'The British and German churches and the perception of war, 1908–1914', *War & Society*, V (1987), 23–44.

—— 'The Great War as ideological conflict—an Australian perspective', *War & Society*, VII (1989), 56–76.

—— 'The "ideas of 1914" in Germany and Australia: a case of conflicting perceptions', *War & Society*, IX (1991), 61–82.

Moulton, H. Fletcher, *The life of Lord Moulton* (London, 1922).

Moyer, Laurence V., *Victory must be ours: Germany in the Great War 1914–1918* (New York, 1995).

Mühlmann, Carl, *Deutschland und die Türkei 1913–1914. Die Berufung der deutschen Militärmission nach der Türkei 1913, das deutsch–türkische Bündnis 1914 und der Eintritt der Türkei in den Weltkrieg* (Berlin-Grunewald, 1929).

Müller, Christian, 'Anmerkungen zur Entwicklung von Kriegsbild und operativ-strategischen Szenario im preussisch-deutschen Heer vor dem Ersten Weltkrieg', *Militärgeschichtliche Mitteilungen*, 57 (1998), 385–442.

Müller, Herbert Landolin, *Islam, Gihad ('Heiliger Krieg') und deutsches Reich. Ein Nachspiel zur wilhelminischen Weltpolitik im Maghreb 1914–1918* (Frankfurt am Main, 1991).

Müller, Stefan von, *Die finanzielle Mobilmachung Österreichs und ihr Ausbau bis 1918* (Berlin, 1918).

Murfett, Malcolm H. (ed.), *The First Sea Lords: from Fisher to Mountbatten* (Westport, Conn., 1995).

—— and John N. Miksic, Brian P. Farrell, Chiang Ming Shun, *Between two oceans: a military history of Singapore from the first settlement to British withdrawal* (Oxford, 1999).

Musil, Robert, *The man without qualities*, 3 vols. (London, 1979).

Myers, Ramon H., and Mark R. Peattie (eds.), *The Japanese colonial empire, 1895–1945* (Princeton, 1984).

Nasson, Bill, 'A great divide: popular responses to the Great War in South Africa', *War & Society*, XII (1994), 47–64.

—— 'War opinion in South Africa, 1914', *Journal of Imperial and Commonwealth History*, XXIII (1995), 248–76.

Naumann, Friedrich, *Werke*, vol. IV, *Schriften zum Parteiwesen und zum Mitteleuropaproblem*, ed. Theodor Schieder (Cologne, 1964).

Neilson, Keith, *Strategy and supply: the Anglo-Russian alliance, 1914–17* (London, 1984).

—— 'Watching the "steamroller": British observers and the Russian army before 1914', *Journal of Strategic Studies*, VIII (1985), 199–217.

—— '"My beloved Russians": Sir Arthur Nicolson and Russia, 1906–1916', *International History Review*, IX (1987), 521–54.

—— '"That dangerous and difficult enterprise": British military thinking and the Russo-Japanese war', *War & Society*, IX (1991), 17–37.

—— *Britain and the last Tsar: British policy and Russia 1894–1917* (Oxford, 1995).

Neitzel, Sönke, *Kriegsausbruch. Deutschlands Weg in die Katastrophe 1900–1914* (Munich, 2000).

—— *Weltmacht oder Untergang. Die Weltreichslehre in Zeitalter des Imperialismus* (Paderborn, 2000).

Nettl, J. P., 'The German Social Democratic Party 1890–1914 as a political model', *Past and Present*, 30 (1965), 65–95.

—— *Rosa Luxemburg*, 2 vols. (London, 1966).

Nevakivi, Jukka, *Britain, France and the Arab middle east 1914–1920* (London, 1969).

Nish, Ian H., *Alliance in decline: a study in Anglo-Japanese relations 1908–23* (London, 1972).

—— *Japanese foreign policy, 1869–1942; Kasumigaseki to Miyakezaka* (London, 1977).

Northern Arts and Scottish Arts Council, *Futurismo 1909–1919: exhibition of Italian Futurism* (Newcastle and Edinburgh, 1972).

O'Brien, Phillips Payson, *British and American naval power: politics and policy, 1900–1936* (Westport, Conn., 1998).

—— (ed.) *Preparing for the next war at sea: technology and naval combat in the twentieth century* (London, 2001).

Occleshaw, Michael, *Armour against fate: intelligence in the First World War* (London, 1989).

Offer, Avner, 'The working classes, British naval plans and the coming of the Great War', *Past and Present*, CVII (1985), 204–26.

—— 'Morality and Admiralty: "Jacky" Fisher, economic warfare and the laws of war', *Journal of Contemporary History*, XXIII (1988), 99–119.

—— *The First World War: an agrarian interpretation* (Oxford, 1989).

—— 'Going to war in 1914: a matter of honor', *Politics and Society*, XXIII (1995), 213–41.

Österreichisches Bundesministerium für Heereswesen und vom Kriegsarchiv, *Österreich-Ungarns letzter Krieg 1914–1918*, ed. Edmund Glaise von Horstenau, 7 vols. (Vienna, 1931–8).

Osuntokun, Akinjide, *Nigeria in the First World War*, London, 1979).

Overlack, Peter, 'Australian defence awareness and German naval planning in the Pacific 1900–1914', *War & Society*, X (1992), 37–51.

—— 'German interest in Australian defence, 1901–1914: new insights into a precarious position on the eve of war', *Australian Journal of Politics and History*, XL (1994), 36–51.

Overlack, Peter, 'The force of circumstance: Graf Spee's options for the East Asia cruiser squadron in 1914', *Journal of Military History*, LX (1996), 657–82.

—— 'Australasia and Germany: challenge and response before 1914', in David Stevens (ed.), *Maritime power in the 20th century: the Australian experience* (St Leonards NSW, 1998).

—— 'Asia in German naval planning before the First World War: the strategic imperative', *War & Society*, XVII (1999), 1–23.

Overstraeten, R. von (ed.), *The war diaries of Albert I, king of the Belgians* (London, 1954).

Owen, Gail L., 'Dollar diplomacy in default: the economics of Russian–American relations, 1910–1917', *Historical Journal*, XIII (1970), 251–72.

Oxford Faculty of Modern History, *Why we are at war: Great Britain's case*, 3rd edn. (Oxford, 1914).

Panayi, Panikos, *The enemy in our midst: Germans in Britain during the First World War* (New York, 1991).

Panichas, George A. (ed.), *Promise of greatness: the war of 1914–1918* (London, 1968).

Pares, Bernard, *The fall of the Russian monarchy: a study of the evidence* (London, 1939).

Paret, Peter (ed.), with Gordon Craig and Felix Gilbert, *Makers of modern strategy from Machiavelli to the nuclear age* (Oxford, 1986).

Parry, Cyril, 'Gwynedd and the Great War', *Welsh History Review*, XIV (1988), 78–117.

Paskauskas, R. Andrew (ed.), *The complete correspondence of Sigmund Freud and Ernest Jones 1908–1939* (Cambridge, Mass., 1993).

Patterson, A. Temple, *Jellicoe: a biography* (London, 1969).

Pavlovich, N. B., *The fleet in the First World War*, vol. 1, *Operations of the Russian fleet* (New Delhi, 1979; first published, Moscow, 1964).

Pearson, Raymond, *The Russian moderates and the crisis of Tsarism 1914–1917* (London, 1977).

Pearton, Maurice, *The knowledgeable state: diplomacy, war and technology since 1830* (London, 1982).

Peball, Kurt, 'Der Feldzug gegen Serbien und Montenegro im Jahre 1914: Armee zwischen Tragik und Grösse', *Österreichische militärische Zeitschrift*, Sonderheft 1 (1965), 18–31.

—— (ed.), *Conrad von Hötzendorf. Private Aufzeichnungen: erste Veröffentlichungen aus den Papieren des k.u.k. Generalstabs-Chefs* (Vienna, 1977).

Pedroncini, Guy, 'Stratégie et rélations internationales: la séance du 9 janvier 1912 du conseil supérieur de la défense nationale', *Revue d'histoire diplomatique*, XCI (1977), 143–58.

—— (ed.), *Histoire militaire de la France*. Tome III, *De 1871 à 1940* (Paris, 1992).

Perrins, Michael, 'The council for state defence 1905–1909: a study in Russian bureaucratic politics', *Slavonic and East European Review*, LVIII (1980), 370–98.

Peters, John, 'The British government and the City–industry divide: the case of the 1914 financial crisis', *Twentieth Century British History*, IV (1993), 126–48.

Pethö, Albert, *Agenten für den Doppeladler. Österreich-Ungarns. Geheimer Dienst im Weltkrieg* (Graz, 1998).

Petit, Lucien, *Histoire des finances extérieures de la France pendant la guerre (1914–1919)* (Paris, 1929).

Petrovich, Michael Boris, *A history of modern Serbia 1804–1918*, 2 vols. (New York, 1976).

Pfeilschifter, Georg (ed.), *Deutsche Kultur, Katholizismus und Weltkrieg: eine Abwehr des Buches La Guerre allemande et le Catholicisme* (Freiburg im Breisgau, 1915).

Philbin, Tobias R., *Admiral von Hipper: the inconvenient hero* (Amsterdam, 1982).

Philpott, William J., 'The strategic ideas of Sir John French', *Journal of Strategic Studies*, XII (1989), 458–78.

—— 'Origines et signification de la stratégie britannique du "flanc nord"', *Guerres mondiales et conflits contemporains*, 180 (octobre 1995), 47–63.

—— *Anglo-French relations and strategy on the western front, 1914–1918* (Basingstoke, 1996).

Pick, Daniel, *War machine: the rationalization of slaughter in the modern age* (New Haven, 1993).

Pitreich, Max von, *1914. Die militärischen Probleme unseres Kriegsbeginnes. Ideen, Gründe und Zusammenhänge* (Vienna, 1934).

Plaut, Paul, 'Psychographie des Kriegers', *Beihefte zur Zeitschrift für angewandte Psychologie*, XXI (1920), 1–123.

Pogge von Strandmann, Hartmut (ed.), *Walther Rathenau: industrialist, banker, intellectual, and politician. Notes and diaries 1907–1922* (Oxford, 1985; first published 1967).

Pokrowski, M. N. (ed.), *Die internationalen Beziehungen im Zeitalter des Imperialismus*, ed. Otto Hoetsch, series 1, ii (Berlin, 1933).

Pomiankowski, Joseph, *Der Zusammenbruch des Ottomanischen Reiches. Erinnerungen an die Türkei aus der Zeit des Weltkrieges* (Vienna, 1928).

Popovics, Alexander, *Das Geldwesen im Kriege* (Vienna, 1925).

Porch, Douglas, *The march to the Marne: the French army 1871–1914* (Cambridge, 1981).

—— 'The Marne and after: a reappraisal of French strategy in the First World War', *Journal of Military History*, LIII (1989), 363–85.

Pourcher, Yves, *Les Jours de guerre: la vie des français au jour le jour 1914–1918* (Paris, 1994).

Pressel, Wilhelm, *Die Kriegspredigt 1914–1918 in der evangelischen Kirche Deutschlands* (Göttingen, 1967).

Prete, Roy A., 'French strategic planning and the deployment of the B.E.F. in France in 1914', *Canadian Journal of History*, XXIV (1989), 42–62.

Prior, Robin, *Churchill's 'World Crisis' as history* (London, 1983).

Pugh, Martin, *The making of modern British politics 1867–1939* (Oxford, 1982).

Raithel, Thomas, *Das 'Wunder' der inneren Einheit. Studien zur deutschen und französischen Öffentlichkeit bei Beginn des Ersten Weltkrieges* (Bonn, 1996).

Raschke, Martin, *Der politisierende Generalstab: die friderizianischen Kriege in der amtliche deutschen Militärgeschichtsschreibung 1890–1914* (Freiburg, 1993).

Rathmann, Lothar, *Stossrichtung Nahost 1914–1918: zur Expansionpolitik des deutschen Imperialismus im ersten Weltkrieg* (Berlin, 1963).

Rauchensteiner, Manfred, *Der Tod des Doppeladlers. Österreich-Ungarn und der Erste Weltkrieg* (Graz, 1993).

Redlich, Joseph, *Austrian war government* (New Haven, 1929).

Regele, Oskar, *Feldmarschall Conrad. Auftrag und Erfüllung 1906–1918* (Vienna, 1955).

Reichsarchiv, *Der Weltkrieg, 1914 bis 1918*, 14 vols. (Berlin, 1925–44).

—— *Der Weltkrieg. Kriegsrüstung und Kriegswirtschaft*, 2 vols. (Berlin, 1930).

Reinharz, Jehuda, 'Science in the service of politics: the case of Chaim Weizmann during the First World War', *English Historical Review*, C (1985), 572–603.

Reith, John, *Wearing spurs* (London, 1966).

Reitz, Denys, *Trekking on* (London, 1933).

Renouvin, Pierre, *The forms of war government in France* (New Haven, 1927).

—— *La Crise européenne et la première guerre mondiale (1904–1918)*, 6th edn. (Paris, 1969).

Renzi, William A., 'Great Britain, Russia, and the straits, 1914–1915', *Journal of Modern History*, XLII (1970), 1–20.

—— 'Who composed "Sazonov's Thirteen Points"? A re-examination of Russia's war aims of 1914', *American Historical Review*, LXXXVIII (1983), 347–57.

[Repington, Charles à Court], *Essays and criticisms*, by the military correspondent of *The Times* (London, 1911).

Ribot, Alexandre, *Letters to a friend: recollections of my political life* (London, [*c*.1925]).

—— *Journal d'Alexandre Ribot et correspondances inédites 1914–1922* (Paris, 1936), edited by A. Ribot.

Riezler, Kurt, *Kurt Riezler. Tagebücher, Aufsätze, Dokumente*, ed. Karl Dietrich Erdmann (Göttingen, 1972).

Ringer, Fritz K., *The decline of the German mandarins: the German academic community, 1890–1933* (Hanover, NH, 1990; first published 1969).

Ritter, Gerhard, *The Schlieffen plan: critique of a myth* (London, 1958; first published 1956).

—— *The sword and the sceptre: the problem of militarism in Germany*, 4 vols. (London, 1970–3).

Rivet, Daniel, *Lyautey et l'institution du protectorat français au Maroc 1912–1925*, 3 vols. (Paris, 1988).

Robbins, Keith, *The First World War* (Oxford, 1984).

Robert, Jean-Louis, *Les Ouvriers, la patrie et la révolution: Paris 1914–1919* (Paris, 1995).

Robinson, Ronald, and John Gallagher, with Alice Denny, *Africa and the Victorians: the official mind of imperialism* (London, 1961).

Roesler, Konrad, *Die Finanzpolitik des deutschen Reiches im Ersten Weltkrieg* (Berlin, 1967).

Rogger, Hans, 'Russia in 1914', *Journal of Contemporary History*, I (1966), 95–119.

Rohkrämer, Thomas, *Der Militarismus der 'kleinen Leute'. Die Kriegsvereine im Deutschen Kaiserreich* (Munich, 1990).

Röhl, John C. G., 'Admiral von Müller and the approach of war, 1911–1914', *Historical Journal*, XII (1969), 651–73.

—— *The Kaiser and his court: Wilhelm II and the government of Germany* (Cambridge, 1994).

—— (ed.), *1914: delusion or design? The testimony of two German diplomats* (London, 1973).

—— (ed.), with Elisabeth Müller-Luckner, *Der Ort Kaiser Wilhelms II in der deutsche Geschichte* (Munich, 1991).

—— and Nicolaus Sombart (eds.), *Kaiser Wilhelm II: new interpretations* (Cambridge, 1982).

Rohwer, Jürgen (ed.), *Neue Forschungen zum Ersten Weltkrieg* (Koblenz, 1985).

Roosa, Ruth Amenda, 'Russian industrialists during World War I: the interaction of economics and politics', in Gregory Guroff and Fred V. Carstensen (eds.), *Entrepreneurship in imperial Russia and the Soviet Union* (Princeton, 1983).

Rosenberg, Arthur, *The birth of the German republic 1871–1918* (New York, 1962; first published 1931).

Rosenberger, Bernhard, *Zeitungen als Kriegstreiber? Die Rolle der Presse im Vorfeld des Ersten Weltkrieges* (Cologne, 1998).

Roskill, Stephen, *Hankey: man of secrets*, 3 vols. (London, 1970).

—— *Admiral of the Fleet Earl Beatty: the last naval hero: an intimate biography* (London, 1980).

Rothenberg, Gunther, *The army of Francis Joseph* (West Lafayette, 1976).

—— 'The Austro-Hungarian campaign against Serbia in 1914', *Journal of Military History*, LIII (1989), 127–46.

Rothwell, V. H., *British war aims and peace diplomacy 1914–1918* (Oxford, 1971).

Rubanowice, Robert J., *Crisis in consciousness: the thought of Ernst Troeltsch* (Tallahassee, 1982).

Rumbold, Algernon, *Watershed in India 1914–1922* (London, 1979).

Rürup, Reinhard, 'Der "Geist von 1914" in Deutschland. Kriegsbegeisterung und Idolisierung des Krieges im Ersten Weltkrieg', in Bernd Hüppauf (ed.), *Ansichten vom Krieg: vergleichende Studien zum Ersten Weltkrieg im Literatur und Gesellschaft* (Königstein, 1984).

Ryan, Stephen, *Pétain the soldier* (Cranbury, NJ, 1969).

Ryder, A. J., *The German revolution of 1918: a study of German socialism in war and revolt* (Cambridge, 1967).

Saatmann, Inge, *Parlament, Rüstung und Armee in Frankreich, 1914/18* (Dusseldorf, 1978).

Sackett, Robert Eben, *Popular entertainment, class, and politics in Munich, 1900–1923* (Cambridge Mass., 1982).

Sanborn, Joshua A., *Drafting the Russian nation: military conscription, total War, and mass politics, 1905–1925* (De Kalb, Illinois, 2003).

—— 'The mobilization of 1914 and the question of the Russian nation: a reexamination', *Slavic Review*, LIX (2000), 267–89.

Sanders, Michael, and Philip M. Taylor, *British propaganda during the First World War 1914–18* (London, 1982).

Sareen, Tilan Raj, *Indian revolutionary movements abroad (1905–1921)* (New Delhi, 1979).

Sayers, R. S., *The Bank of England 1891–1944*, 2 vols. (Cambridge, 1966).

Scham, Alan, *Lyautey in Morocco: protectorate administration, 1912–1925* (Berkeley, 1970).

Scheler, Max, *Das Genius des Krieges und der Deutsche Krieg*, in *Politische-Pädagogische Schriften*, ed. Manfred S. Fring (Bern, 1982; first published 1915).

Schmidt, Martin E., *Alexandre Ribot: odyssey of a liberal in the Third Republic* (The Hague, 1974).

Schmidt-Richberg, Wiegand, 'Die Regierungszeit Wilhelms II', in Militärgeschichtliche Forschungsamt, *Handbuch zur deutschen Militärgeschichte*, vol. V (Frankfurt am Main, 1968).

Schoen, Erich, *Geschichte des deutschen Feuerwerkswesens der Armee und Marine mit Einschluss des Zeugwesens* (Berlin, 1936).

Schöllgen, Gregor, *Escape into war? The foreign policy of imperial Germany* (Oxford, 1990).

Schorske, Carl E., *German social democracy 1905–1917: the development of the great schism* (New York, 1955).

Schubert-Weller, Christoph, '*Kein schönrer Tod…*' *Die Militarisierung der männlichen Jugend und ihr Einsatz im Ersten Weltkrieg 1890–1918* (Weinheim, 1998).

Schulte, Bernd F., *Die deutsche Armee 1900–1914: zwischen beharren und verändern* (Dusseldorf, 1977).

—— *Vor dem Kriegsausbruch 1914. Deutschland, die Türkei und der Balkan* (Dusseldorf, 1980).

—— *Europäische Krise und Erster Weltkrieg. Beitrage zur Militärpolitik des Kaiserreichs, 1871–1914* (Frankfurt am Main, 1983).

Schwabe, Klaus, *Wissenschaft und Kriegsmoral. Die deutschen Hochschullehrer und die politischen Grundfragen des Ersten Weltkrieges* (Göttingen, 1969).

Schwarzmüller, Theo, *Zwischen Kaiser und 'Führer'. Generalfeldmarschall August von Mackensen: eine politische Biographie* (Paderborn, 1995).

Scott, Ernest, *Australia during the war* (Sydney, 1940; first published 1936).

Scott, J. D., *Vickers: a history* (London, 1962).

Seabourne, Teresa, 'The summer of 1914', in Forrest Capie and Geoffrey E. Wood (eds.), *Financial crises and the world banking system* (Basingstoke, 1986).

Seligmann, Matthew S., 'Germany and the origins of the First World War in the eyes of the American diplomatic establishment', *German History*, XV (1997), 307–32.

Semmel, Bernard, *Liberalism and naval strategy: ideology, interest, and sea power during the Pax Britannica* (Boston, 1986).

Seton-Watson, R. W., J. Dover-Wilson, Alfred E. Zimmern, and Arthur Greenwood, *The war and democracy* (London, 1915; first published 1914).

Shanafelt, Gary W., *The secret enemy: Austria-Hungary and the German alliance, 1914–1918* (Boulder, Col., 1985).

Shaw, Stanford J., and Ezel Kural Shaw, *History of the Ottoman empire and modern Turkey*, 2 vols. (Cambridge, 1976–7).

Sheehan, James J., *German liberalism in the nineteenth century* (Chicago, 1978).

Shevin-Coetzee, Marilyn, *The German army league: popular nationalism in Wilhelmine Germany* (New York, 1990).

Showalter, Dennis E., 'The eastern front and German military planning, 1871–1914—some observations', *East European Quarterly*, XV (1981), 163–80.

—— 'Even generals wet their pants: the first three weeks in East Prussia, August 1914', *War & Society*, II (1984), 60–86.

—— *Tannenberg: clash of empires* (Hamden, Conn., 1991).

Sieferle, Rolf Peter, 'Der deutsch–englische Gegensatz und die "Ideen von 1914"', in Gottfried Niedhart (ed.), *Das kontinentale Europa und die britischen Inseln: Wahrnehmungsmuster und Wechselwirkungen seit der Antike* (Mannheim, 1993).

Siegelbaum, Lewis H., *The politics of industrial mobilization in Russia, 1914–17: a study of the war-industries committees* (London, 1983).

Silberstein, Gerard E., *The troubled alliance: German–Austrian relations 1914 to 1917* (Lexington, 1970).

Simkins, Peter, *Kitchener's army: the raising of the New Armies, 1914–16* (Manchester, 1988).

Simon, Rachel, *Libya between Ottomanism and nationalism: the Ottoman involvement in Libya during the war with Italy (1911–1919)* (Berlin, 1987).

Skidelsky, Robert, *John Maynard Keynes*, vol. I, *Hopes betrayed 1883–1920* (London, 1983).

Smith, C. Jay, jr, 'Great Britain and the 1914–1915 straits agreement with Russia: the British promise of November 1914', *American Historical Review*, LXX (1965), 1015–34.

—— *The Russian struggle for power, 1914–1917: a study of Russian foreign policy during the First World War* (New York, 1969; first published 1956).

Smith, Leonard Vinson, 'Command authority in the French army, 1914–1918: the case of the 5^e division d'infanterie', Columbia University Ph.D. dissertation, 1990; published as *Between mutiny and obedience: the case of the French Fifth infantry division in World War I* (Princeton, 1994).

Smith, Paul, (ed.), *Government and the armed forces in Britain 1856–1990* (London, 1996).

Snell, John L., 'Socialist unions and socialist patriotism in Germany, 1914–1918', *American Historical Review*, LIX (1993), 66–76.

Snyder, Jack, *The ideology of the offensive: military decision-making and the disasters of 1914* (Ithaca, NY, 1984).

Soames, Mary (ed.), *Speaking for themselves: the personal letters of Winston and Clementine Churchill* (London, 1998).

Sombart, Werner, *Händler und Helden: politische Besinnungen* (Munich, 1915).

Soutou, Georges-Henri, *L'Or et le sang: les buts de guerre économiques de la première guerre mondiale* (Paris, 1989).

Spiers, Edward M., *Haldane: an army reformer* (Edinburgh, 1980).

Spies, S. B., 'The outbreak of the First World War and the Botha government', *South African Historical Journal*, I (1969), 47–57.

Spitzmüller, Alexander, *Memoirs of Alexander Spitzmüller, Freiherr von Hammerstein (1862–1953)*, ed. Carvel de Bussy (New York, 1987).

Spring, D. W., 'Russia and the Franco-Russian alliance, 1905–1914: dependence or interdependence?', *Slavonic and East European Review*, LXVI (1988), 564–92.

Stanley, William R., 'Review of Turkish Asiatic railways to 1918: some political-military considerations', *Journal of Transport History*, VII (1966), 189–204.

Stargardt, Nicholas, *The German idea of militarism: radical and socialist critics* (Cambridge, 1994).

Stegemann, Hermann, *Geschichte des Krieges*, 4 vols. (Stuttgart, 1918–21).

Steinberg, Jonathan, *Yesterday's deterrent: Tirpitz and the birth of the German battle fleet* (London, 1965).

Steiner, Zara, *Britain and the origins of the First World War* (London, 1977; revised edn., with Kerlin Neilson (London, 2003).

Stengers, Jean, 'L'Entrée en guerre de la Belgique', *Guerres mondiales et conflits contemporains*, 179 (juillet 1995), 13–33.

Stevenson, David, *French war aims against Germany 1914–1919* (Oxford, 1982).

—— *The First World War and international politics* (Oxford, 1988).

—— *Armaments and the coming of war: Europe, 1904–1914* (Oxford, 1996).

—— 'War by timetable? The railway race before 1914', *Past and Present*, 162 (1999), 163–94.

Stoecker, Helmuth (ed.), *German imperialism: from the beginnings until the Second World War* (London, 1986; first published 1977).

Stone, Jay, and Erwin A. Schmidl, *The Boer war and military reforms* (London, 1988).

Stone, Norman, 'Army and society in the Habsburg monarchy, 1900–1914', *Past and Present*, 33 (1966), 95–111.

—— 'Hungary and the crisis of July 1914', *Journal of Contemporary History*, I (1966), 153–70.

—— *The eastern front 1914–1917* (London, 1975).

—— *Europe transformed 1878–1919* (London, 1983).

Storz, Dieter, *Kriegsbild und Rüstung vor 1914. Europäische Landstreitkräfte vor dem Ersten Weltkrieg* (Herford, 1992).

Strachan, Hew, 'The First World War: causes and course', *Historical Journal*, XXIX (1986), 227–55.

—— *The First World War: a new illustrated history* (London, 2003).

—— 'Germany in the First World War: the problem of strategy', *German History*, XII (1994), 237–49.

—— (ed.), *Oxford Illustrated History of the First World War* (Oxford, 1998).

Stromberg, Roland N., *Redemption by war: the intellectuals and 1914* (Lawrence, Kan., 1982).

Stubbs, John O., 'The impact of the Great War on the Conservative party', in Gillian Peele and Chris Cook (eds.), *The politics of reappraisal 1918–1939* (London, 1975).

—— 'The Unionists and Ireland 1914–1918', *Historical Journal*, XXXIII (1990), 867–93.

Stumpf, R., *The private war of Seaman Stumpf: the unique diaries of a young German in the Great War*, ed. Daniel Horn (London, 1969).

Suchomlinow [i.e. Sukhomlinov], W. A., *Erinnerungen* (Berlin, 1924).

Sulzbach, Herbert, *With the German guns: four years on the western front 1914–1918* (London, 1973; first published 1935).

Sumida, Jon Tetsuro, 'British capital ship design and fire control in the *Dreadnought* era: Sir John Fisher, Arthur Hungerford Pollen, and the battle cruiser', *Journal of Modern History*, LI (1979), 205–30.

Sumida, Jon Tetsuro, *In defence of naval supremacy: finance, technology and British naval policy, 1899–1914* (Boston, 1989).

—— 'British naval administration and policy in the age of Fisher', *Journal of Military History*, LIV (1990), 1–20.

—— 'Sir John Fisher and the *Dreadnought*: the sources of naval mythology', *Journal of Military History*, LIX (1995), 619–37.

—— (ed.), *The Pollen papers: the privately circulated printed works of Arthur Hungerford Pollen, 1901–16* (London, 1984).

Summers, Anne, 'Militarism in Britain before the Great War', *History Workshop*, 2 (autumn 1976), 104–23.

—— *Angels and citizens: British women as military nurses 1854–1914* (London, 1988).

Swietochowski, Tamusz, *Russian Azerbaijan, 1905–1920: the shaping of a national identity in a Muslim community* (Cambridge, 1985).

Taslauanu, Octavian C., *With the Austrian army in Galicia* (London, [1918]).

Taylor, A. J. P., *Politics in wartime* (London, 1964).

—— (ed.), *Lloyd George: twelve essays* (London, 1971).

Terraine, John, *Douglas Haig: the educated soldier* (London, 1963).

Thompson, Wayne C., *In the eye of the storm: Kurt Riezler and the crises of modern Germany* (Iowa City, 1980).

Ticktin, David, 'The war issue and the collapse of the South African Labour party 1914–15', *South African Historical Journal*, 1 (1969), 59–80.

Townsend, Mary Evelyn *The rise and fall of the Germany's colonial empire 1884–1918* (New York, 1930).

Trachtenberg, Marc, 'The coming of the First World War: a reassessment', in Trachtenberg, *History and strategy* (Princeton, 1991).

Travers, Tim H. E., 'The offensive and the problem of innovation in British military thought 1870–1915', *Journal of Contemporary History*, XIII (1978), 531–53.

—— 'Technology, tactics, and morale: Jean de Bloch, the Boer war, and British military theory, 1900–1914', *Journal of Modern History*, LI (1979), 264–86.

—— 'The hidden army: structural problems in the British officer corps, 1900–1918', *Journal of Contemporary History*, XVII (1982), 523–44.

—— and Christon Archer (eds.), *Men at war: politics, technology and innovation in the twentieth century* (Chicago, 1982).

Trebilcock, Clive, 'The British armaments industry 1890–1914: false legend and true utility', in Geoffrey Best and Andrew Wheatcroft (eds.), *War, economy and the military mind* (London, 1976).

—— *The Vickers brothers: armaments and enterprise 1854–1914* (London, 1977).

—— *The industrialization of the continental powers 1780–1914* (London, 1981).

Trumpener, Ulrich, 'German military aid to Turkey in 1914: an historical re-evaluation', *Journal of Modern History*, XXXII (1960), 145–9.

—— 'Turkey's entry into World War I: an assessment of responsibilities', *Journal of Modern History*, XXXIV (1962), 369–80.

—— 'Liman von Sanders and the German–Ottoman alliance', *Journal of Contemporary History*, I (1966), 179–92.

—— *Germany and the Ottoman empire 1914–1918* (Princeton, 1968).

—— 'The escape of the *Goeben* and *Breslau*: a reassessment', *Canadian Journal of History*, VI (1971), 171–87.

—— 'War premeditated? German intelligence operations in July 1914', *Central European History*, IX (1976), 58–85.

Tuchmann, Barbara, *August 1914* (London, 1962).

Tunstall, Graydon A., jr, *Planning for war against Russia and Serbia: Austro-Hungarian and German military strategies, 1987–1914* (Boulder, Col., 1993).

—— 'The Habsburg command conspiracy: the Austrian falsification of historiography on the outbreak of World War I', *Austrian History Yearbook*, XXVII (1996), 181–98.

Turner, John, *British politics and the Great War: coalition and conflict 1915–1918* (New Haven, 1992).

—— (ed.), *Britain and the First World War* (London, 1988).

Turner, L. C. F., *Origins of the First World War* (London, 1970).

Uhle-Wettler, Franz, *Erich Ludendorff in seiner Zeit* (Berg, 1995).

Ullrich, Volker, *Kriegsalltag: Hamburg im ersten Weltkrieg* (Cologne, 1982).

Ulrich, Bernd, and Benjamin Ziemann (eds.), *Frontalltag im Ersten Weltkrieg: Wahn und Wirklichkeit* (Frankfurt am Main, 1994).

Unruh, Karl, *Langemarck: Legende und Wirklichkeit* (Koblenz, 1986).

Valiani, Leo, *The end of Austria-Hungary* (London, 1973; first published 1966).

Valone, Stephen J., ' "There must be some misunderstanding": Sir Edward Grey's diplomacy of August 1, 1914', *Journal of British Studies*, XXVII (1988), 405–24.

Vandenrath, Johannes, *et al.*, *1914: les psychoses de guerre?* (Rouen, 1985).

Veitch, Colin, ' "Play up! Play up! and win the war!" Football, the nation and the First World War 1914–15', *Journal of Contemporary History*, XX (1985), 363–78.

Verhey, Jeffrey Todd, 'The "spirit of 1914": the myth of enthusiasm and the rhetoric of unity in World War I Germany', University of California, Berkeley, Ph.D. dissertation, 1991; published as *The spirit of 1914: militarism, myth and mobilization in Germany* (Cambridge, 2000).

Vogel, Jakob, *Nationen im Gleichschritt: der Kult der 'Nationen in Waffen' in Deutschland und Frankreich, 1871–1914* (Göttingen, 1997).

Vogt, Adolf, *Oberst Max Bauer: Generalstabsoffizier im Zwielicht* (Osnabrück, 1974).

Wallace, Stuart, *War and the image of Germany: British academics 1914–1918* (Edinburgh, 1988).

Wallach, Jehuda L., *The dogma of the battle of annihilation: the theories of Clausewitz and Schlieffen and their impact on the German conduct of two world wars* (Wesport, Conn., 1986; first published 1967).

Wandruszka, Adam, and Peter Urbanitsch, *Die Habsburgermonarchie 1848–1918*, vol. I, *Die wirtschaftliche Entwicklung*, ed. Alois Brusatti (Vienna, 1973); vol. V, *Die bewaffnete Macht* (Vienna, 1987).

Wank, Solomon, 'Some reflections on Conrad von Hötzendorf and his memoirs based on new and old sources', *Austrian History Yearbook*, I (1965), 74–89.

Watson, David Robin, *Georges Clemenceau: a political biography* (London, 1974).

Watt, Richard M., *Dare call it treason* (London, 1964).

Watts, Anthony J., *The imperial Russian navy* (London, 1990).

Weber, Eugen, *Action française: royalism and reaction in twentieth-century France* (Stanford, 1962).

Weber, Frank G., *Eagles on the crescent: Germany, Austria, and the diplomacy of the Turkish alliance 1914–1918* (Ithaca, NY, 1970).

Wehler, Hans-Ulrich, *The German empire 1871–1918* (Leamington Spa, 1985; first published 1973).

Weir, Gary E., 'The imperial naval office and the problem of armor prices in Germany, 1897–1914', *Military Affairs*, XLVIII (1984), 62–5.

—— 'Tirpitz, technology, and building U-boats, 1897–1916', *International History Review*, VI (1984), 174–90.

Wells, H. G., *Mr Britling sees it through* (London, 1916).

Westwood, John, *Railways at war* (London, 1980).

Wette, Wolfram (ed.), *Der Krieg des kleinen Mannes: eine Militärgeschichte von unten* (Munich, 1992).

Wheeler-Bennett, John W., *Wooden titan: Hindenburg in twenty years of German history 1914–1934* (London, 1967; first published 1934).

Wilcox, Craig, 'Relinquishing the past: John Mordike's *An army for a nation*', *Australian Journal of History and Politics*, XL (1994), 52–65.

Wild von Hohenborn, Adolf, *Briefe und Tagebuchaufzeichnungen des preussischen Generals als Kriegsminister und Truppenführer im Ersten Weltkrieg* (Boppard am Rhein, 1986).

Wildman, Allan K., *The end of the Russian imperial army: the old army and the soldiers' revolt (March–April 1917)* (Princeton, 1980).

Williams, Rhodri, *Defending the empire: the Conservative party and British defence policy 1899–1915* (New Haven, 1991).

Williamson, D. G., 'Walter Rathenau and the K.R.A. August 1914–March 1915', *Zeitschrift für Unternehmensgeschichte*, XXIII (1978), 118–36.

Williamson, John G., *Karl Helfferich 1872–1924: economist, financier, politician* (Princeton, 1971).

Williamson, Samuel R., jr, *The politics of grand strategy: Britain and France prepare for war, 1904–1914* (Cambridge, Mass., 1969).

—— 'The origins of World War I', *Journal of Interdisciplinary History*, XVIII (1988), 795–818.

—— *Austria-Hungary and the origins of the First World War* (London, 1991).

—— and Peter Pastor (eds.), *War and society in East Central Europe*, vol. V, *Essays on World War I: origins and prisoners of war* (New York, 1983).

Wilson, Jeremy, *Lawrence of Arabia: the authorised biography of T. E. Lawrence* (London, 1989).

Wilson, Keith, 'The British cabinet's decision for war, 2 August 1914', *British Journal of International Studies*, I (1975), 148–59.

—— 'The Foreign Office and the "education" of public opinion before the First World War', *Historical Journal*, XXVI (1983), 403–11.

—— (ed.), *Forging the collective memory: government and international historians through two World Wars* (Providence, 1996).

—— *The policy of the Entente: essays on the determinants of British foreign policy 1904–1914* (Cambridge, 1985).

—— 'Hankey's appendix: some Admiralty manoeuvres during and after the Agadir crisis', *War in History*, I (1994), 81–97.

—— 'Understanding the "misunderstanding" of 1 August 1914', *Historical Journal*, XXXVII (1994), 885–9.

—— (ed.), *The rasp of war: the letters of H. A. Gwynne to the Countess Bathurst 1914–1918* (London, 1988).

—— (ed.), *Decisions for war, 1914* (London, 1995).

Wilson, Trevor, *The downfall of the Liberal party 1914–1935* (London, 1966).

—— 'Britain's "moral commitment" to France in July 1914', *History*, LXIV (1979), 380–90.

—— 'Lord Bryce's investigation into alleged German atrocities in Belgium, 1914–15', *Journal of Contemporary History*, XIV (1979), 369–83.

—— *The myriad faces of war: Britain and the Great War 1914–1918* (Cambridge, 1986).

—— (ed.), *The political diaries of C. P. Scott* (London, 1970).

Winter, Denis, *Death's men: soldiers of the Great War* (London, 1978).

Winter, J. M., *Socialism and the challenge of war: ideas and politics in Britain 1912–1918* (London, 1974).

—— *The Great War and the British people* (London, 1986).

—— *The experience of World War I* (Edinburgh, 1988).

—— (ed.), *War and economic development: essays in memory of David Joslin* (Cambridge, 1975).

Winter, Jay, and Blaine Baggett, *1914–18: the Great War and the shaping of the 20th century* (London, 1996).

Witkop, Philipp (ed.), *Kriegsbriefe gefallener Studenten*, 7th edn. (Munich, 1928).

Witt, Peter-Christian, *Die Finanzpolitik des Deutschen Reiches von 1903 bis 1913: eine Studie zur Innenpolitik des wihelminischen Deutschland* (Lübeck, 1970).

Witt, Peter-Christian, (ed.), *Wealth and taxation in Central Europe: the history and sociology of public finance* (Leamington Spa, 1987).

Wohl, Robert, *The generation of 1914* (London, 1980).

Wolff, Theodor, *Vollendete Tatsachen 1914–1917* (Berlin, 1918).

—— *Tagebücher 1914–1919*, ed. Bernd Sösemann, 2 vols. (Boppard am Rhein, 1984).

Woodward, Llewellyn, *Great Britain and the war of 1914–1918* (London, 1967).

Wright, Gordon, *Raymond Poincaré and the French presidency* (Stanford, 1942).

Wysling, Hans (ed.), *Letters of Heinrich and Thomas Mann, 1900–1949* (Berkeley, 1998).

Ypersele, Laurence van, 'Le 4 août en Belgique: naissance d'un mythe royal. Enquête dans la presse belge', *La Grande Guerre: pays, histoire, mémoire*, 8 (juin 1995), 7–10.

Zagorsky, S. O., *State control of industry in Russia during the war* (New Haven, 1928).

Zechlin, Egmont, 'Friedenbestrebungen und Revolutionierungsversuche: deutsche Bemühungen zur Ausschaltung Russlands im Ersten Weltkriege', *Aus Politik und Zeitgeschichte*, 20/61 (17 Mai 1961), 269–88; 24/61 (14 Juni 1961), 325–37; 25/61 (21 Juni 1961), 341–67.

Zeman, Z. A. B., *The break-up of the Habsburg empire 1914–1918: a study in national and social revolution* (London, 1961).

Ziemann, Benjamin, *Front und Heimat: ländliche Kreigserfahrungen im südlichen Bayern 1914–1923* (Essen, 1997).

Zilch, Reinhard, *Die Reichsbank und die finanzielle Kriegsvorbereitung 1907 bis 1914* (Berlin, 1987).

Zuber, Terence, *German war planning 1891–1914: sources and interpretations* (Woodbridge, 2004).

—— *Inventing the Schlieffen plan: German war planning 1871–1914* (Oxford, 2002)

—— 'The Schlieffen plan reconsidered', *War in History*, VI (1999), 262–305.

—— 'Terence Holmes reinvents the Schlieffen plan', in *War in History*, VIII (2001), 468–76.

Zürcher, Erik Jan, *The Unionist factor: the role of the Committee of Union and Progress in the Turkish national movement 1905–1926* (Leiden, 1984).

Zweig, Stefan, *The world of yesterday* (London, 1943).

INDEX

Black Sea straits, Russian interest in
    62, 75–6
Bloem, Walter 175
Böcklin, Arnold 174
Boer War 18
Boisdeffre, General 124
Bolsheviks 147–8
Bonar Law, Andrew, support for war
    120
Bosnia-Herzogovina:
    Austria-Hungary administration
        of 53, 81
    Austria-Hungary propose
        annexation of 54–5
    crisis (1908-9) 54–8
Boy Scouts 186
Boys' Brigade 186–7
Briand, Aristide 165
British Expeditionary Force 33
Brooke, Rupert 175, 177
Brusilov, A. A 98
Buchan, John 176
Bucharest, Treaty of (1913)
    71, 79
Buchlau agreement (1908) 54–6
Bulgaria 53
    alliance with Serbia 62, 63
    declares independence 55
    declares war on Serbia 71
    declares war on Turkey 63
    and Russia 57, 62
    success against Turks 69–70
Bülow, Bernhard von:
    domestic objectives of foreign
        policy 14
    and financing of navy 27
    and overseas expansion 13
    and the press 131
    resignation 28
    and social Darwinism 171

supports Austria-Hungary over
    Bosnia 56
Bundesrat:
    formation of 7
    Prussian influence in 8
Burian, Stephan Count 55, 70, 97

Cabrinovic, Nedeljko 82
Caillaux, Joseph 35, 42, 76, 99, 165
    and Moroccan crisis (1911) 31,
        32
Caillaux, Madame 99, 115
Cambon, Jules 30, 31, 36, 113
Cambon, Paul 24, 116, 119
Cameron of Lochiel 204
Campbell-Bannerman, Sir Henry 23
Canada 41
Carliol, J W 238
Catholicism 213–15
Chagall, Marc 201
Chamberlain, Houston Stewart 237
Chesterton, G K 221
Childers, Erskine 135, 186
Churchill, Winston:
    and Anglo-German naval rivalry
        43
    and continental strategy 34
    on German fleet 40
    and July crisis 131
    and naval building programme 41
    proposes 'naval holiday' 40
civilization:
    British interpretation of 222
    war as defence of 220–1
Clemenceau, Georges 35, 165, 220
Cole, G D H 178
Colonial Society (Germany) 16
Committee of Imperial Defence, and
        continental strategy 32–3, 34
Conan Doyle, Arthur 221

Romania 53
  and Balkan Wars 71
  and irridentism 71–2
Romanticism 173, 176
Rosenberg, A J 215
Royal Navy:
  and Anglo-French naval talks 34
  two-power standard 17, 26
  uninterested in amphibious
    operations 33
Rumelia, Turkish rule over 53
Russia:
  and anti-Germanism 73–5
  and army expansion 78
  and Black Sea straits 62, 75–6
  and Bosnia crisis (1908-9) 54–7
  and Bulgaria 62
  domestic conditions 102–3
  and France 25; and Bosnia crisis
    (1908-9) 57; military convention
    with 18; Poincaré's commitment
    to 37; support from 63
  and Germany; economic
    hostility 73; limited détente 30,
    62; rejects defensive alliance 19
  and July crisis; general
    mobilization 107; and partial
    mobilization 104–7; reaction to
    Serbian ultimatum 101–5; urges
    restraint on Serbia 100
  and liberal imperialism 74–5
  and mobilization 200–2
  and permissibility of war 76
  and Serbia, support for 64
  and socialism 146–8
  and United Kingdom 18, 76–7;
    Anglo-Russian convention
    (1907) 24–5; and Bosnia crisis
    (1908-9) 57; naval talks 77
Russo-Japanese War 18

Sammlungspolitik 12, 14, 27, 41
San Giuliano, Marquis di 94
Sazonov, Sergei 62, 64
  and July crisis 101, 104, 105, 106–7,
    114
  and strengthening of Entente
    76, 77
Schäfer, Dietrich 219
Scheler, Max 177, 180, 217, 226, 227,
    229, 235
Schiedemann, Philipp 153
Schiele, Egon 174
Schlieffen, Alfred von 69
  and Moroccan crisis (1905) 20
Schöpflin, Aladar 175
Schulz-Gaevernitz, Gerhart von 231
science, subordination to art 173
Scutari, seized by Montenegro 70
Second International:
  Basle conference (1912) 142
  Copenhagen conference (1910)
    142
  formation of 141
  French support of 157
  and general strike 142, 145
  and July crisis 143–4
  and pacifism 142
  and response to war 142
  revolutionary left and war 144
  Stuttgart conference (1907)
    141–2
  and trade unionism 145
  see also socialism
Sembat, Marcel 165
Serbia 53
  and Albania 69
  army of 84, 100
  and Austria-Hungary 57
  and Bulgaria; alliance with 62, 63;
    war with 71